A History of American Life

THE McNEIL CENTER FOR EARLY AMERICAN STUDIES

A HISTORY OF AMERICAN LIFE

IN

Twelve Volumes

ARTHUR M. SCHLESINGER
DIXON RYAN FOX

Editors

CARL BECKER
Consulting Editor

A HISTORY OF AMERICAN LIFE

A HISTORY OF AMERICAN LIFE
Volume VII

THE IRREPRESSIBLE
CONFLICT
1850-1865

BY

ARTHUR CHARLES COLE

PROFESSOR OF HISTORY, WESTERN RESERVE UNIVERSITY

New York
THE MACMILLAN COMPANY

Free society! we sicken at the name. What is it but a conglomeration of greasy mechanics, filthy operatives, small-fisted farmers, and moon-struck theorists? All the northern, and especially the New England states, are devoid of society fitted for well-bred gentlemen. The prevailing class one meets with is that of mechanics struggling to be genteel, and small farmers who do their own drudgery, and yet are hardly fit for association with a southern gentleman's body servant.

Cited from the *Muscogee* (Georgia) *Herald*
by the *N. Y. Tribune*, Sept. 10, 1856.

The free States carry on their government on the principle of the equality of men. We think slavery is morally wrong, and a direct violation of the principle. . . . Slavery is wrong in its effect upon white people and free labor. It is the only thing that threatens the Union. It makes what Senator Seward has been much abused for calling an "irrepressible conflict."

ABRAHAM LINCOLN, at Hartford, March 5,
1860, *Complete Works* (J. G. NICOLAY and
JOHN HAY, eds., N. Y., 1905), V, 330-331.

The fault of the Free States in the eyes of the South is not one that can be atoned for by any yielding of special points here and there. . . . Their crime is the census of 1860. Their increase in numbers, wealth, and power is a standing aggression. It would not be enough to please the Southern States that we should stop asking them to abolish slavery, —what they demand of us is nothing less than that we should abolish the spirit of the age.

[JAMES RUSSELL LOWELL], "The Question
of the Hour," *Atlantic Mo.*, VII (1861),
120.

CONTENTS

CONTENTS

ILLUSTRATIONS

(By the Editors)

EDITORS' FOREWORD

PROBABLY no period of American history has been more thoroughly explored, surveyed and mapped by historians than the decade and a half following 1850, when two great sections of the nation, grown deeply different, profoundly disagreeing as to loyalties, mobilized first argument and then armed men and set out to destroy each other on the battle-field. While the breach was widening, Northern publicists accounted for it in terms of incompatible moral codes. This conception underlay William H. Seward's famous statement at Rochester on October 25, 1858, that it signified "an irrepressible conflict between opposing and enduring forces." Southern writers, on the other hand, saw an irreconcilable difference between two schools of constitutional interpretation, one stemming from the doctrine of Jefferson, the other from that of Hamilton. Jefferson Davis gave this point of view definite expression in his *Rise and Fall of the Confederate Government* (1881). More recently, historians have studied the economic implications of the controversy: the sectional rivalry for control of the public domain, the Southern fear of Northern business enterprise, the South's decreasing influence in the national economic order.

Professor Cole's comprehensive view contemplates these factors, but, seeking to encompass all the aspects of American life throughout that era, it shows that the strife between the sections involved very much more. From his text emerges a picture of two different civilizations contesting, one for supremacy and the other for independence; the one resting on a caste system and slave labor, the other a fluid society based on free wage labor; the one pivoted on the production of a few staple crops, the other grounded on a diversified production of farm and factory; the one aristocratic, indifferent to intellectual achievement and hostile to freedom of opinion, the other democratic, proud of its poets, novelists, scientists and educators; the one living increasingly to itself and clinging to the past, the other responsive to the spirit of the age and frankly experimental in the pattern of its political and social life. It was this deep-reaching "irrepressible conflict" that defeated every effort to patch up mere political difference in 1860-1861 and made the South willing to secede though it still wielded a controlling hand in Congress.

Professor Cole illuminates the daily life of Americans throughout the fifties. Despite the distorting lenses of many nineteenth-century historians his narrative reminds us that people courted and married, went about their business, read and wrote books, laughed, played and prayed, unaware that hosts of young men in blue and in gray would soon confront each other on bloody battle-fields. In the domain of letters, for example, the decade proved one of the brightest in American annals, producing some of the best work of Emerson, Thoreau, Melville, Hawthorne, Whitman, Parkman, Motley and others. The author has properly devoted several chapters to such themes as "Immigration Becomes a National Problem," "The Growing Pains of Society," "Health and Happiness," "Educational and Cultural Advance" and "The Challenge to the Church." Particularly interesting is his constant emphasis on the part that the Middle West played in the varied life of the times. No earlier writer has done so much to redress a balance that never existed save in the historian's mind.

The strategy of warfare Professor Cole leaves to the

military expert. His primary concern is with the impact
of the conflict on the popular consciousness in North
and in South and with its diverse effects on the man in
the ranks. The reader learns of Southern life under
stress of war-time conditions, of civilian welfare activities in the North, of corruption in military contracts, of
the horrors of the battle-field and the circulation of
atrocity stories, of conditions in Northern factories and
of Northern endeavors to raise cotton and sugar cane
to offset the shortage of the Southern supply. Much
that is novel and suggestive appears also in the author's
discussion of the results of the clash of arms on educational efforts and intellectual life.

Professor Cole's laborious mining of contemporary
newspaper files has yielded many a nugget of prime
historical interest. His "Critical Essay on Authorities"
shows to what extent he has utilized diaries, memoirs,
official documents and the latest historical monographs.
The picture he draws of mid-century United States discloses American civilization at its most critical turning
point; the four tragic years of fratricidal bloodshed
heralded the emergence of modern America.

A. M. S.
D. R. F.

THE
IRREPRESSIBLE CONFLICT
1850-1865

THE
IRREPRESSIBLE CONFLICT

CHAPTER I

PROSPERITY AND PANIC

IN the summer of 1850 Americans looked out upon their country with eyes that glowed with pride and confidence. "Manifest destiny" had been realized; the flag had been borne in triumph to the Rio Grande and to the Pacific shore. As if to celebrate this great achievement the mountains of the Far West had loosed a mighty stream of gold. Within the vast empire under the "Stars and Stripes" the forces of political democracy had won under Western leadership a mighty victory. The American example had been enviously cited in the recent revolutionary movements in France, Italy and Germany and, lest others overlook it, the government was soon gratuitously preaching it to Austria and Spain. The old alignment, of East and West, of the complacent settled communities on the one hand and the changing and obstreperous frontier on the other representing to some extent the antipathy of credits and debts was still sensed, but less keenly than in Andrew Jackson's time. For thirty years discerning minds had feared that it might be supplanted by another cleavage, more clear and strict, between the slave-plantation culture of the South and the industrial and small-farm culture of the North. Each had reached a high degree of self-consciousness and it had seemed that their interests might be mutually antagonistic, especially in determining the future of the new land gained from Mexico and thus of national control. But moderate men, representing the varied propertied interests of the nation, were satisfied that—despite the work of agitators and fire eaters—intelligence, forbearance and sentimental nationalism had surmounted all that difficulty when the legislative items just narrowly passed on their own merits were shortly acquiesced in as a great and "final" compromise that should make for national accord. That this apparently perfect balance, this dualism, could not possibly continue with ideals so disparate and aggressive—in fact, that the house was hopelessly divided and on the verge of schism—this in that Indian summer calm could not be realized.

A period of sectional strife gave way to an era of prosperity, which had been gathering through the later forties, an era the like of which no one could recall. The political uneasiness was soon to rise again, but the anodyne of business profits was temporarily to dispel much of its pain. Seven fat years, wherein an international free trade was fed by constantly increasing American production, were followed by a sort of apoplectic spasm, the Panic of 1857, but economic health, welling up from American energy and vast resources, seemed quickly to conquer it, and for three more years the irrepressible conflict was denied by a prosperous and optimistic people. Its manifestations were resented as perversities and those who spoke of trouble were condemned as makers of it.

Much better it was to make money. In those seven years both imports and exports trebled, until each exceeded the annual value of a third of a billion dollars. Three fourths of this trade was carried in American bottoms, and the American merchant marine came at length to outnumber the ships that flew the Union Jack. Banks and bank capital, together with their loans and paper issues, expanded at a rate that betokened an end of the caution of the forties. Nearly fifty millions in gold were added to the coinage each year.[1] Stimulated by such forces as well as by a new system of rail transport, American manufacturing leaped ahead. At the end of the decade a billion dollars was invested in factories, shops and mills, a sum double the capital investment of 1850 and heralding the coming domination of industrialism. This advance, however, was mainly confined to the free states, their output exceeding that of the slave states ten to one.

This abounding prosperity rested upon an expansion of transportation facilities such as the country had never before experienced. The fifties saw the emerging outlines of a genuinely national system of transportation and communication. Crude as the efforts may seem to a later generation, they prefigured the miraculous shortening of distances in the years after the Civil War. Before 1850 means of travel and carriage had consisted largely of scattered short rail lines, occasional canals, navigable streams and badly made roads. Though river improvement seemed a prime necessity, meager state treasuries did not permit reckless ventures in that field and the federal government was dispensing "pork" with painful economy. State roads were often created by legislation, but, with only stakes in the open prairie and blazes on the trees, experience seemed to demonstrate that a state could not legislate a mudhole into a highway.

Through private initiative, plank roads came into sudden favor in the late forties as a quick and easy solution of the transportation problem. General laws were enacted to make easy the incorporation of plank-road associations and stock was eagerly subscribed. Fifty miles of plank road built in 1850 radiated from Chicago in

---

[1] Edit., *Harper's Mo.*, VI (1853), 703; G. W. Curtis, *Potiphar Papers* (N. Y., 1856), 32.

nearly every direction. A traveler up the Illinois River reported almost every town and landing "engaged in constructing plank roads to the interior. . . . The plank road fever fully keeps pace with the railroad excitement." [1] By the middle of 1851 six hundred miles were said to have been built or laid out in Illinois; at a cost of approximately fifteen hundred dollars a mile this involved an investment of nearly a million. While mere child's play as compared with the difficulty and expense of canal or railroad construction or with the facilities afforded thereby, these projects brought immediate results in improving transportation conditions. Within a few years, however, travelers discovered all too easily the limitations of the plank road. [2] The two-inch boards, soon decaying or working loose, added to the hazards of travel. A plank road in good repair promised real relief from prairie mud, but in actual fact muddy water often shot out in all directions every time the horses took a step. Though in the older parts of the country where better roads predominated the Concord wagon and the light open high-wheeled carriage or "buggy" were established American institutions, in the open spaces of the West the prairie schooner and the oxcart were still essential to reliable transportation. Enterprising spirits, it might be noted, tried to adapt their vehicles as "wind wagons" to the constructive use of prairie breezes. [3]

West of the bend of the Missouri, the wagon road and the stagecoach line were all important for the movements of the overland pioneer. Congressmen and news-

[1] *Chicago Tribune*, cited in *Illinois State Register* (Springfield), March 13, 1851. See also U. B. Phillips, *Transportation in the Eastern Cotton Belt to 1860* (N. Y., 1913), 385; *De Bow's Rev.*, XII (1852), 98; J. A. Durrenberger, *Turnpikes* (Valdosta, Ga., 1931), chap. ix.

[2] J. G. Kohl, *Travels in Canada, and through the States of New York and Pennsylvania* (Mrs. Percy Sinnett, tr., London, 1861), II, 227.

[3] *Ohio Statesman* (Columbus), May 27, 1860; *Boston Eve. Transcript*, June 16, 1860.

paper editors might discuss the advantages of a transcontinental railroad and Jefferson Davis as secretary of
war might direct a series of surveys of possible routes to
the Pacific; but all this seemed daydreaming to men who
faced the immediate task of traversing the two thousand miles of plain and mountain that separated the
Pacific Coast from the "States." From them and their
friends and relatives came the demand for an extended
system of federal wagon roads and for better mail service. Imaginative Westerners, indeed, suggested camels,
and when private capital proved unresponsive, Secretary
Davis authorized an experiment to determine the adaptability of this "ship of the desert" to the arid wastes of
the American Southwest.[1] There seems little doubt that
the camel demonstrated his superior usefulness as a pack
and draft animal, but the prejudices and objections of
nearly all classes to "these outlandish brutes" were never
sufficiently dispelled. Instead, long trains of covered
wagons and carts, drawn by from four to six teams of
mules or oxen, made their way across the plains, carrying food, clothing and luxuries as well as needed machinery to the mining camps and other settlements of
the Far West. Freighting fell to the hardened veterans
of the trail who took equal pride in the prowess of
their animals and in their own achievements with crack-
ing whip and resonant profanity. During 1860 nearly
twelve thousand men, eight thousand mules, sixty-eight
thousand oxen and sixty-nine hundred wagons were employed to transport the eighteen thousand tons of freight
across the "Great American Desert."[2]

In the meantime the government was induced to in-

---

[1] See Boston Times, cited in Illinois State Journal (Springfield), Aug.
31, 1849; N. Y. Herald, April 24, 1858; W. L. Fleming, "Jefferson
Davis's Camel Experiment," Pop. Sci. Mo., LXXIV (1909), 141-152.
[2] American Railway Times (Boston), Jan. 21, 1861; Edward Dicey,
Six Months in the Federal States (London, 1863), II, 104.

stall a new system of overland mail. On the first of July, 1850, a monthly mail stage service began between Independence, Missouri, and Santa Fé. Guarded by eight heavily armed men, the ponderous six-mule coach with its mail and passengers struggled over a rough uncertain route hoping to reach its destination in a fortnight.[1] About the same time a postal route opened under Mormon management between St. Joseph and Salt Lake City. In 1857 the postmaster-general awarded to John Butterfield of the Overland Mail Company a contract for a mail service to cover the distance between St. Louis and San Francisco in twenty-five days. Four-horse coaches were to run day and night with relays of fresh animals obtainable at stations located at ten-mile intervals. On September 15, 1858, after a year's preparation but before all the stations had been built on the plains west of Arkansas, this unique semiweekly service was inaugurated over the southern route through El Paso and Fort Yuma. The distance of nearly twenty-eight hundred miles was covered by the first east-bound stage in slightly over twenty-three days, while the west-bound coach rolled into San Francisco a day later.[2] Earlier the same year a weekly mail route began between St. Joseph and Placerville, California, by way of Salt Lake City, over which stages maintained a twenty-nine days' service.

Though all these mails operated at a deficit, there was a mounting demand for more frequent and speedy service. When the government hesitated to assume a heavier burden of expense, the great freighting firm of Russell, Majors and Waddell agreed to undertake a venture

[1] Henry Inman, *The Old Santa Fé Trail* (N. Y., 1897), 146 ff.

[2] "Monthly Record of Current Events," *Harper's Mo.*, XVII (1858), 830. See also L. R. Hafen, *The Overland Mail, 1849-1869* (Cleveland, 1926), 94-96; F. A. Root and W. E. Connelley, *Overland Stage to California* (Topeka, 1901), 13; Curtis Nettels, "The Overland Mail Issue in the Fifties," *Mo. Hist. Rev.*, XVIII, 521-534.

which stands unmatched in the annals of the American frontier. This was an overland pony express mail for the carriage of letters and telegraph messages between St. Joseph and Sacramento. Expert light-weight riders, with runs of from seventy-five to eighty miles upon fleet, hardy Indian horses stationed ten or fifteen miles apart, were to dash over the Platte trail upon a ten-day schedule. On April 3, 1860, the system was inaugurated with riders starting simultaneously from the eastern and the western termini. Ten days later on the last relay from the east the pony-express rider, followed by a band of whooping, shooting horsemen, galloped into Sacramento, which awaited his arrival in a holiday mood. At almost the same moment the east-going express reached St. Joseph where the citizens celebrated the event with a parade of noisy bands, bonfires, fireworks and the inevitable speech making.[1]

Five dollars a half ounce was the tariff upon the tissue-paper letters thus carried. For ordinary postal service, however, the charge was but three cents a half ounce for any distance up to three thousand miles, the rate since 1851 when Congress yielded to the popular demand for cheaper postage. For two of the three-cent pieces authorized by that law, a letter could thus be sent at the slower pace from points upon the Atlantic Seaboard.[2] Meantime the telegraph was making its way into the Far West—the forerunner of the railroad and of the daily mail. In a decade many thousands of miles of wire were erected and at length the fifty independent lines were absorbed in the Western Union Telegraph Company. In January, 1859, not a single wire existed

---

[1] W. L. Visscher, *The Pony Express* (Chicago, 1908), 22-57; G. D. Bradley, *The Story of the Pony Express* (Chicago, 1913).

[2] Letters carried twenty-five hundred miles wholly or in part by sea were charged twenty cents' postage. Clyde Kelly, *United States Postal Policy* (N. Y., 1931), chap. iv.

in Arkansas, but within a year a line to California had already been carried two hundred and fifty miles west of St. Louis.[1] On October 26, 1861, the Pacific telegraph was open, with 3595 miles of wires stretching from New York to San Francisco. It was no mere coincidence that in that month the firm of Russell, Majors and Waddell, now bankrupt, abandoned the operation of the pony express.

In a similar fashion the demand for faster and cheaper ocean mail led to the laying of the first Atlantic cable. In the spring of 1854 Cyrus W. Field of New York induced a group of wealthy friends to join him in the audacious venture of laying a cable by way of Newfoundland and Ireland. After numerous setbacks, the cable having parted on several occasions at the mid-ocean rendezvous where the two sections were to join, a successful splice was made late in July, 1858. Upon the sixteenth of August messages of congratulation and international good will passed between Queen Victoria and President Buchanan. A succession of popular celebrations and demonstrations reached their climax upon September 1, the day set for the formal opening of the cable.[2] Enthusiasts were soon predicting a submarine telegraph on the south side of the Gulf Stream and even telegraphic connections with India. "Good Bye to Steamer News," sang out an influential daily journal, only to learn within a few weeks that the cable had stopped working.[3] Whether the trouble was due to

[1] *Dollar Newspaper* (Phila.), Jan. 12, 1859; *N. Y. Tribune*, Jan. 4, 1860.

[2] *N. Y. Tribune*, Sept. 2, 1858; *N. Y. Herald*, Sept. 2, 1858, Jan. 1, 1859; *National Intelligencer* (Wash.), Aug. 14, 17, 19, Sept. 3, 1858; "Monthly Record of Current Events," *Harper's Mo.*, XVII (1858), 689, 829; T. L. Nichols, *Forty Years of American Life* (London, 1864), I, 22 ff.

[3] *National Intelligencer*, Sept. 4, 22, 30, 1858. For later history of transatlantic cable, see Allan Nevins, *The Emergence of Modern America* (*A History of American Life*, VIII), 86.

faulty insulation or some other technical difficulty was not clear, but Field himself remained undiscouraged.

Better success greeted the efforts to improve water transportation. It was a far cry from the tiny canal boat to the river steamer, still farther to the palatial transatlantic liner which now came into its own. The old sailing time of nearly a month was cut in half, while a maximum ten-day voyage became the objective of the splendid paddle-wheel steamers of the Collins line, an American venture which, aided by a government subsidy, engaged in vigorous competition with the British Cunard mail line. The *Atlantic,* first of the four speedy Collins liners, inaugurated the new service on April 27, 1850; in August, 1852, the *Baltic* made the passage from Liverpool in nine days and thirteen hours. The Cunard line strove desperately, and in time successfully, to meet this competition with new vessels built for speed.[1] The rivalry came to an end in 1858 when the American line, deprived of most of the government subsidy, became insolvent. Those of its ships which had escaped ocean disasters were sold under the sheriff's hammer.[2] First-class passenger ships sailed exclusively from New York, although at the end of the decade the Cunard line was planning to utilize the excellent landing facilities at Portland, Maine, for some of its newest and largest boats. In the later fifties Cornelius Vanderbilt also ventured into the transatlantic passenger field, with steamers to Southampton, Havre and Bremen.

[1] The first newspaper cartoon of Uncle Sam appeared in a New York comic weekly, *Diogenes, Hys Lantern,* March 13, 1852, depicting under the title, "Raising the Wind," the struggle between an American shipowner and the Cunard Company, the latter actively aided by the portly John Bull, while Uncle Sam amiably looked on.

[2] W. W. Bates, *American Marine* (Boston, 1893), 130, 146-147; J. R. Spears, *The Story of the American Merchant Marine* (N. Y., 1910), 265-272; T. C. Grattan, *Civilized America* (London, 1859), II, 172-175; Edmund Patten, *A Glimpse at the United States* (London, 1853), 106-107.

The maritime romance of this era centers about the famous clippers. These long graceful vessels, fully rigged with square sails on all three masts, came in response to the demand for speed by American argonauts eager to reach California. Many of them, more particularly the products of the architectural genius of Donald McKay, were trimmed in mahogany, rosewood and brass, with sumptuous staterooms and cabins. They represented the triumph of New England shipbuilding. Some, faster than racing yachts of today, made over eighteen knots hour after hour; several made eastward runs to Liverpool in fourteen days. The best of the clippers completed the voyage around the Horn in less than one hundred days. Returning, they in many cases first crossed the Pacific to pick up a cargo of the products of China, Japan or the Indies. The record return voyage around the Horn covered the distance to Boston in seventy-six days and five hours.[1] The extensive profits of the "Frisco trade" in the flush times of the early fifties induced Vanderbilt to arrange steamship connections with California by way of the isthmus. The California trip could thus be cut to twenty days or less, until the Panama Railroad a few years later offered further economies in time.

More important perhaps than this spectacular passenger traffic to Europe and California was the fact that the "glorious era" of the merchant marine had arrived. American ocean traffic increased from a tonnage of 1,500,000 in 1850 to nearly 2,500,000 in 1860,[2] and American ships sailed into every corner of the seven seas. It was a final triumph of that seamanship which did not

[1] S. E. Morison, *The Maritime History of Massachusetts* (Boston, 1921), 327-352.
[2] E. R. Johnson and others, *History of Domestic and Foreign Commerce of the United States* (Carnegie Inst., *Contribs. to Am. Econ. History*; Wash., 1915), II, 51.

need to harness the giant steam in the conquest of Father Neptune. Of the 4107 vessels that put into New York in 1853 only 214 were powered by steam; nor did the proportion increase greatly during the decade.

With Parliament's repeal of the navigation acts British markets lay open to the products of New England shipyards. Enoch Train and Company, aided by the egotistical genius of a nephew George F. Train, maintained a successful line of packets from Boston to Liverpool as well as a fast clipper service between Boston and Australia. Young Train dreamed of a great American shipping combine, but found his uncle too conservative to take steps in that direction. This "splendid, dashing looking fellow, with a head like Apollo's, a voice full of music, a hand with an electric thrill in its grasp," was an audacious representative of that "young America," whose virtues he proclaimed in a series of letters written from various spots on the globe and in his books *Young America Abroad* and *Young America in Wall Street*.[1]

By 1860 the American merchant marine had outdistanced, in fair competition, that of Great Britain. The American Navigation Club, an association of Boston shipowners and merchants, issued an untaken challenge for an Anglo-American clipper race from England to China and return. These were the substantial fruits of the seamanship that enabled the yacht *America* to show her keel to the best of the English entries in the international regatta of 1851 and to bring back the cup which the English have ever since tried to recover. English travelers to America saw replicas of the *America* in the trim little schooner-yachts that came as pilot boats

[1] Hiram Fuller, *Belle Brittan on a Tour at Newport, and Here and There* (N. Y., 1858), 227-228, 287-288. See also G. F. Train, *My Life in Many States and in Foreign Lands* (N. Y., 1902), and same author, *An American Merchant in Europe, Asia, and Australia* (N. Y., 1857).

out of New York Harbor to meet transatlantic steamers. The English journalist, William H. Russell, could not refrain from commenting, "How different the graceful, tautly-rigged, clean, white-sailed vessels, from the round-sterned, lumpish billyboys and nondescripts of the eastern coast of our isle!" [1]

The New England fishing industry also scored new triumphs.[2] Gloucester outdistanced Boston in the cod and mackerel fisheries, while the Canadian reciprocity treaty of 1854 proved a great boon to all. Whaling also prospered. A fleet of seven hundred whalers, most of them sailing out of New Bedford, pursued their quarry into tropic heat and Arctic cold. In the spring of 1856 the *E. L. B. Jenney* returned to port after four and a half years, bringing in a valuable cargo of two thousand five hundred barrels of sperm oil.[3] Friends and relatives customarily scanned the pages of the *New Bedford Whaleman* for tidings of absent ones off upon such long cruises.

The coasting trade experienced a similar expansion. Numerous steamers were installed in regular service between Northern ports and the seacoast cities of the South. Trade between the two sections increased fifty per cent in tonnage during the fifties.[4] River steamers plied up and down every navigable stream. In season they stopped day or night at almost every bluff and landing in the cotton belt to pick up bales piled seven or eight tiers high. At such times it might take two and a

---

[1] Patten, *A Glimpse at the United States*, 19; W. H. Russell, *My Diary North and South* (Boston, 1863), 6.

[2] Morison, *Maritime History*, 302-312, 375.

[3] *Boston Eve. Transcript*, May 13, 1856. See also J. R. Spears, *The Story of the New England Whalers* (N. Y., 1910), esp. 323, 324; Perry Walton, *Whale Fishery of New England* (Boston, 1915) ; E. P. Hohman, *The American Whaleman* (N. Y., 1928).

[4] Johnson and others, *History of Domestic and Foreign Commerce*, I, 346-347.

half days to do the trip up the Alabama River from
Mobile to Montgomery, the wild strains of a steam
calliope on the upper deck of the steamboat heralding
its arrival at each landing.[1]

Steamboating upon the Mississippi and its tributaries
also saw bonanza years. The busy shipyards and foundries along the Ohio could not keep up with the demand. One clumsy, slow-moving type of craft, its lower
decks filled with cows, horses, sheep, pigs and poultry,
seemed like a veritable Noah's ark. Others, large trim
vessels with gilded ornamentation and luxurious saloons,
lavished upon their passengers elaborate food and
musical entertainment and made fifteen miles or more
an hour. To be sure, safety was often sacrificed to speed,
particularly when rival boats undertook to race each
other. Usually such contests were impromptu, with the
recognized right of the winner to "carry the broom" of
victory upon her pilot house. But there was danger
enough of a boiler explosion without the additional risk
of a race. Indeed, between explosions, fires and dangerous snags in the river, the average life of a vessel was
only five years. Steamboat disasters upon Western rivers
in 1858 totaled forty-seven sunk, nineteen burned and
nine exploded, with an estimated loss of two hundred
and fifty-nine lives and a property damage of $1,924,-
000.[2] By contrast, canal transportation, the great hope
of the preceding generation, was on a rapid decline.[3]
Yet the canal boat in its slow and humble way still
moved countless tons of traffic. The Illinois and Michigan Canal, connecting the Mississippi system with the

[1] F. L. Olmsted, *The Cotton Kingdom* (N. Y., 1861), I, 275;
Nichols, *Forty Years of American Life*, I, 229; Russell, *My Diary*, 184,
185.

[2] *N. Y. Herald*, Jan. 3, 1859.

[3] See C. R. Fish, *The Rise of the Common Man* (*A History of
American Life*, VI), 75-77.

Great Lakes, contributed the most important example of new achievement in this class.

With the passage of each year, however, all modes of inland transportation seemed increasingly antiquated as compared with the more efficient means of locomotion which a new era of railroad building now achieved. In rapid succession New York, Philadelphia and Baltimore realized their quarter-century-old dreams of rail connections with the West. A series of seven or eight local lines between Albany and Lake Erie became, after 1842, links in the first chain of routes across the Empire State; in 1853 they found corporate unity as the New York Central system.[1] By that time three other roads had penetrated the Appalachian barrier. In 1851 the Erie was completed to serve as a single direct connection between New York and its western terminus at Dunkirk on the lake. By December, 1852, the entire route of the Pennsylvania road was open to Pittsburgh, while five months later the Baltimore and Ohio celebrated the completion of its line to Wheeling, farther south on the Ohio. In that year, too, the Atlantic and St. Lawrence, the beginning of the Grand Trunk system, joined Portland, Maine, with Montreal. The Pennsylvania promptly pushed its rails into Ohio and Indiana while the roads to the north arranged connections with local Western lines.

In the spring of 1852 the Michigan Central and the Michigan Southern entered Chicago from the east. In October, 1853, it was possible for Chicagoans to reach Alton by the combined facilities of three roads. This made the first communication by railroad from New York City to the Mississippi River. On February 22,

[1] Caroline E. MacGill and others, *History of Transportation in the United States before 1860* (Carnegie Inst., *Contribs. to Am. Econ. History;* Wash., 1917), 378.

1854, the completion of the Rock Island and Chicago Railroad was celebrated with due pomp and ceremony at its western terminus, for this formed the first continuous connection between the Great Lakes and the Mississippi. Now, in the flowery language of the after-dinner orator, the iron horse that sipped his morning draft from the crystal waters of Lake Michigan could slake his evening thirst upon the banks of the great river. By the end of the decade, along the western border of Illinois railroad lines with the Eastern connections touched the Mississippi at eight points.

The West had, indeed, opened up a railroad era of its own. Thousands of miles were under construction in the upper Mississippi Valley. Indianapolis and Chicago were the *foci* of numerous lines. The future of Cleveland, of Cincinnati and even of St. Louis seemed bound up with suitable rail connections with the East. Meantime the railroad out of St. Louis crept steadily westward until over two thirds of the distance to Kansas City was covered, while across northern Missouri a road from Hannibal to St. Joseph served as a continuation of the Burlington from Chicago and of a diagonal St. Louis connection. St. Joseph was the western outpost of the railroads in 1860, whence the railway frontier struck across eastern Iowa to La Crosse upon the upper Mississippi.

During the fifties the trackage of the nation more than trebled, reaching a total of over thirty thousand miles. Of these only a third were within the limits of the slave states, while the trans-Allegheny region north of the Ohio, which had been far in the rear in 1850, now outdistanced every other section of the country. Behind this railroad miracle was a combination of forces. Local investors and land speculators, after conceiving an enterprise, rallied the community to its support; farms were mortgaged to assist in the accumulation of capital; counties and municipalities strained their credit to subscribe for stock. In due time came the construction gang; the meadows along the right of way blossomed with tents and shanties where the Irish laborers and their families huddled together in something akin to a state of nature.[1]

Outside capital, Eastern and foreign, usually demanded special privileges as the price of its enlistment. According to critics, "swarms of hungry cormorants" clamoring for special legislation besieged the state capitols, and it was said that the bills pressed by these lobbyists, prepared in New York, were first canvassed by Wall Street men before they were sent on for legislative indorsement. Small Western investors, despite their impressive totals, complained that they were crowded out of their due representation by these metropolitan financiers. Rumors circulated of large corruption funds to compass the defeat of rival projects. Only the general enthusiasm for railroad development prevented a strong reaction in line with Western prejudices against corporation influence.

As the "railroad fever" raged, thousands of miles of track received official sanction that never passed the state of paper projects; others were begun only to collapse of their own weight, sound as well as shaky enterprises going to ruin. Certain ambitious undertakings promised success only in the event of federal aid. In September, 1850, a union of political and sectional forces at Washington secured an epoch-making grant of public lands to the Illinois Central Railroad and to the Mobile and Ohio, two projects that in combination made the appeal of a Lakes-to-Gulf enterprise. This precedent was eagerly seized upon by other railroad promoters. Almost at once legislative bodies wrestled with resolutions re-

[1] Dicey, *Six Months in the Federal States*, II, 140.

questing similar aid for schemes, some as scandalous as others were worthy. Unhappily, Congress did not always show as fine discrimination as when in 1851 it refused to aid an Illinois enterprise whose tireless promoter, in spite of long-standing indorsement by the legislature of that state, had succeeded in putting to work only a lone Irishman.[1]

The service furnished by these newly built railroads varied according to circumstances. Some were constructed to meet an urgent want; the heavy freight and passenger traffic that immediately began often taxed them to capacity. The use of wood for fuel was gradually abandoned and the coal-burning "tank locomotive" eliminated the frequent stops for "wooding-up." [2] Roadbeds were rough and travel was jolty, but wooden rails topped with metal strips were soon replaced by solid iron; steel rails were yet in the future. The approaches to the larger cities were usually double-tracked, and in 1860 the Pennsylvania advertised itself as "the great double track route." [3] Gradually the standard gauge track was adopted. It took some strenuous planning and the suppression of local mob outbursts, known as the "Erie War," to wipe out permanently the well-known "Erie isthmus" where inconvenient transfers of passengers and freight had contributed to local prosperity.

To eliminate unnecessary interruptions, car ferries were provided or the streams bridged, the ferry across the Susquehanna on the Philadelphia-Baltimore route arousing the amazement of foreign travelers.[4] In 1853

[1] A. C. Cole, The Era of the Civil War (C. W. Alvord, ed., The Centennial History of Illinois, Springfield, 1918-1920, III), 47.

[2] J. R. Beste, The Wabash (London, 1855), I, 162; Russell, My Diary, 90; Boston Eve. Transcript, June 16, 1853, Oct. 1, 1860.

[3] N. Y. Tribune, Jan. 4, 1860.

[4] Anthony Trollope, North America (N. Y., 1862), 290.

a suspension bridge was built over the Niagara, a monument to the engineering genius of John A. Roebling. Two years later, to the bitter disappointment of St. Louis interests and of the advocates of a water route to the Gulf, the Mississippi was bridged at Rock Island, and in less than a year one hundred and twenty-five thousand freight cars and nearly seventy-five thousand passenger coaches crossed the trestle. The Rock Island Bridge suit, in which Abraham Lincoln served among the counsel of the railroad, was brought by the combined opponents of such bridges—in support of a steamer which had collided with and set fire to the Rock Island structure—to secure a court ruling that the bridge was a nuisance menacing river traffic. The court's decision for the railroad was influenced by the valuable services the bridge had rendered in improving transportation facilities in the trans-Mississippi region.[1] The outcome was a striking testimonial to the extent that rail transportation was tying together East and West, replacing the older bonds of river transportation that had previously linked the upper and lower sections of the Mississippi Valley.

By 1860 Chicago, the new rail metropolis of the West, had fifteen lines and well over a hundred daily trains. Thirty miles an hour was a common speed for passenger traffic; Chicago and Alton trains averaged twenty-two miles, rarely varying ten minutes from schedule. When a traveler, accustomed to a stage ride of three days and nights from Chicago to the state capital, made the trip by rail in twelve hours, it seemed to him "more like a sketch from some part of the Arabian Nights, than a matter of stern reality."[2] An experi-

[1] A. J. Beveridge, *Abraham Lincoln, 1809-1858* (Boston, 1928), I, 598-605.
[2] *Alton* (Ill.) *Courier*, June 3, 1853, Feb. 22, 1854.

enced tourist in 1854 reported express travel over a succession of five lines from Boston to Cincinnati in forty
hours. In May, 1860, a Michigan-Southern train made
a record-breaking trip between Chicago and Buffalo in
fifteen and a half hours. Passenger fares were commonly
two cents a mile, though they varied according to circumstances of competition. A few roads having a monopoly of traffic charged upwards of three cents, while
the strenuous warfare of rival lines sometimes drove
fares down to less than one cent. A traveler in 1851 reports having been carried from Buffalo to Cincinnati
and supplied with meals for a total of three dollars.[1]

In the early sixties the modern convertible sleeping
car was introduced with a promise of luxury in travel.
Almost immediately the Negro porter made his appearance. The crude cot arrangement seemed well worth the
extra dollar charged, though those who suffered from
the occasional collapse of an upper berth may have
found their enthusiasm tempered.[2] Railroad wrecks and
accidents in general loomed up as a much more serious
risk. Without fences along the right of way, straying
cattle, indifferent to the locomotive's wailing whistle,
caused about half the accidents, though not the more
serious catastrophes. The toll of fatalities mounted at
a rate that occasioned vigorous protests against "reckless" speed.[3] As railroad accommodations penetrated ever
farther into the interior of the country, the bugle blast
and the crack of the stage-driver's whip died out along
the old turnpikes. In June, 1853, the Ohio Stage Coach

[1] Beste, The Wabash, I, 172.
[2] Ferri Pisani, Lettres sur les États-Unis d'Amérique (Paris, 1862),
381. See also Trollope, North America, 111-112; Dicey, Six Months in
the Federal States, I, 57; Francis Tiffany, Life of Dorothea Lynde Dix
(Boston, 1890), 332; A. D. Richardson, Beyond the Mississippi (N. Y.,
1867), 155.
[3] "Editor's Easy Chair," Harper's Mo., XVII (1858), 555; N. Y.
Herald, Aug. 31, 1855; Cincinnati Enquirer, June 8, 1859.

company operating out of Columbus placed their fifty coaches upon the market; after a year's delay an Iowa stage company purchased the entire movable equipment and transferred it overland in a grand cavalcade to a region not yet penetrated by the railroad.

With the advent of the railroad travel for pleasure became a popular pastime. Excursions to near-by points found favor and long-distance journeys attracted extraordinary numbers. So "democratically" were such opportunities embraced that travel in America remained a one-class institution. It might properly be pointed out that the personal contacts in train and hotel brought together Easterners and Westerners rather than Northerners and Southerners and thus contributed psychologically to the new sectional alignment.

The railroads opened up to the world the great granary of the upper Mississippi Valley. The fertile lands of the corn belt of east-central Illinois were untouched until the Illinois Central and other lines connected them with markets in the East that were now as accessible as near-by cities had been a decade before. Five or more puffing locomotives drew the hundred-car train that often carried Western products from Buffalo over the New York Central. Closer bonds with the Atlantic Seaboard by the direct rail route reduced the Westerners' dependence upon the Mississippi outlet and the Southern market. No sudden love replaced the traditional Western hostility to Eastern exploitation, but the double bands of iron welded a steadily growing community of interest. The railroad was one of the most significant forces that combined to weaken the old sectionalism in preparation for the day when the coöperation of West and East was essential to save the Union from disruption.

Meantime the railroads were working miracles within

the West itself. Towns sprang up with mushroom rapidity along the lines that intersected the open prairies. In 1854 West Urbana was a mere depot on the Illinois Central, a year later it was a rising village of a hundred houses, with three hundred more buildings in process of erection, including "two large hotels, six stores, a large furniture ware-house," a Presbyterian church and a schoolhouse.[1] In 1861 it became the thriving town of Champaign with a separate corporate existence. Many a sleepy hamlet of log huts and shanties was thus aroused and converted into a bustling center of activity.

The greatest advantages, however, accrued to the western termini of the new railroads, especially Chicago. This wonder city more than trebled its population in the decade, counting over a hundred thousand souls in 1860. After the completion of the Illinois and Michigan Canal in 1848 the current of trade which had formerly flowed southward through St. Louis turned eastward to the wharves of Chicago. As the hub of the railway system of the Northwest, Chicago further challenged the economic leadership of St. Louis. Rail connections with the Mississippi diverted from the water route the agricultural products of Minnesota, Wisconsin and Iowa as well as of northwestern Illinois. In 1855 Chicago had a grain trade of over twenty million bushels, nearly twice that of its rival on the Mississippi. By 1860 its forest of huge grain elevators gave it a unique place among American cities. It had become the greatest primary wheat depot in the world, the capital of King Corn.

In the course of the decade a cosmopolitan metropolis evolved out of the straggling community that earlier had been constantly menaced by the inundations of river and lake. The city gradually lifted itself by its boot

[1] *Chicago Democrat*, May 5, 1855.

straps, as it were, raising the street level seven or eight feet so as to secure more adequate drainage. Houses were often hoisted bodily to the new grade, although no uniformity of practice prevailed and the pedestrian sometimes had to make his way up one flight of steps and down another. New buildings were constantly being erected, massive stone and brick stores, warehouses and factories, even "palatial" hotels, standing alongside wooden huts and shacks. On the occasion of the Prince of Wales's visit in 1860 Chicago seemed "an extraordinary *melange* of the Broadway of New York and little shanties of Parisian buildings mixed up in some way with backwoods life." [1] By that time Chicago had added to its metropolitan atmosphere the horse-drawn street cars which in the fifties came into use in most Eastern cities.[2] Equipped with fifty-seven hotels in 1855, eight of them "first class," the "Queen City of the West" claimed a consideration as a convention city which received rich recognition in the Republican convention of 1860.

St. Louis, the older Western metropolis, experienced less rapid progress. Yet in the decade it more than doubled its population, reaching a total of 161,000. It was reaping the last great harvest of its strategic position. But with the unbridged Mississippi at its front door it could not effectively connect with the railroad lines that ran to the Atlantic Seaboard. Its future seemed bound up with the development of the overland trade with the Far West, for which it had long been the chief starting point and depot. That the railroad was destined

[1] *Chicago Tribune*, Nov. 12, 1860; N. A. Woods, *The Prince of Wales in Canada and the United States* (London, 1861), 288.

[2] *National Intelligencer*, July 8, 1861. The enthusiastic George F. Train even undertook to introduce this American institution to the cities of England. Train, *My Life in Many States*, 259, 261-262, 270; same author, *Union Speeches* (2d ser., Phila., 1862), 51-54; Alexander Macmillan, *A Night with the Yankees* (n. p., 1868), 16; Dicey, *Six Months in the Federal States*, II, 214-215.

to play an important part in this trade, many Missourians seemed slow to realize.

Though rail expansion proved detrimental to river traffic at the lower points, it gave a great boom to commerce on the upper Mississippi as the railroad came to supply a direct route with Eastern markets. Soon a hundred or more steamboats averaging about two hundred tons were plying the waters in and out of St. Paul.[1] Through passenger tickets between St. Paul and the East evidenced the close coördination of rail and river traffic. While there were still times when as many as one hundred and seventy steamboats loaded and unloaded along the St. Louis levee, much of the upper-river traffic now went eastward over the rails.[2] Indeed, in 1858 certain enterprising "Yankees" established a carrying trade from the Hudson's Bay Company posts in Canada by way of the Red River of the North and the Mississippi to St. Paul and New York, thus reducing communication with London to a matter of four or five months.[3] On the eve of the Civil War William H. Seward, campaigning for Lincoln's election, could prophetically declare to a St. Paul audience that they were living in a region that was destined to become the seat of power for all North America.[4] Rail and sail were great tools of empire-building in the fifties. It was a national tragedy that one important section of the Union could not subscribe to the doctrine, voiced by Abraham Lincoln in his second message, that "steam, telegraphs and intelligence" had wrought a vast territory, with a wide variety of climate

[1] G. B. Merrick, *Old Times on the Upper Mississippi* (Cleveland, 1909), 162-172; Herbert and Edward Quick, *Mississippi Steamboatin'* (N. Y., 1926).

[2] Charles Mackay, *Life and Liberty in America* (London, 1859), I, 226.

[3] T. W. Knox, *Camp-Fire and Cotton-Field* (Phila., 1865), 299.

[4] W. H. Seward, *Works* (G. E. Baker, ed., Boston, 1884), IV, 331-332.

and production, into "an advantageous combination for one united people."

Meantime manufacturing had undergone a rapid development in the Ohio Valley. Assisted by improved transportation and other favoring conditions, the industrial frontier steadily crept westward until it reached the Mississippi. Some four thousand Illinois mills in 1860 had an output worth over fifty million dollars, with Chicago as the center for the manufacture of farm implements and machinery. Peter Schuttler's wagon factory, established in 1843, was known all the way to Texas and to Oregon, while the transfer in 1848 of the McCormick reaper works to Chicago gave it a new point of vantage.[1] The growth of industrialism in the Middle West promised to forge a new link between the upper Mississippi Valley and the Atlantic Seaboard.

In all parts of the North a distinctive feature of factory production was the increasing reliance on cheap and efficient methods. A proud Yankee boasted that his country offered "the best and cheapest farm implements, the best carpenters' tools, the best locks, fire-engines, nails, screws, and axes; the best fire-arms, the cheapest clocks, the fastest steamers and sailing vessels, the cheapest railroads, the lightest wagons, and many of the most useful labor-saving machines in every department of industry."[2] A single machine at Pittsburgh turned out half-pound iron railroad spikes at the rate of fifty per minute, so that a plant with only seven employees had

[1] W. T. Hutchinson, *Cyrus Hall McCormick: Seed Time, 1809-1856* (N. Y., 1930), 250-275.

[2] "Editor's Table," *Harper's Mo.*, XIII (1856), 411. See also V. S. Clark, *History of Manufactures in the United States, 1607-1860* (Carnegie Inst., *Contribs. to Am. Econ. History;* Wash., 1916); Isaac Lippincott, *A History of Manufactures in the Ohio Valley to the Year 1860* (Chicago, 1914); J. L. Bishop, *A History of American Manufactures from 1608 to 1860* (Phila., 1868); E. A. Riley, *Development of Chicago and Vicinity as a Manufacturing Center prior to 1880* (Chicago, 1911).

an output of five tons a day. In another city a factory produced three hundred thousand dozens of common pins a day: brass wire whizzed into a machine to come out with heads and points perfectly shaped, later to be packed in paper packages with a machine that picked out the pins, laid them in rows, and pushed each row into a paper fed by a girl operative. At Hartford in the early fifties Samuel Colt established what soon became the greatest arms factory on the globe. There his famous revolver was manufactured with an array of precision machine tools that soon made the inventor an early world-renowned captain of industry. Simultaneously a new rubber industry developed upon the basis of the sixty patents taken out by Charles Goodyear before his death in 1860. The sixty thousand workers employed in making several hundred India-rubber products produced annually eight million dollars' worth of merchandise. Clocks and watches were turned out by the hundreds in factories with virtually the only handwork that of assembling the parts. House's telegraphic printing machine, a type-setting machine and the Hoe rotary press were only a few of the mechanical contrivances that made easy the transmission and publication of the day's news.[1] Americans at length had an opportunity to display as well as boast of their industrial prowess. In 1851 a great British international exposition, housed in a spectacular "Crystal Palace" at Hyde Park, launched the first of a series of modern world's fairs. There American products achieved triumphs in several fields. "The American Reapers; Bigelow's Carpet Power Looms; Day & Newell's Locks; St. John's Variation Compass

---

[1] Nichols, *Forty Years of American Life*, I, 377-381; Holland Thompson, *The Age of Invention* (Allen Johnson, ed., *The Chronicles of America Series*, New Haven, 1918-1921, XXXVII), 148, 172-173, 190-192; Waldemar Kaempffert, *A Popular History of American Invention* (N. Y., 1924), *passim*.

and Velocimeter; Herring's Safes; and Dick's Anti-Friction Press had no rivals, and afforded conclusive demonstrations of American superiority in utilitarian inventions." [1] Two years later America held her own Crystal Palace exhibition in New York in a structure of iron and glass like that of the English fair.

Not only in manufacturing but also in retail methods a change took place. With the ever greater reach of the railway, the picturesque peddler with his pack of "Yankee notions" played a less conspicuous part in the distribution of commodities.[2] Improved shopping facilities in near-by towns and cities came within reach of more and more Americans. A striking new development was the department store, which made its first appearance in the nation's metropolis when Alexander T. Stewart in 1848 erected a six-story marble palace on an expensive Broadway site. Like the country "general store," of which it was a sophisticated urban counterpart, there was scarcely anything that its counters could not supply. After a dozen years this building was outgrown and Stewart erected a new and larger structure out of the then popular cast-iron materials; at length New York could claim without fear of contradiction the finest store in the world.[3] At the same time, the magnificent jewelry establishments of Tiffany and of Ball and Black displayed lavish stocks of plate and jewelry that betokened an age of gilt and glitter, if not of refinement and taste.

[1] Bishop, *History of American Manufactures*, II, 480.

[2] Richardson Wright, *Hawkers and Walkers in Early America* (Phila., 1927), 23, and *passim*; Kohl, *Travels*, II, 300.

[3] [Isabella L. Bishop], *The Englishwoman in America* (London, 1856), 340-341; Woods, *Prince of Wales in the United States*, 381, 385, 397; Trollope, *North America*, 203; Russell, *My Diary*, 24; Macmillan, *A Night with the Yankees*, 18; G. T. Barrett, *Out West* (London, 1866), 277, 278; *N. Y. Tribune*, Oct. 15, 1860; Nevins, *Emergence of Modern America*, 91-92.

Real-estate speculation was not entirely a frontier phenomenon. The disease ravaged New York City quite as
much as new-fledged Western communities. Many of
the great fortunes of the mid-nineteenth century rested
largely upon land investments. Thus Peter Goelet and
his sons, following in the footsteps of the Astors, reaped
untold wealth from their foresight in buying tracts of
farm and pasture land that adjoined the growing
metropolis in the Fifth Avenue district between
Twenty-third Street and Forty-third.[1] In 1850 the corner of Fifth Avenue and Twenty-third Street was the
site of Madison Cottage, a rural tavern which furnished
a night's lodging for eight cents to guests who were
warned to remove their boots before retiring. So swiftly
did population move northward that in 1858 Amos R.
Eno felt justified in erecting a modern hotel in this same
locality.

Fortunes were accumulating from the most varied
sources. Textile factories in New England and iron
foundries in Pennsylvania produced their captains of
wealth. An enterprising manufacturer made a million
out of patent medicine, retiring to a brownstone palace
on Fifth Avenue which he furnished with a lavishness
intended to excite the envy of his neighbors. In the Middle West the richest man was Nicholas Longworth of
Cincinnati, a wine grower and manufacturer who died
at a ripe old age, in 1862, worth millions in productive
real estate and other investments. This "Bacchus of the
New World" dwelt in a handsome mansion with beautiful gardens, was a liberal patron of the arts and, in a
city famous for the manufacture and sale of whisky,

---

[1] Gustavus Myers, *History of the Great American Fortunes* (Chicago,
1910), I, 97 ff.; J. D. McCabe, *Great Fortunes and How They Were
Made* (Cin., 1872); B. J. Hendrick, *The Age of Big Business* (*Chronicles of America*, XXXIX), 10-11.

was reputed to have done "more for the cause of health and temperance than all the quack reformers." [1]

Some of the new fortunes of the fifties were made possible by gross fraud and corruption. Cities were swindled by contractors in league with the municipal authorities. Franchises were granted to gas and street-car companies that dangled their influence and money before the eyes of pliable avaricious officials. Railroads secured legislative favors by methods that varied from political manipulation to sheer bribery. The Camden and Amboy Railroad maintained its monopoly over the New York-Philadelphia route by an adroit management of local politicians in both political parties.[2] In 1858 the La Crosse and Milwaukee Railroad was charged by a special Wisconsin legislative committee with having passed out bribes wholesale to persons from the governor, who was allotted fifty thousand dollars, down to a number of assemblymen, each of whom received five thousand dollars.[3] Conscientious men deplored the corruption incident to the phenomenal development of industrial America; but comparisons were scarcely fair, for there were no comparable temptations in European countries.

It was not so obvious in that day that the acceptance of a railroad pass involved a questionable obligation. Nearly all public officials traveled on passes. President Buchanan was a shining exception, making it a lifelong practice to decline such favors. Abraham Lincoln, on the other hand, returned his used-up pass on the Alton road, with the facetious comment, "Here's your old 'chalked hat.' I wish you would take it, and send me

[1] Fuller, *Belle Brittan on a Tour*, 49-52; Nichols, *Forty Years of American Life*, I, 154-155.

[2] C. M. Knapp, *New Jersey Politics during the Period of the Civil War and Reconstruction* (Geneva, N. Y., 1924), 184.

[3] D. W. Mitchell, *Ten Years Residence in the United States* (London, 1862), 133.

a new one; case I shall want to use it the first of March." [1] But passes were a petty matter in a day when corruption was gaining such a foothold that a newly elected New York legislator felt called upon to apologize for accepting a position which, previously considered an honor, had now become "an impeachment of a man's standard of honesty." [2] Governor E. Dennison Morgan, a leader of unquestioned integrity, tried by his vetoes to block bills to turn over to George Law and his associates railroad franchises worth a million; but Speaker DeWitt Clinton Littlejohn of his own party led a bipartisan combination which, despite charges of graft, overrode the governor. "That votes were openly bought and sold last winter at the State capital," commented *Harper's Weekly*, June 2, 1860, "that some measures were passed by the aid of money freely paid to numbers of their best friends, while others were defeated by the same corrupt means, is notorious." Horace Greeley flayed Speaker Littlejohn in the columns of the *Tribune* with a resulting charge of libel which the jury failed to sustain. Henry J. Raymond, editor of the *New York Times*, publicly admitted, when he succeeded Littlejohn as speaker, that it had come to be "among the accepted and acknowledged articles of the popular faith, that our legislature is corrupt and corruptible." [3]

If corruption seemed everywhere "a propensity," in the national capital it was "an art." Members of Congress often began by petty manipulation of their mileage and their stationery accounts; next they sold the seat allotments that they drew; and soon their votes were

---

[1] James Buchanan, *Works* (J. B. Moore, ed., Phila., 1908-1911), X, 315; Abraham Lincoln, *Complete Works* (J. G. Nicolay and John Hay, eds., N. Y., 1894), II, 289. Lincoln was its attorney.

[2] Charles Wright (Mountaineer, *pseud.*), *The Prospect* (Buffalo, 1862), 25.

[3] Wright, *The Prospect*, 25-28.

on the market. Corrupt lobby agents then got in their work, having perhaps purchased the aid of six or eight aggressive members. This was the tale told by observant journalists and widely published, much to the astonishment of foreign visitors.[1] Behind the scoundrels who looted the public treasury were the dimly defined figures of others, more adroit but hardly less unscrupulous, who represented the growing victory of the new industrialism. Prosperous citizens of the respectable, churchgoing type winked at the corruption that raised such a stench when it remitted their taxes or when it bargained away to them or their representatives water rights, pier privileges, public-utility franchises or railroad charters. Vanderbilts, Astors, Rhinelanders, Goelets and other proud dwellers on Fifth Avenue witnessed without serious concern the developments that made New York the worst governed city in the Western World.

To many "dollar-worshiping" seemed a national trait as it had never been before. "Every man worships the dollar, and is down before his shrine from morning to night. . . . The frankincense from the temple is ever in one's nostrils," commented an observant Britisher.[2] The philosopher Emerson began to fear lest the rapidly increasing power of accumulated wealth "upset the balance of man, and establish a new, universal monarchy more tyrannical than Babylon or Rome."[3] The prevalent standard of social ostentation, a will-o'-the-wisp pursued by merchants who had not been squeamish about how they had made their pile, affected nearly all

[1] Amelia M. Murray, *Letters from the United States, Cuba and Canada* (N. Y., 1856), II, 198-199; Mitchell, *Ten Years Residence in the United States*, 127, 130-131; Adolf Douai, *Land und Leute in der Union* (Berlin, 1864), 74 ff.; Grattan, *Civilized America*, II, 465-468; Wright, *The Prospect*, 15, 23.

[2] Trollope, *North America*, 183, 185.

[3] Ralph Waldo Emerson, *Journals* (E. W. Emerson and W. E. Forbes, eds., Boston, 1909-1914), V, 285-286.

ranks of society. The times revealed a frantic scramble
for a share in the teeming prosperity, with brains and
nerves always on the stretch.[1] It was a day of fast living, of dissipation and extravagance. In vain the moralist sounded the alarm against the progress of luxury,
"which corrupts the morals and enervates the manhood
of a people, which engenders habits of idleness and
frivolity and turns even industry into unprofitable
channels."[2]

As if to demonstrate that riches had not destroyed
their souls, wealthy individuals more than ever essayed
the rôle of public benefactors. Humanitarian and cultural institutions were recipients of their bounty. Generous gifts and bequests went to colleges, churches, theological schools, benevolent societies, hospitals, and to
relief movements of every sort. The Astor Library, the
Lawrence School at Cambridge and George Peabody's
generous benefactions to Baltimore were only a few evidences that art and literature could flourish in America
"without the aid of kings."[3] To keep such generosity
within bounds, the New York legislature in 1860 provided by law that no person having a husband, wife,
child, or parent should by will bequeath more than one
half of his property to a benevolent, charitable, literary,
religious or missionary society.[4] Liberality on the part
of the wealthy came to be regarded as an outstanding
American characteristic.[5] Cynics like James Gordon Ben-

---

[1] Anon., "Our Sons," *Harper's Mo.*, XVII (1858), 60; anon., "Why
We Get Sick," same mag., XIII (1856), 642-643.

[2] *Providence Journal*, cited in *Washtenaw Whig* (Ann Arbor, Mich.),
Oct. 15, 1851; *Ann Arbor Local News*, March 6, 1860.

[3] "The Lounger," *Harper's Wkly.*, V, 83 (Feb. 9, 1861); P. A.
Hanaford, *The Life of George Peabody* (Boston, 1870).

[4] *Boston Eve. Transcript*, Oct. 5, 1860; *Laws of the State of New
York for 1860*, 607.

[5] Fredrika Bremer, *The Homes of the New World* (N. Y., 1854), I,
357-358; Agénor de Gasparin, *The Uprising of a Great People* (Mary
L. Booth, tr., N. Y., 1861), 55; Trollope, *North America*, 185;

nett of the *New York Herald*, however, issued grave warnings that American education and culture might be tempted to sell its soul in return for such favors.[1]

The golden days of the fifties were not without their uncertainties or interruptions. Indeed, at the end of 1854, when a sudden tightness in the money market had developed, prosperity seemed to have overreached itself. From fifteen to twenty thousand unemployed walked the streets of New York that winter demanding work and denouncing the wealthy classes and their extravagance. In February, 1855, soup kitchens were still in operation, though conditions were rapidly improving. But the lesson of this depression was promptly forgotten. Flush times returned, marked by the usual speculative industrial development, overoptimistic railroad building and wild extravagance of living. In 1857, not without warning, another and more serious day of reckoning arrived. Bankers and business men found themselves helpless in the face of impending economic disaster. In August the storm broke in all its fury. Banks and corporations crashed; railroads became bankrupt; land values dropped sharply; building operations came to a sudden end.

In the rural districts the panic, though forcing trade to shift to a barter basis, caused little real hardship. But in the cities it brought widespread unemployment with resulting suffering from hunger and cold. Thousands shivered in the winter wind as they swarmed the streets of New York's fashionable district to beg for crumbs at rich men's doors. Immigration declined rapidly, while increased emigration reflected a return tide of foreigners who had saved enough money to rejoin friends and rela-

Douai, *Land und Leute*, 226; Macmillan, *A Night with the Yankees*, 22-25.

[1] *N. Y. Herald*, Jan. 1-12, 1859.

tives at home. The really well-to-do, afraid now to display their glitter, acquiesced in an enforced régime of economy, which they made palatable by making it fashionable. Gay "poverty parties" were held in Fifth Avenue mansions, while neighbors, who had lost their all in the crash, moved quietly to cheaper quarters elsewhere.[1] As the state of panic became acute, a spirit of popular discontent stalked abroad. The victims of the economic debâcle displayed a readiness to listen to socialistic and anarchistic agitators. This only caused greater alarm among those in a position to take the lead in the process of recovery, which did not get well under way until the summer of 1858. Yet, for another year and more, hard times lingered.

The most highly organized industries, like the iron mills of Pennsylvania, suffered the worst blows. In the agricultural South, on the other hand, prosperity and good prices for cotton continued, with only occasional bank failures and suspensions as reminders of the economic interdependence of the sections. Excellent cotton crops prevailed, exports increased and Negro slaves sold at prices that exceeded all past figures. All this was in marked contrast to the social revolution that seemed to threaten the industrial areas. The proud spokesmen of the South therefore boasted of the superior soundness of the cotton kingdom. "The wealth of the South," announced J. D. B. De Bow, "is permanent and real, that of the North fugitive and fictitious." [2] Yet the census summary of industrial progress at the close of the decade showed no perceptible trace of the temporary breakdown of 1857.

[1] Fuller, *Belle Brittan on a Tour*, 245, 303.
[2] *De Bow's Rev.*, XXIII (1857), 592.

CHAPTER II

THE LAND OF CHIVALRY

IN the 1850's the black belt of the South, the region of heaviest slave population, attained its highest development, spreading over nearly one third the territory of Dixie. The Negro chattel became part of the agricultural economy not only of the plantations in the fertile river bottoms but also of many small upland farms. Yet never had the lines of social cleavage been so closely drawn. The plantation oligarchy had its nucleus in some three hundred planters, each of whom owned two hundred slaves or more; a group of twenty-three hundred others were lords over a hundred each; while fewer than two hundred thousand owned as many as ten slaves and seventy-seven thousand could each command the labors of but a single Negro. In all the region there were scarcely 384,000 slaveholders in 1860 out of a population of over eight million whites. This meant that slightly more than one out of every four whites was directly or indirectly connected with slaveholding as against one out of three in 1850. Of this number only a quarter of a million enjoyed the full fruits of a plantation system that required a working unit of at least twenty field hands.[1] Many Southerners like Joseph E. Johnston, A. P. Hill and Fitzhugh Lee never owned a slave.

Nevertheless, the plantation ideal more than ever dominated the South. To become a large planter was

[1] *Agriculture of the United States in 1860 (U. S. Eighth Census),* 247.

the aspiration of every ambitious youth. Some nursed this ambition in the squalor of humble hill-country cabins, others in the luxury of comfortable city homes, while the elect awaited their inevitable inheritance on their paternal estates. The planter-aristocrat on his broad acres represented a leisure class that was genial, picturesque and patriarchal. Not all took part in public affairs; even some of the largest planters like Samuel Hairston of Pittsylvania, Virginia, or J. C. Johnson of North Carolina dwelt in contented obscurity.[1] The result is that time has left few traces of men like William B. Goulden, who was reputed to be the largest slaveholder in Georgia.[2] The plantation was the center of social life in the South, though the winter months usually brought a shift to the gayety of a near-by city— Baltimore, Richmond, Charleston, Mobile or New Orleans—and summer a brief respite at some Northern resort or Southern watering place.

One feature of this aristocracy in former times had been its flexibility, evidenced by the ease with which a small farmer, town merchant or sometimes even an ambitious mechanic rose into its ranks. The coming of the railroads led the professional men in the cities sometimes to purchase rural estates and, in the occasional visits of an absentee proprietor, to taste the pleasures of planta-

[1] Hairston, who personally owned nearly two thousand Negroes, had control of one thousand more slaves, the property of his mother-in-law. The annual increase of one hundred a year made it necessary to purchase a large plantation annually on which to settle them. His wealth was estimated at from three to five million. He resided in a beautiful mansion on a magnificent estate. He had a brother in Henry County, Virginia, who owned seven hundred Negroes, and two brothers in Mississippi who owned, respectively, one thousand and six hundred slaves. Another brother in Henry County who had distributed most of his property among his children still owned one hundred and fifty. *Richmond Whig*, cited in *Belleville* (Ill.), *Advocate*, June 21, 1854. See also William Chambers, *American Slavery and Colour* (London, 1857), 194-195.

[2] Goulden is not even mentioned in the works of Ulrich B. Phillips, a native of Georgia and an authority on Negro slavery.

tion ownership. In general, however, the fifties found the landed gentry chary about admitting newcomers to their circles. Not only did the price of slaves and worthwhile land steadily mount, but the *parvenu* was not always welcomed into an aristocracy in which a generation or two of slaveholding had fostered a tradition of birthright.

The best contemporary picture of social stratification is that drawn in 1860 by D. R. Hundley, an Alabama planter. At the top stood the plantation aristocrats. Then came the middle class made up of smaller slaveholding planters, professional men, tradesmen and skilled mechanics. Next followed the yeomen, while separated from them by an almost impassable chasm were the "poor whites." Underneath all were the Negroes, slave or free. Members of the middle class were usually deficient in culture and refinement and, according to Hundley, they "sometimes, from sheer envy and jealousy, entertain a most cordial hatred of those whose attainments and good-breeding they despair of ever being able to emulate." [1] Of this group the skilled artisans were least likely to be slave owners. Their contact with slaves —and with free Negroes—was almost exclusively with those with whom they competed in their work. In the fifties they demanded legislation to prevent such competition, a demand effectively launched at a mechanics' state convention in Georgia on July 4, 1851.[2] But while the proposal was considered in several states, slaveholders were averse to any effort to prescribe the way in which they might employ or hire out their slaves.[3]

[1] D. R. Hundley, *Social Relations in Our Southern States* (N. Y., 1860), 95.

[2] *Savannah Republican*, June 27, July 10, 1851.

[3] In 1859 a skilled mechanic of Columbia, South Carolina, was tarred and feathered and expelled from the community because he had made the remark that slaves should be confined to work on plantations. *N. Y. Tribune*, Jan. 2, 1860.

Signs abounded in the late fifties of an increasing class consciousness among white workingmen, which might have marked the beginning of a revolt against the institution. Thus, in North Carolina, an organized workers' movement challenged a twenty-year-old revenue system because it taxed mechanics' tools twenty times as heavily as slave property.[1]

The yeomanry consisted of small farmers on the hilly fringes of the black belt, where they raised varied crops and lived mainly on "hog and hominy." They represented the surviving influence of the later stages of the frontier. Usually tall, lean, crude, tobacco-chewing, profane, they were also honest and pious, and in number they constituted the backbone of Southern society. Sometimes owning, sometimes hiring, a slave or two, they worked with their children side by side with the Negroes. Their greatest ambition was to become slaveholders; whenever they achieved that status, even on a small scale, they were extremely proud. As they acquired more slaves, they rose in social standing to the middle group. It was from this class, too, that the plantation overseers were usually recruited. In the fifties, however, many of the yeomen, weary of wringing a scant subsistence from a scrap of hillside land, tended to become discouraged and to settle down to habits of sloth and idleness.[2] Traveling through the backcountry of the South from the Mississippi to the James, Frederick Law Olmsted never observed in their homes a "thermometer, nor a book of Shakespeare, nor a pianoforte or sheet of music, nor . . . reading lamp, nor an

[1] W. K. Boyd, "North Carolina on the Eve of Secession," Am. Hist. Assoc., *Ann. Rep. for 1910*, 174-175; Julia A. Flisch, "Common People of the Old South," Am. Hist. Assoc., *Ann. Rep for 1908*, I, 140-141.

[2] J. S. C. Abbott, *South and North* (N. Y., 1860), 146-147. See also F. L. Olmsted, *The Cotton Kingdom* (N. Y., 1862), II, 44; C. G. Parsons, *Inside View of Slavery* (Cleveland, 1855), 113-114.

engraving, or a copy of any kind, of a work of art of the slightest merit." [1] It was to this group and its supposed discontent that Hinton Rowan Helper appealed when in 1857 he published *The Impending Crisis of the South,* in which he challenged "the lords of the lash" as foes "of all non-slaveholding whites, whose freedom is merely nominal, and whose unparalleled illiteracy and degradation is purposely and fiendishly perpetuated." [2]

Helper's failure to arouse the white masses emphasizes the chief paradox of the Southern social system. Though slavery raised ever higher barriers against nonslaveholding whites and in many ways sacrificed the latter to its own prosperity, a greater number of the people than ever before—from the planter capitalists at the top to the willing peasant hangers-on at the bottom—were drawn into some sort of active support of the "peculiar institution." Less than ever before, apparently, did the gentry need to dread leveling agrarian tendencies, or to fear lest they be unhorsed politically by the introduction of the "white basis" of apportioning representation in place of the "mixed" or "federal" system. Indeed, a slaveholding leadership, which included many of the wildest fire eaters in the South, was marshaling in political array the ranks of the unprivileged.

And yet all was not well in the South. The planter leaders realized they could not rely absolutely upon the contentment of the nonslaveholder, especially as, in the fifties, the poor-white class took on more definite outline. An original pioneer stock, drained by the westward movement of its most energetic and ambitious elements, it found itself isolated in the mountainous Appalachian

[1] F. L. Olmsted, *A Journey in the Back Country* (N. Y., 1863), 395, also 259.

[2] H. R. Helper, *The Impending Crisis of the South* (N. Y., 1857), 43-44. James D. B. De Bow replied in a pamphlet entitled *The Interest in Slavery of the Southern Non-Slaveholder* (New Orleans, 1860).

backcountry and in the piny sand barrens of south-central Georgia and eastern Mississippi. Physically undermined by attacks of what was called "malaria," and by a wide range of disorders now known to have been due to the hookworm, some of its members degenerated until they became satisfied with the barest human necessities and with few social enjoyments. At their best, with simple piety and frugality, they eked out a precarious livelihood by tilling a scrubby farm, supplementing its yield with hunting and fishing or by doing occasional chores for a near-by planter. At their worst they ate clay, chewed resin and snuff, drank fiery "rot-gut" whisky, and dreamed on in blissful ignorance of the contempt with which the outside world regarded them.

The planters showed no desire to employ these "hillbillies" at farm labor; nor would the latter have been willing to toil alongside the slave, whom they thoroughly scorned, but over whom they could not always show a marked superiority. Pioneer manufacturers saw in them an available labor supply to bring about in the South the industrial revolution which they foretold. William Gregg employed them in his cotton factory at Graniteville, South Carolina, and gave them a chance to settle the question as to whether ignorance, shiftlessness, and contentment with poverty were inherent qualities or the result of circumstance. Most critics of the poor whites, however, saw little hope for them. Scorned by the groups that surrounded them, the highlanders of western Carolina and of the eastern parts of Kentucky and Tennessee failed to share the general enthusiasm for the "peculiar institution" of the South. Indeed, sometimes they revealed a bitter hatred toward the slaves as well as toward the slave barons. In this attitude the poor white was often encouraged by those who sought his political support. Many a politician wallowed in a demagoguery that attested a degenerate conception of democracy both by the voter and the candidate.[1]

At the very bottom of the social pyramid stood the Negroes, numbering in 1860 over four million. Of these 3,838,765 were enslaved.[2] The institution of chattel slavery can best be interpreted historically as an educational as well as labor system in which, without his consent and in return for his forced labor, the Negro was given his keep and taught some of the elementary lessons of white civilization. By 1850, however, it should have been an open question as to whether or no the institution had outlived its usefulness. There was certainly little in the system to make it keep pace with the march of events; more and more the planter was in a position to realize its economic unsoundness. In a detailed analysis of the Southern system one of the editors of the *Southern Cultivator* frankly admitted that "the amount of labor used on an ordinary Southern plantation is greater per productive acre than the amount of labor used in the most perfectly cultivated portions of Europe" and that "the negro is the investment rather than the land."[3] Under slavery land was soon worn out in an exhausting one-crop agriculture and scrapped. It remained only for the Southerner to realize the signifi-

[1] P. H. Buck, "The Poor White in the Ante-bellum South," *Am. Hist. Rev.*, XXXI, 41-55.

[2] John Cummings, ed., *Negro Population in the United States, 1790-1915* (Wash., 1918), 55.

[3] Commissioner of Patents, *Report for 1860*, 226; D. R. Goodloe, cited in C. D. Wright, *The Industrial Evolution of the United States* (Meadville, Pa., 1895), 151. See also D. R. Goodloe, "Resources and Industrial Condition of the South," Comnr. of Agr., *Rep. for 1865*, 119. Of course, part of the profits of Southern agriculture under slave labor was to be found in the normal slave increase by birth. Negroes increased "like rabbits," Howell Cobb's overseer informed him; it was nothing for the number on a plantation to double in less than a dozen years. U. B. Phillips, *Plantation and Frontier* (J. R. Commons, ed., *Documentary History of American Industrial Society*, Cleveland, 1910-1911, I-II), I, 179.

cance of the fact that the heavy capital investment in labor had no equivalent under a wage system.

Moreover, while the essential needs of the Negro were cared for, the system had little to teach such slaves as displayed signs of initiative and ingenuity. Individuals, to be sure, profited from contact with their masters or from the mechanical employments into which they drifted, either on the home plantation or when hired out to others. But if some were given wide latitude of self-expression, most were lost in the system of absentee ownership with overseer control, such as was common throughout the Lower South. The overseer, generally a semiliterate representative of the humbler white element, was all too often a mere slave driver. Naturally enough, he kept his accounts in terms of dollars and cents and not in human values. Yet one half of the slaves were held in parcels of less than twenty and hence labored under the eye of the owner. From a maze of conflicting testimony by contemporary observers, mainly travelers, it is reasonably clear that the average slaveholder was genuinely concerned for the physical well-being of his "chattels." Some would not allow their slaves to go into the field to pick cotton while the dew was on the plant; some employed white laborers, usually Irish floaters, to do strenuous and unhealthful work such as ditch digging and draining.

As the sectional controversy sharpened, life in thralldom lost many of its mitigating aspects; Southern hearts were hardened by the mere thought of outside dictation or interference.[1] Laws against teaching slaves to read no longer remained dead letters. Police regulations and pre-

---

[1] [Catherine C. Hopley], *Life in the South* (London, 1863), II, 46, 47; Olmsted, *Cotton Kingdom*, II, 350 ff. See also *De Bow's Rev.*, VIII (1850), 22-23, 182-185, 294-296; U. B. Phillips, *American Negro Slavery* (N. Y., 1918), 488, 510; H. M. Henry, *Police Control of the Slave in South Carolina* (Emory, Va., 1914).

cautions for the control of slaves were revised and extended while the machinery for enforcement was strengthened. The curfew became an insistent reality, in Charleston for free Negroes as well as for slaves. Bondsmen attempting to run away were flogged with less mercy than ever. "Judge Lynch" punished the Negro's more serious crimes, sometimes at the stake, with the active approval of sober citizens. All too often the atmosphere reeked with fear and suspicion. As a result greater brutality colored the authority of master over slave.

Yet the lot of the enslaved black was probably not much more unfortunate than that of his free brother in the South. Indeed, an occasional Negro, given his choice, preferred slavery to the uncertainties of freedom.[1] It was hardly for this reason, however, that in 1860 the free colored population of the slave states was only 260,000, a number which represented a smaller rate of increase than that of any other group in the nation. Of these about half were to be found in Virginia and Maryland. Probably the more aggressive and capable ones migrated to the North. At any rate, those who remained had the reputation of being "the most vicious and corrupting element in southern life."[2] They were charged with most of the crimes; nor could the numerous convictions be explained entirely as the result of prejudice or by their lack of civil rights.

Free Negroes were generally confined to menial employments scorned by the whites. From certain skilled occupations they were excluded by law. In some states like Georgia and Mississippi they virtually lacked school facilities, less than ten colored children being enrolled

[1] See the case of Harriet Hall, *Richmond Enquirer*, Feb. 3, cited in *N. Y. Herald*, Feb. 5, 1859.

[2] F. L. Olmsted, *Journey in the Seaboard Slave States* (N. Y., 1859), 125. See also Phillips, *American Negro Slavery*, 449 n.

for the two states according to both the census of 1850 and that of 1860.[1] Inevitably they drifted townward to find employment and escape the restraints of the plantation régime; in the crowded Negro quarters of Washington and New Orleans they developed their own churches, schools and mutual improvement societies. In New Orleans, where the mulattoes outnumbered the pure strain, they were largely skilled workers and, in a community essentially cosmopolitan, received unusual consideration.[2] Both here and in other large cities individuals among them attained a high degree of prosperity and culture. Economic opportunities enabled three hundred and sixty free Negroes of Charleston to accumulate sufficient property to have it listed on the tax duplicates of 1860, while their real-estate holdings were valued at $724,570. One hundred and thirty even owned slaves, to a total of one hundred and ninety.[3]

In all, Southern free Negroes in 1860 owned property valued at twenty-five million dollars. James Roper, natural son of an eccentric English planter, added by his own efforts to his inheritance until he became the largest landowner and the wealthiest man in Jefferson County, Virginia.[4] At least one in every hundred free blacks owned a "chattel" or two, a few controlling parcels of fifty and more. In some cases they purchased relatives to free them; often, however, it was a purely business transaction—nor were they invariably gener-

---

[1] C. G. Woodson, *The Education of the Negro prior to 1861* (N. Y., 1915), 236-237.

[2] The Placide's Varieties Theatre reserved its third tier of boxes for colored persons. *New Orleans Commercial Bulletin*, Jan. 1, 1851. See also Olmsted, *Journey in the Seaboard Slave States*, 14, and Edward Dicey, *Six Months in the Federal States* (London, 1863), II, 114.

[3] Phillips, *American Negro Slavery*, 434.

[4] *Belleville Advocate*, Jan. 3, 1868. See also D. W. Mitchell, *Ten Years Residence in the United States* (London, 1862), 235, and J. A. C. Chandler and others, *The South in the Building of the Nation* (Richmond, 1909-1910), X, 180.

ous masters. In Louisiana certain opulent and refined planters of Negro-French ancestry claimed and were duly conceded the status of Southern gentlemen.[1] In the crisis of 1861 some of the Negro masters publicly declared their unqualified loyalty to the Southern institutions which had enabled them to rise on the shoulders of their fellow blacks.

The presence of free Negroes, however, came increasingly to be regarded by the dominant race as a menace.[2] Many of the twenty thousand slaves manumitted during the decade were set free upon condition of migration to the free states. A demand even arose for legislation to reënslave any blacks who failed to leave. Arkansas enacted such a law to take effect on January 1, 1860. Similar measures were considered in other states, but in Missouri the bill was defeated by the governor's veto, while in Maryland, where the large free colored population intensified the fugitive-slave problem, the voters in 1860 rejected an exclusion proposal submitted by the legislature. Louisiana and Kentucky forbade the further immigration of free blacks. As the day approached upon which the Arkansas law was to go into force, a general exodus of Negroes began. While a few preferred the authority of a master to the uncertainties of seeking a new home, the majority poured into Kansas or took passage up the Mississippi.[3] On January 3 forty-three exiles landed at Cincinnati where a committee representing the colored population bade them welcome. But Illinois and

[1] C. O. Wilson, "Negroes Who Owned Slaves," *Pop. Sci. Mo.*, LXXXI (1912), 492-493. See also Mitchell, *Ten Years Residence in the United States*, 160.

[2] *National Intelligencer* (Wash.), Nov. 1, 1859, Jan. 7, 27, March 13, 18, 27, Aug. 25, Sept. 1, 4, Oct. 31, Nov. 9, Dec. 14, 1860. See also [Hopley], *Life in the South*, I, 156, and Thomas Ellison, *Slavery and Secession in America* (London, 1861), 42, 46.

[3] *Baltimore Sun*, Jan. 7, 1860; A. D. Richardson, *Beyond the Mississippi* (Hartford, 1867), 217.

Indiana, the two nearest free states, had long since closed
their doors to such migrants; nor did the whites of any
other Northern state invite their coming. The pitiful
appeal of a group of these helpless exiles soon appeared
in the public prints; it suggested that many probably
regretted not having accepted their fate in Arkansas.[1]

The South was also becoming troubled about what
had formerly been deemed a highly desirable addition
to her population. Thanks to the part played by North-
ern-born citizens, certain Southern towns had come to
be characterized as "Northern towns." Indeed, many of
the largest slave owners as well as of the influential business and professional men and prominent political
leaders had originally hailed from Pennsylvania, New
York or New England. For a time the push and enterprise of these Yankees had been a spur to many Southerners to go and do likewise. As sectional bitterness increased, however, more and more concern was felt over
the presence of "outsiders." It was soon evident that a
type of espionage was developing by which recent
comers were kept under surveillance. After John
Brown's raid upon Harper's Ferry the tension became
especially strong. Travelers of all sorts were stopped and
compelled to give an account of themselves and their
business in the South. Alleged abolitionists were tarred
and feathered and expelled, while certain unfortunates
were subjected to the extreme penalty of lynch law.[2]
Such conditions not only checked the flow of population
into the South, but caused many local agents of Northern business firms to leave in order to avoid annoyance,

[1] *National Intelligencer*, Jan. 27, 1860; *N. Y. Times*, Jan. 21, 1860.
See also J. B. McMaster, *History of the People of the United States*
(N. Y., 1883-1913), VIII, 430.

[2] Anon., "A Fresh Catalogue of Southern Outrages upon Northern
Citizens," Am. Anti-Slavery Soc., *Publs.*, n. s., no. 14 (1860). See also
Savannah Republican, April 19, 1859; *National Intelligencer*, Sept. 8,
1860; *Mobile Advertiser*, Dec. 23, 1859.

if not positive maltreatment. In this way, too, the years immediately before the war led to a gradual severing of social and economic connections between the sections.

Militant Southerners were not averse to erecting a Chinese wall against the barbarians of the North. They claimed that their section enjoyed the superior opportunities for culture and refinement that only a leisure-class society based upon the exploitation of a servile race could assure. Others, however, pointed to the scanty returns upon the planters' capital, complaining that they could not surround themselves "with comforts and luxuries, and the advantages of education, like other men." [1] In any event, the narrow confines of this culture could not be denied in the face of prevailing illiteracy.

Equally serious was the demoralizing effect of the slavery system upon the initiative of the cultured few. The South at times gave opportunities to courageous thinkers like Joseph Le Conte, scientist at South Carolina College, and Josiah C. Nott, ethnologist at the University of Alabama, in spite of the revolutionary implications of their findings. But it also raised against new and disturbing ideas barriers that not only irked the distinguished Francis Lieber, during the twenty years he occupied the chair of political economy at South Carolina College, but disquieted the bolder spirits of the South like the scientist James Worden of Oglethorpe University, and his promising pupil Sidney Lanier. The trustees of Franklin College, later the University of Georgia, labored for a decade or more to throttle the spirit of scientific revolt, and eventually forced out not only the brilliant Le Conte brothers but the entire faculty. [2]

[1] *Southern Intelligencer*, cited in *De Bow's Rev.*, XXVI (1859), 236.
[2] E. M. Coulter, *College Life in the Old South* (N. Y., 1928), 250-257.

The long-haired Southern youths, served by their Negro valets, had for years attended colleges and universities in greater numbers proportionately than their Northern contemporaries; yet few were inspired to carry on the torch. Higher education in the South, inadequately supported and, perforce, modest in its standards, was largely in the hands of instructors drawn from the North or abroad. The cultural poverty of Dixie caused extensive patronage of Northern and foreign universities. The sectionalism of the fifties, however, bred a demand for greater educational self-sufficiency. Southerners were exhorted to cease sending their youth to Northern institutions, to hire Southern teachers whenever possible, and to utilize schoolbooks published in their own section. As a result, nearly every college and university doubled in attendance, institutions were accorded a more generous support, and new ventures were launched.[1] Most ambitious was the dream of the bishops of the Southern dioceses of the Protestant Episcopal Church, who, under the leadership of Leonidas Polk and with the support of eminent Southerners, projected the "University of the South." In the fall of 1860 the cornerstone of the main building was laid on the chosen site at Sewanee, Tennessee, and contributions toward an endowment of five million dollars were coming in when the war interrupted the promising undertaking.[2]

Yet it was clear that this movement for more colleges and universities would not assure the South a sound educational development. The glorification of the *status*

[1] See anon., "Common Schools and Universities," *De Bow's Rev.*, XVIII (1855), 545-555; Olmsted, *Journey in the Back Country*, 25; Chandler and others, *South in the Building of the Nation*, X, 227-228, and *passim*.

[2] T. D. Ozanne, *The South as It Is* (London, 1863), 193-215; J. W. Du Bose, *The Life and Times of William Lowndes Yancey* (Birmingham, 1892), 318; *N. Y. Tribune*, Feb. 10, 1860; *Baltimore Sun*, Feb. 15, 1860.

quo, the defense of social and economic institutions already threatened by crumbling foundations, could not wisely have been substituted for the search for truth and the spirit of open-mindedness. Francis Lieber gladly left this atmosphere when opportunity beckoned him in 1856 to Columbia College in the North. When Professor B. S. Hedrick of the University of North Carolina was dismissed for having favored the election of Frémont, his academic brethren plodded on in humble subserviency lest they too share the same fate. In 1857 the University of Virginia, forgetful of its rich Jeffersonian tradition, was advertising for a professor of history and literature at a handsome salary, but there were few applicants. Who wants a professorship without freedom of teaching? it was asked.[1] On the other hand, William H. McGuffey, of *McGuffey Reader* fame, served undisturbed as professor of moral philosophy in that institution from 1845 until his death in 1873, despite his Northern origin and moderate antislavery views.

In the same way the South cut itself off from other intellectual contacts with the North. Northern publishers noticed a decline in the sale of their works in the Southern states after 1850, although it was observed in 1851 that there was a sudden increase in orders from South Carolina for works on military tactics.[2] Yet there was no corresponding development of Southern publishing. The recurrent Southern conventions repeatedly indorsed proposals for a publishing agency within the section, and in 1857 even went so far as to provide for a committee to select and prepare a series of Southern schoolbooks "in every department of study, from the earliest primer to the highest grade of literature and sci-

---

[1] *National Intelligencer*, March 3, 1857; *Belleville Advocate*, March 4, 1857.
[2] *Washington Republic*, Sept. 25, 1851.

ence, as shall seem to them best qualified to elevate and purify the education of the South." [1] But the very magnitude of the undertaking, though they hoped to draft the literary talents of McGuffey, Le Conte and others, stood in the way of success. Somewhat later a protagonist of the South, impressed by the influence of works issuing from Harvard scholars in molding opinion, expressed a pious hope that a similar "university press" might be established in Dixie.[2] But it was a byword in Southern literary circles that the planter failed to sustain the various mushroom periodicals that sought his attention. Even the excellent *Southern Literary Messenger* received an uncertain support, while the *Southern Quarterly Review,* started in 1842, reached the end of its resources in 1856.[3]

Cultured Charleston produced little creative literature; its social set looked askance even at William Gilmore Simms who—proud Southron that he was—persisted in his efforts to give the South an indigenous literature. No wonder then that the youthful and rebellious Sidney Lanier chafed at the limitations of his homeland and found a more appreciative Northern audience. Nor did the *ante-bellum* South really glimpse the poetic genius of Henry Timrod and Paul Hamilton Hayne, whose talents were discovered and duly heralded by the generous Simms. Though all these spoke as loyal Southerners, they wrought their success without encouragement from the planter aristocracy.

Similarly, the aristocratic ideal did little to make even a common-school education generally available. North

---

[1] "Southern Convention at Savannah," *De Bow's Rev.,* XXII (1857), 100; *Belleville Advocate,* May 20, 1857; *Hunt's Merchants' Mag.,* XXXIV (1856), 392. The great improvement in Northern school textbooks is noted in *Harper's Wkly.,* VI, 692 (Nov. 1, 1862).

[2] Ozanne, *The South as It Is,* 214-215.

[3] See *De Bow's Rev.,* XXIII (1857), 102.

Carolina, historically less identified with the Negro-slave-plantation system, was unique in promoting public education.[1] In 1853 Calvin H. Wiley was elected first state superintendent of public schools, carrying on his work until after the war with the zeal of a crusader. The considerable fortune of John McDonough went by will in 1850 to the city authorities of Baltimore and New Orleans for the establishment of free schools for the poor. Though there were beginnings of public education in Maryland, Virginia, South Carolina and Louisiana and in the cities of certain other states, these only faintly reflected the educational awakening which had swept through the North and West in the preceding generation.[2] Secondary schools, supported by taxation, existed in such cities as New Orleans and Charleston, but the youth of the South largely attended academies and private schools.

With the increasing tension of the sectional controversy the supply of Northern teachers dropped off. There was much talk of filling the need locally, but there were available in the whole section only two normal schools, one in North Carolina which in 1859 became Trinity College, the other in Charleston dating from 1857. For one reason or another many Southern schools declined visibly during the decade. A writer in De Bow's Review, after perusing the Annual Report of the superintendent of public instruction, announced that a "ten years' trial" of public education in Louisiana had revealed that over half the families of that state would not avail themselves of such opportunities and that the New England system was "not adapted to Louisiana

[1] E. W. Knight, Public School Education in North Carolina (Boston, 1916), 158-190; C. L. Smith, The History of Education in North Carolina (Wash., 1888).

[2] See C. R. Fish, The Rise of the Common Man (A History of American Life, VI), 216-224.

and the South." [1] Some, in their subserviency to the
dominant institution of the South, probably shared the
bitterness of the critic who declared:

> We have got to hating everything with the prefix free,
> from free negroes down and up through the whole cata-
> logue—free farms, free labor, free society, free will, free
> thinking, free children, and free schools—all belonging
> to the same brood of damnable isms. But the worst of
> all abominations is the modern system of free schools,
> which has been the cause and prolific source of the in-
> fidelity and treasons that have turned her [Northern]
> cities into Sodoms and Gomorrahs, and her land into the
> nestling places of howling Bedlamites. We abominate
> the system because the schools are free. [2]

On the other hand, the spirit of Southern sectionalism led to the rapid development of professional training. Commercial education was declared desirable and,
as a new departure, a few professorships of commerce
were established. Medical colleges at Richmond, Charleston, Mobile, New Orleans and Nashville began to flourish. In December, 1859, during the excitement that followed the Harper's Ferry incident, one hundred and
sixty students who had left in a body the medical school
of the University of Pennsylvania and the Jefferson
Medical College transferred to the medical school at
Richmond where they were welcomed with open arms
by the citizens and Governor Henry A. Wise.

Most Southern lawyers had been prepared in law
offices or in Northern universities, but when in 1847 the

---

[1] "The Education, Labor, and Wealth of the South," *De Bow's Rev.*,
XXVII (1859), 278. The article continued: "Some parishes will not
receive any of it. Tensas, for instance, which is taxed $16,000 for the
support of public schools, has 'not a single public school,' says the
Report, 'in it, yet nearly every planter has a school in his own house.' "

[2] *Richmond Examiner*, cited in *Belleville Advocate*, Nov. 6, 1857.

law department of Cumberland University opened at
Lebanon, Tennessee, it rapidly developed until in 1858,
with one hundred and eighty-eight students hailing from
all parts of the South, it was the largest law school in
the United States. Many regretted the lack of theological
seminaries, especially since young recruits to the clergy
were largely Northerners. Accordingly, in 1852 the
Cumberland Presbyterians established a seminary at
Lebanon, and in 1859 the Southern Baptist Seminary
at Greenville, South Carolina, was founded.

The boycott of Northern institutions of higher learning did not reach a significant stage until the war clouds
of 1860-1861 sent the Southern students scurrying back
home. Princeton was regularly attended by so many
Southerners that it was often spoken of as a "Southern
college." Yale, Harvard, Union and Pennsylvania always had numerous registrants from Dixie. Yet none of
these institutions, not even West Point, seemed able to
nationalize the Southerners who attended them. Like
the young classical scholar, Basil L. Gildersleeve, they
eagerly answered the summons to arms to defend their
section and its cherished institutions.[1]

Much of the energy of the South that would otherwise have been directed toward cultural development
went into the defense or glorification of the "peculiar
institution." Few Southerners, whatever the dictates of
their inner conscience, were ready to admit, as it had
been conceded a few generations earlier and as many of
them would admit after the destructive work of a futile
civil war, that slavery was wrong. From the frontier of
Texas Colonel Robert E. Lee might write that slavery
was "a moral and political evil in any country" and that
few in that enlightened age could but acknowledge this

[1] B. L. Gildersleeve, *The Creed of the Old South* (Balt., 1915), 32 ff.

fact; [1] but Lee was superior to or out of touch with the popular psychology that controlled his Southern brethren.

The average Southerner busied himself with revamping the now threadbare arguments in defense of slavery. For his convenience the efforts of its chief protagonists were assembled and published in 1852 under the title, *The Pro-Slavery Argument*. Southern slavery, it was iterated and reiterated, was a humane and beneficent system that well supplied the needs of the black chattels. It extended its patriarchal care to the weak and aged while Northern industrialism callously threw its used-up free labor upon the scrap heap. It guaranteed law and order to the South while Northern almshouses, jails and prisons were filling. It cleared the way to a genuine liberty for white freemen, for it laid the foundations of a cultivated and refined society, intelligently organized in contrast with the sprawling anarchy of the North. Human bondage, moreover, had the stamp of Holy Writ: was this not the testimony of the tenth commandment and the numerous other scriptural references to servants and their duty of obedience to their masters? Slavery had erected the magnificent temple of Solomon; instead of rebuking the practice in abolition sermons Christ and later St. Paul and St. Peter had repeated the injunction of obedience. The wise men of the past, in general, Aristotle and the rest, had proclaimed its value. The Roman Empire had wrought much with slave labor. Indeed, this institution had been an essential of every successful and well-ordered society in history.

As his contribution to the cause, William R. Smith, president of Randolph-Macon College, published in

---

[1] J. W. Jones, *Life and Letters of Robert Edward Lee, Soldier and Man* (N. Y., 1906), 82.

1856 his oft-repeated *Lectures on the Philosophy and Practice of Slavery*. Albert J. Bledsoe followed with his *Essay on Liberty and Slavery* and Thomas R. R. Cobb brought out his *Inquiry into the Laws of Negro Slavery*. There was an increasing use of the ethnological argument—helped by the first intimations of Darwinism—to the effect that the Negro was an inferior race. Abolition, it was argued, meant the Africanization of the South and the end of white civilization there. Though it was a fundamental proposition that only Southerners could understand the problems of race relationship that lay at the root of their social system, the most intensive analysis of this issue was that of a Northern writer, Dr. John H. Van Evrie, who with pseudoscientific gusto declared the Negro to belong to a debased race and slavery to be his normal condition.[1] Other champions, resenting the insinuations of antislavery writers like Harriet Beecher Stowe, entered the lists. In the three years that followed the publication of *Uncle Tom's Cabin* fourteen proslavery novels appeared picturing more favorable aspects of domestic slavery.[2] Somewhat later, with more concern for authentic data, Edward A. Pollard submitted the racy realism of his *Black Diamonds Gathered in the Darkey Homes of the South*.[3]

The Jeffersonian creed of human equality was frankly repudiated by all champions of the Southern system. Slavery was declared the only sure foundation of republican government because of its success in uniting capital and labor. Indeed, the argument logically pointed to the spread of slavery throughout the American republic. The South thus supplemented its defensive tactics with a vigorous offensive. Perhaps the most versa-

[1] J. H. Van Evrie, *Negroes and Negro "Slavery"* (N. Y., 1861).
[2] Jennette R. Tandy, "Pro-Slavery Propaganda in American Fiction of the Fifties," *South Atlantic Quar.*, XXI (1922), 41-50, 170-178.
[3] Published in New York in 1859.

tile and provocative advocate of this point of view was George Fitzhugh of Port Caroline, Virginia. Residing in the rural isolation of a tiny community in tidewater Virginia, he boldly wielded the cudgel in behalf of the "peculiar institution" in a manner quite without a parallel. In the early forties he "became satisfied that slavery, black or white, was right and necessary." He undertook to arouse the South to taking "higher ground in defense of Slavery; justifying it as a normal and natural institution, instead of excusing and apologizing for it, as an exceptional one." Proclaiming himself an enemy to free society, he warned Northern capitalists against abolitionism as the handmaid of a radicalism and agrarianism that was threatening their own vested interests. He urged their alliance, offensively as well as defensively, with the South to stem this tide; slavery is the normal status of the laborer and the Northern states may yet have to introduce it, he argued.[1] This view had just enough currency in the Southern press to act as a boomerang, for Northern agitators seized the opportunity to exhort the wage-earners to scotch the viper, slavery, before it struck at their own freedom. Indeed, for proclaiming this doctrine an editor of the *Charleston Mercury* had the distinction in 1854 of being burned in effigy by the indignant mechanics of the capital of his state.[2]

By this generation also the finishing touches were put upon the Biblical argument for slavery.[3] In its behalf

[1] George Fitzhugh, *Cannibals All!* (Richmond, 1857), 368. See also his *Sociology for the South* (Richmond, 1854), and A. C. Cole, *Lincoln's "House Divided" Speech* (Chicago, 1923).

[2] *Belleville Advocate*, March 15, 1854.

[3] Thornton Stringfellow's *Scriptural and Statistical Views in Defense of Slavery* reached its fourth edition in 1856; in the same year Howell Cobb issued his *Scriptural Examination of the Institution of Slavery,* and other less notable exponents, like the Reverend N. L. Rice, the Reverend W. S. Brown, and Davis Ewart, made their contributions.

the Southern divine invoked the strictest literalism; indeed, the section was well on the road to a religious fundamentalism that repudiated the old Jeffersonian free-thinking tradition. With missionary zeal, on Thanksgiving day, 1860, the Reverend Benjamin Morgan Palmer proclaimed from his pulpit in New Orleans that God had imposed upon the South the duty of maintaining and spreading over the continent the Southern social system.[1] The brilliant but erratic William G. Brownlow, the "fighting parson" of Knoxville, Tennessee, was a staunch defender of slavery, as he was later of the Union and the flag. Lecturing at Memphis in January, 1858, he announced his intention to go on a proselyting mission to the "heathen of New England." Later in the year he met the antislavery clergyman Abram Pryne in public debate at Philadelphia and ran the whole gamut of the scriptural argument.[2] Representing the nonslaveholders of eastern Tennessee, this doughty champion demonstrated the rôle which the yeomanry of the South had come to play in defending the institution.

Brownlow was not the only Southerner to carry the fight into the enemy's territory. Fitzhugh, who enjoyed friendly relations with several abolitionists, keenly relished a battle of words; in 1856 he lectured with some acclaim before the students at Yale, urging for their consideration some of his advanced theories of class relationship. In the same year Senator Robert A. Toombs of Georgia repeated in Tremont Temple, Boston, the thoroughgoing defense which he had made the subject of an earlier address at Emory College, Georgia.

[1] B. M. Palmer, *The South: Her Peril and Her Duty* (New Orleans, 1860). See also W. C. Johnston, *Life and Letters of Benjamin Morgan Palmer* (Richmond, 1906).

[2] W. G. Brownlow and Abram Pryne, *Ought American Slavery to Be Perpetuated* (Phila., 1858).

Among other points he maintained that slavery would cease only when wages descended to a point barely sufficient to support the laborer and his family, so that capital could not afford to own labor; American slavery therefore would "find its euthanasia in the general prostration of all labor." [1] Other spokesmen twitted Northern industrialists with charges of hypocritically evading the fundamental fact that they too were practising slavery. Capitalism, they held, was slavery under the guise of freedom. In palliation of their own "peculiar institution" professional Southerners shed crocodile tears over the pitiful condition of Northern "slaves without masters."

Thus did the South proclaim for a decaying institution more virtues than it had ever before been supposed to possess. Thus did a society deeply fissured by forces of social stratification acquire coherence, if not unity, on the eve of a struggle that was to determine its very right to exist.

[1] Robert Toombs, "Slavery: Its Constitutional Status, and Its Influence on Society and the Colored Race," *De Bow's Rev.*, XX (1856), 602; U. B. Phillips, *The Life of Robert Toombs* (N. Y., 1913), 164.

CHAPTER III

THE SOUTH MILITANT

THE desire of the South to develop its intellectual life apart from the North was closely related to a deepening sense of its economic inferiority to that section. To be sure, the South claimed its share of the prosperity of the fifties. The agriculturalist enjoyed good prices for crops that represented double the output of the preceding decade. The South also still boasted a greater actual and *per-capita* production of corn and pork than the North, even though, in view of its heavier consumption of these products, it continued dependent upon the free states for a considerable supply. But this advantage, too, was rapidly ebbing, while in other crops Dixie had to recognize a growing subordination to the North. The corn and wheat yield on the thousands of backcountry farms that constituted a South within the South was pitifully small as compared with the heavily laden fields of the Western states.

The various Southern staples had clearly defined their habitats. The cotton kingdom, firmly established in the Gulf states, claimed the larger and better portion of the black belt. Only the "sugar bowl" of Louisiana disputed its preëminence, but remunerative prices for cotton served to check the expansion of sugar, as of other crops. Indeed, the uncertain returns of the bumper sugar harvest of 1853 and of the short crop of 1856 discouraged many a sugar planter. Cotton was grown almost entirely with slave labor on plantations of hun-

dreds or thousands of acres. Both slaves and land had
become too valuable for tobacco culture. Tobacco
growers, therefore, could not compete in Mississippi,
Louisiana and Texas with the prosperous cotton
planters of those states; they struggled to maintain their
status in the border states, with Kentucky rapidly gaining on Virginia and likewise a rapid expansion into
Tennessee and Missouri. The one-hundred-per-cent increase in tobacco production in the fifties was largely
accounted for by this westward shift.[1]

"Cotton is King!" proclaimed the proud Southron
who saw production nearly double during the fifties and
reach the five-million-bale record of 1860, an increase
resulting largely from the recent expansion into the
virgin fields of Texas. Few were willing to face the unpleasant fact that the combined cotton, tobacco, rice,
hemp and sugar harvest of 1850 probably did not equal
in value the 1850 hay crop of the North, nearly half of
it raised in New York, Pennsylvania and Ohio.[2] Thus
was the advantage of the unique Southern staple offset
by the varied agricultural output of the North. Moreover, the older portions of the cotton kingdom furnished
ample proof of an artless and exhausting culture. Virgin
tracts were worn out by small planters who, unable to
replenish the fertility of the soil, sold out to wealthier
neighbors and sought new land farther west. The large
planters gave the blasted fields some rest, and credited
themselves with net profits in the form of increased hold-

[1] J. A. C. Chandler and others, *The South in the Building of the
Nation* (Richmond, 1909-1910), V, 164-165, 191-192, 205-211.

[2] H. R. Helper, *The Impending Crisis of the South* (N. Y., 1857),
50-53. Helper's figures on hay and cotton prices are low in comparison
with the quotations in contemporary newspapers and in Commissioner
of Patents, *Report for 1850*. On cotton they are not as low as those in
Hunt's Merchants' Mag., XXVI (1852), 71; cf. *De Bow's Rev.*, IX
(1850), 531. See also Commissioner of Agriculture, *Report for 1862*,
553, which estimates the hay crop of the North as "double in value the
cotton crop."

ings of land and slaves. Such a system was far from efficient. Almost the only modern agricultural implement on the average cotton plantation was the plow. The value of the farm tools upon the standard plantation of one thousand acres and one hundred slaves was well under five hundred dollars.[1]

A few farseeing and courageous spirits worked out upon their own holdings the principles of modern scientific agriculture. As earlier, Edmund Ruffin was the leading exponent of a new and better system. He was convinced that the South's economic and political decline was due largely to a soil depletion which in turn produced a population drain that reduced Southern representation in Congress. Other pioneers of a like mind demonstrated to their own satisfaction methods by which a more fundamental prosperity might yet be attained. In 1854 a generous donor established at Franklin College a professorship of agriculture, a chair first held by Dr. Daniel Lee, editor of the *Genesee Farmer* and of the *Southern Cultivator*.[2]

The fifties brought the culmination of a great agricultural revival in Maryland and Virginia, states in which the farmer had early felt the stern pinch of necessity and been forced to do some fundamental thinking concerning agricultural economy. Artificial fertilization, deep plowing, the use of improved seed and other methods inspired by farm journals, agricultural societies and soil chemists led to greatly increased yields and to marvelous advances in land values. The introduction and wide use of guano worked such wonders that the supply seldom proved adequate. It was reasonably clear from the agricultural revolution which resulted that slave

[1] T. N. Carver, ed., *Selected Readings in Rural Economics* (Boston, 1916), 274.

[2] Chandler and others, *South in the Building of the Nation*, X, 363; Avery Craven, *Edmund Ruffin, Southerner* (N. Y., 1932), 49-72.

labor was not in itself the cause of soil exhaustion. But the outcome none the less was that these two states were rapidly losing their Southern characteristics. The former plantation system began to yield to small-scale diversified farming in which slavery had a steadily declining significance.[1] The market gardens about Norfolk, which supplied New York with early vegetables, offered a striking contrast to the large old-fashioned Virginia farms among which they were scattered.

Cotton culture in the black belt was rewarded by an average price for the decade of between ten and eleven cents in spite of a drop to eight cents in 1851-1852. Good prices for cotton and other staples proved to be the opiate that dulled the wits of the planter of the black belt. Though planters' conventions, such as those of the South Central Agricultural Association, were held at intervals, they aroused scant thought in regard to agriculture. Not only was little done to replenish the fertility of the seaboard lands, but there was little understanding in and about South Carolina of the serious effects of the competition of the more fertile cotton areas of the Lower South. Eleven and twelve-cent cotton, which served to allay the discontent and disunion sentiment of the Gulf states in 1850, furnished South Carolina no such relief. Yet the fire eaters of the Palmetto State failed to grasp the argument of Edmund Ruffin that replenishment of fertility would restore the South to national leadership or prepare it for a prosperous independent national existence.[2] Even with good prices, however, the profits in fertile expanding areas were un-

[1] F. L. Olmsted, *The Cotton Kingdom* (N. Y., 1862), I, 153-154. See also A. O. Craven, *Soil Exhaustion as a Factor in the Agricultural History of Virginia and Maryland, 1606-1860* (Univ. of Ill., *Studies,* XIII, no. 1), 147-161.

[2] Ruffin addressed the fourth annual fair of the South Carolina Institute of Agriculture on Nov. 18, 1852. See Craven, *Soil Exhaustion,* 141.

dermined by other factors that entered into production. Of rather uncertain significance was the enhanced value of land. More evident was the increased cost of slaves, accentuating in the fifties a tendency of the previous half-century.

Superficial evidence of Southern stagnation was noted by travelers who descended the Ohio River and compared its banks: on the one side, the state of Ohio with rapidly advancing prosperity; on the other, Kentucky, no less favored by nature, yet unkempt, squalid and languishing. "Why?" rhetorically asked the visitor. "Because slavery blights all that it touches." [1] Whatever the limitations of such a sweeping comparison, Southerners had to concede its essential validity. More and more they came to face the fact that their section was lagging farther and farther behind the free states in growth and prosperity. Few there were, however, who would attribute this decline to slavery. Those who admitted that it might be a costlier form of labor than the wage system were prone to consider this an indication not of the economic unsoundness, but of the superior altruism, of their civilization.

As increasing social stratification excluded all but the few from the privileges and opportunities of the Southern order, it was natural to charge the section's inferior prosperity against an outside foe—the North. Southern peasants in moments of lucid contemplation might deplore the folly of getting excited over the sectional situation when so few of them actually owned slaves; yet they ordinarily were responsive to the appeals of the fire-eating politician and journalist. Thus arose a cult of

[1] Agénor de Gasparin, *The Uprising of a Great People* (Mary L. Booth, tr., N. Y., 1861), 222. See also Edward Dicey, *Six Months in the Federal States* (London, 1863), II, 65, 76; [Isabella L. Bishop], *The Englishwoman in America* (London, 1856), 126; J. R. Beste, *The Wabash* (London, 1855), I, 231-232.

Southern antagonism to the North and Northerners that
finally reached its climax in the bitter passions of war
time.

"It has, without doubt, become the settled conviction
of large numbers of persons in the slave states, that in
some way or other, either through the fiscal regulations
of the Government, or through the legerdemain of trade,
the North has been built up at the expense of the South."
Thus commented George M. Weston, a fair-minded
Northern analyst of Southern economic life, in his penetrating study *The Progress of Slavery in the United
States*.[1] Evidence of the prevalence of this belief existed
at every hand. It was estimated, with undoubted exaggeration, that the South paid annually in taxation the
sum of fifty million dollars, of which only ten million
was returned in the form of expenditures. Attempts to
determine the total tribute paid by Southerners in their
various economic contacts with the North resulted in
estimates of from one hundred to two hundred million
annually.[2] No wonder the cry was raised that the South
was being impoverished by a degrading vassalage.

Many vivid pictures were painted of this economic
dependence. According to an Alabama journalist,

> At present, the North fattens and grows rich upon
> the South. . . . Our slaves are clothed with Northern
> manufactured goods, have Northern hats and shoes,
> work with Northern hoes, ploughs, and other imple-
> ments, are chastised with a Northern-made instrument,
> are working for Northern more than Southern profit.
> The slaveholder dresses in Northern goods, rides in a
> Northern saddle, . . . patronizes Northern news-

[1] Weston, *Progress of Slavery* (Wash., 1857), 68.
[2] R. R. Russel, *Economic Aspects of Southern Sectionalism, 1840-
1861* (Univ. of Ill., Studies, XI), 190-191. See also J. G. Van Deusen,
Economic Bases of Disunion in South Carolina (Columbia Univ., Studies,
no. 305).

papers, drinks Northern liquors, reads Northern books, spends his money at Northern watering places. . . . In Northern vessels his products are carried to market, his cotton is ginned with Northern gins, his sugar is crushed and preserved by Northern machinery; his rivers are navigated by Northern steamboats, his mails are carried in Northern stages, his negroes are fed with Northern bacon, beef, flour, and corn; his land is cleared with a Northern axe, and a Yankee clock sits upon his mantel-piece; his floor is swept with a Northern broom, and is covered with a Northern carpet; and his wife dresses herself in a Northern looking-glass; . . . his son is educated at a Northern college, his daughter receives the finishing polish at a Northern seminary; his doctor graduates at a Northern medical college, his schools are supplied with Northern teachers, and he is furnished with Northern inventions and notions.[1]

For all this, it was complained, the North repaid the South by abusing and denouncing slavery and slave-holders.

"The South is . . . the very best colony to the North any people ever possessed," insisted R. Barnwell Rhett of South Carolina on the floor of the United States Senate.[2] The "Lord North" of these days was a greater oppressor than the Lord North of the British ministry who turned a deaf ear to the petition of the American colonies in 1775, proclaimed the *Southern Press*, the special organ which Southerners had set up as their mouthpiece at Washington.[3]

An economic readjustment seemed required to relieve the section of this servile relationship. Diversification

---

[1] Cited in F. A. P. Barnard, *An Oration Delivered before the Citizens of Tuscaloosa, Alabama, July 4, 1851* (Tuscaloosa, 1851), 12. See also Russel, *Economic Aspects of Southern Sectionalism*, 48.

[2] *Congressional Globe*, 32 Cong., 1 sess., app., 46.

[3] *Southern Press*, cited in *Washington Union*, Dec. 21, 1851.

through the development of manufacturing and trade facilities was the demand. "Give us factories, machine shops, work shops," Southern champions cried. "Give us artisans, shoemakers, tailors, blacksmiths, etc. Let them be encouraged—well supported, preferred, and a step, an important step in rendering the South independent and prosperous will have been made." "The Encouragement of Home Industry is the 'pillar of cloud by day, and the pillar of fire by night' that must guide the Southern States of this Union through the bewildering and hazardous strife for sectional supremacy which ever and anon convulses the country. The time has come when the Southern people *must* act for the development of their boundless resources, or pay the hated penalty of conscious inferiority, and degradation in the scale of empire." [1]

Diversificationists pointed to unique advantages for manufacturing: plentiful raw material, water power in abundance, and a cheap labor supply in the slave and poor-white population. An increasing number of Southerners, however, after soberly calculating the value of the Union, reluctantly reached the conclusion that disunion and a separate confederacy furnished the only satisfactory solution. In time they lent strength and dignity to the movement of the fire-eating politicians and journalists who were agitating and organizing for secession. The latter argued that diversification could not come about so long as the South was held within the bounds of the Union.

Meanwhile, however, progress was made in manufacturing. The low prices of the late forties seemed to furnish incontrovertible evidence of an overproduction

---

[1] *Natchez Courier*, cited in *Mobile Advertiser*, Aug. 27, 1850; *Nashville True Whig*, cited in *Memphis Eagle*, Jan. 16, 1851. See also A. C. Cole, *Whig Party in the South* (Wash., 1913), 208-209.

of cotton, if not an argument for "bringing the spindle to the cotton." Sales at from five to ten cents per pound meant vanishing profits in the older sections of the black belt. Economic distress not only fed the flames of sectional agitation in national politics, but with many clinched the argument for economic self-reliance. As a result, the middle of the century witnessed the erection of many cotton mills in various parts of Dixie. William Gregg was the outstanding leader in such ventures in the Palmetto State. Alabama also had its industrial pioneers like Daniel Pratt of Prattsville. The neighboring state of Georgia, with its railroads and fifty or sixty cotton factories clustered about Columbus and Augusta, soon acquired the reputation of being the Empire State of the South and furnished an example which its sister commonwealths were urged to emulate.[1]

Dividends of ten and twenty per cent were heralded as the assured profits of factories contiguous to the cotton fields. For a time all such undertakings prospered. Then, in North as well as South, success was threatened by a rise in the price of raw cotton. Overproduction of cotton materials and European competition further contributed to uncertain returns and occasional losses. Especially discouraging was the failure of the Augusta mills toward the end of the decade. By this time, however, conditions seemed to be taking a turn for the better, for a factory in Choctaw County, Mississippi, declared a twenty-nine-per-cent dividend. Yet the South of 1860 had hardly begun to solve the problem of her dependence upon cotton.[2]

[1] *Louisville Journal*, June 25, July 20, Sept. 12, Oct. 2, 1852; *National Intelligencer* (Wash.), Feb. 27, March 27, 1855, Jan. 27, 1858; *Savannah Republican*, April 5, 1853, March 1, 1859; Olmsted, *Cotton Kingdom*, I, 274; Robert Everest, *A Journey through the United States and Part of Canada* (London, 1855), 116-117.

[2] Russel, *Economic Aspects of Southern Sectionalism*, 60-61, 226-227; *New Orleans Bulletin*, cited in *National Intelligencer*, Sept. 30, 1858.

Probably greater success might have been achieved had the same constructive purpose moved all those who brooded over Southern needs and rights. Some, however, eager to strike back at the North, urged commercial nonintercourse or a high discriminatory tax upon Northern goods offered for sale in the South. Governor John B. Floyd of Virginia recommended such a course during the crisis of 1850, and the idea found active supporters in all the cotton states, including such ultra Whigs as Senator John M. Berrien of Georgia and Congressman Thomas L. Clingman of North Carolina.[1] Conservatives, however, deplored the retaliatory spirit which lay back of the proposal; it seemed to many to contain the unwelcome embryo of disunion. When the excitement subsided in 1852 the project dropped from active discussion—to be revived when events again moved rapidly toward a dissolution of the Union.

In the summer of 1860 Governor John J. Pettus of Mississippi advocated nonintercourse as a lever which, properly handled, could "turn New England upside down in six months. Half her population," he argued, "would be paupers from the day the Southern States cease to trade with her." [2] Perhaps the tragicomic corollary to this argument was unduly pressed by the lanky Illinoisian whom the Republicans later nominated as their candidate for the presidency. Addressing a New England audience, Lincoln ridiculed the Southern boycott of Northern articles as dramatized by Senator Mason of Virginia in appearing at Washington in homespun: "To make his proof good for anything, he should have

---

[1] *Richmond Whig*, Jan. 14, 15, Feb. 1, Dec. 7, 12, 1850; *Washington Republic*, Aug. 28, Nov. 16, 1850; *Natchez* (Miss.) *Courier*, Oct. 15, 1850; *New Orleans Bulletin*, June 20, Dec. 30, 1850; *Louisville Journal*, Dec. 11, 13, 1850; *Flag of the Union* (Jackson), Nov. 22, 1850; *Savannah Republican*, Nov. 21, 1850.

[2] *National Intelligencer*, Oct. 23, 1860.

come into the Senate barefoot." "If that's the plan," he added, "they should begin at the foundation, and adopt the well known 'Georgia costume' of a shirt collar and pair of spurs." [1]

The proposed nonintercourse with the North was one factor in the movement for direct trade with Europe. By establishing such a direct traffic, it was argued, the South would save the tribute which had regularly been rendered to the North for allowing its ships, its merchants and its cities to handle the imports and exports of Dixie. In 1852 a weekly journal, the *Cotton Plant*, was projected, with the indorsement of representative Southerners, to advocate this proposal. [2] Every quiet little Southern port town had rosy dreams of awakening from its quiescent state as a "chrysalis of commerce." While most of these ambitious schemes never got beyond the stage of agitation, a few reached the point where prospectuses were issued and subscription books opened, and one or two Virginia projects on the eve of the war attained actual realization. A few lines of sailing packets were more easily established, but by this time even the optimistic realized that the era of steam was at hand. Indeed, Northern steam craft had already begun to absorb the coastwise trade, a development which seemed ominously to offset any slight steps in the direction of commercial independence by the South.

Railroad building offered another field for Southern enterprise. Here as in the North it had long since passed the initial stage of planning. A route between Wilmington, North Carolina, and the Potomac River fifteen miles below Washington and a forked system, by which Chattanooga was connected through Atlanta with Savan-

[1] Abraham Lincoln, *Complete Works* (J. G. Nicolay and John Hay, eds., N. Y., 1905), V, 337, 363.
[2] *National Intelligencer*, April 27, 1852.

nah and Charleston, represented the principal attainments of earlier times. The fifties saw greater achievement. While there were still numerous schemes for joining the South Atlantic tidewater with the Ohio Valley, such hopes were cherished mainly by Virginians who dreamed of making their seaport, Norfolk, the successful rival of New York. Meantime lines were completed which bound together the slave states themselves. One road pushed through the Blue Ridge, linking Richmond with Chattanooga where it connected with the important extension from this mountain base to Memphis. The first Mississippi River connection, however, was not completed until 1857. By the outbreak of the Civil War another east-and-west line through the heart of the cotton belt was in process of completion, tying Vicksburg and Montgomery with the railroads of Georgia and South Carolina. In a similar way north-and-south connections were made not only along the seaboard but also in the Mississippi Valley. The Mobile and Ohio formed almost a national route with access to Chicago, as contrasted with the series of lines joining New Orleans, Jackson, Memphis, Louisville and Nashville. The rate of increased construction during the fifties was actually greater than in the rest of the country, though this was in part because the section had fallen behind in the preceding decade. Distributed over an extensive territory, the railroad mileage jumped from two to ten thousand, equaling in 1860 more than a third of that of the nation.[1]

This transportation development made its contribution to Southern sectionalism. Orators might whip up popular enthusiasm in railroad conventions and through

[1] *Statistics of the United States Including Mortality, Property, etc.* (*U. S. Eighth Census*, 1860), 333; Chandler and others, *South in the Building of the Nation*, X, 654-655.

campaigns of education, but they could not be blind to the fact that the North had clearly outstripped them. They lamented the reluctance of Northern capital, upon which they were largely dependent, to enlist in Southern enterprises. Local capital, though they did not appreciate it, was too largely enmeshed in the slavery system. The rail routes failed to bring the desired relief from one-crop agriculture. On the contrary, the railway enlarged still farther the cotton kingdom, thus intensifying competition in production. The rapid industrial development that was anticipated failed also to materialize.

On the other hand, the railroad did bring outside contacts and accessible markets to the yeoman farmer of certain backcountry districts. As a result, towns like Charlotte, Spartanburg and Athens took on new life, while Atlanta, a crude village in 1850, attained ten thousand at the end of the decade. Strategically located with reference to railroads, it became an important market for the farm produce of northwestern Georgia and the gateway of trade between the eastern cotton belt and the Gulf section.[1] In general, rail transportation meant easier communication and closer contacts. Travel, always a part of every planter's life, lost the romantic flavor of the family carriage or the coach-and-four, with well-groomed horses and sable attendants, but it became more simple and frequent. Social solidarity and political unity within the section were inevitably advanced.

In the effort to coördinate and vitalize the various movements for economic independence, the leaders came together in a series of conventions which betokened the developing germ of Southern nationalism. By the fifties the South had outgrown planters' conventions, railroad

---

[1] *Southern Banner*, June 28, 1860, cited in U. B. Phillips, *Transportation in the Eastern Cotton Belt to 1860* (N. Y., 1913), 392.

conventions and direct-trade conventions of the kind
that reflected the local pride or ambition of a given region. The new leadership called into being the section-
wide Southern Commercial Convention, which met in
annual session after 1852 in various leading cities. This
institution cannot be distinguished entirely in its per-
sonnel or in its point of view from the Nashville Convention of 1850, the belated achievement of the South
Carolina leadership, in which an effort was made to appraise the value of the Union from a political standpoint. From the collapse of the disunion movement of
1850-1851 promoters like James D. B. De Bow, William L. Yancey, the Alabama fire eater, Edmund Ruffin
of Virginia and their like learned the temporary weak-
ness of this method of attack. They were also keenly
alive to the economic issues that demanded consideration. So they brought Southerners together again and
again to debate such proposals as the establishment of a
steamship line to Europe, the encouragement of Southern manufactures and the construction of a Pacific railroad by a southern route.[1]

Yet De Bow and his associates were as much or even
more interested in political remedies, especially in "a
union of all parties in the South for the sake of the
South." They came in due time to dominate the floor
of the convention if they were not, indeed, the life and
soul of the movement. Their activity aroused a challenge
from conservative Southern critics who felt that "to call
together the idle lawyers and jackdaw politicians of the
land and call it a commercial convention is the essence

---

[1] J. W. Du Bose, *Life and Times of William Lowndes Yancey* (Bir-
mingham, 1892), 358 ff.; Russel, *Economic Aspects of Southern Sec-
tionalism*, 123 ff.; W. W. Davis, "Ante-Bellum Southern Commercial
Conventions," Ala. Hist. Soc., *Trans.*, V, 153-202; Herbert Wender,
Southern Commercial Conventions, 1837-1859 (Johns Hopkins Univ.,
Studies, XLVIII, no. 4).

of 'humbug.' " [1] Presently, however, the conservative members dropped away and the disunionists came into control, even numerically. The last meeting, at Vicksburg in 1859, was thinly attended, chiefly by the radical disunionists—"a baker's dozen of peripatetic politicians and windgalled and spavined political economists," commented a caustic critic.[2]

Even though the Southern convention came thus ingloriously to an end, it made a significant contribution to the movement for Southern nationalism. It accustomed the people of the South to ringing pronouncements, such as De Bow's in his presidential address at Knoxville to the effect that the South had rights which its champions were in duty bound to maintain.[3] Many Southerners were more impressed by fire eating and gasconade than by the drastic but simple logic of sober thinkers like Willoughby Newton, a former Whig congressman from Virginia, who in 1858 assured the literary societies of the Virginia Military Institute that the real question for the South was, *"not whether power is usurped by the majority, but whether the Constitution itself has not become effete"*; or, as an editor commented, "not whether any aggression has been committed, or is in process of commission, by the preponderating North, but whether, by the mere fact of such preponderance, the Constitution itself has not become null and void." [4]

The last desperate effort of the Southern convention was to launch a movement for reopening the African slave trade. This seemed the only hope for the further

[1] *Georgia Federal Union*, cited in *National Intelligencer*, April 8, 1859.
[2] *Independent Monitor* (Tuscaloosa, Ala.), June 9, 1859.
[3] See opening presidential address of Aug. 10, 1857. "The Rights, Duties, and Remedies of the South," *De Bow's Rev.*, XXIII (1857), 225-238.
[4] *National Intelligencer*, July 24, 1858.

expansion of the plantation system in the face of the limited internal traffic and the prevailing high prices for slaves. The total transactions involving the transfer of Negro chattels probably averaged less than seventy-five thousand a year. Much of this was an intrastate trade, with the result that the black belt of a state like Mississippi imported only five or six thousand annually.[1] As the chief slave-selling state, Virginia annually exported to other states about ten thousand Negroes.[2] After the slave pens were closed in Washington in 1850, the slave auction at Richmond became one of the memorable sights of the South, comparable with the better known mart at New Orleans. Though some Southerners feared that this trade might drain the Old Dominion of its slave population and thus lead to the abandonment of slavery there, the prevailing high prices of slaves quieted most scruples on this score.[3] Prime field hands worth $1000 in 1850 were listed in 1859 at $1600 and $1700, with an occasional sale at $2000 or better. Late in 1858, at Autaugaville, Alabama, one hundred and fifty Negroes of varying ages and conditions brought an average of $950 per head.[4]

In view of the high prices and the knowledge that vessels were illegally putting out from New York and New England ports to engage in the slave traffic—if only to supply the Brazilian market [5]—Southerners in-

[1] Frederic Bancroft, *Slave-Trading in the Old South* (Balt., 1931), 384-405, esp. 405.

[2] *Alton* (Ill.) *Courier*, July 22, 1858; Adolf Douai, *Land und Leute in der Union* (Berlin, 1864), 313; F. L. Olmsted, *Journey in the Seaboard Slave States* (N. Y., 1859), 54-56; Olmsted, *Cotton Kingdom*, I, 374; T. R. Dew, in William Harper and others, *The Pro-Slavery Argument* (Charleston, 1852), 369-370.

[3] *Savannah Republican*, Jan. 1, Nov. 10, 1849.

[4] *N. Y. Herald*, Jan. 1, 1859; *Ohio State Journal* (Columbus), Jan. 14, 1859.

[5] *Chicago Weekly Democrat*, Nov. 25, 1854; *N. Y. Herald*, March 6, 1855; George Fitzhugh, *Sociology for the South* (Richmond, 1854),

creasingly turned to the thought of formally renewing the trade with Africa. When the filibuster William Walker, as "president" of the republic of Nicaragua, decreed in 1856 the reëstablishment of slavery there and invited the importation of Negroes, Southern ultras set up a chorus of approval.[1] Some undertook to show that the laws banning the African trade operated in a manner unjust to certain states and were therefore unconstitutional; nullification was proposed as a remedy. In general, however, Southerners merely pointed to the inadequacy of the supply and the resulting high price of slaves. An outside source would bring into cultivation millions of acres lying waste; it would check the draining and abolitionizing of the border states and widen the area of slavery by the introduction of new states interested in its maintenance.

De Bow, high priest of this new cult, carried the argument a step further, pointing out that, if the basis of slavery were enlarged, this fact would cause it to embrace "in a direct and tangible interest every member of the community," or, as Edward A. Pollard put it, "it would admit the poor white man to the advantages of our social system," and "give him clearer interests in the country he loves now only from simple patriotism."[2] This concern over maintaining the allegiance of the yeomanry is in many ways the key to the success of the Southern movement of the fifties. The greatest danger of all was, as De Bow wrote Yancey in an

164-166; Theodore Parker, *Works* (Centenary edn., Boston, 1907-1911), XI, 371.

[1] *Charleston Standard*, Nov. 15, cited in *Chicago Weekly Democrat*, Nov. 29, 1856.

[2] "African Labor Supply Association," *De Bow's Rev.*, XXVII (1859), 234; E. A. Pollard, *Black Diamonds Gathered in the Darkey Homes of the South* (N. Y., 1859), 52-53; *Charleston Mercury*, Feb. 17, 1857, cited in T. C. Smith, *Parties and Slavery, 1850-1859* (A. B. Hart, ed., *The American Nation: A History*, N. Y., 1904-1918, XVIII), 296.

open letter, that "when our smaller proprietors and non-slaveholders, amongst the best and most reliable citizens we have, come to examine carefully, they will imagine that there is a tendency at present to consolidate in fewer and fewer hands, the entire control of labor." [1] Such champions anticipated opposition from the larger slave-holders. Yet even some of these were sympathetic. The reopening of the foreign slave trade was discussed at the commercial convention at Savannah in December, 1856, with William B. Goulden as its chief proponent. Henceforth it became a regular feature of the meetings, winning indirect indorsement at Knoxville in 1857 and an unqualified commitment at Vicksburg in 1859. Shortly after the adjournment of the Vicksburg convention, the African Labor Supply Association was organized for the promotion of a lawful slave trade, among its active members being William L. Yancey of Alabama and L. W. Spratt of South Carolina, with De Bow as president. [2]

There were those, however, who could not wait for legal obstacles to be cleared away. [3] Southern juries for years had almost uniformly failed to convict slave traders; nor had federal authorities exhausted every effort to suppress the traffic. The illicit trade opened with new vigor in 1857. Aside from successful ventures, twenty vessels were seized as slavers in the last nine months of the year. In 1858 the United States marshal seized the yacht *Wanderer* and arrested its captain for landing some three hundred naked Africans at Brunswick, Georgia. Charles R. Lamar of Savannah, who had shared in the original venture of the *Wanderer*, now purchased it at auction and continued it in the traffic.

[1] "African Labor Supply Association," 234.
[2] *Savannah Republican*, May 23, 1859.
[3] J. P. Kennedy, *Mr. Ambrose's Letters on the Rebellion* (N. Y., 1865), 164-165.

He also acquired the slave barque *Rawlins,* publicly defying the government to arrest him. In April, 1860, press notices appeared of the *Wanderer* landing a cargo of slaves in Texas.[1]

A little later the barque *Orion* was seized with upwards of eight hundred blacks on board; but, although it was condemned as forfeit and its owners expedited judicial procedure by a plea of guilty, they received only nominal penalties. Soon the *Orion* was back in the traffic, being again captured within six months, this time with a cargo of a thousand. During eighteen months of the years 1859-1860 eighty-five slavers were reported to have fitted out in New York Harbor. Senator Douglas estimated that over fifteen thousand Negroes were thus illegally imported in 1859, while the following year this figure more than doubled.[2] The risk of capture by the British, as well as American, squadrons off the coast of Africa and of conviction for piracy, under the British practice, was offset by the enormous profits and by the approval voiced in Southern quarters. "Speed the pirates," was the benediction of the *Jackson Mississippian,* leading Democratic organ in Mississippi— "Speed the honest 'pirates' in their noble mission to augment the supply of Southern labor, and to obey the injunction to feed the hungry and clothe the naked. The wants of the Southern people, and the requirements

[1] *N. Y. Herald,* Jan. 1, 12, 22, 1859; *National Intelligencer,* Jan. 1, 3-6, 10, 15, May 5, 6, 17, 24, 27, June 1, 4, 19, 20, 1859; *N. Y. Tribune,* May 1, 1860. See also W. E. B. Du Bois, *The Suppression of the African Slave Trade to the United States of America, 1638-1870* (Harvard Hist. Studies, I), 178-183, and J. R. Spears, *The American Slave Trade* (N. Y., 1900), 194.

[2] Du Bois, *Suppression of African Slave Trade,* 179; Gasparin, *Uprising of a Great People,* 31; Henry Wilson, *History of the Rise and Fall of the Slave Power in America* (Boston, 1872-1877), II, 618-619; *Baton Rouge Advocate,* cited in *Chicago Press,* April 26, 1858; [George Fitzhugh], "The Administration and the Slave Trade," *De Bow's Rev.,* XXVI (1859), 144-146.

of commerce, call loudly for more and cheaper negroes and thanks to the adventurous slave traders, they are coming." [1]

Yet the waxing demand for reviving the lawful importation of slaves was probably less a response to real economic need than an expression of the accumulating forces of discontent. The established planter usually had ample room for expansion from the slave increase by birth, while the small farmer who used efficient methods of cultivation was less dependent upon slave labor than was generally realized. Texas, where society was still quite fluid, spoke in no uncertain terms in 1860 by defeating for governor the Democratic candidate who championed a reopening of the trade. Its renewal would probably have severed the last bond that held Virginia to the South. [2]

Though failing to rally the people to their more extreme plans, the fire eaters continued to complain of unjust discrimination against their section and invoked an ever more aggressive assertion of "Southern rights." More responsive was the popular attitude to their charges of Northern connivance in plots to free the enslaved African. All signs of restlessness among the blacks were promptly attributed to the work of abolition fanatics and incendiaries; nor were humble emissaries of freedom always lacking. There seemed signs that an insurrectionary contagion was spreading. While this fear was at its crest, there flashed through the South the frightful news that a band of whites and blacks, led by John Brown, a fanatical abolitionist, had seized a United States arsenal, raised the standard of revolt and liberation and placed guns in the hands of slaves, thus leveling a blow at the forces of law and order and white

[1] Cited in *Belleville Advocate*, Sept. 7, 1859.
[2] *Richmond Enquirer*, May 25, 1858.

security. Defeated in his mad purpose, he had fallen into the hands of the state authorities. What did all this portend? A state of panic, of utter terror, gripped the South. There were nightmares of a second Santo Domingo, the awful details of which were recited again and again. Even after Brown had gone to the gallows and cooler heads began to point with pride to the loyalty of the slaves and the free Negroes of Virginia, the excitement would not down. The hysteria, fed by rumors, mostly unfounded, continued as an important feature of the era when the South was called upon to decide whether her institutions, her civilization, would be safer within the Union or without it.

All this contributed to the final decision of the non-slaveholder. He saw his home and hearth threatened as well as the wives and children of the gentry. His leaders had always warned him of the menace of Negro equality; here was the climax of that menace. No wonder that he was often more zealous for the South than the planter himself. Fear of Negro equality, on the one hand, and the hope of attaining a place in the slaveholders' paradise, on the other, helped to rally the Southern yeomen around the banner of "Southern Rights." They, too, were ready to defend the institution of slavery and to join the movement for national independence, that "Ethnogenesis" which the poet Timrod heralded in 1861.

CHAPTER IV

THE STRUGGLE FOR THE NEW WEST

As has been said, the traditional Western suspicion of the older settled areas had come by mid-century to yield to forces, physical and spiritual, which linked the upper Mississippi Valley to the Atlantic Seaboard. The embattled legions that were to overwhelm the forces of Southern chivalry gained their decisive strength from recruits that poured forth from the farms of the Northwest. The fifties beheld the flood tide of the westward movement. In that decade the total population grew from less than twenty-three million to nearly thirty-one and a half. About one tenth of this gain occurred in states and territories not even listed in the census of 1840, while a million and a half were added from the only slightly older trans-Mississippi states. It is significant that the South, despite its apparent zeal for territorial expansion, was not producing a serious population pressure along its own frontier. Texas, to be sure, experienced a significant growth, and the rush to its lands attracted attention; but there the slaveholders from the older South were outnumbered by the mixed stream of Northerners and foreigners seeking the plains of west Texas.

Each spring throughout the free states a teeming mass of humanity, cattle and wagons pushed over the east-and-west highways and the prairie roads of Illinois and Iowa to new homes in the West. "Movers' wagons! More movers' wagons!" chorused the small boys as they spied another approaching train of migrants. Old settlers turned their homes into taverns with simple accommodations for the travelers. River steamboats, now in their heyday, carried their crowded human cargoes down the Ohio and up the Mississippi. For weeks in 1854 the ferry at Burlington, Iowa, daily transferred some six or seven hundred passengers, many from the older states of the Mississippi Valley—Ohio, Indiana and Illinois. The railroads connecting the Atlantic Seaboard with the Mississippi ran trains of fourteen and fifteen cars, carrying those able to afford the more rapid method of transit.[1]

Minnesota was in 1850 a frontier outpost of six thousand souls; St. Paul, capital of the newly organized territory, a yearling town of a thousand. Soon, however, settlers poured in, ruthlessly expelling the Indians before a fair treaty adjustment could be completed. Villages and towns sprang up and land speculation was rampant. The Panic of 1857, a blessing in disguise, brought the collapse of a fictitious prosperity, followed presently by development on more solid foundations. By 1858 the population of Minnesota was sufficient to win recognition, even from a reluctant South, of its right to statehood. In 1860 its inhabitants numbered one hundred and seventy-two thousand, a cosmopolitan mixture of foreigners and of settlers from the older Northern states.[2]

Farther south the agricultural frontier lingered at the bend of the Missouri. The land beyond the river—the

---

[1] It became noticeable, however, that through trains carried back to the East a heavy passenger traffic, only exceeded by the flood tide of colonists that moved in the opposite direction. *Cleveland Herald*, cited in *Baltimore Sun*, April 25, 1860.

[2] See F. L. Paxson, *History of the American Frontier, 1763-1893* (Boston, 1924), 424-425; W. W. Folwell, *A History of Minnesota* (St. Paul, 1921-1931), II, chap. i; G. B. Merrick, *Old Times on the Upper Mississippi* (Cleveland, 1909), 162 ff.

"Great American Desert" of early travelers—was too scantily supplied with water and timber to compete with the fertile unsettled areas of the old Northwest. It was the home and hunting ground of the American redskin, many of whom had earlier been transported across the Mississippi to make way for the oncoming tide of white settlers. Pioneers following the great trails to the Pacific had sometimes paused to sell forbidden firewater to the Indians, but otherwise they had shown little interest in the region. The red man became adept at beggary and thievery; and occasional raiding parties, not always unprovoked, caused a thrill of terror among the creeping white-canvased caravans. To ease the situation the newly created department of the interior brought together the tribes along the overland trails in a great council in the summer of 1851. In return for presents and the promise of an annual payment of fifty thousand dollars for fifty years, they consented to settle upon designated ranges, agreeing not to commit depredations upon emigrants and recognizing the right of the federal government to build roads and posts at will. It must be said that the Indians observed their obligations, moral as well as legal, more scrupulously than did the government agents.[1]

Hardly had the agreement been made before squatters began to penetrate this region, hoping to acquire legal rights to land. Restless spirits in neighboring states, tempted by high prices offered for their farms, also looked expectantly toward it. Meanwhile, the increasing interest in a transcontinental railroad created a demand for organizing this region into the territory of Nebraska. Missouri advocates of a central route and Stephen A.

[1] J. C. Malin, *Indian Policy and Westward Expansion* (Univ. of Kansas, *Bull.*, XXII, no. 17), 91-94; Stephen Bonsal, *Edward Fitzgerald Beale, a Pioneer in the Path of Empire, 1822-1903* (N. Y., 1912).

Douglas, the great champion of a northern route connecting with Chicago, were equally anxious to remove the Indian barrier and to throw open to settlement the lands through which the road would pass. Placating Southern hostility to the Missouri Compromise restriction, Douglas now proposed the application to Nebraska of the democratic doctrine of popular sovereignty. On May 30, 1854, his measure, the Kansas-Nebraska act, as it was finally called, was duly enacted providing for two territories north of the thirty-seventh parallel.[1] In the territory of Kansas, it was believed, the South could test the strength of the slave institution in the onrush of westward expansion. Nebraska, it was expected, would be commercially tributary to Iowa and, with the aid of a transcontinental railway connecting the North Platte Valley with the rail and water routes out of Chicago, be identified with the North and freedom.[2]

The peopling of Kansas at first differed little from other movements into fertile lands freshly thrown open to settlement. While territorial legislation was pending, immigrants on the left bank of the Missouri impatiently awaited the opportunity to cross over into the new territories. In the middle of March four steamboats descending the Ohio picked up six hundred men, women and children from Pennsylvania, Ohio and Kentucky; reaching St. Louis they found other arrivals competing for transportation up the Missouri.[3] Not long after, large

[1] On the Kansas-Nebraska act, see F. H. Hodder, "The Genesis of the Kansas-Nebraska Act," Wis. Hist. Soc., *Proceeds.*, LX, 69-86, and same author, "The Railroad Background of the Kansas-Nebraska Act," *Miss. Valley Hist. Rev.*, XXII, 3-22. Cf. P. O. Ray, *The Repeal of the Missouri Compromise* (Cleveland, 1909).

[2] See speech of Bernhart Henn, Iowa member of Congress, in *Congressional Globe*, 33 Cong., 1 sess., app., 888.

[3] *National Intelligencer* (Wash.), March 21, 23, 31, 1861. See also W. E. Miller, *The Peopling of Kansas* (Columbus, 1906).

companies of emigrants, old rangers and prospective settlers inexperienced in pioneering, were moving through
the states of the old Northwest with the destinations
"Kansas" and "Nebraska" proclaimed from the canvas
coverings of their wagons.

A new incentive, however, soon entered into the migration to Kansas. In Worcester, Massachusetts, Eli
Thayer aroused the foes of the extension of slavery to
the need of filling the new territory with inhabitants
who would dedicate the region to free labor. In April,
1854, he arranged with Amos Lawrence and other
wealthy opponents of slavery to incorporate, as a business venture as well as a philanthropic enterprise, the
Massachusetts Emigrant Aid Company; the plan was to
colonize free-soil settlers in Kansas and provide them,
at a profit to the promoters, with land, equipment and
supplies.[1] When the original project, a five-million-dol-
lar corporation, failed to attract the necessary capital,
Thayer and his fellow promoters went ahead with a
more modest philanthropic venture designated as the
New England Emigrant Aid Company. Indorsed by
leaders like Horace Greeley, this colonizing idea spread
to other communities. New York City soon had three
organizations: the Kansas League, the American Settlement Company and the Western Emigration League.[2]
News of these activities aroused the people of the frontier towns of Missouri. Kansas, they asserted, should be
reserved for the institutions which Missourians would
naturally carry with them across the western boundary

[1] Eli Thayer, *A History of the Kansas Crusade* (N. Y., 1889), 18,
23-25, 58-59; E. E. Hale, *Kansas and Nebraska* (Boston, 1854), 222;
S. A. Johnson, "The Genesis of the New England Emigrant Aid Company," *New England Quar.*, III, 95-122.

[2] For activities in Washington, see testimony of Daniel Mace, 34 Cong.,
1 sess., *House Rep.*, II, 829.

of their state. Organizations were formed to remove any "abolitionists" who arrived under the auspices of Northern aid societies.

Meantime Missourians crossed into Kansas. Some of them, settling upon lands not yet ceded by the Delaware Indians, founded the town of Leavenworth which in six months became a thriving community of several hundred inhabitants. For a time free-state emigration could not keep up with the tide of proslavery squatters. Most Northern settlers came, and continued to come, unassisted from Ohio, Indiana and Illinois. It was midsummer before the first party sent out by the Massachusetts group arrived; when winter set in, only six hundred settlers had thus been placed in Kansas. These, pitching their tents on the Kansas River, established the town of Lawrence at some distance from the settlements of the Missourians. There, lodged in hastily constructed log cabins, sod hovels and board shanties, this handful of Northerners struck terror to the hearts of proslavery zealots. They were regarded as the vanguard of a horde of mercenaries bent on winning Kansas, not as true pioneers but as the military agents of a fanatical corporation of limitless resources.

Threatened with the exclusion of their human chattels from a territory they claimed as their rightful own, western Missourians organized in secret oath-bound societies to cross into Kansas at a moment's notice to save the "peculiar institution" at the polls. In this way some sixteen hundred men, many of them armed with pistol and bowie knife, entered the territory in November, 1854, and contributed—unnecessarily, as the sequel showed—to a proslavery victory in the first territorial election. In certain border towns the entire male population—doctors, lawyers, merchants and editors as well as the ne'er-do-wells—joined the invasion. When the election of a territorial legislature took place, they again appeared at the polls and swept all before them. The legislature so chosen adopted a drastic slave code based directly upon Missouri statutes.

The struggle, however, had only begun. Northern champions of freedom conjured up in their minds a picture of ruthless "border ruffians" ready for any act of desperation at the behest of the slavocracy. They hastened, therefore, to organize additional colonization companies and aid societies all the way from Maine to the Mississippi. Everywhere volunteers were enrolled, so that by the summer of 1855 Northern settlers formed the majority. Organizing a Free State party, they held a convention at Topeka and drafted a free-state constitution. In the autumn the Kansas Emigration Society of Missouri made a frantic appeal to the South to speed to the rescue. The response came in the formation of Kansas associations in older states like South Carolina, Georgia and Alabama. Major Jefferson Buford of Eufaula, Alabama, recruited a company of three hundred under military organization, selling forty slaves to raise the twenty thousand dollars he had personally pledged to the enterprise.[1] This and other companies arrived in Kansas just in time to swell the military forces of the proslavery authorities who were determined to crush the Free State party.

On May 21, 1856, acting as a posse, they entered the town of Lawrence and left behind a path of destruction. Conceiving himself divinely appointed to avenge the lives lost at Lawrence, John Brown, beginning the train of events which would end at Harper's Ferry, led his sons and a few neighbors to the cabins of proslavery settlers along Pottawatomie Creek, and, dragging five men from

[1] W. L. Fleming, "The Buford Expedition to Kansas," *Am. Hist. Rev.*, VI, 38-48.

their beds, butchered them in cold blood. The entire territory and the Missouri border were soon aflame with exaggerated tales of the sacking of Lawrence and of the Pottawatomie massacre. Both sides rushed to arms. The martial bands of the proslavery party were matched by companies of young Northerners prepared, with Sharps rifles in their hands and the plow and sickle among their baggage, for either peace or war. Henry Ward Beecher, regretful that "anything else should be needed but moral instrumentalities," sent to a colony forming at New Haven not only his blessing and twenty-five Bibles but "the arms required for twenty-five men." [1] Soon Sharps rifles, listed as "Beecher's Bibles," were regarded as standard equipment for every emigrant company.

The Southerners countered with a strict embargo upon traffic up the Missouri River. At various points armed bands stopped, searched and plundered parties of Northern migrants. A Chicago company of seventy-eight men under military organization was twice held up, disarmed, and finally taken to Alton under guard. Such incidents fanned the zeal for aiding the cause of freedom in "Bleeding Kansas." Chicago, where a meeting promptly subscribed a relief fund of fifteen thousand dollars, became the headquarters of a National Kansas Committee organized by delegates from aid societies all over the free states. The Chicago company and other emigrant parties were again fitted out and sent to Kansas by a safer route through Iowa and Nebraska. [2] Meantime among the older settlers of Kansas blood was flowing. Fanatics and ruffians on both sides ranged about stealing, pillaging, burning and killing. Two hundred

[1] N. Y. Tribune, April 4, 1856.
[2] J. C. Malin, "Colonel Harvey and His Forty Thieves," Miss. Valley Hist. Rev., XIX, 57-76.

lives lost, two million dollars' worth of property destroyed—this was only part of the cost of "Bleeding
Kansas." At length in November, 1856, to the relief of
all, federal forces under a more capable governor brought
the reign of terror to a close.

Members of the Free State party had been the chief
sufferers, but they were gaining in numbers every day.
The enthusiasm aroused by the Kansas relief activities
caused a considerable revival of unassisted emigration in
the spring of 1857.[1] Confident of President Buchanan's
support, the proslavery settlers therefore hastened to
press for the admission of Kansas as a slave state before
the reins of political power slipped from their hands.
But the Free State men, at last exercising their rightful
influence at the polls, upset this plan by participating in
territorial politics and in August, 1858, rejecting the
proposed Lecompton proslavery constitution by a vote
of 11,300 to 1788. As a result admission to statehood
was delayed until January, 1861, a time, as it happened, when stark famine, following a devastating
drought, menaced the hundred thousand inhabitants.
Again the cause of suffering Kansas aroused generous
Northerners, the winter of 1860-1861 witnessing a new
campaign of relief.[2] With the upheaval of civil war Kansas was once more a scene of divided loyalties and border
warfare. What wonder that the grim and at times fanatical determination that carried the cause of freedom
through all these vicissitudes created a new home for
Puritanism in the trans-Mississippi West!

While these ill winds were blowing over Kansas, the
twin territory to the north had shown steady progress.
By 1860 nearly thirty thousand people were scattered

[1] Erastus Beadle, *To Nebraska in '57* (N. Y., 1923).

[2] *N. Y. Tribune*, Oct. 10, 17, Nov. 6, 21, 23, 29, Dec. 13, 15, 22,
26, 1860, March 2, April 2, 6, Oct. 10, 1861; *Cleveland Leader*, Sept.
13, 1860.

over the timberlands along the Missouri. The fertile soil produced grain in great abundance, often, however, only to be harvested by the grasshopper. Of a chain of villages Nebraska City was at first the most important, but Omaha City, designated as territorial capital, claimed four thousand five hundred inhabitants in 1865. By that time its growth was proceeding rapidly, partly in anticipation of the completion of the Pacific railroad. In another year, its sidewalks "thronged with returned gold seekers, discharged soldiers, farmers selling produce, speculators, Indians, and other strange characters of border life," it seemed to some "the liveliest city in the United States." [1] To the west lay the undulating prairies and the sand hills with their grasses, still the ranging grounds of innumerable buffaloes. Asked in 1864 whether they considered the territory ready for statehood, the people of Nebraska modestly voted no.

Meantime in 1858 the Indians of the Dakota country in upper Nebraska were induced to sell their old hunting grounds and remove to a reservation. In the next year a few white families arrived and erected pioneer cabins. On March 2, 1861, the region north of the forty-third parallel was cut from Nebraska and, together with the wedge-shaped tract between the Big Sioux and the Missouri River, formed into the territory of Dakota. [2] The five thousand people listed in 1860 dwelt mostly in the lower point of the older area east of the Missouri, which had been cut from Minnesota when it became a state. Conditions in Dakota were soon recognized as peculiarly favorable for wheat growing, Red River grain, often averaging sixty bushels an acre, being unexcelled. Though the frontier normally looked eastward for a

[1] A. D. Richardson, *Beyond the Mississippi* (Hartford, 1867), 564.
[2] M. K. Armstrong, *History and Resources of Dakota, Montana, and Idaho* (Yankton, S. D., 1866), 34-35.

market, Dakota farmers sold their produce mainly to Indian agencies, military posts and mining camps upriver, while those of the Red River Valley sent their products downstream on the steamer *International* to the forts and trading posts of the Hudson's Bay Company in the interior of British America. Agricultural products, including cattle and horses, brought higher prices in Dakota than on the Mississippi River.

The farther West continued to lure the adventurer in ways only less dramatic than the gold rush of the forty-niners.[1] California, the new El Dorado, did not find its stride in gold production until 1853 when sixty-five million dollars' worth was taken from the mines. By this time life in mining settlements had been rendered more orderly by the activities of vigilance committees. In a commonwealth so favored by nature agricultural development was inevitable as disillusioned fortune seekers reverted to the field labors they had abandoned. Farm acreage more than doubled in a decade, while the value of farms and of farm implements leaped at least fifteenfold; the wheat yield, already over five million bushels in 1860, doubled in another five years. In southern California the orange, the fig and other semitropical fruits were found to flourish as in their native clime. The grapevine, free from its common destructive diseases, came also to be cultivated extensively; by 1863 the vineyards of the state totaled nearly three and a half million plants.[2] Much of this development centered in the region of Los Angeles, a city of five thousand; in the

[1] H. V. Huntley, *California: Its Gold and Its Inhabitants* (London, 1856); Ernest Seyd, *California and Its Resources* (London, 1858); L. B. Patterson, *Twelve Years in the Mines of California* (Cambridge, Mass., 1862). For the rush itself, see C. R. Fish, *The Rise of the Common Man* (*A History of American Life*, VI), 308-311.

[2] F. B. Goddard, *Where to Emigrate, and Why* (Phila., 1869), 40; R. G. Cleland and Osgood Hardy, *March of Industry* (J. R. McCarthy, ed., *California*; Los Angeles, 1929), 40, 42 ff.

absence of the real-estate promoter unimproved agricultural lands were available at prices of one or two dollars an acre. Many old Spanish rancheros sold sections of the forty or fifty-thousand-acre tracts which they had exploited in rude feudal ease.

Made a state as a part of the Compromise of 1850, California quadrupled its population in a decade, reaching nearly four hundred thousand in 1860. The mingling of people from all parts of the globe made the commonwealth the most cosmopolitan in the Union. Contacts of California with the East were unusually close. San Francisco prices were quoted in New York papers, some of which published regular California editions. The *New York Herald* claimed San Francisco as the daughter of New York: her merchants were from the Eastern metropolis, her financiers from Wall Street, and her leading journalists from the office of the *Herald*.[1] The city on the Golden Gate had a population in 1860 of about fifty-seven thousand, which nearly doubled by the end of the Civil War. The journalist Samuel Bowles was impressed with the prosperity, culture and refinement of the Pacific Coast and hazarded the guess that San Francisco possessed more college graduates proportionately than any other American city.[2]

North of California the vast agricultural empire of Oregon continued to entice the emigrant.[3] Soon the timber and fishing resources attracted attention; their development was delayed only by the problem of communication with the markets of the world. The population of Oregon increased from thirteen thousand in

[1] *N. Y. Herald*, Jan. 31, 1854.
[2] Samuel Bowles, *Across the Continent* (Springfield, Mass., 1865), iv. See also same vol., chaps. xxvi, xxviii, and Richardson, *Beyond the Mississippi*, chaps. xxvi-xxvii.
[3] W. L. Hill, cited in Goddard, *Where to Emigrate, and Why*, 67.

1850 to over fifty-two in 1860 despite the fact that Washington territory, organized in 1853 out of the region north of the Columbia River, embraced about twelve thousand inhabitants in 1860. Seeking statehood, the people of Oregon on their own motion held a constitutional convention in 1857 at Salem. Remote from the scene of the slavery controversy, these Westerners saw little appeal in the new Republican movement and chose rather to affiliate with the traditional party of the frontier. This fact commended their plans to a national administration generally favorable to Southern interests, and the new state with reduced boundaries secured recognition early in 1859.

Meantime the recently arrived Mormon exiles in Utah reared their desert commonwealth. Under the able leadership of Brigham Young they directed their patient industry toward the agricultural conquest of the arid Great Salt Lake Valley.[1] New proselytes to the Mormon faith, with its generally unpopular doctrine of polygamy, were recruited, partly in the British Isles and other foreign fields. Each year large caravans, arriving by the Mormon trail, were systematically placed as well-organized colonies upon carefully chosen sites. The tracts contiguous to streams were promptly made fruitful by a well-planned irrigation system. By 1865 the system included two hundred and seventy-seven main canals which, built at a cost of less than two million, totaled over a thousand miles and watered one hundred and fifty thousand acres. The farms, small in size, were tilled intensively. Along the canals, connected by good roads, stood tidy towns and villages which boasted of sobriety, industry and excellent school facilities. The humbler followers

[1] George Thomas, *The Development of Institutions under Irrigation* (L. H. Bailey, ed., *The Rural Science Series;* N. Y., 1920), chaps. ii-iv; L. E. Young, *The Founding of Utah* (N. Y., 1923).

of the faith toiled with remarkable industry and perseverance. Those endowed with qualifications for leadership, largely from the more educated and refined minority, held places in the ecclesiastical hierarchy which was dominated by Young, a shrewd and benevolent despot. He was president of the Mormon Church and governor of Utah territory.[1]

Under the unique system of social control the solitude of "Deseret" began to glisten with golden fields. No ready market for the surplus had originally been contemplated, but the gold rush to California provided purchasers at unexpected prices. The Mormons salvaged, or purchased when necessary, discarded baggage, implements, furniture and livestock. They fattened the emaciated beasts of burden and resold them to immigrants who refitted in the Utah settlements. In due time the crops of the Great Basin were transported by ox and mule team to mining camps in Montana, Colorado and Nevada five hundred miles distant. The future promised a transcontinental railroad connection with both the Pacific Slope and the older states.

Salt Lake City was in the sixties a beautifully laid-out community of over fifteen thousand. Public edifices of stone and wood attracted favorable notice. A theater, in which amateurs performed with a skill equal to that of the professional troupes of the day, ranked architecturally with the playhouses of the metropolitan centers of the East.[2] Utah more than trebled its population in a decade, attaining a total of over forty thousand in 1860, a growth based on solid foundations. Its very

[1] M. R. Werner, *Brigham Young* (N. Y., 1925), chaps. vi-xii.
[2] Bowles, *Across the Continent*, 103. See also B. G. Ferris, *Utah and the Mormons* (N. Y., 1854); Jules Remy, *Journey to Great Salt Lake City with Sketches of the History, Religion and Customs of the Mormons* (London, 1861); R. F. Burton, *The City of the Saints, and across the Rocky Mountains to California* (N. Y., 1862).

prosperity presaged the passing of that isolation which the Mormons had deemed necessary for security and independence. "Gentiles" came in to represent the federal government or to head business enterprises, at first with a doubtful welcome from the "saints." The latter desired to rule the territory to their own ends, and federal officials found themselves not only helpless but virtually defied by territorial authorities.

When President Buchanan in 1857 undertook to clear up the situation by displacing Brigham Young as territorial governor, Young and his Nauvoo Legion, composed of all male Mormons from eighteen to forty-five years, attempted to prevent the "invasion" of Utah by the new governor and his fifteen hundred federal troops. During the course of the "Mormon War" that followed, Mormon militia joined with a band of Indians in the cold-blooded slaughter at Mountain Meadows of a hundred and twenty men, women and children, emigrants to California. The news of this massacre and of other outrages upon non-Mormons aroused belligerent feeling in the states, especially in those which had previously expelled the Mormons from their midst. Buchanan and his representatives, however, found that Mormons were evacuating Salt Lake City, leaving to its defenders instructions to apply the torch to every house if the troops entered. After an exciting year the issue was adjusted amicably. Young and the Mormons promised to respect federal authority and a general amnesty was granted. While the tension between Mormons and Gentiles continued, the latter steadily grew more numerous and, as they approached the five thousand mark, they organized social contacts of their own.[1]

Meanwhile other groups of settlers were drawn into

[1] For later developments, see Allan Nevins, *The Emergence of Modern America* (*A History of American Life*, VIII), 141-146.

the mountainous country. When the ebbing of the California fever awakened prospectors from their dreams of glittering wealth, there began an exodus of those unwilling to settle down to agricultural and other normal pursuits there. One group of adventurers, refusing to give up hope, sought the yellow metal in the nooks and crannies of the great American divide. It was they, the backwash of the gold rush, who in time spread the mining frontier over the entire region of the Rockies.[1]

Repeated false rumors of gold discoveries were followed in the fall of 1858 by stories of fabulous finds in the "Pike's Peak Country," identified by the one point of mountain geography generally known on the frontier. While the metal found in the sands of Cherry Creek proved an uncertain reward for the privations and sufferings encountered by the early comers, in the following summer rich quartz veins were discovered in what came to be known as the Gregory district. Even before this the new rush had reached its height. Seasoned prospectors closed in on this new field; border communities sent their restless spirits; and in the Middle West the old scenes of 1849 were reënacted. Thousands left for the gold fields with the slogan, "Pike's Peak or Bust," emblazoned on the canvas of their prairie schooners. Many others had scarcely completed preparations when the news came in May that the fortune hunters were returning in droves with the cry of "humbug."

As a matter of fact, success and disappointment alternated in the new gold country. Rich placer diggings proved limited and yielded few fortunes. When prospecting parties, exploring the near-by mountain range,

<hr>

[1] William Gilpin, *The Central Gold Region* (Phila., 1860); H. H. Bancroft, *History of Nevada, Colorado, and Wyoming* (same author, *Works*, San Fran., 1883-1890, XXV), v-vii ff.

found gold-bearing quartz veins over a large area, the ore was so firmly imbedded in the rock as to require unexpected outlays of labor and capital in setting up stamp mills. The mining company perforce entered the field. Bonanza days seemed over for the average gold seeker, and the exodus threatened to develop into a stampede. Meantime Denver City had been established, a busy, compactly built settlement in a fertile river valley at the very heart of what had been called the "Great American Desert." The census enumerators reported five thousand there in 1860 and found thirty-four thousand more in its general vicinity. With the first rush of settlers a spontaneous movement for local self-government developed, but an early dream of statehood vanished with the dwindling population of the gold fields. Late in 1859, however, the autonomous territory of "Jefferson" was in full operation.

The early years of Colorado, as this territory with reduced boundaries was formally christened by Congress in February, 1861, helped confirm the Eastern concept of the "wild and woolly West." Outlaws and desperadoes, flocking to Denver and the mining camps, for a time held sway. But the order-loving citizens of Denver, as in many other smaller towns, soon organized a vigilance committee which drove out or tamed the rougher elements. Presently came a different source of division, over the question of secession. Rebel sympathizers were active and influential; plot and counterplot became the order of the day. When the crisis passed and the danger of Indian uprisings was allayed, the settlers of Colorado turned more and more to agricultural pursuits. The valley of the South Platte River soon instanced yields of sixty bushels of wheat to the acre, sixty-six of barley, sixty-five of oats and four tons of hay. Mineral wealth and agriculture proved the combination which at length broke up the great mountain empire that had thus far stood in vast isolation.[1]

Meantime a new commonwealth was in the making immediately to the west. In 1858 and 1859 gold prospectors combing the eastern slopes of the Sierra Nevada discovered valuable silver deposits on the sides and at the foot of Mount Davidson, the loftiest summit in the Washoe range. The most important find was the Comstock lode. Miners promptly poured in from all quarters of the compass. Carson City, a flourishing town just off the California trail and a product of the first rush, quickly demanded an independent existence for this new mining frontier. Though the natural associations of the settlers were with California, the silver deposits were largely within the territory of Utah, and neither government was near enough to reflect adequately their wishes or needs. In 1861, therefore, Congress created the territory of Nevada with headquarters at Carson City. Thither came Mark Twain as private secretary to one of the territorial officials; in the mining camp he found ample opportunity for "roughing it" and ample local color for his later volume under that title.[2] Virginia City, with the Comstock lode partly within its limits, was the metropolis of the territory. When the ore-bearing veins of eastern Nevada were discovered in 1862 the thrifty city of Austin grew up at the center of the Reese River mining region. In spite of a small and an uncertain population, a congressional majority anxious to gain votes admitted Nevada to statehood in 1864.

To the south, in the region of the Spanish settlements along the Mexican border, mining was already an old

---

[1] Bancroft, *History of Nevada, Colorado, and Wyoming*, 363-420.
[2] S. L. Clemens (Mark Twain, *pseud.*), *Roughing It* (Hartford, 1872).

story.[1] Of the sixty thousand citizens of New Mexico in 1850 few were Americans and they were of the type that find a fascination in isolation, lawlessness and danger. Most of them were engaged in trading, such as the few hundred at Santa Fé, an almost negligible element in a population mainly Mexican and half-breed. Sleepy, sun-baked Mexican towns revealed plaza, old Catholic church, adobe houses, narrow streets and naked children. Outside, sheep and goats grazed on the hills; the rancheros knew only the most primitive agriculture. Evidences of mineral wealth recalled the Spanish search for El Dorado. But only the more westerly region responded to the mining excitement of the early sixties. There Arizona territory was created in 1863, although yielding in 1870 a population of less than ten thousand.

Far to the north, those nomads of the mountains, the prospectors, were opening up a new gold country along the Snake River. Early in 1861, after finds had been made just across the Washington-Oregon line, over a thousand miners hit the trail for the new field. In 1862 the Salmon River region to the south was the scene of wild excitement; eight or nine thousand miners stampeded to Florence—to leave almost as quickly as they had come. The discovery of the Boise basin drew most of the prospectors to a new district with Idaho City as its main settlement. Boise, at the head of the valley and between the Owykee and Boise mining fields, was founded in 1863 as a staging junction through which nearly all the passengers and supplies had to pass. Soon it gave promise of becoming the commercial center of this region.

Just across the Great Divide miners were prospecting on the upper waters of the Missouri. It was not long

[1] See H. I. Priestley, *The Coming of the White Man* (*A History of American Life*, I), chaps. iii-iv.

before ore was discovered over a wide section about the headwaters of the Columbia, Missouri and Yellowstone rivers. In May, 1863, Virginia City grew up overnight on Alder Gulch and in 1864 Helena was founded at "Last Chance Gulch," each the center of a valuable mining district. In 1863 Congress organized this new inland empire into the territory of Idaho, including the area of the present states of Montana and Wyoming. Mountain ranges, however, divided the territory into two fairly well-defined groups of camps. In response to the pleas of miners east of the Bitter Root range, Congress in 1864 erected the territory of Montana.

Thus in the period from 1849 to 1865 the mining camp made its first real contribution to the Anglo-American frontier. Over one hundred and fifty thousand, with pick and pan, burro, pack and shovel, took part in the quest. Ready to brave almost any hardship to attain sudden wealth and then go back to the East for its enjoyment, few actually returned. The call of the wilderness, the lure of the great out-of-doors, alone detained many. Others found their success bound up in the permanent development of the Far West—in cultivating the fertile valleys or grazing stock upon the nutritious native grasses, in handling supplies, or in selling their labor. Erstwhile miners thus became home builders and the vanguard of a new frontier.

Meanwhile the older regions of the upper Mississippi Valley were becoming the social and economic, as well as the political, heart of the nation. "Westward the star of empire takes its course," truly sang the contemporary Yankee bard.[1] A great influx of new settlers more than replaced those lost to the trans-Mississippi West. Yankee

[1] See poem in Boston Post, clipped in Belleville (Ill.) Advocate, April 25, 1850. He was, of course, doubtless unwittingly, misquoting Bishop Berkeley's poem of a century earlier.

stock from the rock-strewn farms of New England, enterprising sons of other seaboard states and restless pioneers from the upper Ohio Valley, together with sturdy, ambitious and freedom-loving refugees from the Old World, combined to make their contributions to the Mid-West and to hasten the passing of the frontier.

New Englanders often migrated in parties or in well-organized colonies. They first sought their kind in the old Yankee belt along the Great Lakes, thus avoiding the antipathy of critics who charged them with being "sniveling, hypocritical, rascally, white-livered Yankees" afflicted with "cant, humbug, Pharisaism, bigotry, abolitionism, red republicanism." [1] It was not long, however, before they spread out in all directions, even into lower Illinois, that "land of ignorance, barbarism, and poverty." [2] There the Southern bias of the earlier settlers made them less welcome, but missionary zeal inspired many to carry the torch of freedom to light up the darkness of "Egypt." Migrating New Yorkers, Pennsylvanians, Ohioans, Hoosiers and the rest also played an important part. As in the case of Yankee settlers, the older Eastern influences which they brought with them, far from succumbing to frontier experiences and prejudices, came to make a deep impress upon the new environment. Thus the mingling of peoples aided further in breaking down Western suspicion of the Atlantic Seaboard.

The North-South line of cleavage, on the other hand, grew steadily more rigid. Only a few settlers hailed from the states south of the Ohio River; and these, primarily from Virginia, Tennessee and Kentucky, cher-

[1] Adolph Douai, *Land und Leute in der Union* (Berlin, 1864), 245, 247.
[2] Auguste Laugel, *The United States during the War* (N. Y., 1866), 177. See also A. C. Cole, *The Era of the Civil War* (C. W. Alvord, ed., *The Centennial History of Illinois*, Springfield, 1918-1920, III), 14.

ished growing doubts concerning the virtues of slavery. This stream remained insignificant until the oncoming war enlarged the flow, bringing many who felt bitterly resentful toward the South and its institutions. The heart of the South had shifted with the culture of cotton to the Gulf states. A common frontier experience no longer bound these states to those north of the Ohio. The barrier between freedom and slavery was fast becoming more effective than the old mountain barrier between the seaboard and the West.

CHAPTER V

FARM AND FIELD

UNTIL 1860, when for the first time in American history the output of factory, mill, shop and mine exceeded in value that of the farm, agriculture was the bone and sinew of the nation's economic life. Yet, save for the faint beginnings of scientific agriculture which revealed themselves in this period, farming in the North as in the South was fundamentally a process of soil exploitation. Under such a system the advantage lay with the newer unexhausted lands of the West. By 1850 the wheat belt, having passed beyond New York and Pennsylvania, was shifting to the states along the Mississippi and beyond. During the Civil War it leaped across the arid plains and Rocky Mountains to California and Oregon. In the same way corn found a new habitat in the region of central Illinois and eastern Iowa and Missouri—a fertile prairie section where the tall stalks often bore from sixty to seventy-five bushels to the acre.[1] In 1860 Illinois led all other states in both corn and wheat production.

Good crops and favorable prices prevailed generally throughout the decade. The European famine year of 1847 had driven wheat up to $1.25 a bushel; then came a gradual decline until in 1854 the Crimean War, with renewed activity by foreign buyers, restored higher price levels. By that time fluctuating values were be-

[1] P. W. Bidwell and J. I. Falconer, *History of Agriculture in the Northern United States, 1620-1860* (Carnegie Inst., *Contribs. to Am. Econ. History;* Wash., 1925), 333, 348; A. H. Sanford, *The Story of Agriculture in the United States* (Boston, 1916), 223.

coming standardized by Chicago and New Orleans markets. A summer drought in 1854 sent breadstuffs higher than they had been for eighteen years. Normal values were not entirely restored when the Panic of 1857 arrived. Then, however, with crowded cellars and bursting grain ricks agricultural prices dropped to new low levels. The farmer, suffering from the depression, often found it cheaper to burn his corn as fuel than to market it.[1]

With the greatly increased output of the upper Mississippi Valley, the Middle West became the chief granary of the industrial centers of the Atlantic Seaboard and of Western Europe. Chicago, as the largest primary grain depot in the world, served as an agricultural weathercock "showing from whence come the balmy winds of prosperity."[2] Buyers scoured every corner of this new inland empire in order to ship the crops to the giant elevators of the *entrepôt* on the lake. As a means of hurrying the grain to Eastern markets, eighteen of the most prominent mercantile houses of Chicago organized a Merchants Grain Forwarding Association in September, 1857. Extensive speculation began to develop, two chief centers of operation being the exchange at the Board of Trade and a street intersection known as "gamblers' corner." There many a fortune of twenty or thirty thousand dollars was made or lost within a few weeks.

With the humbling of the Eastern states, Illinois won preëminence as the first agricultural state in the Union.[3] Prosperous large-scale farmers like Michael L. Sullivant found it desirable to remove from central Ohio to the

[1] *Rockford* (Ill.) *Republican*, Jan. 21, 1858.
[2] *Illinois State Journal* (Springfield), Sept. 6, 1855; *Ottawa* (Ill.) *Free Trader*, Feb. 18, 1854; *Cleveland Leader*, Aug. 17, 1860; Auguste Laugel, *The United States during the War* (London, 1866), 149.
[3] W. E. Baxter, *America and the Americans* (London, 1855), 219.

Illinois prairies where land was still cheap and the pioneer, with no brush to grub, could raise a full quota of crops the first year.[1] Sullivant acquired holdings of eighty thousand acres in east-central Illinois, sending out from Ohio several well-equipped parties to develop them. Thus, while farms in general were decreasing in size, successful and ambitious individuals competed in accumulating ever larger tracts. Cornfields sometimes attained the size of a few thousand acres. In every direction from their simple but commodious double log houses the owners surveyed their fields, flocks and herds. The results of such large-scale farming seemed miraculous. Deep plowing and cultivation with the latest agricultural implements contrasted sharply with the methods of the average farmer. But there was little regard for the future, little concern over soil exhaustion which seemed extremely remote.

The drain of population into the farther West, together with declining land values and sometimes abandoned farms in Eastern parts, aroused an interest in agriculture rooted in the fundamental instinct of self-preservation. At length agriculture was to be given consideration not as an art but as a science. The value of lime and phosphate as fertilizers became more generally known. The importation of guano had its beginnings as did also the manufacture of commercial fertilizer. By 1859 the entire output of fertilizer factories was valued at $891,344, a clear gain for the decade, yet merely a harbinger of the immense gains to follow.[2] These were the practical results of the application of chemistry to farming.

[1] *Ohio State Journal* (Columbus), May 1, 1856; James Caird, *Prairie Farming in America* (N. Y., 1859), 119; Bidwell and Falconer, *History of Agriculture*, 270.

[2] *U. S. Twelfth Census* (1900), V, p. cxl; X, 562; Bidwell and Falconer, *History of Agriculture*, 320.

At the same time agricultural periodicals multiplied in number and in circulation. Agricultural organizations sprang up everywhere, some content with the homely designation of farmers' clubs. By 1858 over five times as many Northern as Southern groups were listed, with a total of nearly a thousand.[1] While county fairs acquired a greater vogue, state fairs came generally to be held north of Mason and Dixon's line. Five hundred and twenty thousand visitors attended the Connecticut state fair of 1855; the third state fair in Illinois claimed the same year an attendance of fifty thousand.[2] The Missouri state fair at St. Louis in September, 1860, attracted widespread attention because of the presence of the Prince of Wales and his entourage.[3] The United States Agricultural Society, organized in 1852, met annually at Washington, passing its fairs around among the larger cities of the country. For a time the annual reports of the patent office chronicled significant progress in agriculture, the way being thus paved for the organization in 1862, under a separate staff, of a bureau of agriculture in the department of the interior.

A demand also arose for agricultural education. A movement sponsored by Westerners urged the establishment of state agricultural or industrial universities. This was a pet scheme of Professor Jonathan B. Turner of Illinois College at Jacksonville, a preacher and practical agriculturist, who aroused the support of many farmers, mechanics and business men. His Illinois critics denounced his "worse than Utopian dream," and sought to kill it by advocating professorships of agriculture in the existing colleges of the state. In 1852, therefore, Turner proposed that federal aid be enlisted in the form

[1] Commissioner of Patents, *Report for 1858*, 91.

[2] *N. Y. Herald*, Oct. 12, 1855.

[3] N. A. Woods, *The Prince of Wales in Canada and the United States* (London, 1861), 321; *Cleveland Leader*, Sept. 11, 1860.

of a grant of public lands—an idea which promptly became the unique feature of the Turner plan. With tireless energy this sturdy champion won the backing of leaders all over the North. An important ally was found in the Eastern labor forces which had set up a claim for state-supported industrial education to counterbalance the neglect of the children of the masses. With this growing support Elihu B. Washburne and Richard Yates brought Turner's plan to the attention of the patent office and of the United States Agricultural Society as well as to that of congressmen.[1]

The issue was now transferred to Washington. To avoid the ill-feeling of Easterners, who had already come to regard doubtfully the large grants to Western states for schools and other purposes, it seemed wise to have the proposal introduced by an Eastern member. For this reason and the obvious interest of the older states in improved agricultural methods, Representative Justin S. Morrill of Vermont was induced to father a land-grant measure for the endowment of an agricultural and industrial college in every state. Its advocates had the disappointment of seeing the bill pass Congress only to be vetoed on February 24, 1859, by President Buchanan who insisted that Congress did not have the power to give away public land.[2] Three years later, with the nation torn by civil discord, the measure was again carried through Congress and became law with President Lincoln's signature on July 2, 1862. Meantime, state aid had been invoked for the establishment of such institu-

[1] Mary T. Carriel, *Life of Jonathan Baldwin Turner* (Jacksonville, 1911); B. E. Powell, *The Movement for Industrial Education and the Establishment of the University, 1840-1870* (same author, *Semi-Centennial History of the University of Illinois*, Urbana, 1918, I); A. C. Cole, *The Era of the Civil War* (C. W. Alvord, ed., *The Centennial History of Illinois*, Springfield, 1918-1920, III), 240-245.

[2] J. D. Richardson, comp., *A Compilation of the Messages and Papers of the Presidents* (Wash., 1897), V, 543-550.

tions. Pennsylvania State College was legislatively sanctioned in 1854; Michigan Agricultural College, the first of these institutions to be opened (1857), was authorized in 1855; Maryland Agricultural College in 1856; and similar institutions were provided for in New York and Iowa.

In the fifties, too, began the widespread use of improved farm appliances. On many a little farm, especially in the East, the hoe, the spade, the scythe and the flail lingered unchallenged, but elsewhere the work of the husbandman was attended by an increasing clatter of horse-driven machinery. In 1850 the output of such implements amounted to less than seven million dollars; in a decade it increased one hundred and sixty per cent. A succession of improved plows, including wheel plows, had appeared long before 1860; John Deere, a Moline, Illinois, plow manufacturer, annually turned out thirteen thousand of his unusually successful products. The effort to develop a "steam plow," which might turn the prairie sod with more economy than did animal power, caused the Illinois Central Railroad to offer a prize of three thousand dollars for such an achievement. Demonstrations in various parts of the country were often voted satisfactory by newspaper correspondents. A trial was made in 1859 at the Illinois state fair at Freeport in which the Fawkes steam plow, winner of the grand gold medal at the United States Agricultural Fair the preceding year, impressed all spectators, but the judges failed to give it a favorable decision.[1]

The most significant development was the tremendously increased output and use of mechanical harvesters. In both senses Illinois was the "Reaper State."[2] In 1850

[1] Comnr. of Patents, *Rep. for 1859*, 256-258.
[2] "Illinois—The Reaper State," *Chicago Advertiser*, cited in *Illinois State Register* (Springfield), Nov. 6, 1851.

the McCormick Reaper factory was able to turn out but ten machines a day; six years later it was selling four thousand annually. Several other Illinois machines were also on the market, each with at least a neighborhood patronage. The reaper of John H. Manny of Freeport proved to be a formidable competitor of the McCormick product, which, however, had the advantage of certain special patent rights. In 1854 when McCormick sued Manny for infringement upon his patents, a number of other rival manufacturers in the East joined Manny in a legal battle royal, with able patent lawyers on each side, from which Manny emerged victorious.[1]

Whatever the make, the machine was soon necessary equipment for the wheat farmer. A large-scale operator like Michael Sullivant bought reapers in lots of from ten to fifty. In 1860 an observer with the aid of a spy-glass counted one hundred and forty-six reapers at work at one time upon the golden prairies of northern Illinois. There was much discussion concerning the respective merits of different machines, leading to reaper trials to provide more objective data. In 1857 a national contest of reapers at Syracuse, New York, furnished better evidence of remarkable achievements in this field than of the relative merits of competing products.[2] By 1860 nearly all the popular reapers were "self-rakers." The binding attachment was a product of the years immediately following.

The modern two-wheeled horse-power mowing machine virtually dates from the fifties when it reduced the cost of cutting an acre of hay to less than a third. Horse-rakes, tedders and balers were developed in the same decade, while the local newspapers carried alluring ad-

[1] W. T. Hutchinson, *Cyrus Hall McCormick: Seed-Time, 1809-1856* (N. Y., 1930), chap. xviii.
[2] Comnr. of Patents, *Rep. for 1859*, 26.

vertisements of patent grain drills, rotary broadcast seeders, corn planters, patent cultivators, corn shellers and the like. Portable threshers were demonstrated successfully, one American machine winning against all competitors at the Paris exposition of 1855. About 1860 steam power was coming into use in threshing. Thus did the products of American inventive genius herald a great agricultural revolution. Machine methods accentuated the Western specialization in cereal production. A new premium was placed upon large-scale production, giving the advantage to wealthy landowners able to employ a corps of farm laborers. With larger numbers of settlers taking up the minimum claim in public lands, however, the average farm declined considerably in size.

Signs also appeared of a growing diversification of agriculture, especially as the corn and wheat belt moved to fresh regions. A wider range of small grains was grown; under the stimulus of good prices potato acreage increased; market gardening came to the fore; and orcharding assumed a new importance. Fruit-growing centers arose in western New York, along the lake shore of Ohio and in southern Illinois; by 1860 large quantities of apples, peaches and melons were shipped from the farms of "Egypt." Grape culture flourished in the German districts around Alton and Belleville, as also in the Cincinnati and St. Louis areas. California under the same German influence was soon to excel all other wine-growing regions. With the increased output of excellent native wines foreign importation declined. Horticultural societies sprang up in many sections, among them the Northwestern Fruit Growers' Association, formed in October, 1851. Supported almost entirely by residents of Illinois, it met in annual session until 1857 when it merged with the Illinois Horticultural Society, organized in 1856.

A new development in agriculture came with the introduction of "Chinese sugar cane." Under the influence of prophecies that the upper Mississippi Valley would prove peculiarly favorable to its culture, that entire section sought to convert itself into a sugar-growing district. In 1856 J. M. Kroh and a few other farmers in Wabash County, Illinois, planted small plots of this "Chinese millet," "sorgo sucre," or "northern sugar cane," as it was variously called. Their immediate success aroused keen interest. Kroh alone sold seed to over two thousand persons, while his neighbors also disposed of their surplus and seed was distributed by congressmen as favors to constituents. Successful experiments in granulation seemed to make domestic sugar merely a question of the cost of manufacture. The cultivation of sorghum spread through the Middle West where the syrup in due time became a staple of the family breakfast table.[1]

Significant readjustments also took place in stock raising. In 1850 the New York beef market relied upon New York and New England graziers. In the West St. Louis, supplied by large pork growers and by cattle feeders who scoured the surrounding territory, was the chief rival of Cincinnati, the first American "Porkopolis." But with the advent of the railroad New York began to draw its beef more and more from the West. Cattle shipping and meat packing for distant markets became a new source of prosperity for the Mississippi Valley, especially for Chicago with its superior transportation facilities. Cattlemen, driving stock from Missouri, Texas and even Mexico, took advantage of the grazing and feeding facilities of Illinois and Iowa and of the conveniences of the Chicago market. Her rapidly acquired preëminence in beef packing made Chicago in

[1] Cole, *Era of the Civil War*, 82-83.

1860 the greatest general meat-packing center in the West.[1]

Pork raising was a simple industry as carried on in the Mississippi Valley. Hogs were often allowed to run at large upon the streets of the towns as well as in the country. Indeed, it was sometimes a difficult matter to decide to whom a lot of grunting porkers owed allegiance. Nor was there much attention to improvement by breeding. Fortunately the danger of hog cholera or other disease was usually slight. Hogs were the chief means of converting the corn of the West into marketable form.

Except on the Texas plains stock raising proved to be genuinely profitable only when practised on advanced principles. The more enterprising stockmen were beginning to introduce blooded stock, especially pedigreed shorthorns from England, to improve the breed. In Illinois, Kentucky and other states joint-stock companies were formed to import pure-bred animals from Europe. The capital stock of such associations was promptly subscribed and the auctions at which the cattle were sold often netted handsome profits. The business west of the Mississippi prospered from purchases by overland emigrants eager to make provision for stocking their farms in the new country. With the gold rush to California the scarcity of the meat supply in the mining regions led certain Texas stockmen to undertake the long and perilous drive to the Pacific Coast. By the end of the decade, however, wise California farmers were stocking their farms with thoroughbred cattle from the East.

In most parts of the North the horse was coming into his own as the draft animal of the farm. Many older farmers still preferred the powerful but slow-going ox,

---

[1] Cole, *Era of the Civil War*, 83-85; H. C. Hill, "The Development of Chicago as a Center of the Meat-Packing Industry," *Miss. Valley Hist. Rev.*, X, 255-273.

but in a series of plowing and hauling contests featured at certain fairs the horse demonstrated his superior qualities. Special horse fairs were held in different communities. By 1860 there were as many horses as oxen in New England, although bovine supremacy lingered on in the West. Since, however, in that year Illinois and Ohio shared with New York the leadership in the number of their horses, it was clear that the same trend was under way in the Mississippi Valley. Kentucky was a great mule-breeding state, largely for the Southern market;[1] there were many in Dixie who claimed for the long-eared hybrid special merit in agricultural work. As on the southwestern frontier the camel had been advocated as a carrier, various experiments were made in the Southern states, especially in Alabama, to test its adaptability to farming. It was found that the smaller animals could carry two bales of cotton with great ease and that a single camel could readily draw a two-horse prairie plow. In an exciting plowing contest with a mule at Montgomery, Alabama, the camel, to the surprise of the onlookers, won an easy victory. Despite five or six years of experimentation, however, prejudice against these outlandish beasts prevented any widespread use of them.[2]

This trend of agricultural progress had its occasional interruptions. Thus in 1858, following the Panic of 1857, a great meeting of farmers in central Illinois went on record in protest against the fall of prices and the raising of interest and freight rates, all of which it laid at the door of "trading combinations," banks and railways; it urged organization to strengthen the economic condition of farmers and raise them to that "position

[1] Comnr. of Patents, *Rep. for 1850*, pt. ii, 188; "Department of Agriculture," *De Bow's Rev.*, VIII (1850), 387-388.

[2] A. C. Cole, "Camels in the United States," *History Teacher's Mag.*, IV, 156-157.

among the classes of mankind . . . that nature destines them to occupy." [1] Later in the year a "Farmers' Congress," held at Centralia in connection with the state fair, declared that "the producing class should assert, not only their independence but their supremacy." [2] To carry out this purpose, the congress resolved in favor of coöperative wholesale purchasing and selling agencies in the chief centers of commerce. It was another matter, however, to translate this vague aspiration into constructive action.

As in earlier times, the American farmer of the midcentury era tended to seek his profits in the increased value of his land holdings. The migratory habits of the pioneer type were often accentuated by the opportunity to sell lands and improvements at considerable gain, while the more settled husbandman saw few incentives to careful and scientific tillage when new and fertile lands were always available toward the setting sun. Only the unambitious and the dull were disposed to accept conditions as they found them, and they were unfit to introduce the leaven of scientific agriculture.

If the average farmer was a speculator, trading upon the progress of the country, he was an amateur in a decade which was an era of speculation. Never since the thirties had the lure of Western land been more compelling. On the frontier line in Wisconsin and in Iowa, in California, Minnesota and Kansas, wonder towns rose in a fortnight with enthusiastic real-estate champions proclaiming each the future metropolis of the new West. Though these were often "paper" projects, property doubled in price in a few weeks. James W. Forney, the Philadelphia journalist and politician, purchased land—with borrowed money—at the end of Lake Su-

---

[1] *Our Constitution* (Urbana, Ill.), June 26, 1858.
[2] *Rockford* (Ill.) *Register*, Oct. 16, 1858.

perior where a Pacific railroad terminus had been planned, realizing nearly tenfold on one half his holdings. Another Pennsylvanian, George Addison Crawford, laying aside his law practice in 1857, joined a party going on a "spec" to Kansas where he and his associates bought the town of Fort Scott, "a prairie paradise." His own share of the profits promised to surpass "a good many years' salary at my old desk." [1] Attending the land sales at Paoli, he mingled with the crowd where "bowie knives and revolvers looked their prettiest into neighbors' faces" and found there only one of a number of opportunities for profitable investment.

The wounds of "bleeding Kansas" could be traced in part to bitter contests over such expected profits in land values. Upon his arrival Andrew H. Reeder, first governor of the new territory, bought lots in the nascent communities and started Pawnee City on his own account. Chief Justice Samuel D. Lecompte and other territorial officials founded Lecompton and sought to have the capital situated there. Lawrence and other free-state communities were in many ways the projects of Eastern speculators. The promoters of rival communities rejoiced that the local slavery issue promised to bring them steady reënforcements. "If it was not for land and town lot speculations," insisted a disillusioned settler, perhaps with some extravagance, "there would have been no trouble in Kansas." [2]

Similar conditions prevailed in the older regions of the Middle West. Chicago furnished one of the best examples of real-estate mania, house rents there rising to

---

[1] George A. Crawford to Horatio King, July 13, 1857, *Miss. Valley Hist. Rev.*, XIII, 541-544.

[2] *St. Clair Tribune*, May 31, 1855. See also W. E. Connelley, *A Standard History of Kansas and Kansans* (N. Y., 1918), I, 411, and W. C. Abbott, "Political Warfare in Early Kansas," *Journ. of Am. History*, III, 629-630.

twice those for similar New York residences. Stephen A. Douglas, having moved to Chicago, immediately bought large tracts on its outskirts, one of which he later sold at a profit of nearly a hundred thousand dollars. The immigrant Carl Schurz laid out a new Wisconsin farm in town lots and rejoiced in the many inquiries made by prospective purchasers while the work of surveying was going on. Others were content with profits on farm lands. Judge David Davis purchased numerous valuable farms in Illinois and holdings of ten thousand acres in Iowa. William Scully, an Irish landlord, coming to America and buying up Mexican War bounty land scrip at a discount, acquired thousands of acres of fertile prairie land which, with his later purchases, made him the largest alien landholder in the United States. In contrast, the proverbial ineptitude of the poet seemed proved when William Cullen Bryant sold his Illinois property on the Rock Island Railroad for ten dollars an acre shortly before it rose in value to many times that amount. It was estimated that in 1857 more than eight hundred million dollars was invested— though only a quarter of it in cash—in idle Western lands and in lots in proposed cities.[1]

Land speculation was often the main motive of advocates of projected railroad lines. Certain legislators and officeholders made their own investments sure by influencing political action. Governor Augustus C. French of Illinois bought up warrants and, through a dozen friends and agents, acquired lands along the probable route of the Illinois Central Railroad. His interests were also linked with the proposed Atlantic and Pacific, an ambitious cross-state route, whose backers, while pressing their project before the people and the legislature,

[1] D. W. Mitchell, *Ten Years Residence in the United States* (London, 1862), 328.

quietly bought land at strategic points along the route. Uri Manly, one of them, after having waited twenty years for such an opportunity, secured land at the intersection of the Illinois Central and the expected line. When the legislature refused a charter, he complained that he had lost a fifteen-dollar-an-acre accretion on two pieces of four thousand acres in Effingham County, besides the anticipated increase on twenty-three hundred acres in Clark County. "I had made a town—a city where our Road & the Central crossed," he lamented to his colleague in misfortune, Governor French.[1]

Under such conditions extensive inroads were made upon the public domain. On September 28, 1850, Congress donated to the states in which they lay the public swamp lands and lands liable to overflow, a gift totaling nearly two million acres in the case of Illinois alone. Federal land sales jumped from one or two million acres a year to over fifteen million in 1855 at the peak of the speculation. Successive grants in aid of railroad building in the Mississippi Valley totaled over twenty-two million acres by the crash of 1857.[2]

Not only the federal government but individual states, railroad companies and private owners dispensed lands to purchasers. Operations in Illinois suggest the general trend.[3] In annual auctions the state offered to the public the lands that remained of the federal grant in aid of the Illinois and Michigan Canal. A rush to these sales began in 1852; Chicago hotels became crowded, excited competition among the purchasers developed, and the bidding was spirited. In 1853, after a two years' suspension

[1] Uri Manly to French, Sept. 3, Oct. 27, Dec. 17, 1851, Jan. 29, March 2, 1852 (French MSS., McKendree College Library).
[2] J. B. Sanborn, *Congressional Grants of Land in Aid of Railways* (Univ. of Wis., *Bull.*, no. 30), chaps. ii-iv; Thomas Donaldson, *The Public Domain* (Wash., 1884), 269-270.
[3] Cole, *Era of the Civil War*, 85-91.

of the sale of state holdings along the more important railroad lines, the lands were again placed on the market, with preëmption rights for squatter settlers. Meantime heavy cash sales prevailed at the federal land offices aside from thousands of acres entered with Mexican War land grants and with warrants under the bounty land act of September 28, 1850. For a year, while the Illinois Central made its selections under the land grant of 1850, the tracts were withheld from sale, after which there was a heavy rush both by actual settlers and by speculators. Soon all land within the grant was assigned. The poorer federal lands, spurned in the open market, were quickly taken up when Congress in 1854 passed a graduation act which permitted entries at as little as twelve and a half cents an acre. As a result of these activities the public domain in Illinois rapidly disappeared. The Quincy land office was closed in June, 1855; already the Shawneetown district was rapidly approaching the one-hundred-thousand-acre minimum which would terminate its title to a separate office.

This left the Illinois Central the greatest landed proprietor in Illinois. To it, as has been said, the state transferred the federal grant of two and a half million acres, an immense tract scattered through forty-seven counties and equal to ten counties of over four hundred square miles.[1] The lands were divided into four classes: about 50,000 acres, valuable for town sites or because of mineral wealth, were to sell at not less than twenty dollars an acre; 350,000 acres of superior farming land at fifteen; 1,300,000 acres at eight; and the remainder at five. These prices applied to tracts which, lying on the unbroken prairies, had previously been scorned at $1.25 an acre; and while this schedule was being fixed, the government was selling its adjacent holdings at a maxi-

[1] See earlier, 16.

mum of $2.50 an acre. On September 27, 1854, the company opened its Bloomington office which in the first month disposed of 15,242 acres in McLean County at an average price of $9.97. In another year the company was aggressively pushing sales in all parts of the state. By 1857, with its grant half sold, the company had realized fourteen million dollars. Thousands of squatters with improved farms dwelt in southern Illinois on lands along the Illinois Central. The general assembly recommended to Congress that squatters on the federal domain be granted preëmption rights for a period of twelve months, while the company itself pursued a similar policy of generosity toward the *bona fide* settler. In addition it extended long credits to settlers generally and was lenient to purchasers who fell in arrears.

As the public domain disappeared in the older West and the prices of speculative holdings soared, champions arose to present the claims of the landless elements of society. Many citizens viewed with alarm the trend toward a system of tenantry, a system which "tends to separate classes in society; to the annihilation of the love of country; and to the weakening of the spirit of independence." [1] Already by 1850 the landless were the most numerous class in the large cities. The remedy agreed upon by reformers was the grant of free homesteads to actual settlers, thus taking from the capitalists monopoly of the soil. In 1848 the "National Reformers" held an industrial congress and chose as their presidential candidates Gerrit Smith of New York and William S. Wait of Illinois. Later in the year they effected a working agreement with the Free Soil party, which they had previously criticized for its failure to assert "man's inherent and inalienable right to a limited portion of the soil upon which he subsists" as the real and only ground

[1] *Chicago Democrat*, Jan. 22, March 28, 29, 31, 1848.

of "free soil." In 1850 the reformers renewed their campaign and in an industrial congress at Chicago adopted resolutions declaring that "the free land proviso would everywhere, on the cotton plantations of the South, and in the cotton factories of the North, unite all lovers of freedom and humanity and would strip the question of liberty of all prejudices resulting from sectional and partial agitation." These reformers insisted upon the folly of fighting an autocracy that dominated the southern half of the nation while supporting in their own midst "Factory Lords, Land Lords, Bankers, Speculators, and Usurers." On the other hand, they saw the issue of land monopoly behind the slavery question; from this point of view the Wilmot proviso seemed "but a modification of the great principle, that the earth was given for the uses of man; and that, like the other essential elements to existence, no portion of it should be the subject of monopoly." [1]

When Senator Stephen A. Douglas on December 27, 1849, presented a bill to give one hundred and sixty acres of public land to any head of family or widow who would occupy and cultivate them for four years, it was obvious that a radical reform was becoming popular. Soon a series of legislative resolutions, especially from Western states, supplemented the requests of memorialists for a homestead law. Andrew Johnson of Tennessee championed the cause in the House and in the spring of 1852 had the satisfaction of seeing his bill adopted by that body. In the Senate, where the conservatism of the older states found an ally in the fears of the South for its rights in the new territories, the fight was continued without success until 1860 when a variant of the law was blocked by the veto of President Buchanan. It was unconstitutional and unjust, he de-

[1] Cole, *Era of the Civil War*, 90.

clared; it was not fair to the old states, to existing settlers, or to other classes. Moreover, the bill would "open
one vast field for speculation." [1] The Republicans with
a homestead plank in their platform therefore claimed
special consideration as champions of the cause, making
Buchanan's veto an argument in favor of the election of
Lincoln in 1860.[2] Their triumph and the withdrawal
of Southern members made it possible for Congress to
enact the homestead law of 1862. By this measure a free
farm of one hundred and sixty acres could be acquired
by actual settlers after five years' residence. Soon, with
the ever westward press of population, extensive grants
to homesteaders, on the one hand, and to railroad projects, on the other, eclipsed the total earlier purchase by
both settler and speculator. Under this spur the vast
agricultural empire of the upper Mississippi Valley came
into its own.

[1] James Buchanan, *Works* (J. B. Moore, ed., Phila., 1908-1911), X,
443-451.
[2] G. M. Stephenson, *The Political History of the Public Lands from
1840 to 1862* (Boston, 1917), 202-217; E. D. Fite, *The Presidential
Election of 1860* (N. Y., 1911), 226-227.

CHAPTER VI

IMMIGRATION BECOMES A NATIONAL PROBLEM

"SINCE the period when the Gothic tribes, under their hereditary kings, strode down the banks of the Borysthenes, and overwhelmed Greece and Germany and the whole empire of Rome, no migration of men has occurred in the world at all similar to that which is now pouring itself upon the shores of the United States. In extent none, anterior to the Gothic or since, has equaled it. In a single week we have again and again received into the bosom of our society, numbers as great as a Gothic army."[1] The explanation of this phenomenon was less spectacular than this glowing word-picture might suggest. It was to be found in the grim reality of hunger and famine, in instances of political oppression and religious intolerance, that drove their hapless victims into crowded sailing vessels where for forty days, amid filth, disease and death, they awaited their first ecstatic glimpse of the land of opportunity and asylum for the oppressed. This tide of humanity reached its crest in 1854 when over four hundred thousand disembarked in American ports, only to drop away quickly until in 1862, amid the turmoil of civil war, only seventy thousand arrived. New York, the main receiving port, offered shelter to the newcomers in rude sheds on Grosse Isle until 1855 when the state immigration commissioners leased Castle Garden at the foot of Manhat-

[1] Anon., "Revolution or Migration.—The Irish Question," *Democratic Rev.*, XXX (1852), 97.

tan Island. New York and the other North Atlantic states attempted, rather ineffectively, by legislation to shut out persons of questionable physical, mental or moral capacity. New Orleans, where such regulation was especially lax, proved a popular port of entry for those who wished to make their way to the Northwest by the easy Mississippi route. By 1850 it ranked second in the number of its foreign arrivals.

Many of the immigrants were sped on their way by help from others. Governmental authorities in the Old World at times shipped to America the inmates of their almshouses, asylums, hospitals and prisons.[1] Besides public or charitable aid from European sources, remittances sent back by relatives and friends helped to provide outfit and passage money for those who patiently awaited their turn. Irish immigrants sent home funds totaling over a million dollars a year.[2] The sale of prepaid passage tickets, to be forwarded to prospective immigrants, became increasingly common, especially when steamships, as well as sailing vessels, began to transport third-class passengers. After the Inman Steamship Company inaugurated this practice in 1850, the Boston and Liverpool line of packets of Enoch Train and Company promptly made arrangements with Western railroads and Great Lakes steamboats to forward prepaid passengers from Boston to their destination.[3] To stimulate such business steamship companies established agencies at various points throughout the country, especially in Irish

[1] See G. F. Train, *My Life in Many States and in Foreign Lands* (N. Y., 1902), 97-98; J. P. Sanderson, *Republican Landmarks* (Phila., 1856), 80; W. S. French, *Realities of Irish Life* (London, 1868), 122-125; *Savannah Republican*, May 20, 1854; *National Intelligencer* (Wash.), Jan. 25, 1855; *Boston Eve. Transcript*, Feb. 1, 7, 1855.

[2] Lord Dufferin, *Irish Emigration and the Tenure of Land in Ireland* (London, 1867), 36. Cf. Carl Sandburg, *Abraham Lincoln: The Prairie Years* (N. Y., 1926), II, 5-6.

[3] G. F. Train, *Union Speeches* (2d ser., Phila., 1862), 84-85; Train, *My Life in Many States*, 77.

centers. Until 1864 and 1865, however, most immigrants continued to arrive in sailing vessels. Emigrant aid societies or associations in certain Eastern cities assisted in forwarding the strangers to friends in the interior or undertook to find suitable employment for them. In such ways the newcomers were apt to be drawn to the regions where foreign-born communities were already well established and the tendency to neglect the South was confirmed.

The bulk of immigrants, probably seeking a climate and environment similar to that of their nativity, landed at Northern ports and either settled in and about the large coastal cities or proceeded by divers routes into the Middle West. Aliens constituted about a third of the mid-century population of Boston and Philadelphia and nearly half that of New York. Into these cities many of the refinements of Old World culture were transplanted by exiled intellectuals. There, too, in obscurity and in humble occupations toiled for a time a Garibaldi or a Lamartine, and dozens of other political refugees who impatiently awaited a new day of deliverance for the home lands. In 1851 the Magyars of New York City welcomed to this country their great compatriot Louis Kossuth. The cause of Magyar freedom proved popular not only with the French, German, Austrian, Spanish and Italian residents of the chief immigrant centers but also with native Americans of all classes, whose deputations waited upon Kossuth to pay their respects and who made ready response to his appeal for money to aid the revolution of 1852. Never since the days of Lafayette had a foreign visitor received such a public welcome.[1]

[1] Francis and Theresa Pulszky, *White, Red, Black* (N. Y., 1853); W. J. Stillman, *The Autobiography of a Journalist* (Boston, 1901), 142-144; Samuel Longfellow, *The Life of Henry Wadsworth Long-*

At the same time, the larger Eastern cities acted as a sort of filter which kept behind the scum—those unfit or too poor to undertake the journey into the interior. In New York state and Pennsylvania foreign paupers actually outnumbered the native—in New York more than twofold—while the number of criminal convictions of aliens—largely for petty offenses, to be sure—ran in about the same proportion.[1] A similar situation prevailed in New Orleans where the foreign-born nearly equaled the native residents; yet on the police force they occupied three fourths of the places.[2] Immigration agents in Europe often cautioned the deformed and maimed against going to New York where they were likely to be rejected. In the more lenient New Orleans aliens admitted to its charity hospital outnumbered the native-born as much as seven or eight times. Even Western cities were not wholly free from the problem of foreign paupers and criminals. The immigrant population of St. Louis grew until in 1860 it exceeded the native-born by half. Chicago and Milwaukee also had a majority of foreigners while in Detroit and Cincinnati they formed somewhat less than half.

Notwithstanding these facts and the use made of them by ardent nativists, no federal legislation was adopted to combat these evils. In 1855, however, an act was passed to improve the conditions of steerage transportation; and in 1860 an amendment sought to extend much-needed protection to female passengers from annoyance by sailors. Such legislation tended to encourage rather than restrict the flow. Despite the decline of immigra-

---

fellow with Extracts from His Journals and Correspondence (Boston, 1886), II, 204, 211, 221, 222.

[1] *Statistical View of the United States* (*U. S. Seventh Census, 1850*), 163-165; S. C. Busey, *Immigration: Its Evils and Consequences* (N. Y., 1856), 123.

[2] *National Intelligencer*, May 8, 1854.

tion following the Panic of 1857 foreign arrivals averaged no less than 235,000 annually from 1850 to 1860, while their numerous American-born offspring accounted for much of the increase of the native-born. The alien population of New York, Illinois, Michigan, Wisconsin and California formed one fifth of the total in 1860. California, with a percentage as high as thirty-eight, was for a time a veritable Babel of bewitched gold seekers from all parts of the globe, to such an extent that in the very first summer of the rush the native American forty-niners met in council to consider the seriousness of this problem.[1] Wisconsin stood second with over thirty-five per cent of foreign-born.

Dixie received little of this human tide. A few immigrants there were in every Southern city, but only in Baltimore, New Orleans, Louisville and Savannah did they constitute over a third of the inhabitants. Many lingered within the gates of the friendly cosmopolitan metropolis of Louisiana, unable or unwilling to proceed to the interior. In its foreign-born population of sixty-odd thousand in 1860 almost every nationality was represented, the Irish and the Germans together making up about two thirds of all. Into other regions aliens, mostly Irish, drifted from the Northern states, some as migratory laborers and others as adventurers who hoped to return with their savings to the North or West. Now and again one prospered to the point of acquiring land and Negroes and cast his lot with the South. For example, in 1857 John Burnside, a millionaire New Orleans merchant born in Belfast, purchased a vast estate along the Mississippi and became one of the South's largest sugar planters. When secession occurred the mayor of Jackson, Mississippi, was a Democratic poli-

[1] *Illinois State Journal* (Springfield), Oct. 5, 1849.

tician who had been a member of the Young Ireland party of 1848.[1]

Certain regions of the South were the choice of groups that migrated in colonies to the New World. A series of prosperous German settlements brought over thirty-five thousand to Texas, especially in and about Austin, San Antonio and New Braunfels.[2] The last, a uniquely German community, possessed a varied industrial and cultural life. On the Texas frontier the traveler Olmsted was hospitably entertained by German pioneers in whose log cabins grand pianos resounded with the rendition of Beethoven symphonies, whose bookcases revealed thumbed volumes of the classics, and whose every word and gesture bespoke the refinements of an Old World culture.[3] Here and there other immigrant groups were to be found—a colony of French Protestants on a tract of three thousand acres in Monongahela County, Virginia, a Belgian community in Alabama, Irish settlements near Goldsborough, Maryland, near Little Rock, Arkansas, and in Taliaferro County, Georgia.

Yet in 1860 but a half-million foreign-born persons dwelt in the slave states, nearly a third of these in Missouri. The welcome to the realm of slavery was qualified by a nativism that resulted both from Southern fear of the increased political strength that immigration gave the North and from bitterness toward the anti-slavery views emanating from Northern immigrant elements. Only an occasional farseeing Southern statesman understood the need for the introduction of a Northern

[1] W. H. Russell, *My Diary North and South* (Boston, 1863), 268 ff., 298.

[2] G. G. Benjamin, "Germans in Texas," *German-American Annals*, VII, 109 ff.; Moritz Tiling, *History of the German Element in Texas, 1820-1850* (Austin, 1913); R. L. Biesele, *The History of the German Settlements in Texas, 1831-1861* (Austin, 1930).

[3] F. L. Olmsted, *A Journey through Texas* (N. Y., 1857), 430.

or foreign-born industrial population to redress the balance between the sections.[1] For other reasons, however, the border states of Maryland and Virginia sought to encourage immigration and give aid to new arrivals. Virginians even talked of setting up a station at Norfolk for the reception of immigrants from Europe, for whose labor there was an increasing demand in the interior of the state.

Immigration brought to this country a motley horde which many citizens of older stock prophesied could never be transformed into good Americans. A squalid and congested section of cosmopolitan New York housed an Italian colony of two thousand or more, the headquarters from which itinerant peddlers made their recurring pilgrimages into the provinces. The image vender from Genoa, balancing on his head a tray of classic figures, had only less fascination for the small boy of interior towns than the organ grinder from Lucca with his ubiquitous simian companion.[2] These visitors vied for attention with the gipsy bands that roamed the country in their wagon trains, seeking opportunities to pursue their vocation of fortune telling and winning a reputation for petty thievery. In the larger cities the Italians were already establishing themselves as confectioners and purveyors of fruit. Their more distinguished compatriots were often political exiles eager to continue their labors for Italian independence; in 1859 a group of new arrivals from Naples aroused their countrymen in New York City to fresh efforts on behalf of the cause.[3]

---

[1] William C. Rives to William M. Burwell, Nov. 12, 1854 (Burwell MSS., Library of Congress).
[2] H. T. Tuckerman, *America and Her Commentators* (N. Y., 1864), 336 n.; R. U. Johnson, *Remembered Yesterdays* (Boston, 1923), 51.
[3] *N. Y. Herald*, Feb. 22, 1859; *National Intelligencer*, May 20, 1859; *Baltimore Sun*, June 18, 1859; *N. Y. Tribune*, Feb. 20, 1860.

Jewish immigrants, largely from Germany but not always distinguishable from the other nationals of the countries from which they migrated, numbered in the Civil War period perhaps as many as one hundred and fifty thousand. They too dwelt characteristically in the cities. In New York their well-known second-hand clothing shops on Chatham Street and in the Bowery, where they bargained shrewdly with prospective buyers or sellers, were often the stepping-stones, first, to larger establishments in a better district and, then, to the profitable business of importing, wholesaling or clothing-manufacturing. The Jewish peddler started out from New York and by hard work and frugality soon found himself able to substitute for his shoulder pack a small horse and wagon; presently he set up a shop in some town where he often accepted social ostracism as the price of the economic opportunities that were in store for him.[1] In New York and other large cities Jewish residents were assured contacts with their kith and kin and the enjoyment of congregational worship. Cincinnati alone had four synagogues in 1855.[2] Everywhere the more gifted individuals worked their way to places of distinction and standing in the community. August Belmont, financial agent of the Rothschilds, was an outstanding banker and a leader in the Democratic party. Even the South recognized the exceptional merit of eminent Jews like Senators Judah P. Benjamin of Louisiana and David L. Yulee of Florida and Chief Justice Franklin L. Moses of South Carolina. In New York City the Jews were reputed to be persistent theatergoers and generous supporters of worthy musical entertainment.[3]

[1] Theodor Griesinger, *Lebende Bilder aus Amerika* (Stuttgart, 1858), 20, 142-147.

[2] William Rey, *L'Amérique Protestante* (Paris, 1857), I, 252.

[3] See D. W. Mitchell, *Ten Years Residence in the United States* (Lon-

In the fifties Polish settlements were made in Texas and Wisconsin. A number of Bohemians came to America as political refugees after 1848. Hollanders also continued to arrive, usually shepherded by a devoted and zealous pastor. Some went to the prairies of Iowa, but most of them joined in establishing a group of colonies centering about the town of Holland in southwestern Michigan. There they developed a successful agriculture, but turned more and more to mechanical employments.

The French immigrants of the fifties outnumbered the fifty-four thousand residents listed in 1850 as of French nativity. Twenty thousand of these, the largest annual contribution ever made to the American population, migrated in 1851. Some had been refugee revolutionists resident in England, whom the French government wisely furnished with funds to proceed to more distant shores.[1] Others were humble home seekers who combined with French-Canadian immigrants to swell the population of the Gallic-speaking quarters of the cities or to form new settlements of their own. Native Frenchmen increased so rapidly in Chicago that they were able to reproduce many of the social institutions of their mother land. Near by the strong French-Canadian settlement at Kankakee grew steadily with fresh additions from lower Canada, the emigration becoming so considerable that the Canadian government took alarm. Twelve miles up the Kankakee River, at St. Anne, a new settlement from Montreal and Quebec was started in 1852 by Father Charles Chiniquy, a Roman Catholic priest and temperance apostle of note, who acted as the spokesman of

don, 1862), 59; Charles Mackay, *Life and Liberty in America* (London, 1859), I, 322-323; Griesinger, *Lebende Bilder*, 20, 142-147; *N. Y. Tribune*, June 9, 1854, July 12, 1859; George Cohen, *Jews in America* (Boston, 1924), 92-93; M. C. Peters, *The Jews in America* (Phila., 1905), 52-54, 66-70.

[1] Edmund Patten, *A Glimpse at the United States* (London, 1853), 14.

French-Canadian discontent.[1] By 1860 these two settlements included over fifteen hundred families.

In 1849 a company of French communists under the leadership of Étienne Cabet acquired the property of the Mormons at Nauvoo and established an Icarian colony there. Soon upon the fifteen acres of town property and its outlying farm three hundred and forty colonists were housed. The settlement with the remodeled old Mormon Temple as headquarters had excellent educational facilities and a good library, besides workshops, mills and a store at St. Louis for the sale of their textile manufactures. The progress of the colony was chronicled in its official paper, the *Popular Tribune*, edited by Étienne Cabet. So well did the experiment succeed at the start—with a net profit of nine thousand dollars for the year 1852—that it was arranged to make Nauvoo a parent colony for the preparation of similar establishments in Iowa and elsewhere. Soon, however, controversies arose over administrative matters, and the authority of Cabet was challenged by opponents who finally succeeded in deposing him shortly before his death in November, 1856. The outcome of this factionalism was the complete ruin of Icaria, bringing an end in 1859 to this promising experiment in the realization of a nineteenth-century communistic Utopia.[2]

The Scandinavian contribution to American life, hardly more than begun by 1850, grew so rapidly that the decade brought the total number from Norway, Sweden and Denmark to nearly seventy-three thousand. Of these the Norwegians constituted a half. The humble

[1] Charles Chiniquy, *Fifty Years in the Church of Rome* (Chicago, 1886), 614-617, 789-790, 820.
[2] A. C. Cole, *The Era of the Civil War* (C. W. Alvord, ed., *The Centennial History of Illinois*, Springfield, 1918-1920, III), 18-19; W. A. Hinds, *American Communities and Co-operative Colonies* (2d rev. edn., Chicago, 1908), 361-377.

cotter of the Northland, eking from the rocky soil of his ancestral holding a scant living that was constantly threatened by the exactions of the tax collector, at length was stricken by the "America fever." Numerous Scandinavian colonies were founded in northern Illinois, while Chicago acted as a distributing station for other parts of the West. Besides the several thousand Norwegians in the Lake city, Swedes were numerous there and also at Rockford and in settlements in Henry County. A peculiarly colorful group of Swedish pioneers were led by Eric Janson, a bitter critic of the Lutheran state church and a seceder from its ranks. After a period of persecution in the homeland Janson and his followers in 1846 had founded Bishop Hill colony in Henry County as a haven of refuge and the laboratory for a communistic experiment which attained economic prosperity, though at the cost of internal dissension.[1]

Twenty-three thousand sturdy Northmen dwelt in Wisconsin, scattered in all parts. Fredrika Bremer, visiting St. Paul in 1850, visioned Minnesota as "a glorious new Scandinavia"; by 1860 fulfillment seemed well under way with nearly twelve thousand Scandinavians in the new commonwealth.[2] The four westernmost states of the upper Mississippi Valley claimed well over two thirds of the Scandinavian element. The rest were strewn over the North, with two thousand Danes in the region of the Great Salt Lake to which they had been attracted by the evangelism of Mormon missionaries.

[1] The experiment came to an end in 1862. M. A. Mikkelsen, *The Bishop Hill Colony* (Johns Hopkins Univ., *Studies*, X, no. 1).

[2] Fredrika Bremer, *The Homes of the New World* (N. Y., 1853), II, 55-58; same author, *America of the Fifties* (A. B. Benson, ed., N. Y., 1924), 234-237. On Scandinavian immigration, see G. M. Stephenson, *A History of American Immigration, 1820-1924* (Boston, 1926); K. C. Babcock, *The Scandinavian Element in the United States* (Univ. of Ill., *Studies*, III), 66-75; T. C. Blegen, *Norwegian Migration to America, 1825-1860* (Northfield, Minn., 1931), 349-377.

From Britain came the swelling of a stream which had persistently flowed to America from the earliest days of settlement. Scattered over the country with little pride of nationality except for those active in forming patriotic St. George societies, the old English stock was scarcely aware of the four hundred thousand new recruits of the fifties. Many came at the expense of parishes which found in assisted emigration a solution of the problem of poor relief. In the later fifties, too, English capitalists interested in the Illinois Central Railroad used every means to direct emigrants to its lands, with the result that large companies of English farmers and mechanics settled south of Centralia. In 1859 steps were taken in London toward the organization of the "Prairie Land and Emigration Company" with a capital of $2,500,000, the object of which was to purchase prairie land in Illinois and colonize it with English farmers.[1]

The Emerald Isle, smarting under British rule and a grinding economic system, contributed even more largely to the mid-century population.[2] Even in normal times better rewards for the brawn and brain of Irish youth beckoned across the seas where opportunity offered many paths to success. Then, in 1845 and 1846, the potato crop—the main food supply and source of income of the Irish tenants—rotted in the ground before the attack of blighting disease. Gaunt famine stalked the land and gathered its victims by the thousands. Reluctantly but hopefully many embarked for the great republic to the west. The emerald tide doubled, trebled and quadrupled in volume until in 1851 it brought nearly a quarter of a million. Proud Massachusetts with

[1] Cole, *Era of the Civil War*, 21.
[2] W. F. Adams, *Ireland and Irish Emigration to the New World* (New Haven, 1932).

her strong Anglo-Saxon strain received her quota of "paddies" along with cosmopolitan New York and Pennsylvania. Together these three states accounted in 1860 for more than half of the 1,600,000 residents of Irish birth. New York with over two hundred thousand was the largest Irish city in the world.

Celtic immigrants were usually content to live in the poorest cottages and the most crowded tenements, and to them fell the roughest and most menial tasks.[1] As day laborers in the cities and on the railroads and canals and as servant girls in the homes of the well-to-do, their lot seemed little better than that of the Negroes whom they feared and despised as competitors. Yet this sturdy band of humble toilers made an incalculable contribution to the development of the nation's material resources. Some quickly and unostentatiously attained a prosperity that caused them to stand out from the rest. In less than twenty years in America Alexander T. Stewart, the "lucky Irishman," laid the foundations of his tremendous fortune, becoming not only owner of the finest store in the world but also the greatest importer in America and one of the largest real-estate owners in New York. An observing traveler noted the facility of the Irishman in "casting off the original Paddy and becoming a good American, without losing his warm heart and other good Irish qualities, so that many excellent and distinguished men arise from the second generation of these descendants of Erin."[2]

Yet he also discovered a widespread dislike of the Irish on the part of other racial groups, due doubtless to restless and turbulent individuals whose conduct ad-

---

[1] Jeremiah O'Donovan, *A Brief Account of the Author's Interview with His Countrymen, and of the Parts of the Emerald Isle Whence They Emigrated* (Pittsburgh, 1864).

[2] J. G. Kohl, *Travels in Canada, and through the States of New York and Pennsylvania* (Mrs. Percy Sinnett, tr., London, 1861), II, 318.

vertised the race as noisy and quarrelsome, fond of John Barleycorn and bloody street brawls. Again and again the press of the day plied the question: "Why do our police reports always average two representatives from 'Erin, the green soft isle of the ocean,' to one from any other habitable land of the earth? . . . Why are the instigators and ringleaders of our riots and tumults in nine cases out of ten, Irishmen?" [1] Seldom, however, did the inquirer seek the answer to his question in Old World oppression or in the exploitation in America of the Irish immigrant toiler. If Irish "floaters" illegally determined the vote in certain doubtful districts, as they did in Illinois during the Lincoln-Douglas contest, was it not because the railroads or other interested parties shipped construction gangs to these points and sent the floaters to the polls under careful instruction? [2]

Of a different order were those exiles who had staked their all in the struggle for Irish independence, some of them brilliant idealists who espoused the cause of civil liberty and liberal institutions in every form. Local and state Hibernian societies served as agencies for the expression of such ideals as well as of the sense of Celtic brotherhood. Many an Irish patriot held himself ready to join in the redemption of his native land when the hour should strike. The Irish had their own press, their own militia companies; they celebrated St. Patrick's day with parades and extensive ceremonials. Withal they carefully nursed their ancient grudge against Britain and its authority. Not only did the Irish populace in 1860

---

[1] *Chicago Tribune*, Dec. 23, 1853. See also [Isabella L. Bishop]. *The Englishwoman in America* (London, 1856), 119-120; Amelia M. Murray, *Letters from the United States, Cuba and Canada* (London, 1856), II, 103; Robert Everest, *Journey through the United States and Part of Canada* (London, 1855), 87; T. C. Grattan, *Civilized America* (London, 1859), II, chap. i.

[2] Abraham Lincoln, *Uncollected Letters* (G. A. Tracy, ed., Boston, 1917), 94.

decline to turn out on the occasion of the first visit of a Prince of Wales to America, but the sixty-ninth regiment of New York militia under Colonel Corcoran refused to take part in the ceremonies.

Even more numerous than the Irish were the German immigrants. The "forty-eighters," after the unsuccessful revolutionary upheaval of 1848, fled to America to escape the vengeance of the oppressors whom they had assailed. A far greater number of Germans, however, were impelled by the hope of better living conditions or by unwillingness to undergo compulsory military training.[1] In 1852 the arrivals doubled and the stream maintained this new level for the next year, while 1854 brought flood tide. In that year the figure for 1851 trebled, reaching a total of two hundred and fifteen thousand. With the additions of the years that followed, the census enumerators of 1860 listed more than one and a quarter million.

A thrifty sober stock, the German immigrants usually arrived with sufficient capital to permit them to choose the part they wished to play in their adopted country. Except for those remaining in and about New York City or other ports, they proceeded to the states of the upper Mississippi Valley, notably Ohio, Illinois, Missouri and Wisconsin. There they became prosperous farmers, industrious artisans or successful small tradesmen. To be sure, Friedrich Hecker of Baden and other intellectuals who had helped organize the revolutionary movements of 1848 attained only a limited success as agriculturalists; with more knowledge of the classics than of husbandry, they suffered keenly from the hardship of the frontier and came to be known as "Latin farmers." Others, however, combining practical sense

---

[1] M. L. Hansen, "The Revolutions of 1848 and German Emigration," *Journ. of Econ. and Business History*, II, 630-658.

with scientific knowledge, made significant contributions to the development of horticulture and viniculture in America.[1]

The chief German centers were New York, Cincinnati, Louisville, St. Louis, Chicago and Milwaukee. New York housed more Germans than any city in the world except Berlin and Vienna. In these American communities the Teutonic newcomers maintained social institutions in the transplanted atmosphere of the fatherland. In the more isolated German quarters—like the section of Cincinnati "across the Rhine," which a sluggish canal cut off from the heart of the city—peasant types in woolen jackets, blue worsted pantaloons and low-crowned hats dwelt with their squat, stout matrons and numerous offspring in comfortable proximity to their shops and bakeries, their *Biergärten, Restaurationen* and *Turnvereine*. Near by were dancing gardens, music halls and little theaters where the women, with their babes or knitting, sat placidly while their men folk sucked long pipes and sipped their beer.[2] Near by, too, were German Lutheran and evangelical churches and their affiliated parochial schools. Wherever they settled singing societies were promptly organized—a *Männerchor*, a *Gesangverein* or a *Liederkranz*, in which lusty voices combined to produce a spirited ensemble. There were, besides, local musical festivals and annual national festivals, beginning with one at Cincinnati in 1849, in which as many as forty choral societies competed for a grand prize.

More quickly, however, than any other foreign-

[1] Carl Schurz, *Reminiscences* (N. Y., 1907-1908), II, 41-42; A. B. Faust, *The German Element in the United States* (Boston, 1909), II, 37-38, 41-50; G. P. Koerner, *Das Deutsche Element in den Vereinigten Staaten* (Cin., 1880); Gustave Koerner, *Memoirs, 1809-1896* (Cedar Rapids, Iowa, 1909); W. V. Pooley, *The Settlement of Illinois, 1830-1850* (Madison, 1908), 491 ff.

[2] See Edward Dicey, *Six Months in the Federal States* (London, 1863), II, 54-56, 100-101, and Cole, *Era of the Civil War*, 24, 44, 442-443.

speaking group, the German accepted the American pattern of life. From purpose or necessity he abandoned the Old World garb and sought to free himself from dependence upon an alien tongue. The more sophisticated imitated the institutions they found about them. German militia companies were organized—not only black *Jäger* rifles, but Washington rifles, Washington grenadiers and Washington light cavalry. German Odd Fellow lodges and even tribes of German Red Men fostered the fraternal spirit in true American style. Steuben societies were established in honor of the hero who typified the German contribution to American independence.

In these Teutonic circles an atmosphere of revolutionary democracy lingered, especially among the forty-eighters. In 1852 Dr. Gottfried Kinkel, the German revolutionist, teacher and inspirer of the youthful Carl Schurz, toured the country to collect funds for the revolutionary committee which hoped soon to strike another blow. This erstwhile professor of history and literature at Bonn was welcomed with elaborate ovations and generous contributions.[1] With the growing hopelessness of the revolutionary cause, however, most German Americans accepted a permanent place in the great Western republic and undertook to realize therein the ideals they were unable to attain in the Old World. This was evident in the history of the *Turnverein:* its radical political spirit was seldom maintained in its many American chapters; indeed, its national and sectional conventions were little more than gatherings built around exhibitions of gymnastic skill. Yet a visionary fringe was imbued with the socialist philosophy, par-

[1] Koerner, *Memoirs,* I, 573-577; J. G. Gazley, *American Opinion of German Unification, 1848-1871* (Columbia Univ., *Studies,* CXXI), 79-80.

ticularly the new "scientific" brand bearing the label of Karl Marx. This fact sometimes created prejudice against other reforms in which the Germans were interested, causing the free-homestead proposal, for example, to be stigmatized as the "offspring of the German school of socialism and 'higher law' transcendentalism."[1] As a matter of fact, the socialist element was never large, being confined to organizations like the *Freie Gemeinde*, the *Allgemeiner Arbeiterbund* and the Universal Democratic Republican Society with its French and Italian sections.[2]

Rich as was the cultural atmosphere of their communities and content as they were with the surroundings they were able to create, the Germans did not confine their influence within such narrow limits. Often holding the balance of power in elections, they were courted by both political parties. German leaders played a prominent part in Democratic politics and later, revolting against the influence of the "Slave Power," transferred their allegiance to the new Republican movement. The brilliant young Carl Schurz, with a penetrating insight into American politics and with an eloquent command of English that dismayed his native-born opponents, was a potent force in quieting the natural Teutonic repugnance to the Puritanism and nativism of the Yankee element in the Republican party,[3] while in the

[1] Speech of Josiah Sutherland, April 22, 1852, *Congressional Globe*, 32 Cong., 1 sess., app., 731.
[2] Morris Hillquit, *History of Socialism in the United States* (N. Y., 1903), pt. ii, chap. i.
[3] Carl Schurz, *Speeches, Correspondence and Political Papers* (Frederic Bancroft, ed., N. Y., 1913), I, 43-44, 75; Schurz, *Reminiscences*, II, 101; Adolf Douai, *Land und Leute in der Union* (Berlin, 1864), 251; Andrew D. White, *Autobiography* (N. Y., 1905), I, 86, 87; Henry Villard, *Memoirs of Henry Villard, Journalist and Financier, 1835-1900* (Boston, 1904), I, 51, 58, 63. See also George Schneider, "Lincoln and the Anti-Know Nothing Resolutions," McLean County Hist. Soc., *Trans.*, III, 87-91.

politics of Illinois Gustave Koerner was an outstanding figure. The Lutheran and Catholic clergy, on the other hand, exercised a strong influence upon their congregations along conservative lines, seeking in vain to stem the German revolt from the Democratic party.

The German-American press was firmly grounded in the fifties with three or more dailies in New York City, four in Wisconsin and at least one in every other important German center from the coast to west Texas.[1] Many forty-eighters filled the editorial chair with distinction, including Schurz, Friedrich Hecker, Friedrich Knapp, Wilhelm Rapp, Franz Sigel and Caspar Butz. Francis Grund was dean of the newspaper correspondents at Washington, while Henry Villard was a brilliant correspondent of the New York *Staatszeitung* and later of the *Herald* and of the *Tribune*. The work of all these showed clearly that the Germans had turned their backs upon Europe and taken up the issues of the states and of the nation.[2]

Many folk customs of the Germans were quickly adopted by their American neighbors. Lager beer became a popular beverage and the Teutonic brand of Sabbath observance, which included picnics with singing and shooting contests, appealed to the less strait-laced. The Germans also contributed to the gayety of the winter holidays, notably in the case of Christmas, for they were responsible for spreading the Christmas tree and its bounteous offering of toys. Pictures by Thomas Nast, the Bavarian-American artist, depicting the Christmas

[1] Otto Zirckel, *Skizzen aus den und über die Vereinigten Staaten* (Berlin, 1850), 83-84; *National Intelligencer*, Feb. 9, 1852; *N. Y. Herald*, Jan. 26, 1854; *Ann Arbor Local News*, Nov. 3, 1857.

[2] Abraham Lincoln contributed to the establishment of a German newspaper at Springfield and later, having acquired legal ownership by assuming the indebtedness of its financially embarrassed publisher, profited by its support of his candidacy for the Republican nomination. W. E. Barton, *The Life of Abraham Lincoln* (Indianapolis, 1925), I, 422-423.

spirit in early issues of *Harper's Weekly* were popular with young and old.[1] To many shrewd observers of the day the German stock had a notable contribution to make to a new America. A French observer prophesied favorable results from a physical blending of the Anglo-Saxon and the German, "the one too nervous and irritable, the other too heavy and rustic"; in the new race the fine mental and physical qualities of the two stocks would find a better equilibrium.[2] Besides the Old World culture that America so sorely needed, the German brought with him lessons in *Gemütlichkeit* to temper Yankee stiffness and repression. As a contemporary German American asserted, "The better class of Germans are the spiritual leaven to the better Americans."[3] No wonder, then, that most Americans held out a warm welcome to these newcomers.

Through the centuries that Europeans had been peopling America, the yellow hordes of the Orient had continued immobile bystanders. The discovery of gold, however, wrought a change. As many as thirteen thousand reached California in the banner year of 1854. The earlier arrivals engaged in various kinds of work in the mines where they often successfully exploited holdings which white miners did not find it profitable to work. The Chinese more frequently toiled as common laborers, carpenters, cooks and house servants; their restaurants in San Francisco soon became a familiar institution. In 1860 about thirty-five thousand dwelt in the United States, nearly all of them on the coast. The sudden labor needs in Pacific railroad building brought later accre-

[1] Faust, *German Element in the United States*, II, 384-385.
[2] Auguste Laugel, *Les États-Unis pendant la Guerre* (N. Y., 1866), 124-125, 168.
[3] Douai, *Land und Leute*, 256-257. See also Walt Whitman, *I Sit and Look Out* (Emory Holloway and Vernolian Schwarz, eds., N. Y., 1932), 60, 132, 150-151.

tions. In 1864 about three thousand were employed in the construction of the Central Pacific Railroad and the following year saw the addition of two thousand more, although many soon returned to China with their savings.

These Orientals were handicapped by a state license tax of four dollars a month on every foreign miner who had not declared his intention to become a citizen. This regulation reflected an early sentiment against them which was particularly strong among the white miners, a prejudice which resulted in a request by the California legislature in 1854 that Congress enact a capitation tax on Chinese immigrants and otherwise discourage their influx. Certain leading citizens on the Pacific Seaboard even advocated their total expulsion from American soil. Nevertheless, in 1862, when anti-Chinese sentiment had become even more pronounced, a committee of the legislature concluded that the Chinese population had directly and indirectly made a valuable contribution to the prosperity of the state.[1]

Immigration, white or yellow, meant much for American prosperity, whether in the solution of labor needs, in the stimulus to land sales or as an aid to business and industry. Certain observers, however, were dismayed by the size of the stream. Such critics, moreover, found evils that seemed quite to justify their alarm. Some pointed to the physically, mentally and morally defective immigrants—many direct from the lazar houses and jails of Europe—who became parasites on the large cities and seaports. Some were concerned that the for-

---

[1] M. R. Coolidge, *Chinese Immigration* (N. Y., 1909), 21-22, 61, 63; A. D. Richardson, *Beyond the Mississippi* (Hartford, 1867), 450; Samuel Bowles, *Across the Continent* (Springfield, Mass., 1865), 238 ff.; R. M. Smith, *Emigration and Immigration* (N. Y., 1890), 238-239. See also Allan Nevins, *The Emergence of Modern America* (*A History of American Life*, VIII), 375-376, and plate xiv.

eigners in general retained a love for the fatherland and associated together in clannish exclusiveness.[1] Others pointed to the corruption of the foreign-born voter, often not naturalized or with citizenship illegally conferred, and manipulated by the unscrupulous politician.[2] Native workingmen objected to the growing competition with cheap labor. Moreover, in the North Atlantic states, where the Irish with their unusual aptitude and fondness for politics became especially numerous and the Roman Catholic hierarchy powerful and active, there were those who felt that the Roman Church dominated the political thinking of its members and claimed for the pope a temporal allegiance. On the other extreme were the religious liberals, freethinkers and atheists among the newcomers, whose views shocked American orthodoxy. Nor could many of older native stock view with approval the festive Sabbath merrymaking with which Germans often followed religious worship, or European customs in the use of alcoholic liquor which ran counter to the promising prohibition movement of the early fifties.

In addition, many champions of American standards were alarmed at the presence of "red" revolutionists who, political exiles from their native lands, found the American democracy, which they had idealized from the distance, a "mongrel or bogus type" and the United States a sham land of liberty. The more aggressive sort gathered in the cities and organized radical clubs. A German of this type, editor of the *St. Louis Anzeiger des Westens,* in 1851 urged his countrymen to lead in forming a new political party, a proposal which stirred up

[1] Visitors to America, on the contrary, were impressed with the easy assimilation of the alien. See Charles Casey, *Two Years on the Farm of Uncle Sam* (London, 1852), 224, and Dicey, *Six Months in the Federal States,* I, 295-296.

[2] Russell, *My Diary,* 4.

considerable excitement. In 1852 German revolutionary congresses, representing radical groups from various Eastern cities, met at Philadelphia and Wheeling. While neither meeting was a conspicuous success, the following year saw the organization of a League of German Freemen with headquarters at Louisville and branches in many cities of the Northwest.[1] In 1853, after the German radical movements had largely disappeared, New York admirers of the martyred Italian revolutionist, Orsini, launched an international revolutionary association dedicated to liberty, equality, fraternity and the solidarity of nations.[2] Such activities were denounced by conservative Americans who resented all movements to revise their political institutions into the likeness of "the bloody and drunken dream of French and German liberty."[3] Some realized that these agitators were few in number and almost entirely of the vintage of 1848; but others placed responsibility upon the entire foreign-born population. The declaration was frequently made that immigrants were objects of hostility, not on account of either their birth or religion but rather because of "their moral and political idiosyncrasies, hostile to our interests."[4]

In the early fifties a new wave of native Americanism swept over the land from the old nativistic strongholds in the Atlantic cities to the prairies of the West and the cotton fields of the Lower South.[5] The movement in its

[1] National Intelligencer, April 27, 1854; M. W. Cluskey, ed., The Political-Text Book, or Encyclopedia (Phila., 1858), 220-222, 301. See also Faust, German Element in the United States, 187-189.

[2] N. Y. Herald, May 27, 1858, Jan. 13, 1859.

[3] H. W. Davis, The Origin, Principles and Purposes of the American Party (n. p., n. d.), 24.

[4] T. R. Whitney, A Defense of American Policy (N. Y., 1856), 238, 239.

[5] For the earlier nativist movement, see C. R. Fish, The Rise of the Common Man (A History   American Life, VI), 115.

sounder aspects represented a protest against problems which confronted many communities as a result of the tidal wave of immigration.

In an era when the foundations were being laid for the later popularity of the American fraternal order, native-born groups were formed to nurse a pride in American birth and to deplore the coming of the alien. Secret organizations essentially social in character like the Supreme Order of the Star-Spangled Banner, the United Sons of America, and the Sons of the Sires were soon drawn into local politics; presently they joined in an all-embracing secret political "American" party.[1] It bespoke a deep-seated resentment against the part that the alien was allowed to play, whether legally or fraudulently, in the practical working of the American political system and held up the high ideal of protecting American institutions from the "insidious wiles of foreigners." Its secrecy, even as to name and existence, its novelty and its mystery as a ritualistic organization attracted converts everywhere. "Know Nothings," the critics of the movement called them because of their ostentatious reticence as to their purposes.

As the old political parties faced disruption in the early months of 1854 because of the crisis precipitated by the Kansas-Nebraska bill, the Know Nothing organization spread like wildfire over the country. Cabalistic notices of meetings fluttered about the streets of a community, a "reform" ticket appeared in the field and, when the votes were counted, a Know Nothing victory was revealed. Here was a convenient opportunity for an exodus from old-party bondage, especially for the Whigs

---

[1] Whitney, *Defense of American Policy*, 280; J. H. Lee, *The Origin and Progress of the American Party in Politics* (Phila., 1855), 195 ff.; anon., *The Sons of the Sires* (Phila., 1855); Cluskey, *Political Text-Book*, 63.

who beheld the crumbling of their old organization.[1] As the movement grew various evidences of dilution appeared. Only Americans should rule America, according to the original slogan, but in many a Western community it was deemed expedient to include in the favored category naturalized Protestant citizens. In certain states the question of softening the proscriptive features of the Know Nothing platform produced wrangling within the brotherhood. In Illinois, where the one faction was dubbed "Sam" and the other "Jonathan," "Sam" denoted the original and orthodox brand of nativism while "Jonathan" represented the antislavery wing which welcomed all foreigners who would disavow temporal allegiance to the pope. The nativism of the state Know Nothing organ, the *Daily Native Citizen* of Chicago, was so tempered that it was able to commend the proposal urged by the German press that Gustave Koerner be given the Republican nomination for governor.[2]

It was clear that the Know Nothing movement had become a political party, animated by considerations of expediency. After a sensational victory in Massachusetts in 1854 the strength of the American party shifted to the South. In that section the movement was influenced by motives vastly different from those of the founders. Originally, anti-Catholicism was a necessary concomitant, indeed, almost a synonym of nativism. In Dixie, however, where there were few Catholics, most Native Americans disavowed any intention of religious proscription. In Louisiana, where the strong Creole element was largely Catholic, persons of that faith occupied

[1] L. D. Scisco, *Political Nativism in New York State* (Columbia Univ., *Studies*, XIII, no. 2), 86-87, 115; L. F. Schmeckebier, *History of the Know Nothing Party in Maryland* (Johns Hopkins Univ., *Studies*, XVII), 12, 14, 27, 66; A. C. Cole, *The Whig Party in the South* (Wash., 1913), 309 ff.

[2] *Daily Native Citizen*, cited in *St. Clair Tribune*, Dec. 22, 1855.

prominent positions in the local order.[1] In fact, an attempt was made by Southern representatives in the national council of June, 1855, to abolish the religious test; because this did not succeed, the regular Louisiana delegation failed to win recognition by the national organization. Several state organizations in the South now officially disclaimed any anti-Catholic bias, while in Louisiana the nativists nominated a mixed ticket of Protestants and Catholics headed by a Catholic Creole for governor. Meanwhile, after repeated assaults upon the feature of secrecy, the national organization abandoned its dark-lantern existence, and away went password, grip and ritual.[2]

Southerners, as has been said, were sensitive to the bearing of immigration upon the slavery question and sectional controversy. Aware that the extensive population, prosperity and political strength of the North were in large part due to accessions from Europe, they saw that immigration annually endowed the North with an adult population larger than the voting strength of certain Southern states. As a result, they opposed homestead legislation which included aliens in its benefits,[3] and proposals for equal political rights for foreigners in the territories,[4] both of which they interpreted as inducements for further recruitment of Northern strength. As foreign immigrants who came to America instinctively prejudiced against slavery began to vote accordingly,

[1] *Mobile Advertiser*, May 5, June 16, 1855; *New Orleans Bulletin*, March 24, June 1, July 4, 25, 1855.

[2] *Mobile Advertiser*, July 8, Sept. 1, 1855; *Nashville Republican Banner*, June 17, 1855; J. P. Hambleton, *A History of the Political Campaign in Virginia, in 1855* (Richmond, 1856), 483.

[3] G. M. Stephenson, *The Political History of the Public Lands from 1840 to 1862* (Boston, 1917), 149-177, 221-239; Cole, *Whig Party in the South*, 313; Sanderson, *Republican Landmarks*, 177, 191, 198.

[4] *Congressional Globe*, 33 Cong., 1 sess., 1300 ff.; app., 775 ff.; *Mobile Advertiser*, May 28, 1854.

many Southerners regardless of party affiliations beheld in nativism a means of self-defense.[1]

On the other hand, conservative Southerners were attracted to the Know Nothing party because of its promise to evade the slavery question. Throughout the South, too, members of the moribund Whig organization perceived in the new party the possibility of an effective opposition to the Democratic administration. Southern Know Nothings, however, soon demanded unequivocal support of the institution of slavery while Northern members became equally insistent on the other side. Thus by 1856 the national organization split on the very rock it had pledged itself to avoid. The collapse of political nativism on a national scale was immediate and thoroughgoing. In the great seaports, however, the survivals continued to drag out a slowly expiring existence.

Despite the noisy efforts of the "hundred-percenters" the place of the foreign immigrant in America was not effectively challenged. To be sure, certain sensitive spirits among the foreign-born elements found themselves doubtful of the genuine character of their welcome; some even felt themselves objects of contempt. One adopted son claimed that the American press assigned to aliens the rôle of blockheads and knaves; before election, commented another, we are good Germans, but after election day we are only "damned Dutchmen." [2] In general, however, the foreigner was left free to adjust himself in his

[1] Many of these foreigners were ready with expressions of sympathy for the Negro and denounced slavery as a "political and moral cancer." About the time when the Kansas-Nebraska bill was before Congress they began to speak out with especial boldness. The *Illinois Staats Zeitung*, Sept. 20, 1854, issued an appeal for a Republican party, a great American "Liberty Party." *Missouri Republican* (St. Louis), Sept. 25, 1854. See also G. W. Julian, *Speeches* (Indianapolis, 1855), 121.

[2] *Atlantische Studien*, I (1853), 129. See also Edward Jörg, *Briefe aus den Vereinigten Staaten* (Leipzig, 1853), 33; Mitchell, *Ten Years Residence in the United States*, 151.

own way to the land of his adoption. The needs of a nation in the throes of civil war were shortly to give him an opportunity to rise to unsuspected heights of devotion and patriotism.

CHAPTER VII

The Growing Pains of Society

FOREIGNERS swelling the ranks of the wage-earners helped to advance the labor movement. If immigrant workers by their numbers tended to depress the wage scale, at the same time they provided some of the most effective labor leaders of the 1850's, men trained in the industrial struggle abroad. For a time the American movement seemed bogged in a discussion of the relief to be gained from free homesteads. This panacea constituted a major topic of discussion in the series of industrial congresses held during the early fifties, gatherings which more often represented the white-collar reformer than the wage-earner. As the years went on, however, the worker increasingly turned his attention to coping with the more exigent problems of his employment, such questions as wages, hours of labor and conditions of work.

While local unions had come and gone in the preceding decades, especially with the awakening of labor in the late twenties and early thirties, the modern type of union originated out of a heightened emphasis upon efficient and nation-wide craft organization.[1] In 1852, after two years' planning, the printers organized the International Typographical Union. Two years later the stonecutters launched a similar body, and in 1859 the Iron Moulders' Union of North America grew out

[1] For the earlier labor movement, see C. R. Fish, *The Rise of the Common Man* (*A History of American Life*, VI), 271-274.

of the energetic efforts of William H. Sylvis, the most forceful figure in the mid-century labor world. After a walkout in his own foundry Sylvis joined the iron molders' organization and, as its recording secretary, directed its expansion over the United States and into Canada until on the eve of the Civil War the Iron Moulders' Union was credited with being "the largest mechanical association in the world."[1] In contrast with Sylvis, certain boss molders, meeting in 1858 at Albany where three strikes raged, issued a circular to employers of labor throughout the country urging the formation of a "league for the purpose of importing workmen from Europe to take the place of employees, who, under the influence of the union agitation, had become so restless and dissatisfied with their employers as to strike against their interests."[2] That employers generally did not respond to this appeal was perhaps due partly to their knowledge that skilled workers from abroad were amenable to organization and had indeed taken a leading part in unionization. The year 1859 also saw the formation of the National Grand Union of Machinists and Blacksmiths, a body incorporated by Congress, its charter being the only one ever so conferred upon a labor organization.

There was little concern in this new movement for the common cause and solidarity of the working class. The increasing particularism of the skilled crafts contrasted sharply with the glowing ideals of the humanitarians who had recently been proclaiming in the abstract the dignity and the rights of labor. The unskilled and the unorganized were left to shift for themselves. Meantime the new unions set about to attain their own

[1] *Cincinnati Daily Enquirer*, Jan. 8, 1861.
[2] T. V. Powderley, *Thirty Years of Labor, 1859-1889* (Columbus, 1890), 411-412; Mary R. Beard, *A Short History of the American Labor Movement* (N. Y., 1920), 71-72.

objectives, including exclusive control over conditions in their own crafts. The workday in the fifties varied from the eight-hour schedule of a very few well-organized local groups to the fourteen or fifteen hours often demanded of mill hands in New England. A new downward pressure, however, was being exerted along political as well as economic lines. In Massachusetts a long struggle took place for a ten-hour day; and in 1852 and 1853 employers in that and other states saved themselves from more drastic reductions by conceding the eleven-hour day.[1] In certain other states the ten-hour system was legally established, if not effectively enforced. The new speeding-up processes, however, notably through the use of labor-saving machinery, guaranteed enterprising manufacturers against any loss of productivity.

The worker's daily wage for eleven or more hours allowed him usually but a frugal existence with no provision whatever for possible misfortune. The great mass of unskilled labor received a dollar or less a day; trained mechanics seldom more than two dollars. Wage returns, of course, tended to reflect the ups and downs of the general economic situation. For a time in 1850 and again in the dull periods following the business recession of 1855 and the Panic of 1857 wage reductions took place. In the decade as a whole the general level of pay showed an inconsiderable increase of eight per cent.[2]

To seasonal fluctuations of work and total shutdowns in hard times were added the complications of technological unemployment. The sewing machine in its

[1] J. R. Commons, ed., A Documentary History of American Industrial Society (Cleveland, 1909-1911), VIII, 151 ff.; S. P. Orth, The Armies of Labor (Allen Johnson, ed., The Chronicles of America Series, New Haven, 1918-1921, XL), 53-54.

[2] Statistical View of the United States (U. S. Seventh Census, 1850), 164; Hunt's Merchants' Mag., XXVI (1852), 120-121; Mass. Bureau of Statistics of Labor, Annual Report for 1872, 522.

various forms was revolutionizing the manufacture of clothing and even of shoes, forcing the little handicraft shops to give way to more productive processes. Labor-saving inventions were likewise playing havoc with the more exclusive status of the machinist and blacksmith. Machines tended by apprentices or unskilled workers turned out more goods than did trained artisans who hence often found themselves without jobs. This was a new and potent argument for unionization.

As the years rolled by, labor acquired a steadily grow-ing sense of its strength. Even liberals like Greeley, hitherto censorious of the strike and hopeful that labor would solve its problems by producers' coöperation and land reform, came to champion its cause. Collective bargaining spread through the leading trades while the strike was resorted to with increasing frequency. Eighteen hundred and fifty-three was a veritable strike year.[1] When in February workers won a significant vic-tory over the Baltimore and Ohio Railroad, the con-tagion promptly infected other parts of the country. In May over thirty trades walked out in New York City. Even waiters in the metropolitan hotels, and later in Pittsburgh, struck for higher wages. While success in these movements varied, they generally tended to im-press upon the thoughtful public the conclusion drawn by the St. Louis *Missouri Republican,* January 10, 1854, after a local epidemic of walkouts, "that labor is too poorly paid in proportion to the high rates de-manded for the marketing of produce."

The industrial disturbances in 1855 and those fol-lowing the Panic of 1857 proved less successful in pre-venting wage reductions. The walkout on the Erie Railroad was the first in the annals of great railway

[1] J. R. Commons and others, *History of Labour in the United States* (N. Y., 1918), I, 607-610.

strikes. A modern note was sounded when certain strikers on the Marietta Railroad were arrested on a charge of obstructing the mails. Successes won in 1859 in strikes in Massachusetts shoe factories led to a general state-wide movement early in 1860.[1] Previously unorganized, the workers revealed an unsuspected solidarity, even some of the women operatives joining. At length ten thousand out of the forty thousand shoemakers of the state quit work. The strikers held meetings and demonstrations; at Lynn on March 7 several thousand men and women marched in procession carrying flags and banners, accompanied by bands and military and fire companies. Sympathy ran high on both sides, and troops were employed to quell riotings. In the course of the excitement the Reverend G. W. Babcock, pastor of the Unitarian Church in South Natick, was dismissed because of his sympathetic aid to the strikers. The disturbance was extending into adjacent states when the men began to return to their jobs. Despite favorable adjustments with certain manufacturers the strike in the main failed. In terms of material gain the American labor movement on the eve of the Civil War had little improved its position since the beginning of the decade. Yet progress had been made in self-confidence and in a knowledge of tactics, and the foundations laid for more promising advances in the days of war-time prosperity.

The uncertain rewards of labor were reflected in a new problem of urban poverty. Unemployment in a period of high prices brought the helpless and unorganized workers and their families to dire straits. The early winter of 1854, marked by financial depression following a bad drought and high food prices, compelled the

[1] N. Y. Tribune, Feb. 28, March 7, 8, 1860; Baltimore Sun, Feb. 21, 29, March 1, 19, 1860; Mass. Bur. of Labor Stat., Ann. Rep. for 1880, 16-19.

"friends of the poor" to devise alleviative measures.[1] Besides the appropriations of local governments, private charity lent a helping hand, benefit performances were staged, fairs and relief meetings held. Meantime the jobless in New York met almost daily in the parks and listened to the remedies proposed by socialist leaders.

The Panic year of 1857 yielded an even greater harvest of unemployment. In the midst of plenty, with barns and storehouses full of foodstuffs held back because of low prices, twenty thousand workers and their dependents in Chicago faced starvation. In New York and other Eastern cities the distress was, if possible, even more acute. The jobless held hunger meetings and organized demonstrations. "We want work," "Work or Bread," they shouted. Mobs threatened to raid the banks, "plundering shops," as they were branded; one procession marched to Wall Street. Rich men, it was proclaimed, must share with the poor, or muskets would be used. Yet, in spite of the alarm of the authorities who finally stationed police and soldiers to guard public buildings, no violent outbreak took place. Remedies, such as municipal works, municipal bakeries and soup houses and the sale of foodstuffs at cost by the city administration, were discussed from many angles, but little effective relief was accomplished. In the main the workers struggled through the winter as best they could. Unemployment continued well into the spring.[2]

Simultaneously with the appearance of poverty and unemployment the newspapers chronicled a startling crime wave in the larger cities. Petty theft and robbery, previously uncommon, seemed to spread with amazing swiftness, while juvenile offenders multiplied. Young

[1] J. B. McMaster, *A History of the People of the United States* (N. Y., 1883-1913), VIII, 287-288.
[2] McMaster, *History of the People of the United States*, VIII, 297-302; Orth, *Armies of Labor*, 61-62.

boys were caught picking pockets, shoplifting, pilfering wharves and warehouses, and even in more serious criminal acts. Crimes against property became especially numerous, though deeds of violence also increased until it seemed that little value was placed upon human life. New York City was alleged to be the most crime-ridden city in the world, with Philadelphia, Baltimore and Cincinnati not far behind.[1]

Gangs of youthful rowdies in the larger cities, sometimes under the guise of political clubs, threatened to destroy the American reputation for respect for law. Actuated by group loyalty and a spirit of bravado they operated in New York under appropriately picturesque names like the "Bowery Boys," "Plug-Uglies," "Highbinders," "Swipers" and "Dead Rabbits." Philadelphia and Baltimore had their own assortments of hoodlums and turbulent bands. The Maryland metropolis with its "Rough Skins," "Rip Raps," "Blood Inks," "Bloody Eights" and "Butt Enders" enjoyed the unenviable reputation of having more gangsters, and more reckless ones, than elsewhere.[2] The "Crawfish Boys" of Cincinnati and their like saw to it that Western cities could not claim exemption from such ills.

These ruffians found the two great holidays, New Year's and the Fourth of July, peculiarly suited to their purposes. Saturating themselves with liquor, they de-

[1] *N. Y. Herald*, March 7, 1853, April 5, 9, May 2, 1858; *Cleveland Leader*, Aug. 17, 1860; Charles Mackay, *Life and Liberty in America* (N. Y., 1859), I, 35-36; D. W. Mitchell, *Ten Years Residence in the United States* (London, 1862), 143-144.

[2] Mackay, *Life and Liberty in America*, I, 164; Theodor Griesinger, *Lebende Bilder aus Amerika* (Stuttgart, 1858), 225-229; *Atlantische Studien*, I (1853), 161-169, 220-245; W. H. Russell, *My Diary North and South* (Boston, 1863), 252; Anthony Trollope, *North America* (N. Y., 1862), 447; N. A. Woods, *The Prince of Wales in Canada and the United States* (London, 1861), 364. See also Herbert Asbury, *The Gangs of New York* (N. Y., 1928), and C. L. Bran, *The Dangerous Classes of New York and Twenty Years among Them* (N. Y., 1872).

manded complete right of way, rejoicing in the opportunities for fisticuffs when someone, preferably a rival gang, disputed their claims. A regular amusement consisted in attendance upon fires which they were often accused of having started; there they lent their aid to the volunteer companies and rewarded themselves by appropriating everything that struck their fancies. On election day, often in the name of native Americanism, they drove voters from the polls or fell upon groups of foreign-born citizens who banded together for self-protection.[1] Before their boisterous demonstrations the crude police forces of the day were often helpless.

Yet all the ills of society could not be laid at the door of the gangster. Swollen by the victims of poverty and unemployment, beggary grew to astounding proportions. On the streets of New York professional mendicants from abroad—Irish and particularly Germans— plied their trade. Some, coöperating in beggars' clubs, waxed prosperous and retired. In September, 1860, a police drive rounded up nearly five hundred beggars, representing the rag-tag and bob-tail of society.[2]

Gambling took on new forms and more serious proportions. As official lotteries were abolished in all states except Georgia, Kentucky, Missouri and Delaware, private undertakings found a fresh popularity and many victims.[3] It seemed almost that the United States had become the paradise of the swindler. In New York gambling lured its addicts into brown sandstone or marble mansions of Broadway and other fashionable

[1] Mitchell, *Ten Years Residence in the United States*, 165-167; L. F. Schmeckebier, *History of the Know Nothing Party in Maryland* (Johns Hopkins Univ., *Studies*, XVII, nos. 4-5), 43-44. Cf. Fish, *Rise of the Common Man*, frontispiece and accompanying note.

[2] Griesinger, *Lebende Bilder*, 329-335; *Cleveland Leader*, Sept. 14, 1860.

[3] A. R. Spofford, "Lotteries in American History," *Am. Hist. Assoc., Ann. Rep. for 1892*, 183-195.

streets. Sometimes the police descended upon a petty gambling den; but the grand palaces of vice with their professional decoys and their choice victims—returned Californians, Southern planters on their annual visit, and the like—seemed immune from the law's interference. A contemporary claimed that larger sums exchanged hands daily in New York than in a week in the open banks of Europe.[1]

Prostitution stalked abroad at night overrunning Broadway and adjoining streets. There flourished saloons and dingy dance halls where amidst a tawdry glitter the ten commandments were forgotten and "pretty waiter girls" drank with the patrons they enticed. In the basement haunts along the Bowery there existed, under police protection, a shameless exhibition of vice. Apparently many property owners rejoiced in the opportunity to secure a double rent for such miserable quarters. In gorgeously furnished mansions on Mercer Street beautiful women followed the same ancient calling with a refinement that attracted little notice, except that of the Broadway dandies whom they undertook to ensnare.[2]

The moralist attributed the situation to the laxity that prevailed as a result of the growing inclination toward extravagance and dissipation. According to certain sober critics the relation between crime and poverty could not be denied, especially since the winter months with their heavy expenses and unemployment found lawlessness more rife in the cities than other seasons of the year. Some amateur criminologists found cold comfort in the fact that much of the criminality could be traced to the foreign-born, especially in the seaport cities.

[1] Griesinger, *Lebende Bilder*, 191; *Cleveland Leader*, Sept. 18, 19, 1860.

[2] Edward Dicey, *Six Months in the Federal States* (London, 1863), I, 17; Griesinger, *Lebende Bilder*, 73-80, 148-156, 322-328. See also W. W. Sanger, *History of Prostitution* (N. Y., 1858).

One experienced judge held that murders, riots and violent assaults were usually the work of Irishmen, that daring burglaries and highway robberies were ordinarily committed by Englishmen, petty thefts and larcenies by Germans, and adroit forgeries, obtaining goods under false pretenses and similar offenses by Americans.[1]

Police connivance and misplaced executive clemency aggravated the problem. At any rate, conditions had passed beyond the control of the primitive official systems of the time. In cities where policemen were at all in evidence they appeared in ordinary attire except for the official badge, lounging at grocery corners, reading a newspaper, or talking politics with some acquaintance. In times of need they were usually conspicuously wanting, some said because in cowardice they removed their badges and so concealed their official status. In November, 1853, an order of the police commissioners required the policemen of New York, despite vigorous complaints upon their part, to wear an official uniform consisting of a blue cap bearing the number of the officer, a blue swallow-tailed coat with brass buttons, and gray pantaloons.[2] Less than three months later the same attire was imposed upon the protesting police force of Philadelphia. In 1855 uniforms were introduced into Boston, this city adopting a system of surveillance upon the European model, which made Westerners and Southerners call Massachusetts a "police-ridden state." In New York, where the metropolitan police were responsible to police commissioners appointed by the governor, the latter failed to coöperate. Early in 1858 the mayor, com-

[1] *N. Y. Herald*, April 1, 1855. See also [Isabella L. Bishop], *The Englishwoman in America* (London, 1856), 383, 442; Georges Fisch, *Nine Months in the United States during the Crisis* (London, 1863), 52; Amelia M. Murray, *Letters from the United States, Cuba and Canada* (N. Y., 1856), II, 152-153.

[2] McMaster, *History of the People of the United States*, VIII, 69-70. See also Fish, *Rise of the Common Man*, plate xv, and note on pp. xiv-xv.

plaining of the vice prevailing under police protection, organized a special squad under his own direction which conducted a series of raids upon certain notorious gambling houses, lottery offices and other nuisances.

In Western towns and cities police facilities were limited and uncertain. Although well-established places seemed to have surprisingly little crime, upon the mining frontier the gambler and the desperado enjoyed full license until the community took the law into its own hands and by its vigilance committee meted out crude but effective justice. In the rural districts of the Mississippi Valley horse stealing continued to arouse the wrath of impromptu committees which often dispensed lynch law to the thief as promptly as they applied a coat of tar and feathers to the violator of the community standard of morals. In 1854 when the rustlers concentrated their operations upon Missouri, the National Anti-Horse Thief Association was organized to supplement the efforts of local societies.

Nor were the Southern states immune to criminal proclivities. Desperadoes, gamblers, thieves and murderers, operating upon the Mississippi River boats and in the towns that lined the banks, became more and more in evidence as one penetrated the South. In New Orleans crime was so prevalent that the local sheriff declared it "a perfect hell upon earth"; [1] arrests were at times proportionately more numerous than in New York. In other Southern towns somewhat similar conditions existed. Among the dominant groups of the South no formally dispensed justice was swift enough to deal with crimes against white women: prevailing sentiment ruled that the offender be shot down like a dog.

[1] Russell, *My Diary*, 244; James Stirling, *Letters from the Slave States* (London, 1857), 142, 165. See also Murray, *Letters from the United States*, II, 152-153, and Adolf Douai, *Land und Leute in der Union* (Berlin, 1864), 68-69.

According to the same standards of chivalry, the Southern gentleman prided himself upon being a high-spirited duelist, quick to resent any reflection upon his honor. In the North the "code" still lingered among certain circles, but when an affair of honor occurred, the greatest secrecy was attempted and newspaper notices regularly omitted the names of the participants. But Southerners—planters, editors, even congressmen—assuaged their offended pride with open approval of the public.[1] In February, 1851, S. W. Inge, an Alabama Democratic member of Congress, and Edward Stanly, Whig member from North Carolina, settled by a duel differences brought out in a debate in the House. Yet a year later Senator Rhett declined, "as a professor of the religion of Christ," to settle an altercation with Senator Clemens of Alabama by recourse to the code of honor.[2]

In the growing bitterness of the slavery controversy Southern hotspurs flung their challenges at Northern antagonists. Thus in 1856 Preston Brooks of South Carolina challenged Anson S. Burlingame, but, when the Canadian side of Niagara Falls was appointed for the place, he declined to risk making the long journey through the North which remembered with bitterness his brutal assault on Sumner. Two years later an affair between Congressman James B. Clay, son of Henry Clay, and William Cullom, clerk of the House, was amicably adjusted after having created considerable alarm among their friends. In 1860 when Roger A. Pryor, a Virginia congressman and editor, challenged

[1] James Parton, *General Butler in New Orleans* (N. Y., 1864), 259; Lorenzo Sabine, *Notes on Duels and Duelling* (Boston, 1855), 441; B. C. Truman, *The Field of Honor* (N. Y., 1884), 78, 269, 306, 322, 388, 389. See also J. L. Wilson, *Code of Honor* (Charleston, 1858). Cf. J. R. Kendrick, *Duelling: A Sermon Preached at the First Baptist Church, Charleston, S. C.* (Charleston, 1853), 12-15; Arthur Wigfall, *Sermon on Duelling* (Charleston, 1856).

[2] *Congressional Globe*, 32 Cong., 1 sess., 654-655.

John F. Potter of Wisconsin, the latter in a sardonic vein chose bowie knives, whereupon Pryor in disgust refused to fight. The intervention of the authorities who arrested Potter and placed him under bonds to keep the peace, together with Pryor's insistence upon traditional weapons, caused nation-wide excitement, while Republican newspapers enjoyed the opportunity of twitting Pryor with cowardice for refusing.

The extent of crime conditions, particularly in the cities, suggested a connection with the "demon drink." Under the prevailing American custom of "treating," intemperance had long been a feature of community life. There seemed to be a certain freemasonry in tippling— as William H. Herndon put it, "a peculiar tie that binds men together who have drunk bouts together." [1] Liquor establishments of all sorts abounded: saloons with mahogany cases and cut glass, grog shops, "bungholedoggeries," wine shops, summer gardens and the rest, while the well-stocked barroom was a prominent adjunct to every hotel. New York City possessed from seven to fifteen thousand dispensaries; [2] like Chicago and many smaller communities, it had at least one for every hundred inhabitants.

Aroused by the evils of drink and the ostentation of the liquor traffic, a great temperance wave swept across the nation. [3] The apostles of moral suasion still held the field in 1850. They spoke on the open squares of New York on Sunday, often to audiences of sailors and street walkers, and from this center they reached out into the provinces. In 1850 John B. Gough was adding pledge

---

[1] Carl Sandburg, *Abraham Lincoln: The Prairie Years* (N. Y., 1926), II, 116.

[2] Robert Everest, *Journey through the United States and Part of Canada* (London, 1855), 150; W. E. Baxter, *America and the Americans* (London, 1855), 118-121.

[3] See Fish, *Rise of the Common Man*, 260-268, for earlier phases of the movement.

signers in Buffalo and Detroit to the thousands already on his list,[1] while Father Mathew, the Irish apostle of temperance, was enrolling teetotalers with three million signatures as his goal. Pledge-takers belonged to the Sons of Temperance, a secret ritualistic organization, which became a vast "Cold Water Army," their processions in elaborate regalia and their public exercises a feature of nearly all holiday celebrations. From the East the movement spread to the Mississippi Valley and even into the South, "the land of Dixie and whiskey." [2] In the North Carolina legislature applications for charters of the Sons of Temperance were granted in spite of opponents who "quoted from the Bible, Shakespeare, and Hudibras." [3]

The more aggressive temperance advocates, desiring a complete purging of society, urged political action to strike at the root of the evil. The general assembly of Maine led off in 1851 with a state-wide prohibitory enactment known as the Maine liquor law, the first great landmark in this new phase of the crusade.[4] Encouraged by this victory the temperance forces throughout the country began a vigorous agitation to induce other states to take like action. Its most aggressive expression took the form of Maine-law alliances with township and county divisions and active state organizations. Practical men, who at first frowned on the proposal as the propaganda of traveling tract peddlers and of reformers identified with all the incipient "isms" of the day, came increasingly to look upon it as a force that might work incalculable good.

Vermont, Rhode Island and Massachusetts promptly

[1] J. B. Gough, *Autobiography and Personal Recollections* (Springfield, 1870), 261, 514.

[2] William H. Russell to J. C. B. Davis, June 22, 1861, *Historical Outlook*, XVI (1925), 253.

[3] *North State Whig*, Dec. 11, 1850, Feb. 12, 1851.

[4] Ernest Gordon, *The Maine Law* (N. Y., 1919); J. A. Krout, *The Origins of Prohibition* (N. Y., 1925), 283-295.

followed in the footsteps of Maine. Soon the fight was raging in every state.[1] By 1855 every Northern state legislature except New Jersey had approved some form of prohibition. One New York governor vetoed the prohibitory proposal only to be succeeded by another who accepted it; but the law was shortly repudiated by the courts. In Pennsylvania and Illinois the will of the legislature was defeated by popular referenda, the German strongholds in each case holding the balance of power. Pennsylvania, however, later adopted a milder law. Delaware was the only state south of Mason and Dixon's line which succumbed to the Maine-law forces, although Mississippi took a long step in that direction. Certain states like Iowa, Michigan, Indiana and Massachusetts, after having their legislation annulled by the courts because of the unconstitutionality of certain more or less essential provisions, framed new laws. Where laws were upheld there was still the problem of enforcement. In most communities success in this was only temporary.

The contribution of prohibition to the sobriety of a community was insisted upon by temperance champions, but denied with equal vehemence by their critics. More or less impartial travelers testified that liquor continued to be available at hotels and at illicit dispensaries, even in Maine. At some stores, when "striped pig" was called for, wine and spirits were produced; at others they passed under the name of "dusky Ben" or "sarsaparilla."[2] Certain hostelries lived up to their reputation of "temperance hotels," but "temperance boats" plying between New York and Boston did not lack means of quenching the thirst of the persistent. It seemed to many that the chief effect of prohibition was "to deteriorate the quality of the liquor drunk under it," and to double

[1] McMaster, *History of the People of the United States*, VIII, 127-132.
[2] [Bishop], *Englishwoman in America*, 91.

its cost, making its possession the prerogative of the well-to-do.[1] On the other hand, President Walker of Harvard in 1859 incurred the criticism of Wendell Phillips for countenancing the use of wine at a dinner honoring an important guest, while Harriet Beecher Stowe, on the eve of a voyage to Europe, accepted an invitation to dine with the Atlantic Club on the specific condition that no wine be served.[2]

Probably one of the greatest obstacles to real success was the increasing popularity of lager beer. Scarcely known in America before 1850, this mildly alcoholic beverage attained in ten years a wide popularity.[3] Many an American of older stock joined the German immigrant in favoring this thirst-quenching drink. In 1858 suits involving the question of its intoxicating character came before the courts of New York and Massachusetts. When witnesses in the New York case testified to their ability to drink gallons without inebriating effects, the jury acquitted the defendants of illegally selling intoxicants on Sunday, "believing that lager beer, which does not contain more than 3¾ % alcohol, does not come within the provisions of the statute in relation to intoxicating drinks." [4] The Massachusetts supreme court, however, held beer to be intoxicating in the sense of the law.

While the temperance crusaders still held the field, certain Democratic journals and Democratic politicians

[1] N. Y. Herald, Feb. 11, 1858. See also Mackay, Life and Liberty in America, I, 59, 60-61, 217; Murray, Letters from the United States, II, 240, 289; Trollope, North America, 34, 233; J. R. Beste, The Wabash (London, 1855), I, 268; Dicey, Six Months in the Federal States, II, 190; T. L. Nichols, Forty Years of American Life (London, 1864), II, 88.

[2] Sallie Holley, A Life for Liberty (J. W. Chadwick, ed., N. Y., 1899), 172.

[3] Griesinger, Lebende Bilder, 86.

[4] N. Y. Herald, Feb. 5, 1858; National Intelligencer (Wash.), Feb. 8, March 26, 1858. See also later cases, N. Y. Herald, Jan. 1, 1859; N. Y. Tribune, June 2, 1860.

averse to joining in the hue and cry beheld in dismay the nicknaming of their group as the "whisky party." Other Democrats were made restless because of the prominence of the liquor power in the party councils. Their rebellious spirit helped to feed the anti-Nebraska revolt of 1854; temperance agitation found for a time an ally in the antislavery propaganda. Yet this ally was largely to absorb the crusading spirit of the North. By 1856 the temperance wave was rapidly subsiding; efforts to revive it were unavailing. If it was not, like political nativism, a red herring drawn across the trail of the slavery question, it was, for a time, similarly relegated to the scrap heap with other "isms" that had had their day.

Of greater moment was the movement by which American women went forth in quest of fresh laurels. The beauty, intelligence and grace of the genteel female had become a byword among travelers. She was *svelte*— often too slender—diminutive in stature, with a notable pallor except when it was concealed by "false bloom," which feminine wiles well knew how to employ. These delicate creatures, dressed in the height of fashion often with false brows and false hair, seemed like "playthings—dolls treated as if they were unfit or unwilling to help themselves." [1] Even among plain sturdy people the old frontier spirit of equality of the sexes had yielded to a peculiar consideration for the rights of women—a democratic American brand of chivalry that was often tyrannical in its demands upon the mere male and that, in its degeneracy, seemed to breed a selfish and pert female vulgarity.

American women probably spent two or three times as much upon dress as their sisters in England and the

---

[1] Murray, *Letters from the United States*, I, 264-265. See also Walt Whitman, *I Sit and Look Out* (Emory Holloway and Vernolian Schwarz, eds., N. Y., 1932), 111 ff.

Old World. No one seemed shabbily clad; indeed, the West was wholly innocent of class distinctions in clothing. In fashionable circles in the cities there was reflected a steady gain in the influence of French styles, as set forth in *Le Follet* and profusely copied in *Godey's Lady's Book* and similar journals. Parisian gowns and bonnets together with copies of American fabrication were conspicuously displayed by strollers on Broadway and Fifth Avenue. In the very early fifties ladies' dresses steadily increased in length until they became long dangling "street-sweepers." The ridiculousness and expense of the inconvenient, untidy garments awakened a minority protest among the women. Mrs. Amelia Bloomer, editor of the *Lily,* a reform paper advocating temperance and woman's rights, donned a new costume, the chief features of which were an overskirt reaching somewhat below the knees and a pair of moderately full "trousers" gathered in at the ankle with an elastic band or fastened into the boot top.[1] This style was more an adaptation of the pantalette costume worn for years by young girls than an imitation of male attire. It promised, however, emancipation from a garb which did not permit vigorous physical activity and which had caused the men, thus denied the society of women in many of their labors and pastimes, to regard the sex as inferior. There may have been those, too, who were sufficiently feminine to relish the new opportunity of making the best of such charms as a pretty foot and ankle.

Woman's-rights advocates led the way in adopting bloomers. Elizabeth Cady Stanton, daughter of an austere and distinguished judge, wife of a New York senator and mother of four fine boys, shocked all three generations when she performed the surgical operation upon her costume. Her young son wrote from boarding school

[1] "Summer Fashions," *Harper's Mo.,* III (1851), 288.

that he did not want his mother to visit him "in a short dress," while at home the street urchins screamed in chorus: [1]

> Heigh! ho! the carrion crow,
> Mrs. Stanton's all the go;
> Twenty tailors take the stitches.
> Mrs. Stanton wears the breeches.

In the spring of 1851 the new costume took on a sudden popularity. The fashionable set in the cities evinced an interest, qualified only by the fact "that it did not originate in Paris."[2] Newspaper editors commented upon the favorable contrast "with the *pavement-sweeping* robes that were . . . gathering up the dust and mud at every step." [3] Upon the Fourth of July, especially at certain resorts, bloomers, it was said, were out "in full bloom." One editor noticed a number whose garb "did not extend below their 'courtesy benders.' Well, whose business is it?" he asked.[4] Bloomer parties were held to keep up the courage of the innovators, who braved the gaze of the curious and the sharp tongues of the town gossips rather better than they faced the obvious discomfiture of fastidious husbands and relatives. But even the most courageous grew weary of suffering for their convictions. By the summer of 1853 the new garb was being abandoned by all but an occasional zealot in the woman's-rights movement who religiously attended its conventions in full regalia, and by a few who, safe from the public eye, enjoyed the comfort and convenience which the new dress afforded for house work.[5]

[1] Elizabeth C. Stanton, *Elizabeth Cady Stanton as Revealed in Her Letters, Diary and Reminiscences* (Theodore Stanton and Harriot S. Blatch, eds., N. Y., 1922), II, 27-31.

[2] *Ohio Statesman* (Columbus), July 2, 1851.

[3] *Ohio Statesman*, July 5, 1851.

[4] A. C. Cole, "Illinois Women of the Middle Period," Ill. State Hist. Soc., *Trans. for 1920*, 91.

[5] In 1858 there was a sudden revival of the bloomer which was advo-

It has been customary to speak of the bloomer craze of the early fifties and to ignore the hoop-skirt mania that succeeded it. The hoop skirt was introduced with the credentials of the beautiful Empress Eugénie who set the style for the French court in 1853. Originally fashioned in a stiff fabric known as crinoline and set off by billowing petticoats, the garment aimed at a barrel-like effect, which it was found could better be achieved by the use of cane or whalebone reënforcements. Soon other refinements were attempted like gutta-percha cord and wire framework; watch-spring steel hoops were on the market at five cents a hoop. The newspapers chronicled embarrassing experiences of hoop-skirt wearers upon crowded sidewalks, in trains and street cars, and even in church pews. In spite of caricature, ridicule and male disgust the hoop-skirt style, with variations like the floating-bell and the watch-bell skirts, persisted through the Civil War.[1]

The extravagance of feminine toilette and attire evoked considerable comment. Gowns at a hundred dollars and more were frequent purchases; expensive shawls, lace scarfs and other wraps were a common sight; and modish bonnets for street and house wear, generously trimmed with "love-ribbon" and other frills, graced matrons and misses. Low-necked gowns aroused the indignation of moralists. "Women who wear such dresses are seducers," declared "Justitia" in the Cincinnati En-

cated as a costume in keeping with physiological laws that would aid the wearer "in attaining that position side by side with man, . . . his co-worker in life and its duties, . . . and give a more correct idea of the natural proportions of the human form." *Aurora* (Ill.) *Beacon*, April 8, 1858. At the third annual convention of the National Dress Reform Association at Cortlandville, New York, in July one hundred and fifty women delegates appeared in various types of bloomer costume. *Harper's Wkly.*, II, 470 (July 24, 1858).

[1] No critics accomplished the results of Addison of the *Spectator* when he belabored the hoops of Queen Anne's day. See *Ohio State Journal* (Columbus), May 2, 1856.

quirer, June 11, 1859; ten or fifteen years ago such dresses would not have been tolerated except in the theater, added this critic. Some journals were ungallant enough to attribute the Panic of 1857 largely to the extravagance in personal adornment of the fair sex.[1]

Male attire, by contrast, revealed itself essentially stable. The well-to-do and middle classes continued to be partial to loose-fitting black frock coats, often seedy in appearance, but the uncomfortable stove-pipe hat began to pass out in the sixties. Meantime colored satin, velvet, or brocaded vests had a period of popularity. Trousers were usually narrow except when some dapper specimen of Young America returned from Paris to "startle the town" by the looseness of his bags. The chief field of experimentation for males was in beards and mustaches. Among the younger generation goatees and imperials competed for popularity with the full beard, which seems to have received considerable support from the influx of German immigrants and from the tonsorial deficiencies of the mining frontier. Creams and unguents were advertised with assurances of a crop of whiskers and of mustaches in six weeks. In due time the mustache cup was invented "to meet the exigencies of the unshaven lip."[2] When, following his election, Abraham Lincoln decided to introduce a beard into the White House, the issue of beards or no beards seemed to be settled for many who had hesitated. Lincoln's results were so conspicuous that a *Vanity Fair* caricature showed a druggist proudly commending his jars of "Lincoln Whiskeropherous": "Try one of them pots, and in three weeks

---

[1] Mackay, *Life and Liberty in America*, I, 21. See also Beste, *The Wabash*, II, 214-215; Dicey, *Six Months in the Federal States*, I, 305; Trollope, *North America*, 191-193; Russell, *My Diary*, 12; [Bishop], *Englishwoman in America*, 341, 361; Elizabeth McClellan, *Historic Dress in America, 1800-1870* (Phila., 1910), 253.

[2] *N. Y. World*, Oct. 2, 1863.

you'll be as 'arry and 'ansom as 'im." [1] In due time the uncertain toilets of army life were to add an additional argument for beards; never before or since have whiskers had such a vogue in America.

Into the American home many a comfort and luxury was being introduced. Well-to-do abodes ordinarily possessed hot and cold running water, bathrooms, cookstoves and perhaps even hot-air furnaces. Moreover, the drudgery of housework was often turned over to servant girls who worked at a wage of a dollar or two a week. Previously domestic employment had existed upon an essentially democratic basis, the menial status belied by the use of the term "help" instead of "servant." Now, with a mass of Irish and German immigrants available, the native-born abandoned the field and the term "servant," or "hired girl," began to come into general use. The ubiquitous servant girl from Erin often tried the patience of her mistress; Mrs. Lincoln, like many another housekeeper, found her trials with the "wild Irish" enough to breed a strong sympathy for political nativism. [2] As earlier, however, travelers commented upon the appalling tendency of domestic establishments to yield to the superior advantages of boarding houses and hotels, where wives avoided the servant problem and, released from housekeeping duties, were free for more extensive social activities. [3]

The family, indeed, seemed to many in process of disintegration. Early marriages were still the rule, brides

[1] *Vanity Fair*, III, 126 (March 16, 1861). See reproduction in Sandburg, *Abraham Lincoln*, II, 421, and W. E. Barton, *The Life of Abraham Lincoln* (Indianapolis, 1925), I, 515-517.

[2] Sandburg, *Abraham Lincoln*, II, 274.

[3] Mitchell, *Ten Years Residence in the United States*, 196. See also Mackay, *Life and Liberty in America*, 42-43; Murray, *Letters from the United States*, I, 248; Baxter, *America and the Americans*, 90-91; Charles Casey, *Two Years on the Farm of Uncle Sam* (London, 1852), 38, 227; H. P. Batcheler, *Jonathan at Home* (London, 1864), 46; Francis and Theresa Pulszky, *White, Red, Black* (London, 1853), 75-76.

of fourteen being far from uncommon. The editor of the *New York Herald* deplored runaway matches, especially of young girls who "are as worldly minded as men of thirty." [1] Matrimonial agencies like the Caroline Fry Marriage Association and the Bloomer Marriage Association undertook to arrange suitable matches for those unable to do it themselves. Marriages easily and lightly entered upon frequently ended in failure. Some sought relief in a second marriage, often without a dissolution of previous ties, for with easy escape to the Western frontier bigamists were not easily punished. The laws of California made bigamy a mere misdemeanor, and the offender could not be prosecuted unless indicted within one year of the second marriage. A foreign-born observer held that Mormonism was the natural outgrowth of American conditions. However this may have been, over three thousand five hundred men were openly practising polygamy in Utah in 1859, although Congress was becoming increasingly disposed to enact legislation against the custom. [2]

Many of those disposed to test the success of a marriage by the kind of offspring it produced were depressed by the behavior of the younger generation. Emerson quoted a contemporary as saying it was a misfortune to have been born in an age when children were nothing and to have spent his mature life in an age when children were everything. [3] Youngsters of all ages seemed irrepressible. Foreigners were unanimous that modesty and shyness were unheard-of, that children were selfish and willful, spoiled beyond all discipline. A few admired their sturdy independence, the remarkable development

---

[1] *N. Y. Herald*, April 14, 1858.

[2] *Dollar Newspaper* (Phila.), May 25, 1859; *Toledo Blade*, April 10, 1860.

[3] A. W. Calhoun, *A Social History of the American Family* (Cleveland, 1917-1919), II, 67.

of self-reliance and self-management. American moralists lamented the decay of parental discipline and the alarming development of juvenile depravity. "What have the parents or the community to hope from such children?" they asked in despair.[1] Others undertook to reassure them, to set such gloomy observations in a proper perspective, pointing out that under the milder parental régime most of those no longer subjected to the old grim discipline were working out their own salvation.

In any event, family limitation seemed a desideratum to many parents if one may judge from the advertisements, in daily papers and even in the religious press, "of professed abortionists; of pills which 'are sure to procure abortion,' from which 'miscarriage will certainly ensue,' & etc."[2] But a movement of protest against such practices arose, which was supported by Walt Whitman who in his editorial condemnation included those "infernal inventions," "warranted 'to regulate or limit offspring, without injuring the constitution,'" which were said to be patronized by "ladies of fashion and social position." It may be noted that foreigners felt scandalized at the American laxity in regard to the transmission of birth-control information.

The increasing frequency of divorce was widely deplored as a sign of declining morality. Courts and legislatures seemed to be besieged by applicants for matrimonial relief. Divorce laws varied from complete prohibition in certain Southern states to the easy processes of nearly every Western state and territory. Indiana had a statute which a local judge declared was virtually all

[1] Presbyterian Mag., cited in Calhoun, Social History of the American Family, II, 69; Baltimore Sun, Jan., 4, 1858.

[2] Whitman, I Sit and Look Out, 115. See also Griesinger, Lebende Bilder, 265-266, which cites specific contraceptives and abortive medicines; G. W. Sala, My Diary in America in the Midst of War (London, 1865), II, 161; Round Table, I, 178, 242 (March 5, April 2, 1864). See also Fish, Rise of the Common Man, 153-154.

that the advocates of free love could ask. Introduced by the idealist Robert Dale Owen, this law had made that state free soil for unhappy wives and husbands, while outsiders went there to dissolve undesirable unions.[1] In Nebraska a divorce could be had from the legislature for the asking. The probate courts of Utah had full and unlimited power to issue divorces.[2] In New York, on the other hand, divorces were granted only upon proof of adultery. This seemed to many unduly drastic; in 1858 and successive years bills were introduced into the legislature to make willful desertion, separation for a term of years, or cruel or inhuman treatment by a husband endangering life, cause for divorce. When these efforts failed, divorce lawyers advertised in the daily papers their services in obtaining without publicity or change of residence legal divorces from some other state.

The most active champions of "marriage reform" in New York were to be found in the ranks of the feminists. To Elizabeth Cady Stanton the "whole question of woman's rights" seemed to turn "on the pivot of the marriage relation."[3] Her active ally in this cause was Lucy Stone who, in wedding Dr. Henry B. Blackwell in 1855, required the omission of the word "obey" from the ceremony and set an example of retaining the maiden name.[4] Mrs. Stanton introduced a series of resolutions for more liberal divorce at the national woman's-rights convention of 1860, triumphing over the eloquent Wendell Phillips who pronounced her resolutions irrelevant to the feminist cause. Mrs. Stanton, moreover, addressed the New York legislature in favor of a liberal divorce

[1] See Allan Nevins, *The Emergence of Modern America* (*A History of American Life*, VIII), 216, plate ix and note on p. xiii.

[2] A. D. Richardson, *Beyond the Mississippi* (N. Y., 1867), 147-148; *Baltimore Sun*, Jan. 28, 1860.

[3] Stanton, *Elizabeth Cady Stanton*, II, 49.

[4] Alice Stone Blackwell, *Lucy Stone* (Boston, 1930), chap. xi.

bill, which Lucretia Mott and others supported before the committee. Most of the advocates, however, were silenced by a broadside of editorials in the *New York Tribune* in which Greeley opposed liberalization.

Women of the Middle West, who had enjoyed virtual sex equality in the task of conquering the frontier, refused to be demoralized by the leisure which came to them with increasing relief from domestic routine. They merely found larger opportunity for engaging in organizations with varying social objectives. Besides becoming more active in religious movements they formed sewing societies and reading circles. In certain regions like Indiana and Michigan they were the driving force in library associations which they often made exclusively "ladies'" organizations. Many took a leading part in the anti-slavery crusade. At times of stress the sewing society was enlarged into a relief organization, as when the North hastened to the rescue of bleeding and starving Kansas.

In a similar manner women rushed into the temperance movement. To terminate the liquor traffic seemed to them the easiest way of rescuing their sisters from the abuses of drunken husbands. Pleading the cause of temperance gave many women their first experience along literary and oratorical lines. But there was emotion as well as intelligence in their course. Enraged female victims of the saloon oftentimes raised their standard and led in bold assaults upon the offending groggeries. Armed with hatchets, rolling pins, broomsticks, kitchen knives and fire shovels, they routed the enemy, leaving empty kegs and broken glasses to litter the streets. Enterprising journalists retailed accounts of such Amazon raids to an interested public; they doubtless attracted more attention than the efforts of the more decorous temperance advocates.

Above everything else, the times demanded fuller educational opportunities for the sex. Many chafed at a situation that left leisure-class women content to while away their time in the everlasting rocking chair, ready to lay aside fan, light novel, or "fancy work," only to indulge in trifling gossip.[1] In spite of the increasing excellence of the contemporary female seminary or college they insisted that the same opportunities be made available for young women as were found in colleges and universities for men. In response to this demand, but not without extensive criticism and ridicule, Elmira Female College was launched in 1855, the first woman's institution to grant academic degrees. In 1860 at the request of an invalid niece, a school teacher, Matthew Vassar prepared to establish the institution which, delayed by the Civil War, now bears his name.[2]

Meantime the demand grew for the admission of women to regular colleges and universities. Oberlin no longer occupied a unique place as a coeducational institution, although it continued to bear the reputation, based upon its lack of race or sex discrimination, of being "a sort of fanatical way-station between the district school and Harvard University, where men, women, and 'colored people' are all taught together."[3] Gradually the doors of Mid-Western institutions began to open. Antioch College was founded in 1852 with Horace Mann, an aggressive exponent of coeducation, as its first president. Though other colleges followed Antioch's lead, including the State University of Iowa in 1860, the University of Michigan and the legislature of that state

[1] Calhoun, *Social History of the American Family*, II, 73, 83, 89.
[2] J. M. Taylor, *Before Vassar Opened* (Boston, 1914). See also Nevins, *Emergence of Modern America*, 280-281.
[3] Caroline H. Dall, *The College, the Market, and the Court* (Boston, 1867), 381.

coldly rejected pleas for the admission of women.[1] Many felt that such action was entirely sound. On the other hand, Thomas Wentworth Higginson declared in the *Atlantic Monthly* in 1859 that the real issue was, "Ought women to learn the alphabet?"; that "woman must be a subject or an equal: there is no middle ground."[2] It was to be long, however, before this simple logic would be accepted by the many who felt that education would unfit women for domestic duties and social graces.[3] Meantime, in 1852 an American Women's Educational Association was organized.[4]

The champions of the new day became more and more insistent upon the right of women to participate in any honorable and remunerative field of employment. In 1850 women teachers outnumbered their male associates in Massachusetts more than two to one, but the situation there was exceptional. By 1855, however, their pressure upon the teaching profession was being felt generally.[5] In spite of the frequent citation of the traditional doctrine, "It is a shame for woman to speak in the church," she began also to appear in the pulpit. Antoinette L. Brown, an Oberlin graduate of 1847, after having first been refused a license to preach, was ordained pastor of a church in South Butler, New York, where she began a long and active career. Among those who followed her example were Olympia Brown and Lydia A. Jenkins, active Universalist preachers, Phoebe

---

[1] Annie N. Meyer, ed., *Woman's Work in America* (N. Y., 1891), chaps. ii-iv.

[2] T. W. Higginson, *Atlantic Essays* (Boston, 1871), 96.

[3] Holley, *A Life for Liberty*, 120.

[4] See constitution in its *Second Annual Report* (1854), 3-4.

[5] Anon., "Progress of Womanhood," *Harper's Mo.*, XVI (1858), 492-494; H. T. Tuckerman, *America and Her Commentators* (N. Y., 1864), 333, citing Philip Schaff, *Sketch of the Political, Social and Religious Character of the United States of America* (N. Y., 1855).

Hanaford and others. An occasional preacher's wife, like Caroline H. Dall, supplied for her husband during periods of illness or absence.

Dr. Elizabeth Blackwell and other women pioneers in medicine who by sheer persistence had secured their own professional training made numerous converts among the younger generation. The regular medical colleges, however, were not as yet open to women students. In an address at the opening of the new Harvard Medical Building, Oliver Wendell Holmes declared: "If here and there an intrepid woman insists on taking by storm the fortress of medical education, I would have the gate flung open to her, as if it were that of the citadel of Orleans and she Joan of Arc returning from the field of victory." [1] Not all, however, shared his generous impulse. Accordingly, separate medical colleges for women were established at Boston in 1848 and Philadelphia in 1850. Yet as late as 1859 the Pennsylvania Medical Society went on record recommending "the members of the regular profession to withhold from the faculties and graduates of Female Medical Colleges all countenance and support." [2]

Women writers and editors like Jane Grey Swisshelm, Paulina Wright Davis, Anna E. McDowell, Ellen Wentworth, Minnie Myrtle and Fannie Fern urged with their pens a broader field of woman's rights. Bolder spirits like Elizabeth Cady Stanton, Susan B. Anthony and Lucy Stone mounted the lecture platform to plead their many causes. Male prejudice was encountered at every turn; grave professors sometimes refused to address lyceums which scheduled an occasional female lecturer.

[1] J. T. Morse, jr., *Life and Letters of Oliver Wendell Holmes* (Boston, 1897), I, 186.

[2] Dall, *College, Market, and Court*, 185 n. See also articles by F. C. Waite in *New England Journ. of Medicine*, CCV (1931), 1053-1055, 1195-1198.

Most "females" themselves were indifferent or antagonistic. Women delegates, refused the right to speak at a New York state temperance convention, arranged for a women's state temperance convention at Rochester on April 20, 1852. On the other hand, notable representatives of the male sex, generally liberals and radicals like Horace Mann, Wendell Phillips and T. W. Higginson, joined in presenting the plea for woman's rights before the public.

No more outspoken critic of feminism could be found than James Gordon Bennett of the *New York Herald*. He characterized Lucy Stone "and all like her . . . fit inmates for some well conducted private lunatic asylum" and advised her husband to put her there, "where medicine and soothing treatment will extract from her brain that maggot of desire to exhibit herself at the polls." [1] "It is the settled and fixed sentiment of this and all civilized countries," he insisted, "that the rights of women, like her duties, are bounded by her household, that the votes she has to cast must be polled at her own tea table, that her politics must be the principles of domestic economy and that her authority must be over her own children and her servants." [2] This was a widely prevailing masculine point of view.

The woman's-rights agitation excited fresh determination to secure for married women the separate control of their property.[3] By 1860 this movement had succeeded in a number of states, sometimes to the point of granting them control over their own earnings. At the same time feminist leaders kept alive the question of widening the suffrage franchise and of rendering women eligible for office holding. Strenuous but unsuccessful

[1] *N. Y. Herald*, Feb. 12, 1858.
[2] *N. Y. Herald*, April 4, 1858. See also anon., "Woman and the 'Woman's Movement,'" *Putnam's Mo.*, I (1853), 279-288.
[3] For earlier efforts to this end, see Fish, *Rise of the Common Man*, 271.

efforts were made in certain Eastern states, notably Massachusetts and Connecticut, and the question was considered somewhat in Ohio, Wisconsin and Kansas. The one tangible gain of the decade was the granting by Kentucky of the right to vote for school trustees to any widow having a child of from six to sixteen years. The editor of the Montgomery *Alabama Journal*, rejoicing that such heresies were generally confined to the North, published a facetious account of a women's convention at Boston in which he characterized the principal speakers as disappointed old maids who had embraced the excitement of politics because they had no husbands to embrace; two weeks later, however, he found it necessary to print a petition addressed to the Alabama legislature to give women the franchise and the privilege of holding office.[1]

The "isms" that ravaged the country during the fifties evidenced the growing pains of an adolescent nation. Largely confined to the North, their local critics, like Walt Whitman, were usually willing to concede that they were "significant of a grand upheaval of ideas and reconstruction of many things on new bases." [2] Proud Southerners, on the other hand, rejoiced that the land of chivalry had largely escaped the taint of the fads that were sweeping Yankeedom. In less complacent mood they sounded the tocsin of alarm against vagaries of Yankee fanaticism that found their most portentous expression in a militant abolitionism.

[1] *Alabama Journal* (Montgomery), Jan. 2, 16, 1851.
[2] Whitman, *I Sit and Look Out*, 46.

CHAPTER VIII

HEALTH AND HAPPINESS

THE health of the American people in the middle of the nineteenth century reflected the survival of pioneer optimism and neglect. Although the traditional ague and fever prevailed only on the frontier and in rural backwaters, careless and uncleanly conditions in the more thickly settled towns and cities bred diseases which quickly assumed an epidemic character. Hardly any town possessed an adequate drainage system. In bad weather the unpaved streets approached the condition of a quagmire with dangerous sink holes which only the boatman's phrase, "no bottom," fitly described. Absence of civic pride made the gutters the dumping ground for the community rubbish, while back yards and alleys reeked with filth and offal, the environs of public buildings and stores being especially offensive. If the few pavements of the larger cities somewhat simplified the problem of drainage, they did not solve the problem of cleanliness since they were often hidden from sight by accumulations of filth. New York City had perennial difficulty in securing street-cleaning contractors with a real sense of obligation to the community.

Then, too, nearly every city—from the national capital to some budding Western porkopolis—had its hog nuisance or some equivalent.[1] The streets, squares and parks amounted to public pens, hog holes offending the eye and nose at every turn. Local sentiment, as in Spring-

[1] A. C. Cole, *The Era of the Civil War* (C. W. Alvord, ed., *The Centennial History of Illinois*, Springfield, 1918-1920, III), 4.

field, Illinois, often sharply divided over the question of discontinuing this inexpensive system of scavenging. While the hog and antihog forces in city councils debated the issue his swineship contentedly pulled himself out of his gutter wallow, threatening to upset pedestrians as he carefully chose a freshly painted fence to rub off the unctuous matter with which he was plastered. In the fall of 1853 porkers were more numerous on the streets of Springfield than in the pens at the state fairgrounds. The near-by town of Urbana had a record of more hogs than people, and they had at least equal rights with citizens upon the streets.

Hydrophobia was the natural consequence of the packs of dogs that roamed the streets. Ordinances against allowing them to run at large were seldom enforced, for the city dweller was not willing to dispense with the former guardian of the isolated farmhouse and assistant of the shepherd. At times of mad-dog panics men were often employed to kill off the surplus animals at twenty-five cents a head. Troops of rats lived under the wooden sidewalks and were accepted as an inevitable part of the population of public buildings until the horror of an episode like the devouring of a new-born babe in Bellevue Hospital, New York City, aroused the public to action.[1]

Community waterworks increased but slowly, there being only eighty private water systems and sixty-eight public ones when the war began. Yet this number represented a marked gain over the total of eighty-three in existence in 1850.[2] In 1862 the new hundred-acre Croton reservoir, which had been four years building at a cost of two million dollars, assured the nation's me-

---

[1] N. Y. Tribune, April 25, 27, 28, 1860. Cf. issue of Jan. 9, 1860.
[2] E. D. Fite, Social and Industrial Conditions in the North during the Civil War (N. Y., 1910), 217.

tropolis an ampler supply though, unhappily, the tenement districts were often without access to it. Important places like Milwaukee, Providence and Portland had no public provision whatsoever. On the other hand, a public system did not insure pure water. Thus Chicago's water, drawn from Lake Michigan, was often contaminated by filth which the rain washed from manure heaps upon the lake shore; indeed, the zealous apostle of cleanliness was often served with "chowder in his bathtub." Besides, much of the milk sold in Chicago came from cows "fed on whiskey slops with their bodies covered with sores and tails all eat off," a circumstance which enabled an editorial critic to explain "Why so many children die in Chicago." [1] New York's milk supply was also largely a by-product of the local distilleries and the milk dealers were charged with the serious offense of murdering annually eight thousand children. [2]

While the larger cities possessed handsome residential districts in which the streets were paved and kept clean and the sewage was properly cared for, there were also crowded foreign quarters, veritable hives of humanity lacking ordinary comforts and often even necessities. New York in 1850 had 8141 cellars sheltering 18,456 persons. There, as in Boston, about a twentieth of the population lived in damp, dark, ill-ventilated, vermin-infested, underground rooms. [3] By the end of the war fifteen thousand tenement houses had been built in New York, many of them hardly more than "fever nests." Great blocks of slums were owned by men who resisted all sanitary improvements by securing from the Tammany-ridden city health department appointments as

[1] *Chicago Weekly Democrat*, June 4, 1859.
[2] *N. Y. Herald*, June 7, 1858. See also issues of March 30, 1853, May 28, 31, 1858, and April 3, 1861.
[3] C. E. Norton, "Dwellings and Schools for the Poor," *N. Am. Rev.*, LXXIV (1852), 469.

"health officers" in a system of sanitary police provided for in 1860.[1] In protest a "citizens' committee" appealed to the state authorities at Albany and secured an investigation that led to some relief. It is not surprising that New York had the highest death rate of all American cities. It nearly doubled that of London, although the rate for the country at large was probably not much more than half that of England. Other cities like Baltimore, which made rapid strides in reducing the percentage of mortality, seem to have surpassed the metropolis in provisions for sanitation.[2]

"Narrow and crooked streets," asserted a contemporary critic, "want of proper sewerage and ventilation, absence of forethought in providing open spaces for the recreation of the people, allowance of intramural burials and of fetid nuisances, such as slaughter houses, and manufactories of offensive stuffs, have converted cities into pestilential inclosures."[3] The actual record went far to sustain this sweeping indictment. Smallpox was a dread visitor liable to appear anywhere during the winter months; vaccination was possible only to a limited degree and was not compulsory. In the winter of 1860-1861 the contagion raged in Philadelphia, Jersey City and later in New York until summer when the police department checked its spread by providing free vaccina-

---

[1] Andrew D. White, *Autobiography* (N. Y., 1905), I, 107-110; J. C. Dalton, "Disease in Cities," *N. Am. Rev.*, CVI (1868), 355-362; Council of Hygiene and Public Health of the Citizens' Association of New York, *Report upon the Sanitary Condition of the City* (N. Y., 1865); *Am. Medical Times*, IV (1862), 98-99; *Hunt's Merchants' Mag.*, XLVIII (1863), 120-124; D. W. Mitchell, *Ten Years Residence in the United States* (London, 1862), 146, 150.

[2] W. T. Howard, *Public Health and Administration and the Natural History of Disease in Baltimore, 1797-1920* (Wash., 1924), 65, 70, 507; D. F. Wilcox, *Great Cities in America* (R. T. Ely, ed., *The Citizen's Library of Economics, Politics, and Sociology;* N. Y., 1910), 6, 25, 222.

[3] H. W. Bellows, "Cities and Parks, with Special Reference to the New York Central Park," *Atlantic Mo.*, VII (1861), 416.

tion at appointed places.[1] It broke out again in Washington in 1863, especially afflicting the Negroes. President Lincoln had already experienced a mild form of the disease and carried the disfiguring marks upon his face.[2] Yellow fever, for years a threat to the midsummer peace of Southern communities, raged in all its fury in 1855 at Norfolk and Portsmouth, Virginia, and in Louisiana and Mississippi.[3] In the Virginia plague area one out of five died of the fever, its victims often being buried wholesale in trenches without coffins. Its ravages ceased with the arrival of cold weather, in part because by that time nearly everyone had already contracted the disease. Relief for the fever-stricken district was organized in Northern communities, New York alone subscribing a quarter of a million dollars.

The pestilence that left behind the widest path of destruction, however, was the cholera. A year of special calamity was 1849. Making its appearance in the South in the early spring, the disease spread rapidly through the country, decimating the population of many a town and village. Thousands fled panic-stricken before the scourge, while days of fasting, humiliation and prayer were appointed in view of its probable advent. Almost everyone felt, in fact or in apprehension, the unusual depression and other premonitory symptoms. The streets were empty except for the doctors rushing from victim to victim, and the coffin makers and undertakers following closely on their heels. Huge piles of wood were burned in the hope of purifying the atmosphere, the smoke hanging low on the heavy midsummer air. Cold

[1] N. Y. Tribune, July 1, 1861.

[2] H. P. Batcheler, Jonathan at Home (London, 1864), 223.

[3] N. Y. Tribune and N. Y. Herald, Aug. 1-Nov. 15, 1855. See also R. C. Holcomb, A Century with Norfolk Naval Hospital, 1830-1930 (Portsmouth, Va., 1930), 251-273, and W. S. Forest, The Great Pestilence in Virginia (N. Y., 1856).

weather brought relief though Chicago and other Western cities suffered heavy mortalities in the summer of
1850. In 1851 and the succeeding years the disease extended to the Pacific Coast and to communities that had
previously enjoyed relative immunity. But in 1854 it
recurred in even more destructive form in Chicago and
New York City, taking a toll of nearly twenty-five
hundred lives in the latter place.[1]

To bar the influx of such epidemics from abroad, New
York state revived its quarantine station on Staten Island
with regulations for the rigid inspection of every incom-
ing vessel. During a yellow-fever scare in 1858 mobs
twice set fire to the hospital buildings which they considered a menace to health; they were at least successful
in forcing their removal to a more remote point. A sense
of the magnitude of public-health problems led to a
series of quarantine and sanitary conventions in the years
immediately preceding the Civil War and prepared the
way for more adequate measures of protection.[2]

The touching faith of the people in blatantly advertised patent-medicine "cure-alls" continued strong,
although the German migration, by bringing the trained
prescription druggist, exercised a steadying influence
upon American pharmacy. The *Deutsche Apotheke* with
its German-script signboard appeared in many communities; in New York City there was one such institution
for about every fifty families.[3] Dr. Oliver Wendell
Holmes, however, declared in 1860 in a startling address

[1] See contemporary newspapers. See also Cole, *Era of the Civil War*,
216-217; Emmeline S. Wortley, *Travels in the United States, etc., during
1849 and 1850* (N. Y., 1855), 42, 111; Edmund Patten, *A Glimpse at
the United States* (London, 1853), 97, 98; Dalton, "Disease in Cities,"
352, 358.

[2] See Allan Nevins, *The Emergence of Modern America* (*A History of
American Life*, VIII), 319-323.

[3] Theodor Griesinger, *Lebende Bilder aus Amerika* (Stuttgart, 1858),
41; J. G. Kohl, *Travels in Canada, and through the States of New York
and Pennsylvania* (Mrs. Percy Sinnett, tr., London, 1861), I, 36-37.

before the Massachusetts Medical Society his firm belief
that, in view of the prevailing dependence of his profession upon medication, "if the whole materia medica,
as now used, could be sunk to the bottom of the sea, it
would be all the better for mankind,—and all the worse
for the fishes." [1]

Even in the more provincial interior towns there
seemed to be a ready hearing for lectures upon diseases
and sanitary subjects, often announced in lurid posters.
This lent encouragement to the numerous systems of
medicine that promised to correct the "shocking bar-
barity" of old-school practice. Besides the well-known
allopathic and homeopathic sects, usually in hostile array
against each other, hydropaths were active and successful
in the East and in parts of the Middle West. The virtues
of water were proclaimed as a stimulant and a sedative,
as an astringent and an aperient, and indeed as a universal agent for producing beneficial changes in the
human organism. The "water cure" became the refuge
of many who sought relief from strenuous living, while
New Yorkers frequented Dr. R. T. Trall's Hydropathic
Establishment, making it a sort of reform center. [2] Dr.
Trall was also a moving force in a flourishing local
Hygeiotherapeutic Medical School. In addition there
were those who expounded the virtues of galvanic treatment and of electrochemical baths, while still others
espoused a broad eclecticism in medicine. A contemporary critic found the medical profession a bedlam of
"allopaths of every class of allopathy; homeopaths of

[1] Oliver Wendell Holmes, *Medical Essays, 1842-1882* (Boston, 1893),
203; *Ohio State Journal* (Columbus), June 7, 1860; review in *Am.
Journ. of the Medical Sciences*, XL (1860), 462-474.

[2] T. W. Higginson, *Letters and Journals* (Mary T. Thacher, ed.,
Boston, 1921), 37, 38, 56. See also J. T. Trowbridge, *My Own Story
with Recollections of Noted Persons* (Boston, 1903), 181, 197, 199,
and *Ohio State Journal*, Sept. 23, 30, 1851, Oct. 1, 6, 1856, June 21,
1860.

high and low dilutions; hydropaths mild and heroic; chrono-thermalists, Thompsonians, mesmerists, herbalists, Indian doctors, clairvoyants, spiritualists with healing gifts, and I know not what besides." [1]

Without improved facilities for medical training the science of healing could not hope to forge rapidly ahead. In May, 1848, the American Medical Association was organized at Philadelphia in the effort to elevate and systematize medical education by setting up standards higher than the prevailing ungraded courses of at most three terms of from twelve to sixteen weeks.[2] A young New York physician, Dr. Nathan Smith Davis, who had taken the lead in this movement, accepted an appointment to Rush Medical College in Chicago in 1849 in the expectation that it would inaugurate the reform. Defeated after a prolonged contest, he joined in founding the medical department of Lind University and, when the first term opened in October, 1859, he had the satisfaction of initiating a three-year graded course of study.[3] Davis was a pioneer in a field which even the well-established medical colleges of the East were not as yet ready to enter.[4] Hospitals, on the other hand, were beginning to appear in the larger cities. Though their total number remained small, they were credited with being

[1] T. L. Nichols, Forty Years of American Life (London, 1864), II, 363. See also J. G. Jones and William Sherwood, American Eclectic Practice of Medicine (Cin., 1857), and Griesinger, Lebende Bilder, 41-49.

[2] N. S. Davis, History of the American Medical Association (Phila., 1855).

[3] Released from its connection with the university in 1863, this medical faculty continued for six years as an independent institution under the name of the Chicago Medical College and then became the medical department of Northwestern University. N. S. Davis, "The Earlier History of the Medical School," A. H. Wilde, ed., Northwestern University: A History, 1855-1905 (N. Y., 1905), III, 291-312; W. H. Welch, Papers and Addresses (Balt., 1920), III, 121.

[4] Charles Warren, "Medical Education in the United States," U. S. Comnr. of Educ., Rep. for 1870, 384-396; Abraham Flexner, Medical Education in the United States (N. Y., 1910), 8-10.

an important factor in keeping down the death rate. Not only the state and municipal governments but also religious denominations in the bigger centers displayed an interest in this field. Yet as late as 1873 there were only a hundred and forty-nine hospitals in the country, of which one third cared for insane patients.[1]

Despite the improved outlook for community and individual health signs of a serious physical decline attracted thoughtful critics. Personal habits failed to reflect an adequate readjustment to the somewhat leisurely life that appeared with the recession of the frontier and of frontier conditions. Shrunken limbs, crooked spines, weak joints and disproportionate bodies seemed everywhere in evidence. To the editor of *Harper's Monthly* Young America was "a pale pasty-faced, narrow chested, spindled-shanked, dwarfed race—a mere walking manikin to advertise the last cut of the fashionable tailor." [2] Abetted by the national habit of rapid eating, disorders of the stomach multiplied as the people continued to stuff themselves with a rich diet of badly cooked food. Only a negligible minority accepted the teachings of Sylvester Graham, apostle of vegetarianism and especially of the use of whole-wheat bread, who died in 1851. The unique advances in dental surgery reflected the ravages of disease in the wake of a faulty diet.

Thoughtful men pondered what Emerson referred to as "the invalid habits of this country." It came increasingly to be believed that the sorest need of the people was some recreation that would offer relaxation from

[1] M. M. Davis, *Clinics, Hospitals, and Health Centres* (N. Y., 1927), 4-5; W. G. Wylie, *Hospitals: Their History, Organization, and Construction* (N. Y., 1877).

[2] Anon., "Why We Get Sick," *Harper's Mo.*, XIII (1856), 642, 646. See also anon., "Our Sons," same mag., XVII (1858), 58; Harriet B. Stowe, "Sermon on Your Health," *Atlantic Mo.*, XVIII (1865), 85; Elizabeth Blackwell, *The Laws of Life, with Special Reference to the Physical Education of Girls* (N. Y., 1852), 29.

business cares and sedentary employments. The example of England pointed to the value of out-of-door exercise and sport, for Young America in 1850 had not learned how to play in the modern sense. "To roll balls in a ten pin alley by gaslight or to drive a fast trotting horse in a light wagon along a very bad and very dusty road, seems the Alpha and Omega of sport in the United States," declared a contemporary English observer.[1]

Sports found no less worthy champions in New England than Oliver Wendell Holmes, the statesman Edward Everett, and the authors Bayard Taylor and Thomas Wentworth Higginson. Holmes, a puny, asthmatic type, was fond of horse racing, knew the records of the prize ring, and could often be seen rowing upon the Charles River; but the "Autocrat of the Breakfast Table" admitted that a reputation for athletic prowess might easily lead to ostracism from "good" society.[2] Everett enthusiastically advocated "noble, athletic sports, manly outdoor exercises, which strengthen the mind by strengthening the body, and bring man into a generous and exhilarating communion with nature." [3] Higginson, a strenuous young apostle of the cause, launched a series of articles in the *Atlantic*, beginning with his "Saints and Their Bodies." [4]

So strenuously did he press the merits of skating that rigid-minded people sneered at its increasing vogue as "Higginson's Revival." This sport was one of the few

[1] W. E. Baxter, *America and the Americans* (London, 1855), 99; Amelia M. Murray, *Letters from the United States, Cuba and Canada* (N. Y., 1856), II, 250; T. C. Grattan, *Civilized America* (London, 1859), II, 313-314.

[2] T. W. Higginson, *Old Cambridge* (G. E. Woodberry, ed., *National Studies in American Letters*; N. Y., 1899), 92-93; O. W. Holmes, *The Autocrat of the Breakfast Table* (same author, *Writings*, Boston, 1893-1895, I), 170-173. See also Nevins, *Emergence of Modern America*, 223.

[3] Edward Everett, *Orations and Speeches on Various Occasions* (Boston, 1865-1872), III, 407.

[4] T. W. Higginson, "Saints and Their Bodies," *Atlantic Mo.*, I (1857-

that required little inspiration from Old World customs. Popular with old and young and with both sexes, advocates of woman's rights seized upon it as a means of ushering in the new day; some found it an excellent argument for the bloomer costume. Crowds of ten, twenty and even fifty thousand frequented the ponds in the new Central Park in New York. Rinks were built in towns like Roxbury, Massachusetts, while special excursion trains carried a thousand or fifteen hundred Boston skating enthusiasts to Jamaica Pond and other near-by waters.

The fifties also ushered in a new boating era. Races were scheduled, college crews organized. Two of the greatest college presidents of the next generation, Andrew D. White of Cornell and Charles W. Eliot of Harvard, were members of crews in which Harvard and Yale began the tradition of intercollegiate athletics. Optimists even predicted that "if the boating era shall continue for the next five years, the coming generation will relieve America from the odium of physical decline." [1] At a time when graceful clippers carried the flag in record-breaking voyages through the seven seas, it is not surprising that yacht sailing should have become popular along the Atlantic and in the ports of the Great Lakes. Particularly after the *America* returned victorious in 1851, the sport received a great impetus.[2] Yacht clubs were organized in every large city and regattas regularly scheduled.

1858), 582-595; same author, "Physical Courage," same mag., II (1858), 728-737; Sallie Holley, *A Life for Liberty* (J. W. Chadwick, ed., N. Y., 1899), 166-167. See also A. C. Cole, "Our Sporting Grandfathers, the Cult of Athletics at Its Source," *Atlantic Mo.*, CL (1932), 88-96.

[1] *N. Y. Herald*, July 12, 1858. *Cf.*, however, anon., "How to Keep Well," *Harper's Mo.*, XIV (1856), 59-60.

[2] J. D. J. Kelley, *American Yachts: Their Clubs and Races* (N. Y., 1884), 9.

Hunting and fishing had always been a common American diversion, if only as a means of obtaining a supply of food. To some extent, too, they were a business. Venison, selling for three cents a pound in Middle Western communities, was offered in large quantities in the New York market at around ten cents. From as far west as Wisconsin large shipments of game birds were sent to Eastern cities. The element of sportsmanship was better represented in Dixie where planters were apt to spend much of their time in field sports, especially the fox chase and the deer hunt. The game hunting of the Carolinas was known to sportsmen the world over.[1] On the lagoons of Chesapeake Bay wild-fowl shooting was followed with such ardor and success that canvasback duck was a famous Baltimore delicacy. The big game of the Far West attracted parties of British sportsmen who matched their wits with the American buffalo and elk. But the Prince of Wales during his visit in 1860 was content to fill his bags with the prairie hens and other wild fowl of Illinois.[2]

Boxing or prize fighting gained thousands of followers who felt an instinctive admiration for "the manly art of self-defense." Others, however, joined the press in condemning it as "un-American," a brutal importation from England where it held favor as the amusement of a degenerate nobility. Bouts had to be arranged secretly in out-of-the-way places where the authorities would be least likely to intervene. Oftentimes under

[1] William Elliott, Carolina Sports by Land and Water (N. Y., 1859); Captain Flack, A Hunter's Experiences in the Southern States of America (London, 1866).

[2] N. A. Woods, The Prince of Wales in Canada and the United States (London, 1861), 305-306. See also G. F. Berkeley, The English Sportsman in the Western Prairies (London, 1861); Parker Gillmore (Ubique, pseud.), Accessible Field Sports (London, 1869); B. H. Revoil, Shooting and Fishing in the Rivers, Prairies and Backwoods of North America (London, 1865).

cover of excursions into the country a large attendance
was secured for a match. A boxing festival managed by
John C. Heenan, the prize fighter, at Jones's Woods
outside New York drew a crowd of thirty thousand.[1]
Fights, usually continued until a knock-out, often went
to twenty-five rounds or more. One in 1860 ended in
a fifty-nine-round draw.

On October 20, 1858, John Morrissey, destined to
be a future member of Congress, won from Heenan,
called "Benicia Boy," an eleven-round contest for a
purse of five thousand dollars at a point in Canada
eighty miles from Buffalo.[2] In April, 1860, following
Morrissey's retirement, Heenan met in England the British favorite, Tom Sayres, in a championship bare-fist
match which lasted two hours and twenty minutes, although Sayres's right arm was badly injured early in the
fight. In the thirty-seventh round the crowd, sympathiz-
ing with the plucky Englishman, invaded the ring and
stopped the contest. Both battered fighters claimed the
victory in this most celebrated prize fight of modern
times, but the match was officially declared a draw. Three
years later Heenan returned and lost any claims he might
have had to the championship and a ten-thousand-dollar
purse to the Briton, Tom King.[3]

From across the seas also came the game of racquet.
Clubs were organized, but it found favor only among
the wealthy. Cricket, another importation, had enough
followers to make possible contests between local clubs
and international games with British and Canadian
teams. It too failed to interest the average American.
Football was played, but as then conducted the game
was apt to start or end as a free-for-all fight. Foot-rac-

[1] *Cleveland Leader*, Aug. 18, 1860.
[2] Edit., *Harper's Mo.*, XVIII (1858), 127-128.
[3] Bohun Lynch. *Knuckles and Gloves* (N. Y., 1923), chap. **xx**.

ing appealed to many, while Edward Payson Weston in 1861 began his long-enduring reputation as a pedestrian by walking from Boston to Washington in two hundred and eight hours.[1] Bowling, with easy access to liquid refreshments, was a popular pastime both of idlers at watering places and of small-town loafers. Abraham Lincoln sought to while away the time waiting for news of the Republican national convention at Chicago by a game at a Springfield alley, but found the local resources for bowling and billiards entirely exhausted.

At this favorable moment in the annals of American athletics the game of baseball made its appearance. At first a modification of "Old Town Ball," in the early fifties it took on essentially its present form, though with from eleven to thirteen men on a side. It throve as an informal sport among the youth of the land, played largely on cow pastures without gloves or suits. Clubs were organized and spectators turned out to support the home team whether it registered a victory or a defeat. Scores ran large, one of seventy-five to forty-six for a twenty-five-inning game played upon the Boston Common in 1855 being a matter of record.[2] The organization of the National Association of Baseball Players in 1858 marked the beginning of a more regulated development under a definite code of rules; players from cities all over the Union sought admission to its ranks. Every community of any size soon had its own team and the competitive spirit assured a large attendance. High-school and college teams were also organized. Baseball was well on its way to becoming the national game.

Except in New England where horse racing was sup-

---

[1] E. P. Weston, "The Pedestrian" (N. Y., 1862).
[2] Boston Eve. Transcript, May 31, 1855; A. G. Spalding, America's National Game (N. Y., 1911), 57 ff.

posed to have been prohibited in the decalogue, the race track offered entertainment and vicarious exercise to thousands, as it had for many a year. Even Boston in 1862 turned out in force to witness its first horse race in half a century.[1] Classic events of distances of from one half to four miles were held on hundreds of tracks; when twenty-mile races were attempted they were found too exhausting to be profitable or humane. Tar River, a Southern horse, demonstrated unquestioned excellence in the three and four-mile events; Ethan Allen, reputed to be the fastest trotting stallion in the world, was finally defeated in 1859 by Flora Temple, a gangling, disjointed mare of surprising swiftness. Horse racing and breeding were important industries, and followers of the track doubted whether American horses could be outdistanced. But in November, 1857, the *S. S. Arabia* brought news that the American horses Prioress and Babylon had been badly beaten at Newmarket.[2]

Along with outdoor sports came facilities for indoor athletics, a movement which reflected a strong German influence. As has been said, the revolutionary refugees of 1848 and the years that followed brought with them their *Turnvereine* or gymnastic unions, which met in Turner halls for gymnastic drill. By 1860 over a hundred and fifty societies with a membership of nearly ten thousand were scattered over the country. Meantime the thickening population of the cities encouraged experiments with gymnasiums on a commercial basis, while the Y. M. C. A. and similar organizations provided further opportunities. Just on the eve of the Civil War,

[1] *N. Y. Tribune*, July 25, 1862.

[2] *N. Y. Herald*, Sept. 17, 1855; Mitchell, *Ten Years Residence in the United States*, 329. See also Francis Brinley, *Life of William T. Porter* (N. Y., 1860); Nichols, *Forty Years of American Life*, II, 393; Hiram Woodruff, *The Trotting Horse of America* (C. J. Foster, ed., Phila., 1868).

too, while the older generation shook its head and pointed significantly to the back-yard woodpiles, facilities for physical training and education were furnished in institutions like Amherst, Oberlin, Yale and the United States Naval Academy.

But the older generation was not to be immune from the contagion. In 1860 Dr. Dio Lewis, a young Buffalo physician trained at the Harvard Medical School, who had developed a system of "light gymnastics," removed to Boston to offer the boon of exercise to those in greatest need, "old men, fat men, feeble men, young boys and females of all ages." [1] A year later he opened his Normal Institute for Physical Education, the first school in the country to train teachers of physical culture. The zeal of a former advocate of prohibition and woman's rights entered into Lewis's numerous contributions to periodicals and into his work on *The New Gymnastics* (1862). In this and other ways American sport made a new beginning in the decade before the Civil War. That bloody struggle interrupted the normal course of athletic development, although, after the existing organizations had been largely upset, sport received an impetus from the eager way in which the soldiers in the field seized upon it to help pass the monotonous hours of camp life. The American youth had had his taste of athletics and even grim war was not to destroy his new interest in physical competition. [2]

At the same time it must be remembered that most Americans were content with less strenuous amusements. For the younger generation this was the day of the spelling match and of the autograph collector, when few of

[1] F. E. Leonard, *A Guide to the History of Physical Education* (R. T. McKenzie, ed., *The Physical Education Series*; Phila., 1927), 259.
[2] See Nevins, *Emergence of Modern America*, 219-224.

the great and near great denied requests for a signature with a rebuke such as Horace Greeley administered to the youthful Frances Willard.[1] For a time a "coin fever" ran unabated among young and old and numismatic collections sold at fancy prices.[2] Social centers with equipment for checkers, dominoes and other games made their appearance. But the post office and the depot (pronounced dee-poe) served with the church as the chief social centers of smaller communities. When the evening train or the mail arrived, the current of life set in and social amenities were eagerly exchanged.

Meanwhile the mystery of the secret fraternal society strengthened its hold on city folk, and prefigured the place it was later to occupy in the social organism.[3] Usually it was the Masonic order or the Odd Fellows, but newer organizations like the Improved Order of Red Men, the United Order of Friends, the Independent Order of United Brothers and the Sons of Malta also attracted a following. The secret ritualism was one explanation of the remarkable popularity of the Know Nothing party and of the Sons of Temperance. Apart from certain clergymen few seemed to share the hostility of President Jonathan Blanchard of Knox College who classed not only the fraternal orders but even the Sons of Temperance as "anti-Republican in their tendencies and subversive of the principles both of the Natural and Revealed Religion." [4]

The people of the time thoroughly enjoyed the sight of a balloon ascension. Their especial favorite was John Wise of Lancaster, Pennsylvania, "the world renowned

[1] Frances E. Willard, *Glimpses of Fifty Years* (Chicago, 1889), 105.

[2] *Baltimore Sun*, April 4, 1860.

[3] See A. M. Schlesinger, *The Rise of the City* (*A History of American Life*, X), 288-290.

[4] *Western Citizen* (Chicago), Oct. 1, 1850.

aeronaut, who has made *more* voyages *through the Heavens* than any other man." [1] He provided twenty thousand seats at a dollar a person at the place of inflation and ascension, and at a presentation soirée gave away four thousand dollars' worth of gold watches and jewelry to ticket buyers. Another popular entertainer was Blondin, the ropewalker, who among his feats balanced his uncertain way over the roaring falls of the Niagara.

A new era for the American circus and its patrons arrived with the increasing tendency toward consolidation and as more modern facilities were adopted. The smaller troupes traveled the dusty roads of midsummer, but Spaulding and Rogers's new railroad circus with nine cars of its own proclaimed that "team horses and wagons won't do in this age of steam," that its unrivaled entertainment would go "wherever there is a track or a steamboat." [2] At the beginning of the decade the show was advertised as the "People's Circus"; a few years later it was a "European circus, comprising the élite of the European circuses." When the Civil War came Spaulding and Rogers were operating on the Mississippi in a "Floating Palace" which was seized by the Confederates at New Orleans and converted into a military hospital. [3] One of its rivals, E. F. and J. Mabies' Grand Olympic Arena, combined with Nathan's circus to secure more favorable consideration from the public. In the early fifties Barnum's Grand Colossal Museum and Menagerie toured the country attracting thousands although critics denounced the show for not coming up to the

[1] *Ohio Statesman* (Columbus), July 1, 1851.

[2] See reproduced bill in *Boston Eve. Transcript*, July 7, 1923. See also *Ohio State Journal*, Oct. 1, 1856.

[3] E. C. May, *The Circus from Rome to Ringling* (N. Y., 1932), 77-79.

promises of the posters.[1] Later accretions made it one of the dominant shows on tour. In further keeping with the age of steam, the calliope made its appearance to herald the presence of one or another of these numerous claimants to being "the greatest show on earth."

To the more intellectual, chess offered its attractions. In the late fifties chess clubs were organized in many cities and in nearly all the Eastern colleges. These clubs sometimes competed in telegraphic matches. So popular did the game become that the weekly pictorial newspapers devoted columns especially to chess problems and news. Paul Morphy of New Orleans, the ruling favorite, was successful in defeating the best players of Europe and America.[2] Those, however, who sought a nice test of manual dexterity took up billiards. An American school of billiards developed, combining features of both the French and English systems.[3] In January, 1865, Dudley Kavanagh won one thousand dollars and a gold cue in a championship match with William Goldthwaite.[4] Others found their pleasure in card playing or in the new dancing craze. Ordinarily the means for an evening's diversion, cards were the chief daylight pastime of patrons of summer resorts and of travelers upon river steamboats. Reckless and enormous wagers were sometimes laid to add to the excitement of the "friendly game," often to cause it to terminate in bitterness and confusion.

Soirées, cotillion parties and balls were held periodically in every town, with programs of quadrilles,

[1] *Illinois State Register* (Springfield), May 13, 1852, Sept. 1, Oct. 6, 1853.

[2] Edit., *Harper's Mo.*, XIX (1859), 410.

[3] *N. Y. Tribune*, Oct. 1, 1860; W. H. Russell, *My Diary North and South* (Boston, 1863), 540.

[4] *N. Y. Herald*, Jan. 21, 1865.

schottishes and polkas and an occasional waltz before the supper interval. The annual ball of the local military company or of the firemen was often outshone by a series of "grand soirées" given by a properly christened "Pleasure Association" or "Quadrille Association." In 1854 the New Year's festival at Alton, Illinois, took the form of a "promenade concert" with a band from St. Louis, to which seven hundred paid the admission of seventy-five cents and competed for seventy-five prizes. Even in the Panic winter of 1857-1858 ten thousand persons attended the calico dress ball of a New York City benevolent society.[1] Masquerade balls grew so popular that the police authorities, concerned over the attendance of a vicious element, invoked the New York statute against them.

Summer tours through this land of magnificent distances attracted an ever increasing patronage. Rail lines and their steamship connections carried the traveler in luxury to the scenic beauties of the upper Mississippi. The wonders of Niagara were at length within easy reach; there vagrant Indians in gaudy attire lent color to the scene. The visitor was guided down long flights of stairs until he stood where he could observe the full rush of the torrent above him. The *Maid of the Mist* carried passengers to the very vortex of the falls until in the summer of 1861, when the war curtailed the tourist traffic, it evaded seizure for debt by running the rapids only to be sold at the mouth of the river.[2] Meantime swaggering Americans were thronging Europe in great crowds, giving foreigners "a capital notion of our

[1] *Baltimore Sun*, Feb. 6, 1858.
[2] Anthony Trollope, *North America* (N. Y., 1862), 98. See also Russell, *My Diary*, 365; Ferri Pisani, *Lettres sur les États-Unis d'Amérique* (Paris, 1862), 389-390; Auguste Laugel, *The United States during the War* (London, 1866), 133-137; [Isabella L. Bishop], *The Englishwoman in America* (London, 1856), 222.

progress in intellect and refinement," sarcastically commented Walt Whitman.[1]

While the middle class was finding amusement in such ways, no provision met democratically the needs of all classes. For this reason the rougher element and the youth of the large cities avidly responded to the appeal of the public dance halls which reaped a golden harvest. Some critics of "such sinks of iniquity," "these branches of Satan's den," demanded their immediate extirpation,[2] others their more effective police regulation at the expense of the keepers. It was nevertheless noted that "those cities which extend the largest amount of patronage to amusements, do the greatest amount of business and attract the most visitors."[3] Chicagoans were only human, therefore, in taking pride at the close of the Civil War in the expenditure of a half-million dollars a year for the city's organized amusements.

At the same time the upper social crust was reshaping itself again. In the Northern states leadership fell to a new aristocracy of wealth. Fortunes made in trade and industry, in railroad building and in Western land speculation lined Fifth Avenue with brownstone and marble palaces. Even in Boston worth was coming to be measured in terms of dollars. An "Office of Heraldry," set up in New York, sought to indulge the vanity of those who wished to claim a share in the aristocratic tradition.[4] The reigning queens of society invoked exclusiveness and a vast array of charity fairs, balls and concerts to maintain their thrones. When the Prince of Wales toured the

[1] Walt Whitman, *I Sit and Look Out* (Emory Holloway and Vernolian Schwarz, eds., N. Y., 1932), 104. See also anon., "Are We a Polite People?", *Harper's Mo.*, XV (1857), 390, and edit., same mag., XVII (1858), 122.

[2] *New Orleans Commercial Bulletin*, Jan. 18, 1851.

[3] *Cairo Democrat*, Oct. 1, 1863.

[4] Robert Everest, *Journey through the United States and Part of Canada* (London, 1855), 51.

country in 1860, the guest lists of the great balls in his honor in New York and Boston revealed those who had "arrived" socially.[1] Everywhere the society set found diversion in elaborate dressing, in sumptuous formal dinners where choice liquors were lavishly dispensed, in conspicuous patronage of the theater and opera, and in extravagant dancing parties.

In Dixie the older planter class gloried in an aristocracy of birth; already the initials "F.F.V." were universally understood. Southern society dominated the winter season at Washington. The graciousness of the Southern matron and the charm of her daughter, together with an unstinted hospitality which cost many a Southern member of Congress a small fortune annually, made life at the national capital take on some of the fascination of a European court.[2] All Washington paid court to Harriet Lane, President Buchanan's niece and mistress of the White House. When Senator Stephen A. Douglas in 1856 married the popular Southern belle, Adèle Cutts, their home became an acknowledged center of the social life of the capital. The February horse races at Charleston were widely known and followed as an important item on the social calendar. Especially brilliant were the balls staged for the élite in attendance. The St. Cecilia ball, the most select and fashion-

[1] Elizabeth F. Ellet, *Queens of American Society* (5th edn., N. Y., 1870); Woods, *Prince of Wales in the United States*, 394 ff.

[2] Mrs. Clement C. Clay, *A Belle of the Fifties* (Ada Sterling, ed., N. Y., 1904); T. C. De Leon, *Belles, Beaux and Brains of the '60's* (N. Y., 1909); Elizabeth F. Ellet, *The Court Circles of the Republic* (Hartford, 1869). Life at the capital was a continual round of balls, dinners and receptions. "It seems to me that Washington never goes to bed; never gets up entirely sober. Indeed, there is not time between one entertainment and another," declared a clever commentator upon the life of the day. Hiram Fuller, *Belle Brittan on a Tour at Newport, and Here and There* (N. Y., 1858), 29.

able of all, admitted only the best accredited outsiders.[1]

Membership in this upper ten thousand required participation in the fashionable summer hegira to approved seaside resorts or to Saratoga Springs. Newport, once a thriving commercial town, was now in its glory as an American Brighton, the most fashionable sea-bathing resort in the country. Originally visited chiefly by Southern planters and their families, it found increasing favor with New York patrons. More and more the wealthy notables built their own summer homes—cottages, villas and mansions stretching along the beach for two miles. Dressing, flirting, dancing, riding and bathing furnished the chief amusements. Of these bathing was the newest and the most distinctive pastime, the women clad in clumsy white ankle-length pantalettes and red frocks with long sleeves, the men in costumes rather more abbreviated but less picturesque.[2] So garbed, mixed bathing of men and women seemed harmless enough. Ordinarily the male companions took charge of the ladies in the surf, at times "handing about their pretty partners as if they were dancing water quadrilles."[3] A resort at Old Point Comfort, however, confined the men to one stockade built out into the water, while in another alongside, shrieks, screams and laughter betrayed the ladies at play.[4] At certain beaches nude bathing, signalized by a red flag fluttering in the breeze, was provided for the men during the early afternoon—or napping—hours.[5]

[1] J. M. Mackie, *From Cape Cod to Dixie and the Tropics* (N. Y., 1864), 93, 99.

[2] See Nevins, *Emergence of Modern America*, frontispiece and plate ix, g.

[3] Murray, *Letters from the United States*, I, 37.

[4] "Domestic Intelligence," *Harper's Wkly.*, II, 470 (July 24, 1858).

[5] J. R. Dix, *A Hand-Book of Newport, and Rhode-Island* (Newport,

Nahant, a cool rock rising up out of the sea fourteen miles from Boston, was the favorite resort of wealthy and cultured Bostonians. Reputed for its repose and its freedom from the fast set, it was none the less dominated by an aristocracy whose dinner parties indicated the bounds of the socially elect. Fashion also frequented the enormous caravansaries at Saratoga Springs, the great American Spa. There notables like Mrs. Harrison Gray Otis, Boston's social leader, exchanged courtesies with the élite of the land. At Saratoga, as at Newport, Southern women were conspicuous for their beauty, breeding and intelligence, while their husbands were active among the managers of the great summer balls. A million and a half dollars were spent annually as tribute to the attractions of this resort and to its social standing. Some sought to reinvigorate their systems by regular drafts of the mineral waters that had first brought fame to this backcountry community. Others sought more stimulating beverages. Bowling too had its devotees, even among overdressed belles who sought escape from boredom, while cards and gambling were accepted masculine diversions. Like Newport and Nahant Saratoga was avoided by thousands who felt only disgust at the assumption by a few ruling fashionables of the right to monopolize everything in the way of privilege. Many of these sought out mountain retreats or the resorts along the Jersey Coast. Cape May was popular with a large following of New Yorkers and Philadelphians while Atlantic City was just beginning its phenomenal growth in the late fifties. Coney Island too was rapidly acquiring fame for its roasted clams and sunburned bathers.

1852), 72-75; Charles Mackay, *Life and Liberty in America* (N. Y., 1859), I, 103; Fuller, *Belle Brittan on a Tour,* 159.

Wealthy Southerners, as has been said, had long furnished a valuable patronage to the Northern resorts. Summer Newport was often referred to as a Southern community; a conservative proslavery atmosphere prevailed in the hotels they patronized and even in the churches they attended. In 1858 Senator Jefferson Davis of Mississippi joined a congenial group of prominent Southerners who regularly sojourned near Portland, Maine. As sectional feeling grew sharper, however, the Southern fire eaters insistently demanded a boycott of Northern resorts. Dixie had mountain and seaside attractions of her own, they pointed out. At the same time sensitive Southerners reported an increasingly rude reception upon Northern visits. "We are treated worse in the North than if we were foreign enemies," lamented the editor of the *Richmond Whig.* "Let us with one accord stay home and spend among our own people." [1]

Under this impetus wealthy planters began to erect summer places at the already popular mineral springs in the Virginia mountains, Fauquier White Sulphur Springs becoming especially fashionable. In 1855 a number of Southerners formed a stock company to develop Southern resorts, particularly a spring at Montgomery, Virginia, a few miles from the Tennessee line, where they hoped to create a "Southern Saratoga." [2] A few years later, a number of small watering places with attractive summer residences grew up along the Gulf coast of Mississippi, a convenient location for inhabitants of New Orleans and for planters of the interior. [3] Thus, as the decade drew to a close, the spirit of sectionalism was in-

[1] *Richmond Whig,* July 23, cited in *N. Y. Herald,* July 28, 1858.
[2] *N. Y. Herald,* Aug. 20, 1855.
[3] T. D. Ozanne, *The South as It Is* (London, 1863), 231-233.

vading even the sphere of pleasure and recreation. Formerly, leisure-class Americans from both sections rubbed elbows and learned the lesson of tolerance as they exchanged social courtesies and ideas at Saratoga and Newport. But unobserved by the statesmen, coming events disclosed how badly frayed had become the bonds of fraternal feeling and mutual esteem.

CHAPTER IX

EDUCATIONAL AND CULTURAL
ADVANCE

IMPROVING on the pioneer labors of the preceding
generation, the Americans of mid-century strengthened
and extended the democratic system of education which
they inherited.[1] The West, which Horace Mann believed destined to be the "seat of empire," was eager to
secure the benefits of the victories recently won in the
older states.[2] In 1850 only a few schools were available
in the West and terms were often three months or less.
Over two thirds of the buildings were log houses, many
of the rest mere shanties or temporary shacks. In one
Illinois county the average worth of twenty-one buildings was sixty-five dollars. Now, however, came rapid
development. The organization of a public system under
state superintendents of instruction and the principle of
free education were promptly adopted. Wisconsin's first
constitution (1848) opened the doors of the schools
freely to all. Indiana and Ohio followed in 1852 and
1853. The next year Illinois made provision for a state
school tax, for unlimited taxation, and for a free school
term of six months in every district. The number of
schools doubled and trebled, while enrollment increased
even more rapidly. Soon Illinois was boasting that only

[1] See C. R. Fish, *The Rise of the Common Man* (*A History of American Life*, VI), 200-227.
[2] B. A. Hinsdale, *Horace Mann and the Common School Revival in the
United States* (N. M. Butler, ed., *The Great Educators*, N. Y., 1898),
247.

one child of school age in fifteen was not in attendance and that the average term was nearly seven months.

This expansion produced an inevitable dearth of available instruction. The National Educational Society therefore, through its agent, ex-Governor William Slade of Vermont, coöperated in enlisting well-trained Eastern young women as missionaries in the cause of education. In a period of eleven years nearly five hundred "Yankee school-marms" were sent into the West, which welcomed them with salaries only half those of their male associates, many of them, too, New Englanders. The complaint of Western advocates of education was not only that the supply of young women was insufficient, but that once arrived they married. "Instead of teaching other folk's children, [they] soon find employment in teaching their own." [1] Others, however, had deeper doubts as to the plan. Some educational leaders suggested that such teachers were bound to bring in a spirit of condescension growing out of their lack of sympathy with Western habits, customs and feelings. Certain Democratic politicians, including the great Douglas who had himself come to Illinois as a Vermont schoolmaster, expressed fear that these selected emissaries of New England, and therefore probably of abolition, would mold the youth into the likeness of "canting, freedom-shrieking" Yankee demagogues.

Such ungenerous criticism proved unwarranted, but at any rate it furnished an argument for a local supply of teachers. The colleges of the West were not able to meet the demand, nor were their graduates specifically trained for teaching. This situation led to the founding

[1] A. C. Cole, *The Era of the Civil War* (C. W. Alvord, ed., *The Centennial History of Illinois*, Springfield, 1918-1920, III), 234-235; anon., "Board of National Popular Education," *Am. Journ. of Educ.*, XV (1865), 271-274; Mae E. Harveson, *Catherine Esther Beecher* (Phila., 1932).

of normal schools, the West following along the paths marked out by aggressive Eastern leaders.[1] Michigan acted in 1849, Illinois in 1857, Minnesota in 1860, with other states presently doing the same. Teachers continued, however, to be sadly underpaid though salaries advanced greatly during the decade. In Wisconsin, for example, the average pay of men rose from $15.22 a month in 1850 to $24.20 in 1860, of women from $8.97 to $15.30.[2] An increasing professional spirit developed; county institutes and state institutes as well as teachers' associations were organized, and such organs as the *Ohio School Journal* (1852), the *Illinois Teacher* (1855) and the *Indiana School Journal* (1856) came to exercise an important influence on educational thought.

In most Eastern states the "rate-bill" lingered in whole or in part. This practice involved a charge upon parents to supplement the school revenues and prolong the school term, and was assessed in proportion to the number of pupils in each family. While provision was made for its remittance in the case of parents who could not pay, there were many whose pride kept them from declaring their need and whose children were therefore kept out of school. In New York state the issue of free schools was fought out in a series of popular referenda in which the city voters advocating tax-supported schools met heavy opposition from the rural counties and from the supporters of the parochial system. The result was a compromise which continued the state rate bill in effect—it was not repealed until 1867—and at

[1] Anon., "American Normal Schools," *N. Y. Teacher*, n. s., II (1861), 337-344; R. G. Boone, *Education in the United States* (N. Y., 1889), 132-133; E. G. Dexter, *History of Education in the United States* (N. Y., 1904), 376; E. P. Cubberley, *Public Education in the United States* (Boston, 1919), 290-293.

[2] E. D. Fite, *Social and Industrial Conditions in the North during the Civil War* (N. Y., 1910), 247 n.

the same time authorized such school districts as wished to do so to provide free schools by local taxation. Under this arrangement New York City organized a system of free schools. In June, 1853, therefore, the Public School Society of that metropolis, which had maintained an extensive system on its own account, decided that its goal had been achieved and agreed to surrender its schools to the local board of education. Nowhere, aside from a mild requirement in Massachusetts, was there as yet the feature of compulsory attendance.[1] The educational forces of New England were leavened by the lofty idealism of that Yankee transcendentalist Amos Bronson Alcott. In many respects a hopeless visionary, as superintendent of schools at Concord he introduced into the curriculum singing, calisthenics and physiology and wrote educational reports that were widely read for their sane and stimulating progressivism.

For the average boy and girl of 1850 public education ended in the common schools. Some fortunate few continued their training in the private or semiprivate academies that were just reaching the zenith of their development. But the city high school was steadily increasing in importance. The number of such public institutions rose during the decade from a few dozen to some three hundred. The son of the day laborer and of the artisan began to share educational opportunities that had often been regarded as a peculiar monopoly of the privileged minority. Except in a few conservative communities like Boston, girls took their places in the classrooms devoted to this more advanced training. The high

[1] S. S. Randall, *History of the Common School System of the State of New York* (N. Y., 1871), 220-228, 312-313; Francis Adams, *The Free School System of the United States* (London, 1875), 47, 78; J. M. Wightman, comp., *Annals of the Boston Primary School Committee* (Boston, 1860); W. O. Bourne, *History of the Public School Society of the City of New York* (N. Y., 1870), 579-590; Boone, *Education in the United States*, 330; Hinsdale, *Horace Mann*, 296.

school had its early origins in New England, but the democratic West promptly appropriated the idea and established secondary schools in its growing cities.[1]

The high schools, like the academies, were generally college preparatory schools. Simultaneously in this decade before the Civil War nearly a hundred institutions of higher learning were founded, a record unrivaled in the annals of American education. Most of the new colleges were located in the South, with its growing distrust of the North and Northern schools, and in the West, the newer parts of which were now ready for refinements undreamed of during the frontier stage. These were largely denominational colleges which adopted the traditional curriculum and the prevailing methods of study. Yet the spirit of innovation and revolt was also abroad. Many attacked the existing form of higher instruction and called for a more practical education on the European model. Scores of American students, most of them destined to become college professors, had studied in German universities.[2] From them and others came a demand that the colleges, which seemed to many "the headquarters of conservatism," keep pace with the rapid progress of human knowledge; that science be given a place alongside classical studies; that better libraries and laboratories be provided; and that more freedom in the choice of studies be allowed.[3]

[1] E. D. Grizzell, *Origin and Development of the High School in New England before 1865* (N. Y., 1923), esp. 272-279; John Swett, *American Public Schools, History and Pedagogics* (N. Y., 1900), 74-75; W. E. Baxter, *America and the Americans* (London, 1855), 162-163; Cubberley, *Public Education in United States*, 196-198; State Commissioner of Public Schools of Ohio, *Seventh Annual Report* (1860), 45-52; *Baltimore Sun*, Feb. 15, 1858.

[2] C. F. Thwing, *The American and the German University* (N. Y., 1928), 42-43.

[3] Henry James, *Charles W. Eliot* (Boston, 1930), I, 72, 94; F. A. P. Barnard, "On Improvements Practicable in American Colleges," *Am. Journ. of Educ.*, I (1855), 174-185; J. D. Dana, "Science and Scientific

Henry P. Tappan, president of the University of Michigan from 1852 to 1863, proclaimed the virtues of the German universities and of European systems of thought, until critics branded him the most completely foreignized specimen of an abnormal Yankee that they had ever seen, and in due time forced his dismissal.[1] But under his aggressive administration progress was the order of the day. A course in civil engineering was established, the first chemistry laboratory in America was set up in 1857, and in the same year Andrew D. White was appointed to one of the first chairs of history to be created in an American university.[2] These and similar pioneering ventures caused the enrollment to jump in a decade from a mere handful of students to more than five hundred in 1860; in another five years it more than doubled again. Students flocked from all parts of the country to what an Eastern educator, an orator at the Harvard triennial festival in 1866, called

the only seminary in the country whose liberal scope and cosmopolitan outlook satisfy the idea of a great university. Compared with this, our other colleges are all provincial; and unless the State of Massachusetts shall see fit to adopt us, and to foster our interest with something of the zeal and liberality which the State of Michigan bestows on her academic masterpiece Harvard cannot hope to compete with this precocious child of the West.[3]

Schools," same mag., II (1856), 350; C. A. Bristed, "Five Years in an English University," *N. Am. Rev.*, LXXV (1852), 79-80.

[1] Elizabeth M. Farrand, *History of the University of Michigan* (Ann Arbor, 1885), 112-113.

[2] Andrew D. White, *Autobiography* (N. Y., 1905), I, 42.

[3] E. H. Hedge, "University Reform," *Atlantic Mo.*, XVIII (1866), 299. See also *Michigan Alumnus*, XXXIII (1926), 104. Of his own college Dr. Hedge remarked: "Harvard College is simply a more advanced school for boys, not differing essentially in principle and theory from the public schools in all our towns. In this, as in those, the principle is coercion. Hold your subject fast with one hand, and pour knowledge into

But Harvard, with a faculty made up of men of scholarly distinction, some of them of international repute, remained in the foreground of higher learning. It showed its ability to outgrow old traditions by creating a chair of modern languages to which first Henry Wadsworth Longfellow and later James Russell Lowell were appointed. The vitality of collegiate education in this era, indeed, seemed to depend upon courage to break new ground. Graduate work had its faint beginnings. In 1861 Yale awarded the first American degree of doctor of philosophy. In many places mathematics and the ancient languages were compelled to yield to the demands of the age and make room for modern languages and the new physical sciences.

The advance of knowledge became increasingly indebted to members of college faculties. When Darwin's *Origin of Species* was published in 1859 the entire first American edition sold within a fortnight. Professor Louis Agassiz of the Harvard faculty promptly reiterated his loyalty to the theory of immutability and proclaimed Darwinism "a scientific mistake, untrue in its method, and mischievous in its tendency." [1] At the time Joseph Le Conte, an American scientist trained under Agassiz, was working at the University of South Carolina on a theory of the origin of species by natural selection. Agassiz's own scientific labors attracted such favorable notice that a bequest of $50,000, supplemented by popular subscriptions totaling $75,000 and by a legislative grant of $100,000, made possible at Harvard University a permanent museum of comparative zoology

him with the other. The professors are task-masters and police officers, the President is chief of the College police."

[1] "Professor Agassiz on the Origin of Species," *Am. Journ. of Science and Arts*, XXX (1860), 154. See also Asa Gray's review in same mag., XXIX (1860), 153; B. J. Loewenberg, "The Reaction of American Scientists to Darwinism," *Am. Hist. Rev.*, XXXVIII, 687-701.

to house the collections of this indefatigable worker.[1] Astronomical science as practised at Harvard, where extensive experimentation in stellar photography was being undertaken, aroused the interest of a trio of wealthy Chicago merchants to the point of causing them to provide a local observatory with a telescope somewhat larger than the instrument at Cambridge.[2] Meantime, while Asa Gray, the noted Cambridge botanist, was writing the *Botany of the United States Pacific Exploring Expedition,* and pleading for a fair and favorable consideration of Darwin's theories, Henry Shaw, a retired St. Louis merchant, devoted his time to building up a botanical garden near his home which was to develop into an invaluable laboratory for scientific study. The Smithsonian Institution, too, rapidly expanded its work and its influence as a national clearing house for scientific activities. When a disastrous fire in 1865 destroyed building and records, its evident value insured its prompt replacement.

The appeal of the spectacular accounts for the unusual popular interest in the polar explorations of Dr. Elisha K. Kane. An extensive traveler as an assistant surgeon in the United States navy, he accompanied the United States Grinnell expedition in 1850-1852 in search of the ill-fated Sir John Franklin.[3] On May 30, 1853, he set sail from New York in the brig *Advance* in command of the second Grinnell expedition and during an absence of two years reached Cape Constitution, the highest point attained up to that time by a sailing

[1] *N. Y. Herald,* Jan. 12, 13, 1859; *Dollar Newspaper* (Phila.), April 20, 1859; H. H. Ballard, "History of the Agassiz Association," *Science,* IX, 93.

[2] Auguste Laugel, *The United States during the War* (London, 1866), 139.

[3] Henry Grinnell, a prosperous New York shipowner, fitted out this expedition at his own expense and bore a large part of the expenses of the second voyage.

vessel. The American public, of course, thrilled more over the hardships endured in these expeditions than it did over the valuable additions which they made to scientific knowledge.

In 1860, aided by a considerable endowment from a local donor, Yale began to transform its school of applied chemistry into the Sheffield Scientific School.[1] Technological and professional education made further headway with the establishment of the Chandler Scientific School at Dartmouth, the school of mines at Columbia University and the school of technology at Lehigh University. Colleges of pharmacy arose in Cincinnati (1850), Chicago (1854) and St. Louis (1864) to supplement those in the East. Dental schools were established in Philadelphia and New York, while medical colleges, representing one or another of the various systems of healing, came to be available in every corner of the nation. Meantime law schools more than doubled in number, and Columbia and the University of Michigan established more thorough courses and inaugurated a more systematic study of law. Yet it was possible for a friend of Rufus Choate to state in 1860 that "there is not enough in the whole science of law to occupy a mind like his for a month." [2] The private commercial college also made its appearance in the larger cities with the promise of elevating its graduates to at least the lower levels of the white-collar occupations.

Inevitably the hydraheaded slavery question made its way into nearly every college community in the land. In the East, where traditions were conservative, college faculties generally frowned upon antislavery agitation,

---

[1] T. C. Mendenhall, "Scientific, Technical and Engineering Education," N. M. Butler, ed., *Education in the United States* (Albany, 1900), II, 24-25.

[2] T. W. Higginson, *Letters and Journals* (Mary T. Thacher, ed., Boston, 1921), 71.

advocating compromise. President Theodore Dwight Woolsey of Yale was one of the few outstanding leaders in that section who braved public sentiment by condemning the fugitive-slave law and other concessions to slavery. In the Middle West, on the other hand, many colleges were hotbeds of antislavery feeling. Oberlin, which long since had opened its doors to the few Negroes who applied for admission, saw its enrollment under the impulse of the controversy leap to over twelve hundred in 1850, a new record in college attendance. But Horace Mann with a similar but more radical venture at Antioch College in the same state met with serious obstacles which hastened his death in 1859.[1]

President Jonathan Blanchard of Knox College, one of the most persistent abolitionists in Illinois, roused an opposition in his board of trustees which might have resulted disastrously for him except for the fortuitous vacancy of six places which made it possible to add "good, honest, upright anti-slavery men" to safeguard his position for the future. In 1860 when this crusader accepted the presidency of Wheaton College, Illinois, he first made sure that the trustees would keep faith with their antislavery declarations. At Jacksonville President J. M. Sturtevant of Illinois College took the stump in 1856 for Frémont and "bleeding Kansas." Though the college was surrounded by a conservative community which comprised many of Southern origin, the strongly antislavery faculty went so far as to dismiss a student who insisted upon his right to include in a Junior Exhibition oration remarks deploring Northern agitation and rejoicing in the election of Buchanan as auspicious for future tranquillity.[2]

[1] Hinsdale, *Horace Mann*, 242-264; Mary Mann, *Life of Horace Mann* (Boston, 1865), 402 ff.

[2] Julian M. Sturtevant, *Autobiography* (J. M. Sturtevant, jr., ed., N. Y., 1896), 279-282; C. H. Rammelkamp, "The Reverberations of

Meantime there were numerous signs of a demand for a type of adult education adapted to the needs of the plain people. The workers in many communities had already established mechanics' institutes, which sometimes accumulated excellent libraries and offered special vocational training. In other instances, like the Albany Manual Labor University, people's colleges or labor colleges had been attempted. In 1857, through the generosity of Peter Cooper, the Cooper Union was founded at New York to give practical instruction to the working classes. At once hundreds of students representing every industrial field enrolled and thousands came to use the reading rooms.[1] Evening schools, successfully inaugurated in New York in 1848 by the Public School Society, were rapidly extended under the control of the board of education. Boston followed this lead in 1854 first under private, then under public, auspices. Not only were the "three R's" and other elementary subjects taught, but the instruction in bookkeeping and architectural drawing suggested a timid entry into the field of vocational training.

Formal educational institutions were supplemented by debating clubs and literary and philosophical societies as agencies of popular instruction. On the eve of the war the lyceum reached the height of its glory despite the fact that it lacked the effective organization of a later day.[2] Scarcely a town in the North and Middle West failed to provide a winter course of from twelve to twenty or more lectures. Here, in assemblages listening intently to popular discussions of literature, reform or

the Slavery Conflict in a Pioneer College," *Miss. Valley Hist. Rev.*, XIV, 450-451; same author, *Illinois College: A Centennial History* (New Haven, 1928), 101-118.

[1] *N. Y. Tribune*, Jan. 21, Feb. 1, 1860.

[2] See Fish, *Rise of the Common Man*, 225, and Allan Nevins, *The Emergence of Modern America* (*A History of American Life*, VIII), 238-239.

the achievements of science, one might see a middle-class culture in process of formation. Emerson, Beecher, Gough, Greeley, Agassiz, George W. Curtis and Bayard Taylor were favorites of audiences which came together to secure instruction as much as entertainment. The doors of these "people's colleges" were open to scholars whose bold opinions excluded them from the sober precincts of higher learning, for "the home of real thought was outside, not inside the college walls," as one liberal contemporary declared.[1]

Many an American gleaned his education and drew his inspiration chiefly from the printed page. In the cities the tax-supported free library began to take hold. In 1854 the Boston Public Library, authorized in 1848, opened its doors, and within fifteen years was dispensing one hundred thousand volumes. In 1854, too, the Astor Library in New York City opened. Made possible by a generous bequest from John Jacob Astor and aided by later gifts from the Astor family, it was long the largest library in the country. In 1857 the Peabody Library in Baltimore was established. When a disastrous fire in 1851 destroyed two thirds of the collections of the Library of Congress, a new and safer building was acquired and annual appropriations of ten thousand dollars enabled it to add in eight years fifty thousand volumes. By 1863 the country contained one hundred and four libraries of over ten thousand volumes each, a decided gain from the forty in 1849.[2]

The enthusiasm was shared by the West where libraries were soon set up in communities as remote as Leavenworth, Kansas. Township libraries, often direct adjuncts of the schools, were provided for by law in

[1] T. W. Higginson, *Atlantic Essays* (Boston, 1871), 61-62. See also Carl Schurz, *Reminiscences* (N. Y., 1907-1908), II, 157-158, and Anthony Trollope, *North America* (N. Y., 1862), 222.

[2] Fite, *Social and Industrial Conditions*, 253 n.

several states. Their avowed object in Michigan was "to diffuse information, not only or even chiefly among children or minors, but among adults and those who have finished common school education." [1] It became traditional in Indiana that such collections helped to develop the literary talent and the intelligence of the reading public of that state.[2] In the decade the public libraries of the nation increased eightfold, to over one thousand, while their volumes multiplied fivefold, reaching a total of nearly eight million. In 1856 a group organized the Chicago Historical Society which after a year reported a collection of eleven thousand, largely the gift of members and friends. In time its accumulating bundles of maps and papers and its shelves of books were proudly displayed to distinguished foreign travelers like the Prince of Wales.[3]

By private individuals books were being purchased at a rate that contributed to the increasing prosperity of the American publisher. The bookstore in New York or such an establishment as that of Ticknor and Fields in Boston was the natural resort of cultured patrons and of literary celebrities; but even Albany, the gateway to the West, had several extensive shops that provided for the intellectual wants of travelers on the line of the great trek into the interior. Chicago had three thriving bookstores including one which claimed to be the largest in the Middle West. The shops of this and other Western cities often carried an extensive line of English

[1] F. W. Shearman, *The System of Instruction and Primary School Laws of Michigan* (Lansing, 1852), 420.

[2] R. U. Johnson, *Remembered Yesterdays* (Boston, 1923), 26. Dr. Henry B. Blackwell, husband of Lucy Stone, in a single year established fifteen hundred "Farmers' Libraries," consisting largely of the publications of Augustus Moore, in the school districts of Illinois. Alice S. Blackwell, *Lucy Stone* (Boston, 1930), 194, 196-197.

[3] Laugel, *United States during the War*, 139, 161. See also *Boston Eve. Transcript*, Oct. 6, 1860; U. S. Bureau of Education, *Public Libraries in the United States of America* (Special Rep., Wash., 1876), 893.

classics and current publications, while the Yankee book peddler sold sets of standard works in the more isolated communities.[1] Even the humble frontier cabin generally had "some newspaper, some book, some token of advance in education."[2]

In the absence of an international-copyright law almost every important work that issued from the English press was promptly reprinted in a "pirated" American edition. Dickens, Tennyson, Scott and Thackeray enjoyed a particular vogue. But alongside of them flowered a native literature that commanded enthusiasm at home and respect abroad. The English critic no longer risked the tantalizing inquiry, "Who reads an American book?" Inspired by the intimacy and cordiality of their contacts with one another, the Boston-Concord-Cambridge school of poets, novelists and historians ripened into maturity and fulfilled the promise of their earlier efforts.[3] Longfellow, serious-minded Harvard professor, turned from the tedium of the classroom to give poetic form to American tradition in "Hiawatha," "Miles Standish," "Paul Revere," fit successors to "Evangeline" and all promptly adopted by the people as their own. Whittier, the shy Quaker poet of Amesbury, consumed his energies in a burning devotion to the crusade against slavery and found William Cullen Bryant, the New York poet-editor, a worthy associate in this cause. James Russell Lowell was well launched as the poet of Yankee speech when he was assigned editorial direction in 1857 of the new *Atlantic Monthly,* the organ of the Boston literati

---

[1] J. G. Kohl, *Travels in Canada, and through the States of New York and Pennsylvania* (Mrs. Percy Sinnett, tr., London, 1861), I, 4-6, 36; II, 196-201; Trollope, *North America,* 270, 271. Cf. Higginson, *Atlantic Essays,* 12-13.

[2] Trollope, *North America,* 128, 144; Agénor de Gasparin, *The Uprising of a Great People* (Mary L. Booth, tr., N. Y., 1861), 60-61; Baxter, *America and the Americans,* 84-85.

[3] See Fish, *Rise of the Common Man,* 246-255.

and an exponent of good literature and of reform. The appearance in its pages of Oliver Wendell Holmes's "Autocrat of the Breakfast Table" increased the public admiration for the "Beacon Street wit" and Harvard medical-school professor.

From the shaded lawns of Concord Emerson, America's greatest mystic, continued to leaven the lump of New England Brahmanism. The quiet village had become the Mecca of would-be disciples of all sorts, "devastators of the day," he called them. Cranks and fanatics mingled with sober reformers and men of letters. But Emerson was no mere closet philosopher. In 1855 he contributed an antislavery address to the Tremont Temple series and following the assault on Sumner and the martyrdom of John Brown he publicly declared his sympathy for these dauntless leaders. He joined in the preparation of a memoir of Margaret Fuller Ossoli (1852) and in 1855 urged from the platform that the laws be purged of "every barbarous impediment to women." [1]

Like Emerson, the youthful Thomas Wentworth Higginson saw the salvation of the national literature in the introduction of the American spirit.[2] It was no mere chance that Nathaniel Hawthorne's genius came to bloom in the American setting of his *Scarlet Letter* (1850), followed closely by *The House of the Seven Gables* (1851) and *The Blithedale Romance* (1852). The inspiration for his next great success, *The Marble Faun* (1860), however, came from the beauties of Italy after a decade largely spent abroad in the consular service. Emerson's disciple, Henry D. Thoreau, made a distinct contribution in his *Walden, or Life in the Woods*

[1] O. W. Holmes, *Ralph Waldo Emerson* (Boston, 1885), 209-223.

[2] Higginson, *Atlantic Essays*, 66-67; H. T. Tuckerman, *America and Her Commentators* (N. Y., 1864), 288-289.

(1854) by bringing the great out-of-doors within the range of literary subject matter. Emerson continued to write essays on "Nature," but he had no knowledge and love of beauty such as this apostle of paganism who could live on sunshine and a handful of nuts and dilate for hours on "Autumnal Tints." [1] A few years after Thoreau had sounded this note, a company of New England intellectuals, including Emerson, Lowell, Agassiz and William J. Stillman, the artist, founded the Adirondack Club in the solitude of twenty-two thousand acres purchased at a state tax sale for six hundred dollars. [2] This philosophers' club in the mountain forest had all the brilliant literary Bohemianism of the Radical Club, the Saturday Club and the Atlantic Club of Boston and of the Century Club of New York in which congenial sets of the literati met for mutual inspiration. The complacency of the conservative Saturday Club, however, caused Holmes to complain, "We do nothing but tell our own stories; we never discuss anything." [3]

From the pen of Herman Melville, a writer who stood aloof from the charmed circles of the New England intellectuals, came tales with the tropical glow of the South Seas, and at length, in 1851, his masterpiece, *Moby Dick, or the White Whale*, describing with great power and realism Captain Ahab's demoniacal pursuit

[1] Sallie Holley, *A Life for Liberty* (J. W. Chadwick, ed., N. Y., 1899), 167; Higginson, *Letters and Journals*, 43, 105; F. B. Sanborn, *Henry D. Thoreau* (Boston, 1910), 242-260; W. H. Venable, *Beginnings of Literary Culture in the Ohio Valley* (Cin., 1891), 120.

[2] W. J. Stillman, *The Autobiography of a Journalist* (Boston, 1908), 280-282, 289, 332; Higginson, *Letters and Journals*, 123-124.

[3] T. W. Higginson, *Old Cambridge* (G. E. Woodberry, ed., *National Studies in American Letters*; N. Y., 1899), 104. See also Stillman, *Autobiography*, 224-225, 252, 281; H. D. Stoddard, *Recollections, Personal and Literary* (N. Y., 1903), 217, 241, 260; John Bigelow, *Retrospections of an Active Life* (N. Y., 1909), II, 232 n.; E. W. Emerson, *The Early Years of the Saturday Club, 1855-1870* (Boston, 1918).

of the invincible whale.[1] Kindred in spirit to both Thoreau and Melville was the poet of plain but sturdy American democracy, Walt Whitman. His *Leaves of Grass* appeared in 1855 to the disgust of self-appointed champions of decency. In Middle America, however, these poems found eager and appreciative readers like Abraham Lincoln, at a time when that section was intruding a continental element into the national mind in anticipation of a distinctive American genius.[2]

Transappalachia, indeed, was revealing an amazing if uncertain zeal in literary self-expression. Its political, agricultural and even family journals had from an early day shown marked leanings in that direction. But during the forties special publications with literary interests sprang up in quick succession, Chicago alone witnessing at least one such venture every year. The Western interest was vigorously proclaimed by editors of Yankee origin in successive salutatories and editorial statements. "The GREAT WEST," announced the *Literary Budget* of Chicago on January 7, 1854, "in her undulating prairies, deep-wooded highlands, mighty rivers, and remnants of aboriginal races, presents topics teeming with interest to every reader, and big with beautiful scenes for the artist's eye. The West is full of subject-matter for legend, story, or history."[3] It seemed clear, wrote a poet and compiler of poetry, that the West had

[1] Lewis Mumford, *Herman Melville* (N. Y., 1929). See also his *The Golden Day* (N. Y., 1926).

[2] H. B. Rankin, *Personal Recollections of Abraham Lincoln* (N. Y., 1916), 124-127.

[3] See also *Chicago Gem of the Prairie*, Feb. 26, 1848; Dorothy A. Dondore, *The Prairie and the Making of Middle America* (Cedar Rapids, Iowa, 1926), 194-209, 239-287; W. T. Coggeshall, *Poets and Poetry of the West* (Columbus, 1860); H. E. Fleming, "The Literary Interests of Chicago," *Am. Journ. of Sociology*, XI, 377-408, 499-531, 784-816; XII, 68-118; Venable, *Beginnings of Literary Culture*; R. L. Rusk, *Literature of the Middle Western Frontier* (N. Y., 1925).

"a symphony to utter, whose key-note is already struck, and which is to make the world pause and listen." [1] But that Eastern ties and influence remained was evident in 1860 when Moncure D. Conway, a young native of Virginia, set up in Cincinnati, the oldest literary center in the West, *The Dial: A Monthly Magazine for Literature, Philosophy, and Religion*. This journal frankly aspired "to be an Avatar" of the earlier Boston organ of the same name, a fact which Emerson recognized when he sent a succession of contributions to it.

The "cracker-box philosophers," with their homely sallies about the foibles of the day, also made their contribution to Americanism in literature. Their efforts were characterized by a crudity and exaggeration that sacrificed accurate portraiture to achieve a humorous effect. The average reader of the fifties still enjoyed *The Sayings and Doings of Samuel Slick*, the Yankee clock maker and peddler, or the pungent humor in the *Letters of Major Jack Downing of the Downingsville Militia*. A new crop of American humorists also made their appearance. In 1856 was published *Plu-Ri Bus-Tah, a Song by No Author, Perpetrated by Q. K. Philander Doesticks* (Mortimer Thompson), and in the next year the excellent social satire of William A. Butler, *Nothing to Wear*, a popular humorous poem which was promptly followed by *Nothing to Do, an Accompaniment of Nothing to Wear*. The pretentious ignorance of the garrulous Mrs. Partington who played with words too large for safety added to the general merriment.[2] "Partington Pearls" became the chief stock in trade of the American wit.

But the fun makers who drew the most laughs and

---

[1] Coggeshall, *Poets and Poetry of the West*, cited in Venable, *Beginnings of Literary Culture*, 123.

[2] B. P. Shillaber, *Knitting Work: Web of Many Textures by Ruth Partington* (Boston, 1859).

guffaws were David Ross Locke and Charles Farrar Browne, both Ohio writers and journalists imbued with the Western tradition. The former, as Petroleum Vesuvius Nasby, humble spokesman of the "poor white trash," offered penetrating observations upon the woes of the politicians during the national crisis of the sixties. Browne, for his part, concocted the droll figure of Artemus Ward, that genial and versatile showman whose broad sallies and slender witticisms had even greater success in arousing the risibilities. Like most of their predecessors they resorted to a phonetic spelling which brought their wit and wisdom within the easy appreciation and comprehension of the populace.[1] The contributions of Artemus Ward to *Vanity Fair* did much to insure the success during the early Civil War period of that satirical weekly which represented a distinctly higher level of humor than the *Comic Pictorial* and the other ephemeral publications that preceded it.[2] To the dry wit of the Sam Slick type of Yankee and the broad humor of the black-face minstrel were thus added the naïve comments of the backwoods philosopher. Indeed, the three figures were drawing together to constitute the great trio of American literary comedy.[3]

Next to riotous fun the average American craved hair-

[1] C. F. Browne, *Artemus Ward: His Book* (N. Y., 1862); H. R. Haweis, *American Humorists* (N. Y., 1882); Jennette Tandy, *The Cracker-Box Philosophers in American Humor and Satire* (N. Y., 1925), 132-141. The popular demand for humorous literature even led to the publication in 1864 of a *Cyclopedia of Commercial and Business Anecdotes, Remarkable Traits and Humors, etc.*, by Frazar Kirkland. The favor that greeted cracker-box humor also encouraged more serious effort at satire. In 1853 Nathaniel P. Willis published his *Fun-jottings*. In 1856 George H. Derby brought out his *Phoenixiana* and followed it at the close of the Civil War by *The Squibob Papers*. Even more effective were the sallies at American social conditions by George W. Curtis in "The Potiphar Papers" as published in *Putnam's Mo.* and brought out in book form in 1856.

[2] Anon., "American Comic Journalism," *Round Table*, I, 33 (Feb. 13, 1864); D. C. Seitz, *Artemus Ward* (N. Y., 1919), chap. iv.

[3] Constance Rourke, *American Humor* (N. Y., 1931), 98.

raising thrills. Nor did writer and publisher fail to cater
to this need. Beginning in 1850 the country storekeeper
found it easy to sell cheap paper-bound tales of city
wickedness and of the thwarted attempts of side-
whiskered villains of sartorial perfection to seduce innocent maidens.[1] The earlier success of certain Western
romances suggested another field. A restless literary
swashbuckler named Edward Z. C. Judson set out in
the late forties to retail the products of his own experience and imagination in the pages of a weekly story
paper called *Ned Buntline's Own,* on the theory that
"trash for the masses" instead of art for the critical few
was the secret of literary success. The adventures of his
gallant hero and of other similar worthies were soon
appearing serially in Eastern weeklies, and "Ned Buntline" with an income of twenty thousand a year was
living in ease in New York.[2] In 1860, too, the enterprising publishing house of Erastus F. and Irwin P.
Beadle, following successes with the *Beadle Dime Song
Book* and the *Dime Joke Book,* launched the large-scale
distribution of cheap paper-back novels. Their editor
Orville J. Victor overhauled the manuscripts of varying
merit that poured in and paid fifty dollars or more for
the tales he selected. The flavor of American life, especially of the frontier, was in these thrillers. One of the
most popular was Mrs. Metta V. Victor's *Maum Guinea
and Her Plantation Children,* a pathetic tale of slave life
which Lincoln, Seward and Henry Ward Beecher read
and praised and the English edition of which ran up to

[1] Edmund Pearson, *Queer Books* (N. Y., 1928), 166-181.
[2] Venable, *Beginnings of Literary Culture,* 293-295. Judson had a
notable Civil War career as chief of scouts; he later rambled through
the West with Buffalo Bill and Wild Bill Hickok, whom he then introduced to a rapidly growing circle of admirers. Gilbert Patten, "Dime
Novel Days," *Saturday Eve. Post,* CCIV, 33, 36 (March 7, 1931).

one hundred thousand copies. These tales, selling at a dime, foreshadowed the prolific breed of "dime novels" of later years, being full of second-rate gentility and scrupulous in their observance of the prevailing moral proprieties.[1] In four years five million were put into circulation, including several volumes of biography, largely of frontier heroes.[2]

Meantime the more dignified historic muse took pride in the productive pens of her devotees, largely New Englanders. Richard Hildreth completed in 1856 the *History of the United States* which he had begun in the preceding decade, while George Bancroft after a twelve-year interruption resumed a similar task, the end of which was to prove nearly a quarter-century away. Younger historians impelled by the same patriotic interest also gained recognition. Francis Parkman began his life study of the romance of the colonial frontier, the first fruits of his labors appearing in his *Conspiracy of Pontiac* (1851). In 1858 the initial volume of John G. Palfrey's *History of New England* was published, but failed to prove an immediately profitable venture. When John Lothrop Motley began in 1856 to bring out his *History of the Rise of the Dutch Republic,* he also gained a place among American historians. Meantime the skillful pen of William H. Prescott was depicting the fortunes of *Philip II.* Most of these writers had stylistic distinction that made their work popular. They were part of that galaxy of literary talent that bespoke for the American republic an era of real cultural achievement.

[1] See Nevins, *Emergence of Modern America*, 235-236, and A. M. Schlesinger, *The Rise of the City* (*A History of American Life,* X), 264-265.

[2] Review by William Everett in *N. Am. Rev.*, XCIX (1864), 303-309; Edmund Pearson, *Dime Novels* (Boston, 1929), 50-52; H. M. Robinson, "The Dime Novel," *Century,* CXVI (1928), 62-63. The 1859 song book was published by Irwin P. Beadle.

Every bookstall in Britain, said an English writer, was beginning to groan under "the products of the American mind."[1]

During the fifties, too, new periodicals began to flood the parlor table of the American home. *Harper's New Monthly Magazine* with the varied appeal of its generously illustrated pages achieved a remarkable success and soon had one hundred and seventy thousand subscribers. *Putnam's Magazine* made its appearance in 1853, but Boston lacked a monthly worthy of her literary tradition until the *Atlantic Monthly* was founded four years later. Though some felt there was little demand for a first-class literary periodical, an American publisher found it a profitable venture to reissue various British and even Scotch reviews.[2]

The challenging editorial pens of Henry Ward Beecher and Theodore Tilton gave new popularity to the *Independent* which had been appearing since 1848; with nearly a hundred thousand subscribers it soon became more than a mere religious weekly. In the fifties three pictorial weeklies made their appearance in New York with rather unusual acclaim. The success of Robert Bonner, who acquired the *New York Ledger* in 1851, in building up a constituency of three hundred thousand purchasers of his four-cent weekly was based as much upon his lavish advertising in the newspapers as upon the galaxy of talent that he recruited as contributors.[3] Frank Leslie, transferring his editorial labors from Boston, founded *Leslie's Illustrated Newspaper* in 1855

[1] Baxter, *America and the Americans*, 85.

[2] *N. Y. Herald*, Jan. 7, 1854, Jan. 11, 1859; Edmund Patten, *A Glimpse at the United States* (London, 1853), 103.

[3] See contemporary newspapers esp. *N. Y. Herald*, May 13, 15, 1858; *Ann Arbor Local News*, Jan. 19, 1858; also T. L. Nichols, *Forty Years of American Life* (London, 1864), I, 334. "Fanny Fern," an eccentric strong-minded female, on the one hand, and Edward Everett, appealing for funds to purchase Mount Vernon, were Bonner's great drawing cards.

upon the model of the *London Illustrated News*, but found it profitable also to print lurid crime pictures that anticipated the modern tabloid. *Harper's Weekly*, started two years later, was able to trade upon the widespread popularity of the *Monthly* that had preceded it. More sensational even than *Leslie's* was the *National Police Gazette*, a five-cent illustrated weekly launched in 1845 by the redoubtable George Wilkes, journalist and crusader extraordinary. Making good his promises of "a most interesting record of horrid murders, outrageous robberies, bold forgeries, astounding burglaries, hideous rapes, vulgar seductions," with a skill that won the applause of Greeley and other contemporaries, he turned his lance against his pet aversions—the temperance and blue-law movements, prize fighting and immigrant "shaving"—as well as against the many lurid sins of the underworld. With increasing success the *Gazette* came to have agents in forty towns and cities who popularized its issues with the aid of barber shops and encouraged readers to submit for publication choice morsels of local scandal.[1]

Numerous magazines made their appeal to special groups—to women, to children, to reformers and religionists, to scientists and others. Although there was little net increase during these years, ephemeral ventures succeeded one another in rapid succession. Perhaps most characteristic of the era were the magazines for women, led by *Godey's Lady's Book* which reached the height of its influence under the editorship of Mrs. Sarah J. Hale.[2] Their most recent growth, however, was in the West. Cincinnati as well as Boston had its *Ladies' Repository*, Chicago its *Lady's Western Magazine and Garland of*

[1] Walter Davenport, "The Nickel Shocker," *Collier's*, LXXXI, 26 ff. (March 10, 1928).

[2] Ruth C. Finley, *The Lady of Godey's* (N. Y., 1931). See also Fish, *Rise of the Common Man*, 151, 224.

the Valley, and other communities their *Garlands, Lady's Books, Museums* and *Cabinets.* Strong-minded "editresses" invited their sex to learn of life's proprieties and to contribute fireside gleanings of a literary flavor. As a result "impeccable ladies, trained by the long line of periodicals addressed to them, stood complacently ready to assume the literary dictatorship of the country." [1]

More widely read than magazines, however, were the newspapers. The press was "a vast engine of national education, not over-delicate in its machinery, but still working out its object." [2] The three thousand and more journals of 1860, doubling the figure of 1850, evidenced a decade of extraordinary political agitation. Editorial giants—Greeley of the *New York Tribune,* James Gordon Bennett of the *Herald,* Henry J. Raymond of the *Times,* Samuel Bowles of the *Springfield Republican*— and their younger Western confrères, Joseph Medill of the *Chicago Tribune* and Murat Halstead of the *Cincinnati Commercial,* undertook to guide an excited electorate through the labyrinths of the sectional controversy. A galaxy of special correspondents reported the latest developments at the national capital and at times distinguished editors appeared in person to observe the proceedings of Congress. Journalism was rapidly enlarging its functions. [3] An elaborate organization of reporters, special correspondents, telegraphic news, steam-power

[1] Bertha M. Stearns, "Early Western Magazines for Ladies," *Miss. Valley Hist. Rev.,* XVIII, 319-330. See also her "Reform Periodicals and Female Reformers, 1830-1860," *Am. Hist. Rev.,* XXXIV, 678-699.

[2] Edward Dicey, *Six Months in the Federal States* (London, 1863), I, 50. See also same work, I, 27-40; Adolf Douai, *Land und Leute in der Union* (Berlin, 1864), 234-236; Baxter, *America and the Americans,* 81-84; D. W. Mitchell, *Ten Years Residence in the United States* (London, 1862), 27-29, 211; *National Intelligencer* (Wash.), Sept. 15, 1858, July 30, 1860; *N. Y. Tribune,* Feb. 9, 1860; *N. Y. Herald,* April 24, 1861.

[3] W. G. Bleyer, *Main Currents in the History of American Journalism* (Boston, 1927), chaps. vii-x.

presses and ubiquitous newsboys served papers like the *Herald* and the *Tribune* as they purveyed the news garnered from the highways and byways of the world. These two journals came to have a circulation larger than that of all the dailies published below the Potomac. The tremendous daily circulation of the *Herald* centered in New York and the great cities of the East; the one hundred and seventy-six thousand copies of the weekly *Tribune* furnished gospel for untold thousands of homes in the North and West.

Other characteristics of modern journalism also made their appearance. Private affairs occupied an increasingly large part in the public prints; detailed publication of court proceedings whetted the public appetite for sensational news. In the spring of 1850 editors and readers alike reveled in the mystery and sentimentalities of the trial of Professor John W. Webster, a Harvard chemistry instructor who murdered and disposed of the body of his wealthy friend, Dr. George Parkman, while two years later the press retailed the crimination and recrimination of husband and wife in the Forrest divorce case. In 1859 Daniel E. Sickles, member of Congress from New York, was placed on trial for the murder of a United States district attorney who had seduced his wife. Column after column of the testimony was published in papers all over the country before the defendant was acquitted. Shortly after the election of 1860 the celebrated Burch divorce case occupied an amount of newspaper space limited only by the excitement of the sectional crisis. In all these cases reiterated headings and italic emphasis featured the write-ups; soon a modest type of display headline was utilized in the *Times* as even more effective in contrast.[1]

---

[1] N. A. Woods, *The Prince of Wales in Canada and the United States* (London, 1861), 390; Caroline H. Dall, *The College, the Market, and*

The accounts of sensational happenings usually went out by telegraph, and editors who had scruples about printing such news were often too thrifty to consign to the wastebasket items which many readers craved. In general, news by wire was still a novelty and a source of considerable expense. Brief dispatches were usually packed into a heterogeneous column under some such heading as "Latest by Telegraph," "Morseographic," or "Latest Streak by Lightning." Many regretted, however, that Morse's invention was the medium for so many false reports.[1] Probably a new record in telegraphic news —and newspaper expense—was made by the correspondents of the metropolitan dailies who in 1860 accompanied the Prince of Wales on his American tour.[2] The telegraph also made possible the beginnings of systematic weather forecasting when in 1858, upon the basis of newly developed meteorological principles, Joseph Henry, secretary of the Smithsonian Institution, began to collect and map telegraphic weather records.

More commendable than the popular taste in newspapers was the growing interest in good music. A significant contribution came from the German immigrants, hundreds of whom made a living by giving musical instruction at a dollar a lesson, although they did not always regard this humble rôle as much superior to that of the Italian organ grinder. As the popularity of the piano grew, a number of piano manufacturers of German birth, including Henry Steinway of New York and William Knabe of Baltimore, founded their establishments. The fruits of these labors were summed up in the

the Court (Boston, 1867), 81; Harper's Mo., IV (1852), 563; N. Y. Herald, July 13, 1858; Savannah Republican, April 18, 19, 23, 1859.

[1] Nashville Republican Banner, Sept. 19, 1851; Sumner to Bigelow, Aug., 1852, Bigelow, Retrospections of an Active Life, I, 126.

[2] S. R. Fiske, "Gentlemen of the Press," Harper's Mo., XXVI (1863), 366; [Catherine C. Hopley], Life in the South (London, 1863), I, 137.

proud boast of a Yankee exile in England: "Music is more cultivated in America than in any country in the world except Germany. . . . There are ten piano fortes in every American town or village to every one in England." [1] Under the same stimulus vocal and instrumental music progressed.[2] The older orchestras began to fill up with German performers. New organizations like the Mendelssohn Quintette Club of Boston came to have a wide vogue.[3] In 1855 William Mason and Theodore Thomas formed the Mason-Thomas string quartette to give chamber concerts in New York City. Ole Bull, the noted Norwegian violinist, was one of the few instrumental artists of the first order to tour the country in this period.

Opera at length became a regular feature of the social season in New York, Boston, Philadelphia, New Orleans, Chicago and even San Francisco. In 1850 a troupe brought from Havana by Señor Marty set a new standard for operatic production in New York City. Rival companies headed by Madame Marietta Alboni and Madame Henrietta Sontag were soon vying for public favor.[4] Italian opera had the greatest vogue, but English companies introduced such entertainment to less fashionable audiences in the vernacular. Chicago had an

[1] Nichols, *Forty Years of American Life,* II, 396; Thomas Ryan, *Reminiscences of an Old Musician* (N. Y., 1899), 131. *Cf.,* however, Charles Mackay, *Life and Liberty in America* (N. Y., 1859), II, 145; *Atlantische Studien,* I (1853), 95-97.

[2] See Fish, *Rise of the Common Man,* plate viii, c., and J. T. Howard, *Our American Music* (N. Y., 1931), 216-231.

[3] Ryan, *Reminiscences,* 92, 103, 162, 167; *Boston Eve. Transcript,* Feb. 14, 1855.

[4] Alfred Bunn, *Old England and New England, in a Series of Views Taken on the Spot* (Phila., 1853), 201. Some of the public doubtless agreed with the New York wag who declared:

> The only difference, no doubt
> Twixt Sontag and Alboni
> Is that the one eats sauerkraut
> The other macaroni.

opera war in the season of 1859-1860 between an English troupe and an Italian company. Even American talent began tentatively to invade this difficult musical field. In 1855 Elsie Hensler, a native Bostonian who had won notable successes in Italy, made her début in New York as a prima donna. In the spring of 1856 the Italian composer Luigi Arditi brought out "La Spia" based upon Cooper's novel, while two years later "Leonora," the work of an American composer William H. Fry, was presented with fair success at the Academy of Music.[1]

Music for the millions and opera houses with five thousand seats became slogans of the day. Boston acquired a new music hall early in the decade; Philadelphia citizens were soon subscribing to a new $220,000 opera house; while Brooklyn formally opened an Academy of Music in 1861 with a performance of Italian opera. Not to be outdone, Chicago achieved a great structure that combined an opera house, art gallery and studio building. Nor did the American producer stint the payment of his artists; monthly salaries of from four hundred to a thousand dollars exceeded the level of the European market. With such heavy expenses ventures were not uniformly successful, although the New York season of seventy-odd performances that followed the Panic of 1857 netted a handsome profit.[2] Box-office receipts of over $2000 were common while Grisi and

[1] Luigi Arditi, *My Reminiscences* (London, 1896), 32; Mackay, *Life and Liberty in America*, II, 147; Hiram Fuller, *Belle Brittan on a Tour at Newport, and Here and There* (N. Y., 1858), 293-294. The so-called "colored opera," which during the fifties met with widespread popularity in Boston, New York and interior cities, seems to have combined with the talents of Negro singers a considerable "budget of whimsicalities and heel and toe exercises." See C. E. Russell, *The American Orchestra and Theodore Thomas* (N. Y., 1927), 21, 23; *N. Y. Herald*, Oct. 12, 1855, Feb. 10, 1858.

[2] *N. Y. Herald*, April 2, 1858; Fuller, *Belle Brittan on a Tour*, 293.

Mario in the opera "Norma" drew a house at $4225 at Boston on January 23, 1855.[1]

After the opera season in New York and adjacent cities had closed the artists usually went about the country on concert tour. The way had been paved for them by the American visit of Jenny Lind, who came heralded by that master showman P. T. Barnum as "the Swedish nightingale," "the second Santa Caecilia," "the angel of the stage." The remodeled interior of Castle Garden, with accommodations for over six thousand, proved inadequate for her first concert on September 14, 1850. In the twenty months that followed, the largest halls from Boston to New Orleans and from Charleston to St. Louis failed to provide space for the millions who flocked to see as well as to hear the celebrity.[2] The years that ensued held generous welcome for Alboni, Sontag and other capable artists who, with less of ballyhoo, went on tour through the country. The child prodigy, Adelina Patti, was a general favorite from New York to California.

Numerous companies of black-face minstrels traveled out of Boston and other centers to offer entertainment to less exacting music lovers.[3] The sad sweet music of Stephen C. Foster's songs captivated the audiences that assembled to hear Christy's Minstrels, or Wood's, or others of the troupes that went on tour. Foster made arrangements to furnish Christy with his compositions

[1] Eugene Tompkins, *History of the Boston Theatre, from 1854 to 1901* (Boston, 1908), 34.

[2] P. T. Barnum, *Struggles and Triumphs* (N. Y., 1871), chaps. xvii-xxii; J. T. Trowbridge, *My Own Story* (Boston, 1903), 162, 164, 166.

[3] William Davidge, *Footlight Flashes* (N. Y., 1866), 127; Elizabeth C. Stanton, *Elizabeth Cady Stanton as Revealed in Her Letters, Diary and Reminiscences* (Theodore Stanton and Harriot S. Blatch, eds., N. Y., 1922), II, 31; Fuller, *Belle Brittan on a Tour*, 333-336; Carl Wittke, *Tambo and Bones* (Durham, 1930), chap. iii.

in advance of publication. He soon scored such successes as "Massa's in de Cold, Cold Ground," "My Old Kentucky Home" and "Old Dog Tray." One hundred and twenty-five thousand copies of the last sold within a few months.[1] In due time an even greater popular vogue greeted "Dixie" when on short notice words were set to the tune in 1859 by Daniel D. Emmett as a hooray "walk-around" song for Bryant's minstrels.[2]

Less progress was made in the development of a native drama of enduring merit. The uncertain financial returns of the American playwright at a time when his rights of authorship were without adequate copyright protection may have tended to discourage productivity. In December, 1853, "The Gladiator," one of the three or four romantic tragedies which Dr. R. M. Bird had written for the histrionic talents of his friend Edwin Forrest, was given its thousandth performance; yet for it the able author received only two thousand dollars.[3] Whatever the reward, plays of ephemeral appeal, written by Americans, appeared in great profusion. The historical drama, especially patriotic tales of the Revolution and of the War of 1812, still had a certain vogue, while the Mexican War, the Mormon migration and the settlement of California furnished fresh themes for similar treatment.

[1] Bunn, *Old England and New England*, 212.

[2] The music of this pulsating air was derived apparently from an old English ditty which had been taken up in the South, first by Negro roustabouts who sang as they loaded and unloaded the steamboats on the Mississippi levee. A Southern version, similar to Emmett's, seems to have appeared in 1858 from the pen of W. S. Hayes, clerk in a Louisville music store, which promptly issued the song and sold thousands of copies in the South before the outbreak of the Civil War. C. B. Galbreath, *Daniel Decatur Emmett, Author of "Dixie"* (Columbus, 1904). *Cf.* T. J. Firth, "Who Was the Author of Dixie? That Honor Belongs to a Southern Man—His Name Was Will S. Hayes," Memphis Chamber of Commerce, *Journ.*, VII (1924), 31-36, 40.

[3] A. H. Quinn, *A History of the American Drama from the Beginning to the Civil War* (N. Y., 1923), 244-245.

The taboo upon the slavery question in respectable circles was suddenly dispelled in 1852 by Harriet Beecher Stowe's *Uncle Tom's Cabin,* dramatic versions of which, heralded by sensational headings of theatrical placards, threatened to monopolize the stage in the North. For night after night and week after week it held the boards in the cities, while companies toured the provinces with tents capable of seating as many as five thousand spectators. In the closing years of the decade the temperance play, "Ten Nights in a Bar-Room," adapted from T. S. Arthur's book of the same title, began a long career. Greeley must have discounted these two pieces when he asserted that the stage, the traditional ally of liberty and humanity, had failed to support the antislavery cause and the temperance movement.[1] Indeed, the injection of moral purpose into histrionic performances helped break down the ancient prejudice against the stage. When a Hartford judge in 1852 refused a permit for theatrical presentations on the ground that they were dangerous to morality, several newspapers spoke out in protest. Even the church took a more tolerant attitude toward the drama. A prominent clergyman actually proposed a Christian theater for the production of the right type of plays, although a critic suggested that this was like a proposal to establish a "holy Hell." [2]

Besides "Uncle Tom's Cabin," other plays dealing with slavery scored successes, notably J. T. Trowbridge's "Neighbor Jackwood," a fugitive-slave tale which held the Boston stage for eight years, and, especially, "The Octoroon" (1859), one of a number of

[1] Horace Greeley, *Recollections of a Busy Life* (N. Y., 1868), 205-206.

[2] *Atlantische Studien,* I (1853), 136; *N. Y. Herald,* March 2, 1853, July 8, 1858; edit., *Harper's Mo.,* XXVI (1863), 564. See also Reverend F. Wilson, *Popular Amusements, or How Far May a Christian Indulge in Popular Amusements* (Charleston, 1856), 30-38.

popular dramas from the pen of Dion Boucicault, a young playwright of Irish birth who in 1853 with his actress wife, Agnes Robertson, cast his lot with the American stage. Boucicault aided in the movement which secured more adequate protection to dramatists in the copyright law of August 18, 1856.

Various versions of the stage Yankee with his whimsicalities and verbal oddities continued to furnish inspiration for obscure writers and provide rôles for actors like Joshua H. ("Yankee") Silsbee who in 1850 presented the character Jonathan before London audiences on over a hundred consecutive nights. Another conspicuous success was "Our American Cousin" which ran more than sixty performances at Philadelphia in the season of 1858-1859. In 1859 the third Joseph Jefferson made up his own version and created the title rôle of "Rip Van Winkle," already a popular and well-established theme upon the American stage. Another contribution to a distinctively native school of play-wrighting came with the comedy of life in a large city, new versions of which appeared with great popularity. The combat-loving volunteer fireman, the swaggering Bowery "B'hoy," the pathetic seamstress of New York, the parvenu grand dame and the proud heiress of Broad Street (who duly became the "fireman's bride") were among the characters presented with varying degrees of pathos and humor.[1] Scathing criticism of the selfishness of fashionable society, a popular theme in a democratic country, was set forth in such pieces as Mrs. Bateman's "Self."

New York had, besides other places of amusement, eight regular theaters with a total capacity of nearly fifteen thousand seats, the Broadway Theater being unique in its location upon the street that was destined

[1] Quinn, *History of American Drama*, 294-336.

to become the "Great White Way." "The surest barometer of public prosperity is the state of public amusements," declared the *New York Herald* of October 9, 1855, comparing the poor season of the preceding winter with theatrical receipts of nearly ten thousand dollars for a single night. Every sizable city had one or more theaters, although many New England communities were content to limit entertainment to lectures and concerts. Even in the Western wilds provision was made for the drama. As has been said, the Mormons, recognizing the stage as the ally of the tabernacle, erected a theater that was a triumph of art and enterprise. San Francisco attracted to its large and handsome playhouses some of the brightest musical and dramatic luminaries of the age. Soon every successful mining town had a theater, if only an unplastered room above a saloon like that which Denver in 1860 called the "Apollo Theatre."

At a time when the "star" system prevailed and when native talent was still likely to be neglected for visiting English celebrities,[1] Edwin and John Wilkes Booth, the two handsome American-born sons of Junius Brutus Booth, came to share the fame of their father and of Edwin Forrest as portrayers of the tragic muse. Henry Placide, the American comedian, won his greatest triumphs during this period, while Charlotte Cushman in her classic rôles of Lady Macbeth and Meg Merrilies continued to be the idol of the serious-minded playgoer. Laura Keene also had her admirers and soon had a New York theater bearing her name, sharing this distinction with James W. Wallack and William C. Burton.[2]

The terpsichorean art also developed a following—its critics suggested, among "blacklegs, men about town,

---

[1] Nichols, *Forty Years of American Life*, II, 396.
[2] Brander Matthews and Laurence Hutton, eds., *Actors and Actresses of Great Britain and the United States* (N. Y., 1886), 57-76, 221-223.

worn-out roués." [1] The ballet made its appearance, featuring Lola Montez, the Spanish dancer, whose arrival was preceded by tales of lurid adventure in the courts of Europe. An ingenious producer soon brought out a "Mormon extravaganza"; it was a trashy affair but tremendous houses were attracted by "the short petticoats of Brigham's harem." [2] Next, reviving a popular entertainment of the late forties, came a production called "Model Artistes" in which a company of young women, "sans both petticoats and pants" but clad in the inevitable tights, offered Biblical and classical *tableaux vivants* and

> Did nightly crowds delight
> By showing up their handsome limbs
> At fifty cents a sight. [3]

Soon, despite an occasional police raid, the burlesque "fury" raged in nearly every Bowery establishment. [4] Even the two theaters of Chicago had their performers in tights and short garments, endeavoring to rival the graceful evolutions of the well-remembered Elssler. [5]

Smaller communities without regular theaters contented themselves with Shakespearean readings, with amateur entertainment, or with the efforts of roving performers. The choice of entertainers included "Yankee" Silsbee, Winchell the humorist, Antonio Kaspar, the magician and juggler, "The Faker of Siva" with his *soirées mysterieuses*, and their kind. The amazing exhibitions of John S. Rarey, the famous horse tamer who had conquered the notoriously vicious English thoroughbred Cruiser, became the wonder of Europe and

---

[1] Edit., *Harper's Mo.*, VI (1853), 559.
[2] Fuller, *Belle Brittan on a Tour*, 310.
[3] Seats on the stage were $3.00. *N. Y. Herald*, Jan. 1, 1859.
[4] *N. Y. Tribune*, July 3, 1860.
[5] See Fish, *Rise of the Common Man*, 146.

America alike. At times, too, collections of curiosities and monstrosities, best known of all, the exhibits of Barnum headed by the redoubtable General Tom Thumb, were sent to the provinces for display.

Popular interest in the stage reflected a craving for entertainment rather than an enjoyment of artistic form. All indications pointed to a slow development of an appreciation of art for its own sake. Art stores in New York existed for the sale of mirrors and gold frames, or of steel engravings, lithographs and cheap oil paintings, in standard sizes turned out wholesale under factory conditions.[1] The firm of Currier and Ives sold untold thousands of colored lithographs of race horses, clipper ships, locomotives and other aspects of the American scene. Little did their owners think that they would be dug from storeroom and attic to serve a twentieth-century vogue![2] More pretentious were the huge rolls of painted canvas that were exhibited throughout the country—the "Panorama of Eden," the "Classical Panorama of Roman History," a "Panorama of China," the "Sacred Panorama of Pilgrim's Progress," the "Panorama of the Mississippi River," the "Moving Mirror of the Overland Route to California." Ball's "Pictorial Tour of the United States," an antislavery work, depicted in twenty-three thousand feet of canvas the scenic beauties of the country and the woes of slavery. At the same time the "instantaneous" photographic art of the fifties found a skilled exponent of the new wet-plate process in Mathew B. Brady, a former master of the daguerreotype. At his New York studios and the

[1] See comments in Douai, *Land und Leute*, 239; Theodor Griesinger, *Lebende Bilder aus Amerika* (Stuttgart, 1858), 179-189; *Atlantische Studien*, I (1853), 106-109.

[2] W. A. Weaver, *Lithographs of N. Currier and Currier & Ives* (N. Y., 1925-1926); Russel Crouse, *Mr. Currier and Mr. Ives: A Note on Their Lives and Times* (N. Y., 1931).

Washington branch established in 1858, the most eminent Americans of the day sat for their likenesses. In spite of the increasing market for photography portrait painting, under German and French influence, also prospered. Itinerant artists, often German immigrants, found employment in painting local celebrities, decorating the paddle boxes or the cabins of Mississippi steamers and, at times, in nothing more inspiring than sign painting.

At a higher level the budding genius of American artists sought the stimulus and instruction of the Düsseldorf masters. Throughout the period the Düsseldorf gallery in New York made important contributions to the improvement of the public taste.[1] In 1851 Emanuel Leutze, the foremost local representative of the school, painted his "Washington Crossing the Delaware." Albert Bierstadt, another German expatriate, found inspiration in the Far West for a series of mountain pictures, often on large canvases, thus leading to what has been called the grandiose school of American painting. Meantime Asher B. Durand, J. F. Kensett, and William and James McDougal Hart of the "Hudson River School," inspired by a simple love of nature, continued to reflect the growing spirit of American nationalism in colorful reproductions of scenic beauties. Jasper F. Cropsey, a brilliant young landscape painter who entered the National Academy in 1851 at the age of twenty-six, but who for the six years after 1857 lived largely in London, was soon well known on both sides of the Atlantic for his exquisite "Autumn on the Hudson."[2]

[1] C. H. Caffin, *The Story of American Painting* (N. Y., 1907), 81, 103-117; Eugen Neuhaus, *The History and Ideals of American Art* (Stanford, 1931), 82-84, 137-144; *Round Table*, I, 169 (Feb. 27, 1864). For the "Hudson River School," see Fish, *Rise of the Common Man*, 232.

[2] Woods, *Prince of Wales in the United States*, 406; Clara E. Clement

About 1860 the Barbizon or Fontainebleau school of French art began to attract American artists.

To some foreign critics, however, the artistic genius of America was better revealed in sculpture.[1] This field was sufficiently popular to induce the actress Charlotte Cushman to head a little clique of American women sculptors at Rome who aspired to challenge the supremacy of the male artist; Harriet Hosmer was the ablest of this group.[2] But in a day when William Page's notable portrait of "Venus" had to be given a special exclusive showing to the gentler sex, there was little to encourage the free expression of the sculptor's art.[3] William W. Story and Randolph Rogers carried on the classic traditions of Powers and Greenough but, like their contemporary William Rinehart, spent most of their time abroad.[4]

If the American nation had become by 1860, as some friendly foreign visitors admitted, "the most generally educated and intelligent people on the earth," [5] this was due not only to the operation of the rapidly expanding public-school system but also to the less formal intellectual and cultural influences that ramified in almost every direction. Carl Schurz ascribed the high average of intelligence in large part to the fact that "the individual is constantly brought into interested contact with a greater variety of things, and is admitted to active participation in the exercise of functions which in

and Laurence Hutton, *Artists of the Nineteenth Century and Their Works* (Boston, 1879), I, 173.

[1] Fredrika Bremer, *America of the Fifties* (A. B. Benson, ed., N. Y., 1924), 255; Mackay, *Life and Liberty in America*, II, 142.

[2] Stillman, *Autobiography*, 359. See also Lorado Taft, *The History of American Sculpture* (J. C. Van Dyke, ed., *The History of American Art*, I, N. Y., 1903), 204-211.

[3] *Baltimore Sun*, Jan. 20, 1860.

[4] H. N. Fowler, *A History of Sculpture* (N. Y., 1923), 389-392.

[5] Bishop Fraser, cited in Adams, *Free School System of the United States*, 238.

other countries are left to the care of a superior authority." [1]

Less reassuring was the circumstance that the cultural advance of these years was sectional in character. For the most part the South, hampered by its caste system, its undigested mass of poor whites and enslaved blacks, its growing antagonism to the free states, remained unaffected by the new currents of civilization. It did not share in the movement for popular education; it took a negligible part in the lyceum movement; it supported few magazines or publishing houses; it had little of a creative nature to contribute to science, scholarship, letters and the arts. More and more it lived to itself, closed in by tradition and by loyalty to a social institution which it alone in all the civilized world maintained and defended. The widening breach between the sections thus reached beyond political acerbities into the very substance of life itself.

[1] Schurz, *Reminiscences*, II, 79.

CHAPTER X

THE CHALLENGE TO THE CHURCH

THE American church of the fifties enjoyed its greatest development in the upper Mississippi Valley where it represented one of the refinements that followed in the wake of the frontier. In the flush times of this decade one thousand church edifices were built annually, most of them simple frame structures. Many congregations were still without provision for regular preaching, but the humble, zealous itinerant preacher, pioneer in the work of evangelizing the raw West, reached a large scattered constituency by "riding circuit." The quaintly heroic Peter Cartwright was at the age of seventy still duplicating upon the Illinois prairie some of the feats of his prime. On one occasion he rode ninety-four miles through almost incessant rain, preached to several congregations, and received as quarterage fifteen cents and, by way of table expenses, a dozen apples.[1]

The large field for missionary work in the Middle West was recognized by all religious denominations, most of which maintained formally accredited representatives in the field. The American Home Missions Society and the American Missionary Association also sent out agents,[2] though supporting them so meagerly that they had need of all their Christian fortitude. Such missionaries worked almost entirely in communities of

[1] A. C. Cole, *The Era of the Civil War* (C. W. Alvord, ed., *The Centennial History of Illinois*, Springfield, 1918-1920, III), 249; Peter Cartwright, *Autobiography* (W. P. Strickland, ed., N. Y., 1857), 470 ff.

[2] Lewis Tappan, *History of the American Missionary Association* (N. Y,. 1855).

fair size and left the rural regions virtually untouched. The remoter areas were reached by agents of the American Bible Society and by *colporteurs* sent out by the American Tract Society. The latter attempted a somewhat more intimate religious contact with the people, making what were in many cases virtually pastoral visits with religious exhortation and prayer.

In the process of providing specially trained religious leaders, the denominational college and the theological seminary came into their own. As has been shown, such institutions sprang up on every hand, especially in the West. Within five years Chicago and its vicinity secured five new ones. Northwestern University and the Northwestern Biblical Institute were inaugurated by the Methodists, the University of Chicago by the Baptists, the Chicago Theological Seminary by the Congregationalists, and McCormick Theological Seminary by the Presbyterians. Soon attendance richly justified these pious enterprises. In 1860 four Presbyterian seminaries averaged well over one hundred students each, while the infant institution at Chicago had an enrollment of eighteen.[1]

Nearly all denominations expanded in membership, at the same time meeting rivalry in a proliferation of minor sects. In the country at large the Methodists stood in the lead although Methodism in the West seemed to suffer from neglect by the central organization. After a decade of controversy which caused their leaders to be expelled from the fold, the Free Methodist Church was organized in 1860 out of a group of western New York dissenters known as "Nazarites." Meanwhile, in 1858, two reform elements among the Presbyterians effected a union

---

[1] *Baltimore Sun,* Feb. 24, 1860. A contemporary estimate listed 747 educated ministers in the South and 10,702 in the North. D. W. Mitchell, *Ten Years Residence in the United States* (London, 1862), 211, 212.

which produced the United Presbyterian Church. The Baptist churches continued to display a strong frontier influence, while the Disciples of Christ, even more typical of the pioneer spirit in religion, experienced steady growth.[1] Renewed enthusiasm was inspired by the Western tour in 1853 of the Reverend Alexander Campbell, founder of the denomination. By the end of the Civil War the membership of this denomination approached the half-million mark.

German and Scandinavian immigration into Middle America hastened the growth of Lutheranism in northern Illinois and in Wisconsin, Iowa and Minnesota. The German settlers replaced the losses in the East of their countrymen who had dropped away, while the Scandinavians formed congregations and, in due time, synods of their own. In 1853 the Norwegian Evangelical Church of America was organized by representatives of Wisconsin congregations; seven years later the Scandinavians of northern Illinois withdrew from the northern Illinois synod of the Lutheran Church and formed the Scandinavian Augustana Synod.[2]

The extensive migrations of the New England element brought large numbers of Congregationalists into the West. The first general convention of American Congregationalism, held in Albany, October, 1852, formally declared at an end the old "Plan of Union" with the Presbyterians and called for fifty thousand dollars for the erection of new churches in the states west of Ohio.[3]

[1] Robert Richardson, *Memoirs of Alexander J. Campbell* (Phila., 1870), II, 601-602; W. W. Jennings, *Origin and Early History of the Disciples of Christ* (Cin., 1919), 325.

[2] J. L. Neve, *A Brief History of the Lutheran Church in America* (Burlington, Iowa, 1916), 388-391, 437-438; J. M. Rohne, *Norwegian American Lutheranism up to 1872* (N. Y., 1926), 136-179; G. M. Stephenson, *The Religious Aspects of Swedish Immigration* (Minneapolis, 1932), chap. xiii.

[3] Williston Walker, *A History of the Congregational Churches in the United States* (Philip Schaff and others, eds., *The American Church*

Congregations under their own name began to increase rapidly, especially in the "Yankee" belt along the lower Great Lakes.[1] Already in April, 1851, a Congregational church had been organized in Chicago when the repudiated antislavery members of the Third Presbyterian Church, most of whom had New England Congregationalist antecedents, set up for themselves. Two other congregations established places of worship in the city during the decade.[2] The Middle West also helped train one of the most influential Congregational ministers of the East. Young Henry Ward Beecher, fresh from Indiana where his triumphant revivalism had led to a call to Plymouth Church, captivated his sedate Brooklyn congregation by his oratory and received a salary that rapidly mounted to $5000 and, later, to $12,500. Beecher was soon a collector of paintings, bronzes, books and precious stones, and lived in an atmosphere of refulgence, if not extravagance. Every seat in his immense church was usually occupied; pew rentals went at a premium at the annual auction. High-salaried preachers, high pew rentals, paid singers and expensive organs made stern moralists wonder whether the worship of Mammon had not crept into organized Christianity.[3]

The Episcopal Church had its stronghold in the East; the West was less hospitable to its ritualism and elaborate ceremonial. When Bishop Henry J. Whitehouse succeeded the popular pioneer Bishop Philander Chase of Illinois in 1852, a heated controversy soon waged

History Series, N. Y., 1893-1897, III), 382-383; A. E. Dunning, Congregationalists in America (N. Y., 1894), 337.

[1] Dunning, Congregationalists in America, 423 ff.; T. O. Douglass, The Pilgrims of Iowa (Boston, 1911), 143-144; Warren Upham, ed., Congregational Work of Minnesota, 1832-1890 (Minneapolis, 1921), 47-51.

[2] Cole, Era of the Civil War, 247.

[3] N. Y. Herald, May 18, June 30, 1858; Georges Fisch, Nine Months in the United States during the Crisis (London, 1863), 55.

between the new bishop and low-church critics who attacked him as teaching "Tractarian and Semi Romish Errors." [1] In 1858 the low-church party set up an organ in Chicago, the *Western Churchman,* to combat the influence of the official publication, the *Chicago Herald.*

The fifties also saw much Sunday-school activity. Every denomination undertook to add to its own schools. The Congregational Church formed a western Sabbath School agency in 1853 and sent a number of agents into the West.[2] The American Sunday School Union had in its service hundreds of missionaries attached to various denominations.

The Roman Catholic Church grew lustily in the larger cities, mainly from recruits of Irish and other immigrants. In cities as diverse as New York and Cincinnati from a third to a half of the population were Catholics. Particular efforts were made to insure religious provision for the Middle West. Certain leaders, including Archbishop Hughes of New York, hoped that Catholic colonization beyond the Appalachians might save the poor and degraded Irish from the grog shops and squalor of Eastern cities and, at the same time, strengthen Mother Rome. Meantime the Jesuits and other representatives of the Propaganda undertook an active educational campaign through their rapidly increasing colleges, seminaries and female academies. These

[1] Laura C. Smith, *Life of Philander Chase* (N. Y., 1903), 339-340; *Aurora Beacon,* Oct. 25, 1860; *Church Record,* Jan. 1, Sept. 15, Oct. 1, 1859, Aug. 15, Nov. 1, 1860.

[2] Marianna C. Brown, *Sunday School Movements in America* (N. Y., 1901), 45-58, 118 ff.; E. W. Rice, *The Sunday School Movement, 1780-1917, and the American Sunday School Union, 1817-1917* (Phila., 1917); J. W. Alexander, *The American Sunday School and Its Adjuncts* (Phila., 1856); Addie G. Wardle, *History of the Sunday School Movement in the Methodist Episcopal Church* (N. Y., 1918), 84; William Rey, *L'Amérique Protestante* (Paris, 1857), 104-107; Agénor de Gasparin, *The Uprising of a Great People* (Mary L. Booth, tr., N. Y., 1861), 60; Fisch, *Nine Months in the United States,* 81.

were in many ways in the vanguard of female education, a fact which, together with the low cost, led many Protestant families to send their daughters to them.[1]

But this great church did not enjoy an altogether peaceful growth. Protestant forces, anxious to convert Catholics to their own groups, organized in 1849 the American and Foreign Christian Union and immediately inaugurated an active campaign. In 1853 Monsignor Bedini, nuncio of the pope, visited the United States to settle a dispute between a church at Buffalo and the bishop of the diocese. Having upheld the claims of the hierarchy, he traveled about the country visiting the episcopal sees in the silken purple robes of his office. During the first part of his tour he was received with much *éclat,* but later, when Italian and German revolutionary exiles proclaimed his part in the ruthless suppression of the revolution in Bologna, street demonstrations burned him in effigy and denounced papal authority. Other bold critics appeared, who, having renounced their Catholic faith and allegiance, now lashed the pope, the church and all its works. In 1851 and 1852 Lahey, "the monk of Latrappe," went about exposing the alleged evils of the confessional, while a year later Alessandro Gavazzi, an Italian ex-priest and revolutionary exile, with the applause of Protestant clergymen conducted stormy meetings in his purpose "to destroy the Pope." [2] Toward the end of the decade Father Chiniquy after a long and bitter contest with the bishop of Chicago led his congregation out of the Church and soon became an active and noted anti-Catholic.[3]

[1] Fredrika Bremer, *America of the Fifties* (A. B. Benson, ed., N. Y., 1924), 191-192; J. R. Beste, *The Wabash* (London, 1855), II, 99, 222, 332; *Ohio State Journal* (Columbus), May 16, 1856; Sister Monica, *The Cross in the Wilderness* (N. Y., 1930).

[2] *N. Y. Tribune,* March 21, 30, 31, 1853; J. B. McMaster, *A History of the People of the United States* (N. Y., 1883-1913), VIII, 78-81.

[3] Cole, *Era of the Civil War,* 17; Charles Chiniquy, *Fifty Years in*

The anti-Catholic crusade was carried to the public highway when the street preacher took up the attack. One of the most picturesque of these figures was John S. Orr—the "Angel Gabriel" he announced himself as he summoned his audience with the blasts of his trumpet. Great crowds turned out to hear him on the streets of New York and Brooklyn and of various Massachusetts towns. Unless the police were out in force, his preaching was the almost inevitable occasion for a pitched battle between Irish defenders of the faith and the "Angel's" forces with bricks, paving stones, clubs, fists and even revolvers as weapons.[1] Soon, however, these were episodes in the larger clash between the organized nativists and their opponents.[2]

Religious liberalism was the exception rather than the rule. The Universalists established a successful publication, the *New Covenant*, at Chicago in 1848 and increased their Illinois churches from seven to thirty during the fifties, while the Unitarians grew from four to eleven. But Horace Mann, founding Antioch College as "the only [Western] institution of a first class character which is not directly or indirectly under the influence of the old school theology," was appalled to find only one Unitarian society in a state of two million people.[3] That there were limits to theological liberalism also in the East was evident when Professor Alpheus Crosby of Dartmouth lost his position because of a pungent letter to the American Tract Society denying the eternity of future punishment.[4] When in 1858 a

the Church of Rome (N. Y., 1886), 668-669. See also his *Forty Years in the Church of Christ* (N. Y., 1899).

[1] *N. Y. Herald*, April 24, 1854; *N. Y. Tribune*, June 13, 1854.

[2] See earlier, 142-146.

[3] B. A. Hinsdale, *Horace Mann and the Common School Revival in the United States* (N. M. Butler, ed., *The Great Educators;* N. Y., 1898), 263.

[4] T. W. Higginson, *Letters and Journals* (Mary T. Higginson, ed.,

group of New Englanders held a convention at Hartford "for the purpose of freely canvassing the origin, authority and influence of the Jewish and Christian Scriptures," such rank blasphemy produced an outburst of indignation which encouraged the students of a neighboring denominational college to visit upon it the wrath of a mob.[1] In certain communities small bands of bold spirits gathered annually on January 29 to celebrate the birthday of Thomas Paine.[2] In general, however, free thinking was left to the German and other foreign radicals. *Freie Gemeinde* were formed upon the model of similar congregations in Germany, and in 1859 these local groups organized a union with Philadelphia as headquarters.[3]

More acceptable to the mid-century religious temperament was the new influence represented by the Young Men's Christian Association which entered the United States and Canada when in December, 1851, branches after the English model were formed in Montreal and Boston. Aided by a decided tendency upon the part of young men in the cities to organize for intellectual and moral improvement, its growth was rapid. By the end of the decade associations existed in two hundred American cities. From the start it exercised a strong influence for a unified and practical Christianity.[4]

Boston, 1921), 40-41. A latitudinarian sermon before the theological class at Cambridge could arouse strong antipathy. Samuel Longfellow, ed., *Life of Henry Wadsworth Longfellow* (Boston, 1886), I, 321-322.

[1] W. P. and F. J. Garrison, *William Lloyd Garrison, 1805-1879* (N. Y., 1885-1889), III, 383.

[2] Over one hundred admirers of this early American iconoclast assembled to celebrate his one hundred and twenty-fifth anniversary in Ann Arbor, a college town where the leading Protestant denominations combined to enforce an extremely churchly regimen upon the young university and the community. *Ann Arbor Local News*, Feb. 2, 1858; *N. Y. Herald*, Feb. 4, 1854.

[3] A. B. Faust, *The German Element in the United States* (Boston, 1909), II, 428.

[4] L. L. Doggett, *History of the Young Men's Christian Association*

The mental excitability of Americans seemed to lend itself to many kinds of religious fervor and metaphysical inquiry. Thus the cult of spiritualism experienced a rapid rise. It originated in Rochester with the Fox sisters, the young children of a western New York family, who claimed to act as media for communication with the dead through certain mysterious rapping sounds by which questions put to them were answered.[1] The fame of the Rochester spirit rappings spread over the nation. In 1850 the Fox sisters gave exhibitions in New York City with some of the most eminent men of the nation among their visitors. Persons like William J. Stillman, the artist, and Thomas Appleton, the publisher, became sincere spiritualists, while Horace Greeley gave generous space to the movement in the columns of the *Tribune* and professed at least to maintain an open mind.

Soon a veritable craze was abroad, spreading from Maine to California.[2] Mediums appeared everywhere ready to exhibit spirit manifestations. In 1852 spiritualists began to hold a series of conventions at Boston, Worcester and Cleveland. By the end of the year a dozen and more spiritualist periodicals were in circulation, including the *Seraphic Advocate,* the *Spiritual Telegraph,* the *Spirit Messenger* and *Light from the Spirit World.* The printing press groaned under the pamphlets and books that were being issued, with their exciting tales and their "research" data. In 1853 a great conference was held at Springfield, Massachusetts, with some three

---

(N. Y., 1919), 106-140; F. D. Erb, *The Development of the Young People's Movement* (Chicago, 1917) ; Rey, *L'Amérique Protestante,* 350.

[1] Patrick Kearney, "The Fountain of Spiritualism," *Am. Mercury,* IV (1925), 331-336.

[2] T. C. Grattan, *Civilized America* (London, 1859), II, 355-372; Francis and Theresa Pulszky, *White, Red, Black* (N. Y., 1853), I, 298-308; Bremer, *America of the Fifties,* 203, 334-336; W. J. Stillman, *The Autobiography of a Journalist* (Boston, 1901), 179-197, 236; *Atlantische Studien,* I (1853), 67-70, 134, 145-149, 216-218.

or four hundred "rappers" and other mediums communing with spirits of all ages, all countries and all languages. To many it seemed religious fanaticism gone mad. Indeed, the newspapers began to chronicle numerous instances of suicide and insanity growing out of the excitement. Insanity seemed to increase where the movement was strongest. Presently, however, spiritualism went the way of other "isms." In 1854 the national Senate refused to give serious consideration to a petition signed by fifteen thousand asking for the appointment of a commission to investigate the phenomena of "occult forces." Within a few years a mere handful remained of the million or more adherents which the cult had optimistically claimed in 1853.

Although violent religious emotionalism was becoming more and more a rarity, the revival continued to be an accepted pastime of the closing weeks of the long, dreary rural winter, just as the camp meeting was an escape from dull summer monotony. But the sudden and widespread distress occasioned by the financial crisis of 1857 sharpened the consciousness of sin of many who felt that the Heavenly Father was visiting divine vengeance upon a selfish and materialistic nation.[1] As the theaters closed and other normal means of amusement slipped from the impoverished grasp of habitual seekers after diversion, a new religious interest gripped persons usually least susceptible to such an influence. In the early part of 1858 a spiritual awakening was perceptible throughout the country. Revival meetings attracted community-wide interest; tens of thousands of conversions were reported. For a time only one class seemed immune. "While pugilists, rowdies, and burglars are converted, the revivals have not made the slightest impression upon the hardened sinners of Wall Street,"

[1] *Ann Arbor Local News*, Nov. 3, 1857, March 16, 1858.

lamented a New York editor.[1] Soon, however, it was evident that the spirit of prayer had penetrated even the countinghouse, where the pious hoped that it would continue to dwell.

"Prayer meetings sprang into existence in private houses, stores, shops, theatres, and even in lofts and cellars," noted one observer.[2] But the particular feature of the "Great Revival of 1858" was the large daily union prayer meeting held in nearly every city. Suddenly despoiled of their prosperity, the people turned to God and began to pray. Spontaneity and sincerity marked these gatherings; the pastors did not need to take the initiative. Neither ecstacies nor convulsive sobs were necessary to show that the human soul had been reached. Except in rural communities there was a singular freedom from the extravagances and the wild excitement that had formerly attended such awakenings. The freedom from sectarianism and the perfect cordiality with which preachers and laymen of different churches labored together seemed to herald a new day of religious coöperation.[3]

The "Great Awakening" of 1858 called attention to the growing secularization of the Sabbath, a relaxing of time-honored practices due to the cosmopolitan spirit that prevailed in the large cities and the frontier carelessness that lingered in the West. If Boston still had compunctions against allowing theatrical performances on Saturday night, New Orleans went so far as to impose no Sunday restrictions upon the drama, upon horse rac-

---

[1] *N. Y. Herald*, March 14, 1858.

[2] *N. Y. Herald*, Jan. 1, 1859.

[3] Gasparin, *Uprising of a Great People*, 67, 86; A. P. Marvin, "Three Eras of Revivals in the United States," *Bibliotheca Sacra*, XVI (1859), 291; "Monthly Record of Current Events," *Harper's Mo.*, XVI (1858), 833. The Methodists gained in 1858 more than 100,000 members above the normal annual increase. Wardle, *History of Sunday School Movement*, 93.

ing or other forms of amusement. Even smaller communities sometimes took on a gala atmosphere on the Lord's day, militia companies in uniform parading to music while groups of young folk spent the day in merrymaking, and their elders quenched their thirst through the side-door entrances of the liquor shops. Conditions in other cities were often like those in Chicago:

Here in Chicago, we have fifty-six churches open on Sunday . . . but at the same time, there are no less than eighty ball rooms, in each of which a band plays from morning till midnight. . . . In addition to these activities we have two theatres, each with its performers in tights and very short garments. . . . Saloons . . . do a thriving business through side entrances.[1]

"The German with his love of music and song, with his joy in God's free nature, with his bent for companionship and *Gemütlichkeit*, with all his memories of a Sunday in the old *Heimat*," seemed the peculiar foe of the puritanical Sabbath.[2] In the summer months he and his friends repaired in festive mood to near-by picnic grounds; or they took in one of the "sacred concerts" scheduled at German theaters where the sacred music was limited to a few selections between acts; or they went to a *Wirtshaus*, where the bugles blared out a Strauss waltz and where, amid the clinking of glasses, men and women drank beer while watching the gymnastic stunts or antics of variety performers. The Sabbatarian forces condemned such sacrilege and offered up special prayers "in behalf of this portion of our popula-

[1] *Chicago Daily Times*, cited in *Mound City* (Ill.) *Emporium*, Nov. 12, 1857; cf. *Chicago Democrat*, May 13, 1858.
[2] Theodor Griesinger, *Lebende Bilder aus Amerika* (Stuttgart, 1858), 118-120; Hermann Wimmer, *Die Kirche und Schule in Nord-Amerika* (Leipzig, 1853), 106.

tion, to reclaim them from this fatal error."[1] Such reclamation, however, made little progress. Even the socially minded American found an appeal in this new gospel of the joy of life. When therefore the German's right to his special form of Sunday observance was threatened, sturdy champions among the native elements of the population sprang to his aid.

Other conditions also menaced the church's monopoly of the Sabbath. Railroads and newspapers represented the encroachments of commercial enterprise. A Northwestern Sabbath Convention at Chicago in May, 1854, denounced the danger of desecration by Sunday trains as more appalling than that from any other source. Objection was also made to the running of horse railway or omnibus lines. As the Sabbatarian movement gained strength from the "Great Awakening," Horace Greeley joined the reformers in their protest against the sale of newspapers on Sunday. But his rival James Gordon Bennett rejoiced that a concerted campaign of Sabbatarians and the police commissioners had not caused the circulation of the *Sunday Herald* to decrease.[2] The editor of *Harper's Monthly* deplored the narrowness of the Sunday restrictionist, insisting that urban life required a new version of the Christian conception, that the Sabbath was made for man "for his moral, intellectual, and physical good."[3] It became more and more evident that on this score the Sunday-observance movement could not stay the hands of the clock of time.

The Christian church of the North wavered as it faced the even more serious challenge flung by the abolitionist crusaders. Leading divines, even in the North, denounced the abolitionists as apostles of atheism and

[1] *Alton* (Ill.) *Courier*, May 23, 1854. See also American and Foreign Sabbath Union, *Permanent Sabbath Documents* (Boston, 1851).
[2] *N. Y. Herald*, May 31, June 6, 21, 1858.
[3] Edit., *Harper's Mo.*, XVII (1858), 262.

anarchy and proclaimed that the institution of chattel slavery had the sanction of Holy Writ. President Nathan Lord of Dartmouth College appealed to his fellow preachers of all denominations to stem the tide of abolition, while Bishop John Henry Hopkins built up an elaborate defense of slavery on scriptural and historical grounds. The Reverend Nehemiah Adams returned to New England from a three months' visit in Dixie thoroughly converted from his antislavery views and prepared to win over others by his sweeping defense of the South. The Reverend Philip Schaff depicted slavery as a wholesome training school for the Negro from the lowest state of heathenism and barbarism to some degree of Christian civilization.[1]

The antislavery forces found it no easy matter to meet the scriptural argument for slavery. William Jay, the veteran abolitionist, contended that the proslavery texts were incorrect translations;[2] but this did not undermine the confidence of theological doctrinaires who accepted without question the verbal inspiration of the King James text. The leaders of the American Anti-Slavery Society in 1858 agreed without any real enthusiasm to a proposal by Mrs. Stowe that a tract be issued concerning the Bible and slavery; all present seemed relieved to learn that the task could be delegated to the proponent's brother, Charles Beecher. In 1860, too, an able work appeared from the pen of the Reverend George B. Cheever on *The Guilt of Slavery and the Crime of Slaveholding.*

[1] *Liberator* (Boston), March 23, 1860; Gasparin, *Uprising of a Great People,* 76. See also J. H. Hopkins, *A Scriptural, Ecclesiastical, and Historical View of Slavery* (N. Y., 1864); Nehemiah Adams, *A Southside View of Slavery* (Boston, 1854); Philip Schaff, *Slavery and the Bible* (Chambersburg, Pa., 1861); Samuel Seabury, *American Slavery . . . Justified by the Law of Nature* (N. Y., 1861).

[2] William Jay, *An Examination of the Mosaic Laws of Servitude* (N. Y., 1854).

As early as the 1840's two major denominations had split upon the rock of slavery and driven their Southern brethren into independent organization.[1] Only the Roman Catholic Church seemed free from the agitation,[2] although its next of kin, the Protestant Episcopal Church, proud of its conservative spirit, also succeeded in steering a safe noncommittal course.[3] It was an easy matter for churches organized in independent congregations without central legislative bodies to practise the gospel of "no fellowship with slave-holders." Moreover, most Baptist, Congregational and Unitarian churches were controlled by elements unequivocally committed to the gospel of freedom. The Western Unitarian Conference at Alton in 1857 did not allow the certain danger of the secession of the St. Louis delegation to prevent the adoption of a strong antislavery report.[4] It is significant, too, that a group of Quakers of Chester County, Pennsylvania, opposed to the conservative stand of their brethren, formed a yearly meeting of Progressive Friends and undertook the freest discussion not only of slavery but also of war, marriage, prisons, property and other established institutions of the day.[5]

[1] For the split in Methodist and Baptist churches, see C. R. Fish, *The Rise of the Common Man* (*A History of American Life*, VI), 289-290.

[2] As a matter of fact many of the Catholic clergy and laity seemed to be opposed to the war when the crisis came. They detected signs that the war crusaders had marked popery as the next victim to follow slavery. John M'Keon, a New York lawyer, collected and published evidence that satisfied him that "when the knife is taken from the throats of the Southern people, it will be turned to the throat of every Catholic in the North." See *Cincinnati Enquirer*, Jan. 2, 16, 1864; *Harper's Wkly.*, VIII, 2 (Jan. 2, 1864). Surviving anti-Catholic sentiment made for grave suspicion that this fear reflected a Roman Catholic complicity in the rebellion. See extraordinary charges in Chiniquy, *Fifty Years in the Church of Rome*, 686-687, 691, 695, 700-702, 706, 714-715.

[3] When the war came, however, the Southern dioceses seceded with their states. S. D. McConnell, *History of the American Episcopal Church* (N. Y., 1891), 361.

[4] *Chicago Daily Democratic Press*, May 21, 1857.

[5] *N. Y. Tribune*, June 2, 1854; Higginson, *Letters and Journals*, 73-

Official spokesmen of the Methodist Episcopal Church North commonly pointed to the record of its earnest but conservative protest against the evil of slavery. On the other hand, probably as many as two hundred thousand slaves were owned by its members. Many zealous antislavery men from Northern conferences demanded that the general rule in regard to slavery be made more drastic so that the church might be freed entirely from its "criminal" connection with the institution. This issue was pressed against a declining opposition until the general conference at Buffalo in 1860 adopted a new rule in which, without excluding slaveholders from its communion, it admonished members "to keep themselves pure from this great evil, and to seek its extirpation by all lawful and Christian means." [1]

While the Old School Presbyterians, true to their traditional conservatism, ignored the slavery question, the New School group continued in the early fifties the tactics of trying to appease the antislavery forces by mild condemnations of slavery.[2] The radical element, however, proposed to refuse fellowship to the slaveholder, a program much too strenuous for the cautious leaders of the church and influential laymen like Cyrus H. McCormick, patron of the Theological Seminary at Chicago. Finally, in 1857 when the general assembly voted strong condemnation of a proslavery report of a Kentucky presbytery, six Southern synods with about two

77; Rufus M. Jones, *The Later Periods of Quakerism* (London, 1921), II, 596.

[1] *Ohio State Journal*, May 28, 1860, May 7-10, 1860; Methodist Episcopal Church, *Journal of the General Conference for 1860*, 425-426; J. M. Buckley, *A History of Methodists of the United States* (Schaff and others, eds., *American Church History Series*, V), 501; W. W. Sweet, *The Methodist Episcopal Church and the Civil War* (Cin., 1912), 38-40.

[2] R. E. Thompson, *A History of the Presbyterian Churches in the United States* (Schaff and others, eds., *American Church History Series*, VI), 133-135.

hundred churches and fifteen thousand communicants withdrew. With the opening of the Civil War the Old School Presbyterians of the South organized a separate church of their own.[1]

An especial effort was made in the West to enlist the various missionary agencies under the banner of freedom. An important figure in the controversies that arose was President Jonathan Blanchard of Knox College. Convinced that "the heart of action in the Church" was the missions, he declared that from them "the foul spirit of Slavery must be dislodged before it will be *cast out of the Church.*"[2] Accordingly, beginning in 1847, he led a fight at the annual meetings of the American Board of Commissioners for Foreign Missions in favor of barring slaveholders from the mission churches.[3] These efforts proving fruitless, the Illinois Wesleyan Missionary Conference commended the uncompromising antislavery position of the American Missionary Association and urged affiliation with it instead of the formation of rival societies. President Blanchard showed, however, that even this body permitted membership of slaveholders. Meanwhile antislavery Baptists felt impelled to organize the American Baptist Free Mission Society. As a result a group of extreme opponents of slaveholding fellowship, meeting at Chicago in July, 1852, formed the Free Mission Society for the Northwest. For the same reason the Western Tract Convention was organized in 1859 out of antislavery seceders from the conservative American Tract Society.[4]

[1] L. G. Vander Velde, *The Presbyterian Churches and the Federal Union, 1861-1869* (*Harvard Historical Studies*, XXXIII), pt. ii, chaps. i-iii.

[2] *Western Citizen* (Chicago), March 18, 1851.

[3] C. K. Whipple, *Relations of the American Board of Commissioners for Foreign Missions to Slavery* (Boston, 1861).

[4] *Western Citizen*, March 25, June 24, Sept. 2, 1851, June 1, July 20, 1852; *Chicago Democrat*, Oct. 19, 1859.

Meanwhile the common cause of freedom was tending to break down the denominational barriers that separated the Christian antislavery forces. Deprecating the adoption of expediency as a substitute for the spirit of Christ, the crusaders could not but feel that the slavery issue was of more importance than sectarianism. As a result a Christian Anti-Slavery Convention assembled at Cincinnati in April, 1850; in July, 1851, an even more enthusiastic session of two hundred and fifty delegates met at Chicago with Blanchard in the chair. Though the Christian Anti-Slavery Convention disappeared as the conservative reaction set in, it was revived in October, 1859, as the Northwestern Christian Anti-Slavery Convention.[1] Again Blanchard was a leading figure, calling the assemblage to order and justifying his support of the Republican party.

On less drastic tests of their devotion to human liberty the clergy of the nation spoke out with greater courage. Though ministers were oftentimes silent or apologetic, a strong note of protest sounded from many pulpits at the passage of the fugitive-slave law of 1850. Four years later the clergy burst out in wrath against the Kansas-Nebraska act as an assault on freedom. A memorial signed by five hundred clergymen of the Northwest denounced Douglas for "want of courtesy and reverence toward man and God."[2] Promptly conservative editors and politicians deplored the tendency of churchmen to leave their sacred calling and incite partisan strife. "When ministers enter the arena of politics, and associate themselves with the corrupt and lying hypocrites who lead the black republican party, and utter seditious harangues from the pulpit, they are no longer entitled to that respect that their sacred calling

---

[1] Cole, Era of the Civil War, 223-224.
[2] Congressional Globe, 33 Cong., 1 sess., app., 654.

commands," declared the *Signal* of Joliet, Illinois, when four of the local clergy participated prominently in a Republican meeting.[1] Such warnings probably restrained the timid at a time when radical abolitionists were wondering whether the cause of freedom could triumph except upon the ruins of the church.[2] Henry Ward Beecher, a brilliant barometer of popular progressive currents, answered critics by advancing the doctrine that any topic introduced into the pulpit became thereby consecrated. Mock slave auctions at his church vividly dramatized many of the horrors of chattel slavery.[3]

Thus the outbreak of the war found most branches of the Christian faith embroiled by the slavery controversy. As the paramount moral question of the day it was regarded by churchgoers on one side of the Mason and Dixon line predominantly from one angle and by those dwelling on the other side predominantly from another; and both groups of Christians espoused their convictions with a sense of inner righteousness and high scriptural sanction. However reluctant organized religion may earlier have been to enlist in the sectional strife, it failed to stay the tide of revolt and division when the national crisis appeared.

[1] *Joliet* (Ill.) *Signal,* June 17, 1856.
[2] J. C. Stiles, *Modern Reform Examined* (Phila., 1857), 274-275.
[3] W. C. Beecher and Samuel Scoville, *A Biography of Henry Ward Beecher* (N. Y., 1888), 283-300.

CHAPTER XI

FANATIC AND DOUGHFACE

THE outstanding fact in the antislavery cause of the fifties was the awakened conscience of the masses of the free states. Yet at the beginning of the decade public opinion, wearied of agitation, was susceptible to nearly any appeal for political quiet. Not only conservatives and compromisers, not only business men with Southern connections, but most Northern critics of slavery were, for the time, ready to sacrifice their ideals in order to maintain their loyalty to the Constitution and the Union. Many could say with Abraham Lincoln: "I confess I hate to see the poor creatures hunted down and caught and carried back to their stripes and unrequited toil, but I bite my lips and keep quiet." [1]

To be sure, minority elements continued to agitate. The enactment in 1850 of a fugitive-slave law which denied the Negro not only trial by jury but the right to testify or to summon witnesses in his own behalf, and which imposed drastic penalties upon persons who attempted to assist him, caused consternation in the North. Many thoughtful citizens refused to condone such a clear violation of the principles of common justice. "I say solemnly that I will do all in my power to rescue any fugitive slave from the hands of any officer who attempts to return him to bondage," cried the outraged Theodore Parker. [2] Massachusetts abolitionists men-

[1] Abraham Lincoln, *Complete Works* (J. G. Nicolay and John Hay, eds., N. Y., 1905), II, 282.

[2] Theodore Parker, *Speeches, Addresses, and Occasional Sermons* (Boston, 1861), III, 154.

tioned by name heroic fugitives living in Boston and defied efforts to return them to slavery. "The edict of Nebuchadnezzar, setting up the golden image to be worshipped, on pain of the rebellious being cast into the den of lions, was just as obligatory as is the fugitive-slave law of Congress. . . . Its enforcement on Massachusetts soil must be rendered impossible." [1] Even conservative journals prophesied that the law would be a dead letter.

In other parts of the North friends of freedom also rallied in indignation meetings and circulated petitions for an immediate repeal. Thus, the Chicago common council with only two dissenting votes pronounced the law cruel, unjust and unconstitutional, a transgression of the laws of God. Yet two days later a popular audience in the same city which greeted Douglas, a supporter of the statute, with hostile jeers and hisses, was actually won over and induced by his bold defense to vote an express repudiation of the common council. [2]

When the fugitive-slave measure was enacted, probably twenty thousand Negroes were quietly dwelling in the free states, in comparative safety from the masters whose authority they had fled. [3] They constituted less than a tenth of the Northern free colored population, a stock considerably diluted by white blood. Its growth in a decade to a quarter of a million represented in considerable part the normal expansion of a fairly prolific race, for there was no unqualified welcome in the border free states for the surplus free Negro population of the states across the Ohio. [4] Indeed, Illinois in 1853 reën-

[1] *Liberator* (Boston), Sept. 27, 1850.

[2] A. C. Cole, *The Era of the Civil War* (C. W. Alvord, ed., *The Centennial History of Illinois*, Springfield, 1918-1920, III), 72.

[3] For this and other estimates, see W. H. Siebert, *The Underground Railroad* (N. Y., 1898), 235-237.

[4] John Cummings, ed., *Negro Population in the United States, 1790-1915* (Wash., 1918), 55.

forced its black code by imposing a heavy fine upon every Negro who entered the state and providing that, in default of payment, the Negro should be auctioned off to the person bidding the shortest period of service in return for payment of the fine. This seemed, even to a Southern journal like the *New Orleans Bee*, "an act of special and savage ruthlessness," and within the state it found few open champions. The *Ottawa Free Trader*, claiming that it would establish a peonage system more heartless and cruel than Southern slavery, declared, "We should like to see the man that would mount the auctioneer's block in this town and sell a free man to the highest bidder."[1]

Such a law could never have been enforced against a hostile public opinion. But the electorate of the state had in 1848 given authority for Negro exclusion by a vote of 50,261 to 21,297. The law, therefore, was actually applied in certain cases, and Negroes seeking homes on the prairies of Illinois were put upon the block. In 1857 a free mulatto named Jackson Redman was arrested in St. Clair County and found guilty of violating the act; notices were accordingly posted about the streets of Belleville offering Redman for sale at public auction. Only the interposition of Gustave Koerner, the German Republican leader, who advanced $62.50 to cover the fine and costs, saved the victim from the penalties of the law. Such cases generally aroused widespread indignation in Illinois, although apologists were not altogether lacking.[2] In other border districts, too, Northerners were alarmed at the heavy burdens caused

---

[1] *Ottawa* (Ill.) *Free Trader*, Feb. 26, 1853; Cole, *Era of the Civil War*, 225-226.
[2] Cole, *Era of the Civil War*, 226; Gustave Koerner, *Memoirs, 1809-1896* (T. J. McCormack, ed., Cedar Rapids, Iowa, 1909), II, 30-31; N. D. Harris, *The History of Negro Servitude in Illinois and of the Slavery Agitation in That State, 1719-1864* (Chicago, 1904), 188.

by a sudden influx of free Negroes. In 1860 citizens of western Pennsylvania circulated petitions to the legislature requesting the enactment of legal restrictions.[1]

The decade of the fifties was an era of marked progress for the Negroes in the North. Without large accretions from outside, they were more free from disintegrating forces and were better able to justify their presence in communities where they had established themselves. They became, in private homes and in hotels, "the pleasantest servants in the country," said the Englishman Dicey, echoing a general testimony.[2] Both the proud mistress of a Fifth Avenue mansion and the Mercer Street "Madam" insisted upon colored maids.[3] At times at an approved hotel a Negro head waiter with quiet dignity directed a staff of white waitresses;[4] more often, however, he marshaled a squad of ostentatious assistants of his own race and sex. The mulatto barbers at Willard's Hotel in Washington and elsewhere plied their trade with the assurance that comes only from birthright. New accomplishments in mechanical fields overcame some of the prejudice against Negro artisans. Occasionally successful colored merchants, bankers and lawyers climbed to prominence and in some instances married white women. John V. De Grasse, a Boston physician educated both in America and in France, was formally admitted to the Massachusetts Medical Society in 1854. Robert Purvis, a very light, well-mannered mulatto with a Scotch education, raised prize poultry at his fine country home in Pennsylvania.[5]

[1] *National Intelligencer* (Wash.), Feb. 14, 1860.
[2] Edward Dicey, *Six Months in the Federal States* (London, 1863), I, 65-81.
[3] Theodor Griesinger, *Lebende Bilder aus Amerika* (Stuttgart, 1858), 150.
[4] J. G. Kohl, *Travels in Canada, and through the States of New York and Pennsylvania* (Mrs. Percy Sinnett, tr., London, 1861), I, 34-35.
[5] G. W. Williams, *History of the Negro Race in America, 1619-1880*

In the main, however, the Negroes had to be content with the humble rôle of hewers of wood and drawers of water, despised if not degraded. In spite of Frederick Douglass's ringing admonition, "Learn trades or starve!" many of those who had trades were compelled to abandon them on account of prejudice against their color.[1] Though "the one picturesque element in the dull monotony of outward life in America," they formed "a race apart, a strange people in a strange land."[2] Living in wretched hovels in obscure corners of the towns and cities, they were generally excluded from hotels, from street cars and from cabin passage on boats. The color line was also drawn in the theater, at the lyceum, and even in almshouses, schools and churches. Thrifty and sober or not, they were scorned by white workers, even by the crudest of the newly arrived immigrants.[3] The latter feared as well as resented Negro competition. Race hatred often broke out in towns along the Ohio; in 1857 the populace of Mound City, Illinois, undertook to drive out the Negro residents once and for all.[4]

As these facts suggest, the growing antislavery sentiment in the North did not necessarily imply a wholehearted acceptance of the Negro by the whites. The

(N. Y., 1883), 134; C. G. Woodson, *A Century of Negro Migration* (Wash., 1918), 94-99; Sallie Holley, *A Life for Liberty* (J. W. Chadwick, ed., N. Y., 1899), 101-102; G. F. Train, *Union Speeches* (2d ser., Phila., 1862), 78.

[1] *Frederick Douglass' Paper* (Rochester, N. Y.), March, 1854; B. C. Bacon, *Statistics of the Colored People of Philadelphia* (Phila., 1856), 15.

[2] Dicey, *Six Months in the Federal States*, II, 35; Charles Mackay, *Life and Liberty in America* (N. Y., 1859), II, 137-138; D. W. Mitchell, *Ten Years Residence in the United States* (London, 1862), 158-161; *Atlantische Studien,* I (1853), 192-194.

[3] Agénor de Gasparin, *The Uprising of a Great People* (Mary L. Booth, tr., N. Y., 1861), 57; Georges Fisch, *Nine Months in the United States during the Crisis* (London, 1863), 126.

[4] Cole, *Era of the Civil War*, 227; F. U. Quillan, *The Color Line in Ohio* (Ann Arbor, 1913), 61.

voters of Iowa rejected a Negro-suffrage clause drafted
to form a part of the constitution framed in 1857. Elsewhere efforts to secure for him equal rights before the
law proved abortive; even many members of the Republican party were frightened by the specter of "Negro
equality" which their opponents charged them with
harboring. There were Northern Democrats like D. J.
Van Deren, editor of the *Mattoon* [Illinois] *Gazette,*
who frankly declared his preference for the enslavement
of the Negro in Northern states to the extension of civil
and political equality. In 1857 came the great blow of
the Dred Scott decision in which the Supreme Court
ruled that a Negro could not be a citizen.

Meanwhile, abetted by antislavery extremists, the
Negroes developed a greater race consciousness and as-
sertiveness. Meeting in convention at various points in
the North they shouted defiance at the fugitive-slave act.
Their celebrations on August 1 of the anniversary of
West Indian emancipation became a regular event.[1] A
number of ex-slaves, supplementing the work of Frederick Douglass with harrowing tales of their experiences,
made their contribution to the abolitionist movement.[2]
While certain Negro leaders rejected the idea of colonization in all its forms, others looked more favorably upon
the scheme, some few joining the ventures at Haiti and
in Liberia.

Marked progress was made in educational facilities.
Humble ventures of the race itself were followed by
separate public schools. In 1855 Charles Sumner and
other opponents of "caste schools" secured a Massachu-

[1] *Cleveland Leader,* July 24, 25, 31, Aug. 1, 1860; J. W. Massie,
America: The Origin of Her Present Conflict (London, 1864), 185-187.
[2] Frederick Douglass, *My Bondage and My Freedom* (N. Y., 1855);
Austin Steward, *Twenty-Two Years a Slave and Forty Years a Freeman*
(Rochester, 1857); Solomon Northup, *Twelve Years a Slave* (N. Y.,
1855); anon., *The Experience of Thomas Jones, Who Was a Slave for
Forty-Three Years* (Boston, 1850).

setts law which proclaimed that there must be no distinction in the educational system on account of race,
color or religion.[1] Several institutions for higher education were soon available, the fruits of the philanthropy
of patrons like Gerrit Smith or of certain religious denominations. Wilberforce University near Xenia, Ohio,
was a notable Methodist contribution of this period. In
1858 Negroes rejoiced in the ordination of one of their
race as a bishop in the Methodist Episcopal Church.[2]

A new menace to the tranquillity of the Northern
black man came when the fugitive-slave law excited to
activity not only the slave hunter but also the kidnaper.
Southern Illinois was for a long time the special hunting
ground of man stealers. Scores of free men of colored
skin were sold into bondage by organized bands which
operated the more boldly because the Negroes would not
be admitted to the witness stand. Matters became so serious in the vicinity of Cairo that the mayor called out
the citizens to break up the operations of a local gang
of armed kidnapers who worked in league with a Missouri band.[3] In 1860 the kidnapers found easy victims
among the free Negroes of Kansas who had fled the
Arkansas exclusion-or-reënslavement law.[4]

No less ominous was the appearance of the slave
hunter in Negro settlements farther North. A panic ensued among even the older colored residents, and a considerable exodus began to the safer haven of Canada.[5]
But many who had for years industriously plied their

[1] C. G. Woodson, *The Education of the Negro prior to 1861* (N. Y.,
1915), 319, 325, 329; W. O. Bourne, *History of the Public School
Society of the City of New York* (N. Y., 1870), 594-595, 665 ff.;
Holley, *A Life for Liberty*, 168.

[2] *National Intelligencer*, Oct. 29, 1858.

[3] Cole, *Era of the Civil War*, 228.

[4] *Ann Arbor Local News*, Aug. 21, 1860.

[5] Theodore Parker, *Works* (Centenary edn., Boston, 1907-1911, XI),
335-336; Siebert, *Underground Railroad*, 193-195.

trades in friendly communities were not to be frightened away by idle rumors. Some even listened with approval to abolitionists who urged them to defend their rights by force if necessary. Thus it happened that federal police authorities often pursued fugitives to some Northern Negro settlement only to find that their victims had been secreted or hurried off to the Queen's dominion. At times, too, a band of dusky brethren, desperate in the face of the new menace to their peace and security, snatched a victim from the clutches of his captors, carrying him off to safety.

When the long arm of slavery reached into the North to recover its human victims, it encountered all the obstacles which sympathy for a hunted human animal could throw in its way. Law-abiding citizens accepted dangerous assignments in the more or less loosely organized "Underground Railroad" that moved the fugitive in slow stages toward the promised land of freedom. But when the victim had been run down and the badge of federal authority was enlisted to effect his return to the South, interference usually ended. In November, 1851, however, citizens of Syracuse under the lead of Gerrit Smith, wealthy member of Congress, and the Reverend Samuel J. May stormed the prison in which Jerry, an industrious Negro mechanic, had been thrown pending trial as a fugitive, rescued the prisoner and sent him on his way to Canada.[1] But law-abiding citizens joined in denunciation of such mob violence and declared their intention of upholding the law. The new slave-catching code seems to have been acquiesced in by all "respectable" elements in the North.

Not long after, the elections of 1852 revealed a startling setback for the political antislavery movement. Supporting in Senator John P. Hale of New Hampshire

[1] E. E. Sperry, *The Jerry Rescue* (Syracuse, 1924).

a candidate of firm but moderate antislavery propensities, the Free Soil vote fell off by half. For the time
being many earnest idealists, who had with Garrison
opposed political methods, could not help but conclude
that "Garrison's was the better way." [1] "Abolitionists
are not numerous, nor probably ever will be," declared
Edmund Quincy at the eighteenth annual meeting of the
Massachusetts Anti-Slavery Society, "but there are
enough to keep an everlasting protest against slavery.
Our business is to continually ring the bell, and to be
showing up the rottenness of the system." [2]

Just in the midst of this lull in the crusade for freedom appeared the most effective revelation of the seamy
side of chattel slavery. From the soul and pen of Harriet
Beecher Stowe flowed the stirring protest of *Uncle
Tom's Cabin or Life among the Lowly*. She knew the
institution of slavery as it had revealed itself in Kentucky
across the Ohio River from her Cincinnati home. She
and her family had aided the fleeing slave as he sought
freedom under guidance of the North Star. In the burning language of genius she reached the hearts of millions
who had previously cared very little about the Negro's
lot in bondage. The serial that ran for nearly a year in
the issues of the antislavery *National Era* became in
1852 the great "best seller" of that epoch. As already
noted, a dramatic version appeared every night for
months upon the New York stage and soon had a hearing in nearly every city and town in the North.

The story's influence penetrated to the slaves themselves. In the border states, when they heard the pathetic

[1] Holley, *A Life for Liberty*, 92.
[2] *Liberator*, Feb. 1, 1850. See also Webster's statement: "No drumhead, in the longest day's march, was ever more incessantly beaten and
smitten, than public sentiment in the North has been, every month, and
day, and hour, by the din, and roll, and rub-a-dub of Abolition writers
and Abolition lecturers." Daniel Webster, *Writings and Speeches* (Boston, 1903), X, 165.

tale, they dreaded all the more the possibility of being sold "down river" and dreamed more brightly of the joyous freedom of Canada. Under such an influence one April night in 1853 twenty-five "chattels" in Boone County, Kentucky, struck out across the Ohio.[1] Others were aroused to the same decision by apostles of freedom who at the risk of their lives carried their gospel into the very heart of the cotton kingdom. A few bold spirits like Dr. Alexander M. Ross busily labored in states from Virginia to Mississippi, urging Negroes to try for their freedom and supplying them with information for the attempt. Even on the eve of the Civil War, despite large rewards for his arrest posted in several Southern communities, Ross continued his hazardous operations.[2]

Slaveholders in Maryland claimed to have suffered heavily as a result of such forays notwithstanding the rigid application of lynch law upon all persons suspected of "tampering with slaves." One county in the state claimed to have lost in 1856 sixty slaves worth at least sixty thousand dollars. A series of mass meetings and conventions in 1858 and 1859 considered this problem. Whether as a result of these efforts or not, the annual loss of Maryland reported in the census of 1860 was but 115, far less than one half that recorded in the preceding census. So too the figures for the entire South dropped off by nearly one fourth and totaled only 803. It is probable, however, that the combined forces which undermined the stability of slave property entailed an average loss of well over one thousand for each year of the decade.

Meanwhile there had occurred an active revival of the antislavery movement. The year 1854 marked the turn-

[1] N. Y. Herald, April 20, 1858.
[2] A. M. Ross, Memoirs of a Reformer, 1832-1892 (Toronto, 1893), 42-74; same author, Recollections and Experiences of an Abolitionist (Toronto, 1876).

ing point. In March Joshua Glover was rescued from the authorities at Milwaukee by a mob whose leaders, afterward arrested, were acquitted by the state supreme court on the ground that the fugitive-slave law was unconstitutional.[1] Later in the same year, the hot-headed young idealist Thomas Wentworth Higginson led an infuriated band in a vain attack upon the federal courthouse at Boston for the purpose of freeing Anthony Burns, an arrested fugitive; all attempts to visit upon Higginson the penalties of the law failed. When in 1858 in the "Oberlin-Wellington" rescue the Puritan conscience of the Western Reserve intervened to save a fugitive, the ringleaders, including an Oberlin professor, were convicted of violation of the act of 1850, but the danger of a serious collision between the state and federal authorities led to their release.[2] There followed in October, 1859, the case in which leading citizens of Ottawa, Illinois, participated in the rescue of a fugitive, seven of the rescuers being promptly indicted by the federal grand jury. John Hossack, one of the most prominent of the group, was tried first and found guilty by the federal district court; in October, 1860, he and his associates were given small jail sentences as well as fines. Increasingly Northerners came to hate the slave-catching law and by the same token were convinced that the encroachments of slavery must be checked.

The year 1854 also saw the leadership of the antislavery cause taken out of the hands of the abolitionist extremists and transferred to practical politicians. Before this date the antislavery movement in politics had seemed a failure. Now, in the popular disillusionment and party chaos that came when Stephen A. Douglas sponsored

[1] Siebert, *Underground Railroad*, 284, 327-333.
[2] J. R. Shipherd, comp., *History of the Oberlin-Wellington Rescue* (Boston, 1859).

the Kansas-Nebraska measure, a way to real success was opened through the launching of the Republican party. The new party proclaimed its unalterable purpose to check the canker of slavery that seemed likely to eat out the vitals of the nation. It not only absorbed the scattered remnants of the old Free Soil party and those Whigs who in the collapse of their own party rallied to the cause of human rights, but it enlisted a large bloc of Northern Democrats who felt that Douglas's apostasy had destroyed every claim upon their continued allegiance. So too in time voters who had followed the will-o'-the wisp into the Know Nothing party learned that there was after all but one real issue, that of slavery and its future status in the republic.

The Republicans were enemies of the further extension of slavery, not abolitionists. They generally admitted that the South could justly claim an adequate fugitive-slave law. Indeed, the supreme court of Massachusetts containing five Republican judges unanimously pronounced the act of 1850 constitutional, while the jury that convicted John Hossack in the Ottawa case was made up of eight Republicans and four Democrats and was not over two hours in reaching its verdict. Yet these law-abiding enemies of the slave power were not without weapons which they could wield. With perhaps ironical respect for the law they placed tantalizing obstacles in the way of the slave catchers by withholding the coöperation of state authorities. Statutes, known as "personal-liberty laws," were enacted in virtually every state that fell under Republican control. These laws undertook to nullify the effect of the fugitive-slave act by such devices as guaranteeing jury trial, by authorizing writs of *habeas corpus* to alleged fugitives under arrest, by forbidding state officials to coöperate in the process of rendition and by prohibiting the use of local jails for the confinement of fugitives. So too in 1860 the New York court of appeals ruled in the Lemmon case that slaves were freed by being carried into a free state.[1] A Democratic state like New Jersey, on the other hand, had a fugitive-slave law of her own to supplement the federal statute.

Northern Democrats, when charged with being "doughfaces," trucklers to the slave power, generally retorted that the "Black Republicans" or "kinky-heads" were converts to rank abolitionism. In reality, the abolitionists would have none of such timid brethren; they were made of stronger stuff. They not only bore witness to the sinfulness of slavery, not only refused fellowship to slaveholders and defenders of that institution, but they scorned all compromises with "tyranny." Declaring a union which sanctioned slavery accursed of God, William Lloyd Garrison in 1854 publicly burned a copy of the United States Constitution and proclaimed the slogan, "The Union must be dissolved."[2] From this archapostle of abolition and his followers arose a Northern demand for disunion, for a confederacy free from contamination with slaveholders. Summons for a national disunion convention was issued; various meetings to promote disunion were held in the later years of the decade.[3] Even those abolitionists who acknowledged the wisdom of wielding the political weapon against slavery were not always content to accept the moderate leader-

[1] Henry Wilson, *History of the Rise and Fall of the Slave Power* (Boston, 1872-1877), II, 641-642.

[2] W. P. and F. J. Garrison, *William Lloyd Garrison, 1805-1879* (N. Y., 1885-1887), III, 412. See also copies of the *Liberator*, and T. W. Higginson, *Letters and Journals* (Mary T. Thacher, ed., Boston, 1921), 77-79. John Jay declared the Union "at present a most grievous curse to the American people." Bayard Tuckerman, *William Jay and the Constitutional Movement for the Abolition of Slavery* (N. Y., 1894), 154.

[3] *Liberator*, June 20, 27, 1856, Jan. 15, 23, 30, Feb. 6, 1857; *N. Y. Tribune*, June 3, 1856; *Chicago Tribune*, Sept. 29, 1857.

ship represented by Republican nominees for office. Yet few of them agreed with Garrison when he editorially gibbeted Lincoln as the "slave-hound of Illinois" because he had admitted the South's right to an effective fugitive-slave law! [1]

The Republicans were strong enemies of disunion from whatever quarter it was proposed. They found valuable recruits in working-class elements previously devoted to the Democracy. Northern wage-earners had thus far displayed little sympathy for the Southern slave. But now they were made to see the slave power standing across their own path, not only thwarting their demands for free land or equal rights to the soil but threatening the very social and economic foundations of free society. Republican leaders were not slow to point a warning finger at the Southern "mud-sill" theory of society, with its corollary that slavery was the normal status of the laborer, black or white. Effective use was made in 1856, their first presidential campaign, of the argument that the advocates of this doctrine were allied with the Democratic party.[2]

Republicans seemed to be coming slowly to a conclusion long since reached by Southern champions of slavery on the one hand and by their abolitionist enemies on the other. "'Tis not possible that our two forms of society can long coexist. . . . Social systems, formed on opposite principles, cannot endure," wrote George Fitzhugh, Virginian.[3] From the North Ralph Waldo Emerson could paraphrase the Southern philosopher: "I do not see how a barbarous community and a civilized community can constitute a state. I think that we must get rid of slavery or we must get rid of freedom." Con-

---

[1] *Liberator*, June 22, 1860.
[2] A. C. Cole, *Lincoln's "House Divided" Speech* (Chicago, 1923), 30.
[3] George Fitzhugh, *Cannibals All!* (Richmond, Va., 1857), 154.

tinuing with increasing emotion he made his own preference clear:

> Life has no parity of value in the free state and in the slave state. In one it is adorned with education, with skillful labor, with arts, with long prospective interests, with sacred family ties, with honor and justice. In the other, life is a fever; man is an animal, given to pleasure, frivolous, irritable, spending his days in hunting and practicing with deadly weapons to defend himself against his slaves and against his companions brought up in the same idle and dangerous way.[1]

Republicans were thus drawn into even more advanced ground upon the slavery issue. On June 17, 1858, Abraham Lincoln, the prophet of the Illinois prairies, declared in his famous "house-divided" speech his belief that "this government cannot endure permanently half-slave and half-free." Somewhat later in the same year William H. Seward, the outstanding Republican leader, declared that the radically different social systems of the North and the South were headed for a collision, "an irrepressible conflict," as a result of which the United States would "sooner or later, become either entirely a slave-holding nation, or entirely a free-labor nation." For this forecast—and Lincoln strenuously insisted it was a forecast rather than a program of action—the Illinois leader denied for himself and Seward any originality. "That same idea was expressed by the *Richmond Enquirer*, in Virginia in 1856,—quite two years before it was expressed by the first of us," he declared.[2]

---

[1] Anon., "The Sumner Case," *Littell's Living Age*, L (1856), 376-377.

[2] Speech at Cincinnati, Sept. 17, 1859, Lincoln, *Complete Works*, V, 214-215; New Haven Speech, March 6, 1860, same vol., 358; J. E. Cairnes, *The Slave Power* (N. Y., 1862), 163 n.; Cole, *Lincoln's "House Divided" Speech*, 5-10.

In 1860 Seward, perhaps with working-class votes in mind, again pointed to the fundamental conflict between what he now chose to call the "labor states" and the "capital states." Lincoln, who had frequently expressed fear lest in this conflict "the white man's charter of freedom" be at stake, rejoiced, as he told Connecticut audiences during a shoe strike, "that a system of labor prevails in New England under which laborers can strike when they want to. . . . I like the system which lets a man quit when he wants to, and wish it might prevail everywhere. One of the reasons why I am opposed to slavery is just here." [1]

Under the pressure of such arguments many wage-earners, previously attracted to the Democratic party, entered the ranks of the much-reviled "Black" Republicans. At the same time, as Lincoln and the Western leaders forced a repudiation of nativistic doctrines, the Germans of the Middle West made complete their revolt from the Democracy. The Republicans organized the moderate antislavery forces about the proposal to confine the "peculiar institution" within existing limits. The party found itself the special beneficiary of the Panic of 1857, responsibility for the hard times having been laid at the door of the Democratic administration. The elections that followed revealed Republican gains from the spirit of discontent. In Pennsylvania, where the party had previously made slight headway, the unemployed iron workers joined the leaders of the industry in a demand for tariff protection from foreign competition. Making this the issue in the fall elections of 1858, they accomplished the defeat of all but three of the Democratic candidates for Congress. Though the Philadelphia district did not join in repudiating what had for decades been the dominant party, the conserva-

[1] Lincoln, *Complete Works*, V, 360.

tive leadership, economic and political, there as elsewhere
was thoroughly frightened.

Now at length the relationship of Northern capitalism to the slave power of the South was made entirely
apparent. On the one hand stood those industrial forces
of the North which were demanding a protection that
they could not expect the South to concede. On the other
hand stood the merchants with large credits upon their
books to Southern purchasers, the bankers with extensive loans in the South and the manufacturers whose
products found a ready sale there. All these had ample
reason for concern over the rapid alienation of the two
sections, an alienation which they charged largely against
the Republican party. For some time self-interest had
been impelling the representatives of wealth and conservatism to undertake the task of saving the Union by
curbing the menace of what they sweepingly called
"abolitionism." President Buchanan invoked this force
in support of the administration plan to admit Kansas
under the Lecompton constitution. "The defeat of the
bill," he urged, "would alarm the fears of the country
for the Union, reduce the value of property and injuri-
ously interfere with our reviving trade." [1]

Thomas P. Kettell, former editor of the *Democratic
Review*, now undertook an elaborate analysis of the
rôle played by the South in Northern prosperity. A vast
array of statistics seemed to show that the profits of New
England shipping together with Northern banking and
manufacturing required a continuance of Southern
patronage; therefore the North must not insist "upon
manufacturing morality as well as woolens, and fitting
the South with new principles as well as shoes." [2] This

[1] James Buchanan, *Works* (J. B. Moore, ed., Phila., 1908-1911), X,
200-201.
[2] T. P. Kettell, *Southern Wealth and Northern Profits* (N. Y., 1860),

was the most formal and elaborate of innumerable efforts to convince the North of the importance of a conservative position upon the slavery question.

It was quite obvious that the business interests of Philadelphia and New York were bound up with the economic life of the cotton states. New York, the chief broker of Southern cotton, seemed in many ways "a prolongation of the South." [1] There were some who extravagantly pointed out that, with the loss of Southern trade, the great metropolis would be "no more than a fishing village." [2] As the crisis approached Wall Street cried out: "Without the South we are ruined." [3] So also orders from Dixie played an important rôle in the economic life of Boston. The *Boston Post* reckoned the sales of New England products in the South at sixty million dollars annually beside the impetus given to shipbuilding by the Southern trade. "In every point of view," it declared, "New England seems to have been made for the South, and the South for New England. How could either live and flourish without the other?" [4] The countinghouses of State Street, in the mother city of the Puritans, set a conspicuous example of groveling servility to "King Cotton."

The excitement that developed in the South following John Brown's raid upon Harper's Ferry very much disturbed the normal business relations between the two sections. As has been said, Yankee peddlers and traveling representatives of Northern merchants and manufacturers were received with growing suspicion and even

73; A Merchant of Philadelphia (*pseud.*), *The End of the Irrepressible Conflict* (Phila., 1860).

[1] Gasparin, *Uprising of a Great People*, 76-77, 162.

[2] *Newark Mercury*, Feb. 11, 1861, cited in C. M. Knapp, *New Jersey Politics during the Civil War and Reconstruction* (Geneva, N. Y., 1924), 52.

[3] [Catherine C. Hopley], *Life in the South* (London, 1863), I, 140.

[4] *Boston Post*, Dec. 21, 1859.

hostility. The cry, "Don't trade with the North," went up and orders began to fall off. The *Atlanta Confederacy,* with the aid of *"true* Southern born men in New York," published a blacklist of antislavery firms in the Northern metropolis and announced its intention to supervise the boycott locally. A "white list" of "sound, Constitutional houses" was also prepared from which Southern merchants were urged to purchase their goods.[1]

Conservative Northern newspapers told of factories having to discharge workmen on account of the lack of orders from the South; these were the inevitable results of Northern "fanaticism," it was argued.[2] A group of Connecticut manufacturers, duly impressed by this information, met on January 18, 1860, and adopted resolutions condemning the spirit of sectionalism. Soon Union meetings were held in every Northern city and "white lists" were prepared of Northern firms that had enlisted to check the forces of "Black Republicanism." A few like Abraham Lincoln denied the alleged loss of Southern trade; speaking of the shoe trade of Connecticut, he declared: "Orders were never better than now!" [3] But Lincoln was only partly correct. It was later evident that, in line with Southern preparations for the impending revolution, large freight shipments moved into Dixie in the winter of 1859-1860. Many of these were second orders, part of a process of hoarding supplies for the future in anticipation of the time when the slave states

---

[1] *N. Y. Tribune,* Jan. 23, 1860; [Hopley], *Life in the South,* I, 122.

[2] *Dollar Newspaper* (Phila.), Dec. 14, 1859; *Baltimore Sun,* Jan. 14, 1860; *Philadelphia Journal,* cited in *Baltimore Sun,* Jan. 2, 1860. The *N. Y. Journal of Commerce,* Jan. 24, 1860, issued similar warnings. Gerard Hallock, one of its editors, was strongly in sympathy with the South. See Robert Stiles, *Four Years under Marse Robert* (N. Y., 1903), 36, and *Dictionary of American Biography,* VIII, 158.

[3] Lincoln, *Complete Works,* V, 362.

would no longer pay tribute to their Northern economic exploiters.[1]

Throughout the presidential campaign of 1860 powerful forces of Northern capital were arrayed against the candidacy of the Illinois rail splitter. Conservative fears seemed borne out early in November when the news came of the suspension of the oldest banking house in Baltimore. "The panic of 1860 has commenced in earnest," commented a New York journal. "This state of things is the harbinger of what may be expected in case Lincoln should be elected. . . . The merchants of New York should give heed to those signs of the times, and strive, with might and main, for the success of the Union ticket." [2] The belated meeting on November 5 of a group of New York merchants favorable to Lincoln's election was a rather equivocal demonstration of Wall Street support.[3] The Illinois standard bearer was privately under powerful pressure from the commercial and manufacturing interests of New England "to barter away the moral principle involved in this contest, for the commercial gain of a new submission to the South." [4] As in 1856, funds were poured into Pennsylvania, the pivotal state. August Belmont and other Democratic Wall Street bankers gave generously of their means to save Pennsylvania and the nation from a political revolution. Old-line politicians in the Republican ranks, like Thurlow Weed, admitted that Pennsylvania had been lost in 1856 only because the Democrats had expended fifty thousand dollars more than the Republicans were

[1] New Orleans Picayune, Sept. 10, 1859; N. Y. Herald, Oct. 28, Nov. 28, 1859, Feb. 4, 1860; Savannah Republican, March 22, Aug. 31, 1860.

[2] [Hopley], Life in the South, I, 127.

[3] N. Y. Tribune, Nov. 6, 1860.

[4] J. G. Nicolay and John Hay, Abraham Lincoln (N. Y., 1890), III, 280.

able to raise. Now the latter left no stone unturned, even collecting funds from the beneficiaries of the New York City railroad franchises.[1]

The Republican victory on election day seemed a great blow to American prosperity. Trade with the South reached a complete standstill; the wheels of industry ceased for the moment to turn; securities at the stock exchange went topsy-turvy; money became excessively stringent as the banks, fearful of another panic, called in their loans. The future was dark and uncertain. Was the economic development of the nation to be sacrificed to maudlin sentimentality and blind fanaticism? This was the question upon the lips of conservative men of affairs.

The moneyed interests of the North, hysterical at the thought of secession, favored preserving the Union at any price, particularly since disunion was likely to be accompanied by the forfeiture of Southern debts.[2] There was owing upon the books of Northern merchants and bankers a Southern debt of two or three hundred millions of dollars; nor was there any evidence of a disposition to pay those obligations as they fell due. Indeed, as Southerners beheld the utter terror of Northern creditors at the specter of repudiation, disunion began to offer even greater attractions than mere relief from long-continued economic exploitation and a time-worn crusade.[3] Journals like the *Clayton* (Alabama) *Banner* advanced the argument that it was *"treason to the South to pay money,* or in any way *encourage,* aid or abet the transfer to the hostile section of so important a weapon

[1] Charles Wright (Mountaineer, *pseud.*), *The Prospect* (Buffalo, 1862), 20.

[2] *N. Y. Herald,* Nov. 29, Dec. 10, 1860; *Springfield* (Mass.) *Republican,* Nov. 17, 24, 1860; L. T. Lowrey, *Northern Opinion of Approaching Secession* (Smith College, *Studies,* III, no. 4).

[3] Anon., "The Commercial Revulsion," *De Bow's Rev.,* XXXI (1861), 93. See also *New Orleans True Delta,* Nov. 20, 1860.

of attack and defense." Many were induced to favor a general "smash-up" that would wipe out their liabilities to Northern creditors.[1]

Northern argument that the South was not really in earnest, that talk of disunion was an ancient brand of bluff and braggadocio, and that repudiation could easily be met by confiscation of Southern property in the free states did not relieve these fears. Loudly in petitions and mass meetings the "doughface" spokesmen of Northern capital begged for the acceptance of a scheme of compromise that would satisfy the South and save the Union. Lincoln was never quite sure until he entered office that the Eastern leaders even of his own party could be kept from yielding to such entreaties. When in due course the lower tier of Southern states effected their withdrawal from the Union and Lincoln assumed the reins of administration at the most trying time in the nation's history, "the upper world of millionaire merchants, bankers, contractors, and great traders" rejoiced that the Republicans were at length suffering "for their success."[2]

Lincoln's election, indeed, inaugurated a revolution which played havoc with many existing institutions, political, social and economic. But the brunt of the upheaval fell upon the states that had taken their stand for a static, agrarian civilization in which the institution of chattel slavery held the place of paramount importance. Some Southrons consoled themselves with the thought that they were of the blood of a master race, a noble Norman stock not to be crushed by Northern Puritans of vulgar Saxon origin. They repudiated all

[1] *Clayton Banner*, cited in *N. Y. Tribune*, Dec. 28, 1860; William Watson, *Life in the Confederate Army* (N. Y., 1888), 70, 71. Cf., however, W. C. Corsan (An English Merchant, *pseud.*), *Two Months in the Confederate States* (London, 1863), 111, 133.

[2] W. H. Russell, *My Diary North and South* (Boston, 1863), 21.

thought of brotherhood with the Yankees; this was no fratricidal war but a renewal of the hereditary hostility between the "two races engaged." Let not the "Saxonized maw-worm" bring his taint to the soil of the South.[1] Others, like Senator Wigfall of Texas, accepted as compliment and not reproach the description of their section as a primitive but civilized agricultural community. If, they claimed, it lacked not only a commercial marine, manufacturing and the mechanic arts but also any real cities, literature or even press, it was by choice.[2] In such an atmosphere, of course, the plantation system and the institution of chattel slavery might flourish, although then only with the reins of power in the hands of its ardent exponents and champions. But amid the whirl and rush of modern industrial civilization its doom was certain.

[1] *Boston Eve. Transcript*, July 28, 1862; *Southern Literary Messenger*, cited in *Belleville* (Ill.) *Advocate*, Feb. 5, 1864; William Alexander, "Elements of Discord in Secessia," Loyal Publication Soc., *Pamphlets*, no. 15 (1863), 1-7, 11-12.
[2] Russell, *My Diary*, 179.

CHAPTER XII

MARSHALING THE GRAY HOST

FOR three decades and more spokesmen of the South had protestingly portrayed the economic penalties of its minority status in the Union. Yet Southerners were traditionally content to let the patent office at Washington speak for the North as long as the capitol was the symbol of their own section. In the words of *De Bow's Review*, "politically we are the most suspecting, wide-awake people on the face of the globe—economically the most careless and unsuspecting." [1] The fire eaters and "chivalry" politicians found their strength in this addiction to politics. During the fifties with telling effect they had put a positive tone into the disunionist propaganda by appealing to a spirit of Southern nationality that existed in every sense but the political. They rejoiced, too, that their appeals could rally even the non-slaveholders against the menace of the antislavery crusade, often at junctures when large planters remained unperturbed and wanted only to be left alone. One non-slaveholder queried whether it was not "perfectly farcical that the people who own slaves should be perfectly quiet, and we who own none should be lashing ourselves into a rage about their wrongs and injuries." [2] Now and again in the general stores and barrooms of the backcountry the red-hot stove became a busy "target

[1] Anon., "Southern Patronage to Southern Imports and Domestic Industry," *De Bow's Rev.*, XXIX (1860), 231.
[2] Robert Toombs, Alexander H. Stephens and Howell Cobb, *Correspondence* (U. B. Phillips, ed., Am. Hist. Assoc., *Ann. Rep. for 1911*, II), 142.

for tobacco-practice" and dealers recorded unprecedented
sales of the popular weed, for "in moments of mental
disturbance"—such as the secession crisis—"the tobacco-
chewer eats inordinately of his favorite narcotic." [1]

The political "revolution" of 1860, which sent Abraham Lincoln to the White House, transferred to the
North the reins of power previously held to a surprising degree by Southern men and Southern sympathizers.
Southern conservatives could see no serious menace in
the mere fact of Lincoln's election and counseled patience
unless some overt hostile act were taken. Extremists, on
the other hand, like the editors of the Charleston Mercury, proclaimed the direct consequences to Southern
rights and Southern honor and declared their unwillingness to believe or accept any assurances that might come
from the president-elect.[2] Southerners generally, including Alexander H. Stephens, were alarmed that the triumphant party had made the subject of slavery the "central idea" in a platform of principles which aimed "to
put the institutions of nearly half of the States, under
the ban of public opinion and national condemnation." [3]

After long contemplation of sufferings from economic
discrimination, they had become acutely sensitive to
what Senator Judah P. Benjamin in 1856 called "the
incessant attack of the Republicans, not simply on the
interests, but on the feelings and sensibilities of a high-
spirited people by the most insulting language, and the

[1] N. Y. Tribune, Dec. 24, 1860. Meantime an unusually heavy tide of
emigration was daily rolling westward "bound some for Texas, some for
Missouri, and some for the Lord knows where." Shelby (Tenn.)
Expositor, cited in N. Y. Herald, Dec. 4, 1860. On emigration from slave
to free states, see N. Y. Tribune, Nov. 30, 1860.

[2] Charleston Mercury, cited in National Intelligencer (Wash.), Oct. 24,
1860.

[3] Henry Cleveland, Alexander H. Stephens in Public and Private
(Phila., 1866), 151-153.

most offensive epithets." [1] Much of the aggressiveness
of the "chivalry" politicians of the fifties was the result
of the effort to compensate for this wounded pride.
"Southern honor" was at stake; in its behalf there could
be no excess of zeal. Therefore little exact analysis
needed to be made of the alleged menace to slavery. The
fire eaters preferred what the *Nashville Republican Banner* at first derided as "sublimated abstractions," although when the issue of state "coercion" was raised in
April, 1861, the same editorial pen found vent in similar fulminations. [2]

Contemporary assertion of the constitutional right of
peaceful secession was one of the commonest of these
abstractions. The doctrine was written into formal pronouncements. According to this argument the burden
of responsibility for an armed clash would rest upon
the North. But Southern champions were not unwilling
to face the serious possibility of conflict. For a decade
"The Sword" had been toasted in South Carolina as
"The arbiter of national disputes. The sooner it is un-
sheathed in maintaining Southern rights, the better." [3]
"No nation has ever yet matured its political growth
without the stern and searing experience of civil war,"
William H. Trescott had declared in 1850. [4] "If war
does come," added Edward B. Bryan, "it will be an
open, rigorous and determined war, between two great

[1] *Congressional Globe*, 36 Cong., 2 sess., pt. i, 212. See also E. D.
Keyes, *Fifty Years' Observation of Men and Events* (N. Y., 1884), 425;
Pierce Butler, *Judah P. Benjamin* (Phila., 1906), 207. See indictment
of Virginia by *N. Y. Tribune* and comment of *Richmond Enquirer* in
N. Y. Tribune, March 7, 1854; *Richmond Enquirer*, cited in *Liberator*
(Boston), April 7, 1854.

[2] *Nashville Republican Banner*, Nov. 9, 1860, May 7, 1861.

[3] *Natchez* (Miss.) *Courier*, July 25, 1851.

[4] W. H. Trescott, *The Position and Cause of the South* (Charleston,
1850), 16. See also Langdon Cheves, *Speech in the Southern Convention
at Nashville, Tennessee, November 14, 1850* (Nashville, 1850), 20-22.

nations; the one defending all that is sacred, the other the Lord knows what." [1] Those who cradled the Southern Confederacy were therefore more than mere closet philosophers.

The day of compromise passed despite the active efforts of its advocates in and out of Congress. Determined to preserve the prosperity which depended upon the continued coöperation of the South, financiers of New York, Boston and Philadelphia supplemented the conservative politicians in their efforts to quell Northern sectionalism. But large and imposing Union meetings, and even a general tendency toward greater moderation in the North, were not enough to quiet the storm that had been loosed.

The winter of 1860-1861 witnessed the secession of the lower tier of seven slave states. A month and more of anxious waiting after Lincoln's inauguration ended in war being precipitated by the events in Charleston Harbor. There, after a futile resistance, the little federal garrison at Fort Sumter surrendered to a Southern force. As this news flashed through Dixie the people went wild with joy. Processions of singing and shouting revelers marched up and down the streets; later the celebration was adjourned to clubs, restaurants, bars and taprooms. It seemed a favorable omen that one little state could successfully defend the sacredness of her soil; how then could the North—even with the seventy-five thousand volunteers for which Lincoln now called—expect to subjugate a united South? [2] Under this impelling logic and in view of reiterated hostility to any attempt at state coercion, the upper tier of states—Virginia, Tennessee, Arkansas and North Carolina—successively arrayed themselves on the side of Southern independence.

[1] E. B. Bryan, *The Rightful Remedy* (Charleston, 1850), 151.
[2] *N. Y. Tribune*, April 27, 1861.

Secessionists had early made ready to defend their rights by force. Military preparedness had been a matter of serious concern in the crisis of 1850-1851. Military education then took on a more serious aspect. Literary institutions like La Grange College were converted into military academies.[1] Virginia Military Institute at Lexington, under patrons like Professor Jackson whose sturdiness was to win him the name of "Stonewall," became second in reputation only to West Point. In the excitement following John Brown's raid Virginia and near-by regions were put "on a war footing."[2]

During the presidential campaign, in anticipation of Lincoln's election, companies of "minute men" were formed in South Carolina; blue-cockaded recruits drilled and paraded in the principal centers of the state. With the news of the "Black Republican" victory organizations of "minute men" also appeared in New Orleans and other cities while efforts were made to transform into effective military units the militia that had existed largely on paper. Orders for weapons and munitions were placed with dealers in New York and New England as well as in Baltimore. These developments, together with movements to boycott other Northern goods and to expel suspicious Northerners, stirred the popular pulse and created something of a mob spirit that the advocates of secession promptly capitalized. The news of the South Carolina ordinance of secession was hailed by noisy salutes and enthusiastic demonstrations which brought new recruits. Confederate flags were flung from private dwellings and public buildings, even in states that had not yet seceded.[3] Home guards were organized in nearly every city or town, ready to act upon rumors

[1] J. A. Wyeth, *With Sabre and Scalpel* (N. Y., 1914), 160-161.

[2] *Richmond Dispatch*, cited in *N. Y. Herald*, Jan. 7, 1861.

[3] [Catherine C. Hopley], *Life in the South* (London, 1863), I, 283, 284.

of incendiary fires and servile insurrection which the existing nervous tension bred. In some communities the secretly organized "chivalry leaders" varied their excited discussions with target practice, using as a mark a board roughly hewn into the shape of a man and designated as "Old Abe." Meantime the state legislatures gave legal authorization for properly equipped military forces.

The celebration of the Sumter victory was followed by more serious tasks. War had to be made in earnest if the Southern Confederacy was to take its place in the family of nations. Previously there had been idle talk, even in Richmond, of a grand march on the capital at Washington.[1] Now it was urged that Southern hearth and home be safeguarded against "the invading hosts of the damned Abolitionists."[2] President Jefferson Davis called for one hundred thousand troops, later for four times that number. Volunteers poured into the recruiting offices from plantation homes and yeoman farms. Clumsy yokels as well as sleek, dandyish youths with long, flowing locks enlisted in the ranks to fight the battles of Southern chivalry. Within a year half the eligible male population had responded to the appeal to arms.

In six months the South had achieved an apparent unity out of the diversity of sentiment that had prevailed at the time of secession. Most of those who had urged that the sectional fight should be continued within the Union had acquiesced in the separatist decision of their respective states. The conservative planter who still shook his head and quietly lamented the passing of better days was left undisturbed in his rural isolation, but the zealous Union man quickly felt the adverse judgment of the community, visited upon him perhaps by vigilance

[1] *Richmond Enquirer*, April 13, 1861, cited in A. B. Moore, *Conscription and Conflict in the Confederacy* (N. Y., 1924), 4-5.
[2] R. S. Tharin, *Arbitrary Arrests in the South* (N. Y., 1863), 81.

committees and other emissaries of King Mob. In due time conscription and exile reduced the numbers of both types; some Louisiana Unionists even preferred refuge in the swamps to involuntary service in the Confederate army.[1] Of those who remained at home many kept silent, hoping to escape the penalties of disloyalty to the Confederacy.

Throughout the war the mountain fastnesses and valleys of "Alleghania," centering around western North Carolina, northern Alabama, and eastern Tennessee, formed the chief stronghold of the Unionists.[2] This was an isolated region of little cotton culture and slaveholding where a mild antislavery sentiment had earlier cropped out. There, spokesmen like George W. Lane and R. S. Tharin of Alabama and Andrew Johnson, "Parson" Brownlow, and the Reverend N. G. Taylor of Tennessee openly defied the "cotton nobility." Others when forced into "secesh" service took their vows "from the teeth out." In communities torn by dissension the Union sympathizers awaited the succor of the federal army; meantime their ranks were depleted by refugee migration to Northern states, by enlistments in the Union forces, and by the ravages of a guerrilla warfare which they waged mountain-style with their Confederate neighbors.

Lurid tales were recounted in Northern parts of the maltreatment and sufferings of these loyalist dissenters.[3]

---

[1] A number of exiles hurled their printed broadsides at the Southern disunionists and appealed to the people upon whom they declared the political leaders had forced secession and civil war. See W. G. Brownlow, *Sketches of the Rise, Progress, and Decline of Secession* (Phila., 1862); Tharin, *Arbitrary Arrests in the South;* J. W. Hunnicutt, *The Conspiracy Unveiled* (Phila., 1863); R. J. Walker, *American Slavery and Finances* (London, 1864).

[2] J. W. Taylor, *Alleghania* (St. Paul, 1862); H. T. Tuckerman, *America and Her Commentators* (N. Y., 1864), 277-278. Jones County, Mississippi, was a hotbed of Union sentiment.

[3] *E.g.,* anon., "The Terror at the South," *Harper's Wkly.,* VII, 802

In eastern Tennessee both sides intermittently harassed and abused their opponents and at times burned, pillaged and murdered. Two or three thousand local Union noncombatants were said to have suffered martyrdom. In 1863 James Longstreet's hungry army cleared the country of its food supplies; when it retreated before A. E. Burnside's forces, starvation and destitution stared the rejoicing Unionists in the face. Only generous contributions from the North rescued the unfortunate from their plight.

The fighting Union bushwhackers of Alleghania furnished a striking contrast to the mild-mannered Quaker brethren of the North Carolina meeting and other conscientious objectors whom the Southern authorities tried to recruit despite their well-known gospel of peace in war time. Their conscientious scruples and their generally Union sympathies were often put to the most severe test. That none suffered complete martyrdom at the hands of the military authorities they felt could only be attributed to the protection of an "overruling Providence." [1] Under the injunction to feed the hungry and clothe the naked, even neutral Quakers often gave aid and shelter to Unionist refugees and escaped federal prisoners. The latter also encountered Union men who were secretly organized, sometimes despite their acceptance of Confederate service, to assist in passing on such fugitives along an "underground railroad" to friendly hands and to eventual safety within the Union lines.[2]

(Dec. 19, 1863) ; anon., "Union Refugees in the Louisiana Swamps," same mag., VIII, 310 (May 14, 1864) ; Western Sanitary Commission, *Report on the White Union Refugees of the South* (St. Louis, 1864), 3-39; Loyal Publication Society, *Pamphlets*, no. 73.

[1] Anon., *A Narrative of the Cruelties Inflicted upon Friends of North Carolina Yearly Meeting during the Years 1861 to 1865* (London, 1868). A Confederate statute exempted members of recognized pacifist sects who furnished substitutes or paid a tax of $500. E. N. Wright, *Conscientious Objectors in the Civil War* (Phila., 1931), 104 ff.

[2] William Burson, *A Race for Liberty* (Wellsville, Ohio, 1867), 45,

As has been said, certain venerable and distinguished sons of the South like James L. Petigru of South Carolina and Judge Garnett Andrews, a large Georgia slaveholder, refused to have any part in the war that they opposed and were left unmolested out of respect for their gray hairs or because they were regarded as amiable and harmless dotards. Younger blood, however, was given no choice. Under the circumstances many preferred to fight for the Union. The advancing federal armies brought Northern state recruiting agents who operated in active rivalry to credit the new recruits to their own commonwealths, sometimes offering bounties greater than those available to their own citizens.[1] In the course of the struggle nearly three hundred thousand white Union soldiers were enrolled from the slave states. The border states and Tennessee were especially generous in this respect while even Alabama furnished over two thousand white recruits. Some of these had seen service in the Confederate forces but, like Jeremiah Clemens who had been a major general in the Alabama militia, had experienced a change of heart and welcomed an opportunity to change sides.

But a year of war, with little in the way of definite accomplishment, dulled the enthusiasm of many for participating on either side of the struggle. Yet the Southern forces that had suffered and fought in trench and camp sorely needed reënforcement. Accordingly, in April, 1862, despite their strong state-rights predilections, the legislative representatives of the Confederacy adopted a

64 ff.; T. W. Humes, *Loyal Mountaineers of Tennessee* (Knoxville, 1888), 198. See also W. B. Hesseltine, "The Underground Railroad from Confederate Prisons to East Tennessee," East Tenn. Hist. Soc., *Publs.*, no. 2, 55-69.

[1] F. A. Shannon, *The Organization and Administration of the Union Army* (Cleveland, 1928), II, 76, 77. See also Abraham Lincoln, *Complete Works* (J. G. Nicolay and John Hay, eds., N. Y., 1905), X, 166, 167.

policy of conscription which, amended in September, rendered liable to draft all able-bodied males between the ages of eighteen and forty-five. Numerous exemptions were authorized, including state and Confederate officials and persons engaged in war industries or in what were deemed essential occupations. Under these arrangements many continued to evade military service. By one device or another, including in some cases self-imposed physical disabilities, probably one hundred and fifty thousand persons were exempted from active military service in the area east of the Mississippi River.[1]

Professions like teaching—when twenty or more pupils were under tutelage—acquired new popularity even with those who had previously scorned the art of the pedagogue. The privileged status of apothecaries resulted in shops that boasted of "a few empty jars, a cheap assortment of combs and brushes, a few bottles of 'hair dye' and 'wizard oil' and other Yankee nostrums"; soon they anticipated their modern counterpart in having even greater resemblance to variety stores or produce depots.[2] Some found no way out except through the employ of substitutes. Here was a profitable field for brokers, as the market price of a soldier soon mounted to fifteen hundred dollars and three thousand dollars; professional misfits and deserters found their places as raw materials of the trade. Under the "twenty-nigger" clause many slaveholders escaped for a time the hardships of camp and battle-field while resenting any suggestion that this was "a rich man's war and a poor man's

[1] Cf. J. C. Schwab, The Confederate States of America (New Haven, 1913), 198; Moore, Conscription and Conflict in the Confederacy, esp. 108; Bela Estvàn, War Pictures from the South (N. Y., 1863), 162-163.

[2] Columbus (Ga.) Weekly Sun, Sept. 2, 1862, cited in Moore, Conscription and Conflict in the Confederacy, 55, 56.

fight." It was estimated in September, 1864, that "over 100,000 landed proprietors and most of the slaveholders are now out of the ranks," a condition which, though doubtless exaggerated, caused ominous mutterings to reverberate through the Confederacy.[1] In due time the government remedied the more flagrant abuses and in the last year of the war the man power of the South was more effectively mobilized. The government maintained in active service a fighting machine that averaged about four hundred thousand men. Probably a grand total of well over a million served under the Stars and Bars in the course of the bloody struggle.[2]

The Confederate soldiery did not, however, constitute an altogether enthusiastic fighting force. Caste barriers were felt to exist not only between officers and privates—with an often "shameful disregard" of the humble musket bearer by those in authority [3]—but also among the rank and file where the sensitive exemplar of chivalry chafed at having to share the lot of rough, uncouth countrymen.[4] The latter, conscious that those who had no direct stake in slavery constituted three fourths of the defenders of the Confederacy, in turn resented the implied superiority. Smoldering class hatred sometimes flared up on the arrival of rumors that wealthy exempts at home were "grinding the faces of the

[1] J. B. Jones, *A Rebel War Clerk's Diary* (Phila., 1866), II, 281.

[2] T. L. Livermore, *Numbers and Losses in the Civil War in America, 1861-1865* (Boston, 1901), 63. See also C. B. Hite, "The Size of the Confederate Army," *Current History*, XVIII (1923), 251-253; A. B. Casselman, "Numerical Strength of the Confederate Army," *Century*, XLIII (1892), 795, and "How Large was the Confederate Army," *Current History*, XVII (1923), 653-657; R. H. McKim, *The Numerical Strength of the Confederate Army* (N. Y., 1912).

[3] Randolph Abbott Shotwell, *Papers* (J. G. deR. Hamilton, ed., Raleigh, 1929-1931), I, 128-129, 169-170, 187-188, 444; J. H. Browne, *Four Years in Secessia* (Hartford, 1865), 42, 43; William Watson, *Life in the Confederate Army* (N. Y., 1888), 339.

[4] Shotwell, *Papers*, II, 73.

poor with their extortions and their speculations." [1]
There were increased mutterings against the conscript
officers of the "Jeff Davis Secession Aristocracy." [2]

Those who fought in the ranks were clad in a great
variety of colors and costumes; but the bright plumage
of many an original outfit soon disappeared in the ruck
of war and weather. Replacements came from a multitude of sources. Many were glad to don captured federal
uniforms even though at the grave risk of being mis-
takenly shot by Confederate bullets. The increasingly
used gray uniform was often of a tobacco or butternut-
colored homespun which, when a little rusty, seemed
"the ugliest imaginable style of dress." [3] From the beginning there was a shortage of overcoats and blankets
while the supply of shoes was never adequate. Lee's
army crossed the Potomac in the late summer of 1862
with thousands of his men *barefooted, blanketless, and
hatless!*" [4] If Southern sympathizers in Maryland considered joining the Confederate cause, the impulse was
thoroughly routed by the appearance of this Falstaffian
horde. The real tragedy of these ragged troops, however,
came with the onset of bitter winter weather.

Hunger constantly menaced the gaunt recruits of
Dixie. Regular rations were scant enough from the start
and, because of the poor management of the commissariat, often failed of delivery. After the spring of 1863
reduced allotments became a necessity. The generosity
of the country people often supplied the deficiency and
shipments from home sometimes broke prolonged fasts
just when starvation seemed at hand. Raids upon Union

[1] A. B. Moore, *History of Alabama and Her People* (N. Y., 1927),
I, 542-543.

[2] See *North Carolinan Times*, cited in *N. Y. Tribune*, Aug. 3,
1864.

[3] Shotwell, *Papers*, I, 385. *Cf.* J. W. Thomason, jr., *Jeb Stuart*
(N. Y., 1930), 263.

[4] Shotwell, *Papers*, I, 314.

supply centers and foraging also supplemented local stores. The Confederate cavalry, to which no beef was issued over a period of eighteen months and more, subsisted chiefly on corn, with an especial fondness for roasting ears in season.[1]

In other particulars as well the Confederate forces suffered from inadequate arrangements for their health and physical well-being. Many of the better trained city physicians promptly enlisted and were given commissions for active service. On the other hand, in the rural areas anyone who possessed a small stock of medicines, a few recipes and a knowledge of how to bleed a patient was accepted as a military doctor.[2] For a time the Confederates rejoiced that the Yankees were the chief sufferers as the malarial mosquitoes fought for their Southern homeland. But in the fall of 1862 yellow fever decimated the population of Wilmington and smallpox soon raged violently in the Confederate capital. Supplies of quinine and other necessary medicines threatened to fail despite some success in smuggling from the North and through the blockade. The Confederate government established laboratories to relieve the shortage and was fortunate in being able to enlist the services of the Le Contes in the laboratories at Columbia, South Carolina, which became the chief local source of supply.[3]

After a battle all the doctors who could be spared from cities like Richmond hurried off to the field. For miles around every dwelling served as a hospital. In Richmond public buildings and even tobacco factories sheltered the sick and wounded, sometimes to a total of

[1] Wyeth, *With Sabre and Scalpel*, 202; A. L. Long, *Memoirs of Robert E. Lee* (N. Y., 1886), 637.

[2] W. C. Corsan (An English Merchant, *pseud.*), *Two Months in the Confederate States* (London, 1863), 70-71.

[3] Joseph Le Conte, *Autobiography* (W. D. Armes, ed., N. Y., 1903), 184.

thirty thousand and more. Overworked army surgeons became hardened to the neglect which they were often powerless to correct. In general, little attention was directed to the most elementary sanitary precautions. To be sure, many an angel of mercy appeared among the volunteer nurses; Sally Tompkins, the Florence Nightingale of the South, was commissioned captain for her unwearied ministrations.[1] But the South never developed an elaborate civilian volunteer organization to parallel the Sanitary and Christian Commissions of the North.

With all the hardships of field and camp and with the enemy penetrating farther and farther into Dixie, the drain of desertion impaired the strength of the Southern legions. The urge to desert was not a matter of simple disloyalty. Ill-fed, barefoot, homesick and war-weary soldiers could not have been expected to maintain a satisfactory morale. Discontent made rapid headway. Backcountry farmers and mountain yeomen increasingly resented the mandates that issued from the ruling class of the black belt. Often under the impelling need of their families for food and clothing they fled to the rescue. At times they sought relief from military routine in swamp and forest or mountain fastness. There, in desperate bands, they resisted the efforts of the Confederate authorities to hunt them down. Some sought the enemies' lines to taste the more generous treatment of federal generals. In all, at least two hundred thousand deserters were lost to the Confederate ranks. Desertion it was which virtually undermined the conscription policy of the Southern Confederacy.[2]

An effective mobilization of all the available resources of the Southland was never attained. War materials and

---

[1] J. S. Wise, The End of an Era (Boston, 1899), 394.
[2] Ella Lonn, Desertion during the Civil War (N. Y., 1928), 21-36; Moore, Conscription and Conflict in the Confederacy, 129-130.

supplies were the obvious first need. Every type of weapon was promptly turned to account. The recruit usually appeared for service with a nondescript gun or revolver; even double-barreled shotguns were equipped for service with bayonets. The first extensive munition supply came from the federal forts and arsenals which were taken over following secession. Though one hundred and fifteen thousand stands of arms had been sent for storage in Southern arsenals in the spring of 1860 by Secretary of War Floyd, most of these were condemned muskets, as were those he sold to various Southern states after Lincoln's election. The Confederate leaders made haste upon the secession of Virginia to seize the United States arms factory at Harper's Ferry, but the federal commander destroyed the arsenal and most of the machinery in the armory building before abandoning it. Throughout the war Southern victories in the field usually involved the capture of arms and ammunition needed to replenish scanty supplies.[1]

In the placing of orders for arms and munitions in Europe Southern purchasing agents were for some time favored over their Northern rivals. Even after the increasing effectiveness of the blockade made difficult the delivery of foreign purchases, the Confederate authorities used the leverage of cotton sales to compel blockade runners to include a proper share of war materials in their cargoes. For adequate supplies, however, emphasis had more and more to be laid upon local factories that the war brought into existence or into greater importance. Richmond, with the Tredegar works and other plants, became an important center from which a line of ordnance works was established by 1863 reaching into the Lower South.[2] Selma, Alabama, like the Columbus

---

[1] Shotwell, *Papers*, I, 247-248, 279, 324.

[2] Kathleen Bruce, "Economic Factors in the Manufacture of Confed-

and Augusta section of Georgia, witnessed an important development of munition manufacturing. Powder factories—some private and some government institutions—were set up all over the South, the most important being the government plant at Augusta. With infinite ingenuity and resource the ordnance department under General Josiah Gorgas, a native of Pennsylvania, was soon able to meet the demands made upon it, so that shortages in the field were due largely to the problem of distribution rather than of supply. When the dearth of metals threatened to curtail production, the South responded to the stirring appeal of General P. G. T. Beauregard to spare the church and plantation bells that they might be molded into cannon. In the same way copper kettles, brass door knobs, lead and old iron implements were contributed.[1] The rails of the horse-car street railroad in Richmond were sacrificed for the manufacture of armor for a gunboat.

The war, particularly the shutting out of foreign goods by the blockade, made a necessity out of the oft-proclaimed virtue of Southern self-sufficiency. As new ventures in iron, textile, glass and paper production were launched, loyal Southerners chose to believe that their economic problems were finding a solution. A cheerful optimism prevailed in official and unofficial circles until well into the war.[2] With the editor of the *Richmond Enquirer* they believed that this would "deprive the hated Yankee man and the hyena Yankee woman of

erate Ordnance," *Army Ordnance*, VI (1925), 168-170, and *Virginia Iron Manufacture in the Slave Era* (N. Y., 1931) ; Josiah Gorgas, "Notes on the Ordnance Department of the Confederate Government," Southern Hist. Soc., *Papers*, XII (1884), 67-94.

[1] [Hopley], *Life in the South*, II, 292, 338; *The War of the Rebellion: A Compilation of the Official Records of the Union and Confederate Armies* (Wash., 1880-1901), ser. 4, II, 502.

[2] W. W. Malet, *An Errand to the South in the Summer of 1862* (London, 1863), 38, 75; Corsan, *Two Months in the Confederate States*, 123, 124, 268-272; [Hopley], *Life in the South*, II, 86, 131, 247.

their immemorial market." [1] "Augusta drills," "Atlanta shirtings" and "Graniteville sheetings" set the standard in textiles. Although cotton operatives were exempted from military duty, the head of the Graniteville mills soon complained that Congress allowed only a seventy-five-per-cent profit.[2] The products of the paper mills were usually very crude and rough, though newspaper publishers rejoiced when they found even this supply adequate for their most economical needs.

In the later years of the war the success of the Union arms greatly reduced the number of Southern factories. Northern generals were not unaware of the contribution they might make along these lines toward the throttling of the South. General W. T. Sherman not only burned the cotton factories at Rosswell, Georgia, but—quite unnecessarily, it would seem—transported the four hundred young women operatives beyond the Ohio in order to make certain that production would not be resumed in that vicinity.[3] This unfortunate instance of the deportation of innocent and helpless females seems to have been overlooked by historians of American warfare.

The effective mobilization of the South's material resources depended in large part upon the adequacy of its transportation system. The railroads consisted mainly of short lines operated under a particularism that prevented them from achieving the effective military co-ordination that was secured in the North.[4] Rolling stock and trackage deteriorated rapidly under the heavy war-

---

[1] *Richmond Enquirer*, Aug. 20, cited in *Cincinnati Daily Commercial*, Sept. 6, 1864.

[2] Jones, *A Rebel War Clerk's Diary*, I, 203.

[3] *Richmond Examiner*, Aug. 11, cited in *Cincinnati Daily Commercial*, Aug. 19, 1864. See also *Official Records of Armies*, ser. 1, XXXVIII, pt. i, 70; pt. v, 92-93, 104.

[4] See C. W. Ramsdell, "The Confederate Government and the Railroads," *Am. Hist. Rev.*, XXII, 794-810, and J. F. Rhodes, *History of the Civil War* (N. Y., 1917), 370-374.

time traffic, nor was it possible to develop an adequate replacement by local efforts.[1] Not a single bar of railroad iron was rolled in the Confederacy during the war. The rails of less important lines were sometimes torn up to serve a greater need and Confederate troops often covered their retreat by the wholesale destruction of tracks and bridges. This was supplemented by the havoc wrought by the Union armies. In particular, Sherman's soldiers were past masters in this work, burning the ties and fences to heat the rails which they then wrapped around a tree trunk or a telegraph pole and transformed into "hair-pins" and "cork-screws."[2] The federals captured eleven locomotives at Vicksburg which, after being overhauled and repainted, were christened "General Grant," "Abraham Lincoln" and the like.[3] One of the most daring exploits of the war was the attempt of a group of twenty-four young Union raiders in northern Georgia under J. J. Andrews to cut the line of the Memphis and Charleston Railroad, an attempt which ended in a bold but unsuccessful effort to run off with a Confederate railroad train.[4] With such a multitude of handicaps it was manifestly impossible for the railroads to play their proper rôle of not only guaranteeing adequate supplies, but also of equalizing the varying degrees of plenty and shortage that often existed in different parts of "rebeldom."[5]

[1] *Official Records of Armies*, ser. 4, I, 145; II, 382, 501; III, 9, 575; Southern Hist. Soc., *Papers*, II (1876), 121.

[2] J. T. Trowbridge, *My Own Story* (Boston, 1903), 306, 308; Eliza F. Andrews, *War-Time Journal of a Georgia Girl, 1864-1865* (N. Y., 1908), 47; Regis de Trobriand, *Four Years with the Army of the Potomac* (Boston, 1889), 691. See also *N. Y. Times*, March 30, June 2, 1863.

[3] *Columbus* (Ohio) *Gazette*, Jan. 15, 1864.

[4] J. S. C. Abbott, "Heroic Deeds of Heroic Men," *Harper's Mo.*, XXXI (1865), 164-174.

[5] W. L. Fleming, *Civil War and Reconstruction in Alabama* (N. Y., 1905), 178.

The people of Dixie, fighting for hearth and home, were prepared to make their many sacrifices to the cause of Southern independence. Yet they did not achieve— or at least maintain—that high degree of unity and morale which was essential to a successful revolution.

CHAPTER XIII

THE BATTLE CRY OF FREEDOM

THOUGH the voters of the North had elected Lincoln to office, it had been with no thought that his first task would be to organize a war against their brethren of the South. Conflicting opinions marked the weeks that intervened before he took hold. Democrats of doughface leanings openly proclaimed their sympathies with the South against a North that was "hopelessly abolitionized," and justified secession. "As Democrats, we claim exemption from service in this Black Republican war," declared the *Joliet* (Illinois) *Signal*, January 15, 1861. "Let the Black Republicans . . . do the training, and fighting if necessary, for it was their party that brought the calamity upon the country. We trust that the Democratic members of our Legislature will vote against arming and drilling our people to prepare for murdering and butchering their Southern brethren."

Other Northerners of the "hopelessly abolitionized" type rejoiced with Greeley at the opportunity to "let the erring sisters depart in peace." If some of these talked of the South's right to self-government and self-determination, it is clear that their deeper motive was to rid the nation of responsibility for an undesirable institution. Thus Wendell Phillips renewed the old slogan of "No union with slaveholders!" and saluted the new day: "All hail, . . . Disunion!" [1] Meanwhile still others made

[1] Wendell Phillips, *Speeches, Lectures and Letters* (Boston, 1891), ser. 1, 356, 370. See also *Liberator* (Boston), Jan. 12, 1861; Agénor

304

frantic efforts, in public and in private, to compromise
the differences between the two sections. Apparently
only a few realized the fruitlessness of such attempts.
"Liberty & Slavery," declared Lincoln's erstwhile law
partner with inexorable logic, "are *absolute* antago-
nisms; and all human experience—all human philosophy says—'Clear the ring & let these natural foes—
these eternal enemies now fight it out.' " [1] "We live in
revolutionary times," added Horace White of the *Chicago Tribune,* "and I say God bless the revolution!" [2]

Six weeks after the first native Kentuckian was in-
ducted into the presidential office the bloody struggle
that had been so long impending was precipitated at
Fort Sumter. Lincoln promptly sent out a clarion call
for defenders of the Union, thus ending much of the
futile discussion and wrangling between leaders of the
various factions in the North. Doubt and hesitation vanished. Men knew that the Union was what they cared
for most and the flag was what they held most sacred.
Many of Garrison's supporters wheeled into line, now
seeing in war a means of delivering the Negro from
bondage. Garrison struck out his famous editorial cap-
tion proclaiming the Constitution "a covenant with
death and an agreement with Hell" and later explained
that, since these two allies had seceded with the South, "I
am now with the Government to enable it to constitu-
tionally stop the further ravages of death, and to extin-

de Gasparin, *The Uprising of a Great People* (Mary L. Booth, tr., N. Y.,
1861), 180, 184-185; Elizabeth C. Stanton, *Elizabeth Cady Stanton
as Revealed in Her Letters, Diary and Reminiscences* (Theodore Stanton
and Harriot S. Blatch, eds., N. Y., 1922), I, 180; Ida H. Harper,
Life and Work of Susan B. Anthony (Indianapolis, 1898), I, 208;
F. J. and W. P. Garrison, *William Lloyd Garrison* (N. Y., 1885-1889),
IV, 2-9.

[1] W. H. Herndon to Trumbull, Dec. 21, 1860 (Trumbull MSS.,
Library of Congress).

[2] Horace White to Trumbull, Dec. 30, 1860 (Trumbull MSS.).

guish the flames of hell forever." [1] For a time the abolitionists called off their meetings—including the customary May anniversary of the American Anti-Slavery
Society—feeling that they could afford to "stand still,
and see the salvation of God" [2] as the mighty current of
popular feeling against slavery set in.

Likewise organized Christianity rallied to the support
of Mars. Protestant pulpits thundered denunciation of
the rebellion. Mary A. Livermore later recalled congregations applauding "sermons such as were never before
heard . . . , not even from radical preachers." [3] The
Y.M.C.A. at Cleveland gave consideration to the question, "Under what circumstances is war justifiable?" but
a local preacher had already published a sermon on "The
Christian Necessity of War" and a good Catholic father
was soon christening a big gun with the comment: "The
echo of its voice would be *sweet music*, inviting the children of Columbia to share the comforts of his father's
home." [4] As clergymen eloquently proclaimed "the sub-
limity of the present crisis" and fervently offered prayers
for God's aid to President Lincoln and the Northern
cause, the line between politics and religion quickly dissolved. Later the Northern clergy in general were to be
an important factor in the pressure upon President Lincoln for emancipation. [5]

[1] W. L. Garrison, "The Abolitionists and Their Relations to the War,"
Pulpit and Rostrum, nos. xxvi-xxvii, 46 (March 1, 1862). See also
Liberator, April 19, 1861, Jan. 14, 1862; Phillips, *Speeches, Lectures
and Letters*, ser. 1, 396 ff.

[2] Garrisons, *William Lloyd Garrison*, IV, 20-21.

[3] Mary A. Livermore, *My Story of the War* (Hartford, 1889), 88.

[4] Edward McPherson, *Political History of the Great Rebellion* (Wash.,
1865), 517; *Cleveland Leader*, May 29, June 3, 1861; W. H. Russell,
My Diary North and South (Boston, 1863), 371-372; Frank Moore, ed.,
The Rebellion Record (N. Y., 1861-1868), II, "Incidents," 42-43.

[5] Lincoln's last public statement before his emancipation proclamation
was to a committee from the religious denominations of Chicago, which
asked that he issue such a document. Abraham Lincoln, *Complete Works*
(J. G. Nicolay and John Hay, eds., N. Y., 1905), VIII, 28-33.

With such emotions surging in their breasts little room was left for the higher interests of Christ's spiritual kingdom, though a few independent churches sprang up to serve as houses of worship "wherein the pure and peaceable Gospel of Christ shall be preached, unmixed with politics, fanaticism or other foreign matter." [1] While religious bodies passed resolutions urging the proclamation of universal freedom, the constituent churches, as those of the Central Ohio and the North Ohio Methodist Conferences, lost members steadily, offsetting the important gains of the fifties. Nor did recovery come promptly with the termination of hostilities and the demobilization of the troops in spite of the fact that during the winter of 1863-1864 a new religious spirit began to manifest itself in a series of revivals which added new members, especially from the youth of the land. [2] It was near the end of the decade before the losses of the war period were recovered. [3]

Meanwhile the organized peace movement, confronted with the actuality of war, withered before the hot blasts of passion. The American Peace Society for the first time in its history found itself without a quorum at its anniversary meeting in May, 1860. A year later it was reconciling itself to a war it had been powerless to prevent, arguing that no peace man could "ever be a rebel or lend the slightest countenance to rebellion" and insisting that the struggle was not a war in the sense of its taboo. [4] Few persisted in their pacifist views like

[1] *Cincinnati Enquirer*, Jan. 8, 22, 26, 1864; *Columbus* (Ohio) *Gazette*, Jan. 22, Feb. 19, 1864; *N. Y. Tribune*, Jan. 6, 1864.

[2] E. D. Fite, *Social and Industrial Conditions in the North during the Civil War* (N. Y., 1910), 307-309. Cf. Georges Fisch, *Nine Months in the United States during the Crisis* (London, 1863), 56-57.

[3] Allan Nevins, *The Emergence of Modern America* (*A History of American Life*, VIII), 343-344.

[4] E. L. Whitney, *The American Peace Society* (Wash., 1928), 111-114; M. E. Curti, *American Peace Crusade, 1815-1860* (Durham,

that great internationalist of the period, Elihu Burritt. It was not until the war was over that the society announced it found "in the sad and terrible experience of these four years no reason to change any part of our principles or our policy, but much to confirm our belief of their essential correctness, wisdom, and necessity." [1]

In harmony with the lightning change of public sentiment volunteers answered Lincoln's call in numbers that threatened to embarrass the governors of several Northern states. It seemed like a rising *en masse* in spite of the antiquated militia laws that encumbered the statute books. Old militia organizations that had existed on a skeleton basis to satisfy a fondness for display in drills, parades, military balls and funerals were now transformed into active units. Leading citizens formed new companies under their personal command. Recruiting offices were opened in every town and hamlet. Newspaper advertisements and editorials summoned the patriot to the colors; blazing posters proclaimed the glories of military service; and mass meetings supplied the final touch to crowd psychology.

Soon the air thrilled with sound of fife and drum and with the music of the military band. The streets became colorful with red, green, blue, yellow and even pink Zouave uniforms with their baggy Turkish trousers and tasseled fez caps. Then, after tearful but proud partings, this motley horde was transported to the national capital or to some border camp where the real work of making an army out of the citizen soldiery began. There seemed little of the "swash-buckler bravado" or swagger of the Southern cohorts among these

1929), 223; Gerrit Smith, *Sermons and Speeches* (N. Y., 1861), 193-198; *N. Y. Tribune*, May 24, 30, 1861.
[1] Whitney, *American Peace Society*, 115.

Northern recruits, though, hardly more than their Southern brethren, did they realize the difficulties of the task before them.[1]

Despite the loyal outpouring of native sons from all parts of the North the Union army seemed "an amalgam of nations." Indeed, to William H. Russell the native-born seemed slow to enter the ranks while the Irish and German elements were, he thought, "fighting con amore and pro dolore (viz. 11 per mensem)."[2] Military adventurers—Hungarians, Austrians, Poles, Spaniards, Italians and others—flocked to America to secure commissions.[3] The government scarcely dared refuse their requests for fear they would seek service with the Confederates. The Orleans princes, the Comte de Paris and the Duc de Chartres, were assigned to George B. McClellan's staff where they sought a practical knowledge of military affairs. Many German officers secured assignments under Frémont, the favorite general of the German Americans. Certain military units, dubbed Les Enfants Perdus because of their inclusion of "black sheep" soldiers of fortune from every nation, were officered mainly by foreigners. In the case of General Louis Blencker's division commands were given in four different languages.[4] Above the measured tread of marching

---

[1] Russell, My Diary, 374; Anthony Trollope, North America (N. Y., 1862), 130-132; Adam Gurowski, Diary (Boston, 1862-1866), I, 40; J. F. Rhodes, History of the Civil War, 1861-1865 (N. Y., 1917), 341.

[2] W. H. Russell to J. C. B. Davis, Sept. 25, 1861, Historical Outlook, XVI, 255; Russell, My Diary, 358. These foreign-born had constituted a fair share of the peace-time regular army. Russell, My Diary, 4; J. G. Kohl, Travels in Canada, and through the States of New York and Pennsylvania (Mrs. Percy Sinnett, tr., London, 1861), I, 16.

[3] Russell, My Diary, 334, 341, 483, 580, 583; Carl Schurz, Reminiscences (N. Y., 1907-1908), II, 338-340; Edward Dicey, Six Months in the Federal States (London, 1863), II, 47, 48; John Bigelow, Retrospections of an Active Life (N. Y., 1909-1913), II, 276, 341-342.

[4] Dicey, Six Months in the Federal States, II, 21; Thomas Wentworth Higginson, Letters and Journals (Mary T. Higginson, ed., Boston, 1921), 199.

feet rang out in lusty rivalry the songs of nations over the sea. The ranks of Colonel Abram Duryee's New York Zouaves in their ludicrous uniforms and the more nattily attired Fifty-fifth New York Regiment were filled with French devotees of the "Marseillaise." The regimental bands with their German musicians played tunes dear to the fatherland as well as American military marches and, indeed, the lively strains of "Dixie." [1]

Since the German settlers of the West had developed their antislavery sentiment to a point where they seemed to outabolitionize even the New Englanders, it is not strange that they made a notable contribution to the saving of the American Union. [2] German regiments, often built around Turner organizations, appeared in every large city, while German-American officers like Schurz, Sigel, Rosencranz and Steinweler proved good drillmasters and strategists.

It was not for love of, or pity for, the enslaved African that the Irish poured into the army. Indeed, Negro emancipation was the great bogy of the Irish paddy who feared that the Northern states might be flooded with free blacks with resulting competition for jobs. [3] In the hearts of these sons of Erin there burned a consuming passion for Irish freedom. The Hibernian order had nursed this sentiment since its inception in 1851. It was supplemented shortly by the American branch of the secret Fenian Brotherhood under John O'Mahoney who directed the collection of money and arms and the organization of an invisible Irish army

[1] G. A. Townsend, *Campaigns of a Non-Combatant* (N. Y., 1866), 249; Dicey, *Six Months in the Federal States*, II, 4.

[2] Trollope, *North America*, 414; Auguste Laugel, *The United States during the War* (N. Y., 1866), 166; Russell, *My Diary*, 5.

[3] Edits., *Harper's Wkly.*, V, 802 (Dec. 21, 1861); VI, 530-531 (Aug. 23, 1862); *N. Y. Tribune*, July 11, Aug. 5, 1862. This was the cause of the bitter antipathy revealed in the New York draft riots of 1863.

scattered through the chief Northern cities. In 1863 an Irish Republican organization upon the American model was launched with headquarters at New York City, which levied taxes and contributions, issued bonds, organized its army and made every preparation to strike for Irish independence.[1]

Many an Irishman felt that service in the Union army was but a preparation for the great day of Ireland's deliverance. When the war began Colonel Michael Corcoran of the Sixty-ninth New York militia promptly took the field with his Irish battalion; over a year later, after his exchange by the Confederates as one of the prisoners of Bull Run, he raised an Irish legion and was made brigadier general.[2] Companies and regiments for an Irish brigade were promptly tendered in the summer of 1861 from cities like Cleveland, Detroit, Boston and Philadelphia to serve the endangered Union in preparation "for the cause which is still more desperately in peril."[3] But the more immediate bread-and-butter needs of the Irish at home had to be attended to in the spring of 1862 when distress became acute and relief societies made their appearance in Northern cities.[4] Active Irish enlistment had meantime slowed down, especially when there was no assurance of separate Hibernian units. But the bravery of the Irishman in battle was a matter of general comment.[5]

Doubtless thousands of these foreign-born defenders

[1] Mabel G. Walker, The Fenian Movement, 1859-1872 (Ph.D. thesis, Ohio State Univ., 1929).

[2] See handbill appeal anent Corcoran's capture, etc., N. Y. Daily News, July 26, 1861.

[3] Cleveland Leader, Sept. 9, 18, 1861.

[4] N. Y. Tribune, May 23, 26, 1862, May 4, 5, 7, 1863; Chicago Tribune, March 17, 1863.

[5] John White, Sketches from America (London, 1870), 358. See also G. E. Pickett, Soldier of the South: War Letters to His Wife (A. C. Inman, ed., Boston, 1928), 30-31.

of the Union, like countless of the native-born, were reluctant, if not unwilling, recruits. The bounties so generously offered by federal, state and local governmental units lured many into service and tempted not a few repeatedly to enlist and desert for the profitable returns of "bounty-jumping." When in 1863 the counterattractions of an industrial boom forced the federal government to resort to conscription, many reluctantly acquiesced in the necessity of a military service that offered meager rewards compared with wage-earning.[1] Still others employed all the arts of evasion to escape the necessity of an enlistment which the well-to-do were able to avoid by paying the three hundred dollars exemption fee. In the early months of the draft the enrolling officers encountered all sorts of obstacles to the performance of their duties from every ingenious artifice to open violence. The extensive opposition in New York City led to the draft riots of July, 1863, which were finally quelled only by drastic employment of military force. In the course of the war over two and a half million men served under the colors with mingled emotions as well as doubts as to whether the objective of their efforts was to preserve the Union or to free the black chattels of the South.

The problem of the conscientious objector to military service was a relatively small one but none the less vexatious.[2] Earnest Quaker apostles of peace not only proclaimed "the plain scripture testimony against all wars," but some even refrained from voting because to do so might indirectly implicate them in violations of their principles. Contemporary and later notices compliment

[1] F. A. Shannon, *The Organization and Administration of the Union Army* (Cleveland, 1928), I, 295-323; II, 11-174.

[2] Shannon, *Organization and Administration of the Union Army*, II, 247-260.

the "fighting Quakers," who in the eyes of their brethren "sinned by bearing arms," and the sacrifices they made under arms. More significant, however, was the fate of those who persisted in their conscientious scruples, enduring not only the ridicule of a hostile public but often the abuse of the drill sergeant, if not of their fellow recruits.[1] The true objector did not seek the easy way out of conscript service by the commutation clause or the right of substitution.

In the draft of 1862 some states exempted all Quakers and members of similar sects, while certain other states permitted exemption in return for a payment of two hundred dollars. Elsewhere no distinction was made. In November, 1863, after considerable pressure from the Friends, Secretary of War Stanton proposed a commutation fee for objectors that would provide a special fund for freedman relief; when this was rejected by spokesmen of the dissenters, Stanton professed to be annoyed by their abstractions. In the conscription law of February 24, 1864, however, provision was made for assigning conscientious objectors to hospital work or to caring for the freedmen. Even this concession did not satisfy the more extreme of the dissenters. In general, the war department tried to avoid making an issue of specific cases. Sterling champions of their rights were found in Senators Sumner, Wilson, Ten Eyck and Lane and in Thaddeus Stevens in the lower house. Lincoln himself showed sympathy with, and understanding of, objectors and promised Eliza P. Gurney to do "the best I . . . can, in my own conscience, under my oath to the law."[2]

[1] Cyrus Pringle, *The Record of a Quaker Conscience* (R. M. Jones, ed., N. Y., 1918) ; *Congressional Globe*, 38 Cong., 1 sess., 225. Cf. A. J. H. Duganne, *The Fighting Quaker* (N. Y., 1866).

[2] E. N. Wright, *Conscientious Objectors in the Civil War* (Phila., 1931), 62 ff.; Lincoln, *Complete Works*, X, 216.

Few subscribed to the harsh formula that they should be made to "fight, pay, or emigrate." [1] In the South, where the issue was more closely drawn, leaders like Assistant Secretary of War John A. Campbell did what they could to alleviate the sufferings of pacifists who were caught in the toils of conscription.

More troublesome than the problem of the conscientious objector was that of the deserter. Untold thousands of the latter became a veritable plague to the civil and military authorities of the Union as well as of the Confederacy. Deserters were not of necessity unwilling conscripts dragged into the fray; ardent recruits of the bounty-jumping persuasion furnished their full share. Desertion increased with conscription, of course, though even the volunteers of 1861 and an amazing number of their officers indulged in the practice.[1] Criminal types and arrant cowards were numerous enough and they sowed seeds of discontent among their fellows. The facts of officer absenteeism and of civilian profiteering weakened enthusiasm for a cause which, on both sides, became vague in the mind of the private soldier. Soldiers deserted singly and in groups of varying size. The second winter of the war opened with over one hundred thousand absent without leave from the Northern armies; the average monthly desertion for the remainder of the war was over five thousand. The grand total was roughly two hundred thousand.

While each side encouraged desertions from the enemy, desperate efforts were made to check it in their own ranks. Thousands of troops were detached to hunt down absentees, an unpleasant task in which the "tears and screams of wives and children" often touched the tender

---

[1] *Congressional Globe*, 37 Cong., 3 sess., 995.
[2] Regis de Trobriand, *Four Years with the Army of the Potomac* (Boston, 1889), 284-285.

chords of those detailed to that duty.[1] The death penalty was increasingly applied in the later years until executions became an almost daily occurrence. Deserters from both armies were scattered over the Confederacy, especially in the mountain region and in backcountry districts, where bands of them often held sway or added their contribution to the local guerrilla warfare.[2]

Another ugly phase of the Northern military effort was revealed in the profiteering and graft involved in equipping and supplying the army.[3] Under pressure of the national need the government paid almost any price for supplies and handsome profits were harvested, especially by the political allies, personal friends and relatives of those who awarded the contracts. If some served their country with active conscience, others robbed without stint. Many commodities could be secured by the government only through middlemen and go-betweens and the latter oftentimes bought at the lowest prices regardless of the quality of the article. Aged, blind, spavined and ringboned nags constituted the vast bulk of a delivery of cavalry horses. For sugar the government sometimes received in considerable part sand; for coffee, rye or some worse substitute; for leather, a paperlike substitute; for muskets and pistols, the refuse of shops and of foreign armories and, in certain cases, even condemned arms previously disposed of to the contractors who resold them.[4]

[1] J. W. Bowyer and C. H. Thurman, The Annals of Elder Horn (N. Y., 1930), 46.

[2] Ella Lonn, Desertion during the Civil War (N. Y., 1928), 62-76, 181-182; Shannon, Organization and Administration of the Union Army, I, 177-180, and passim.

[3] N. Y. Tribune, May 25, 1861; Russell, My Diary, 344, 374, 389.

[4] "Government Contracts," 37 Cong., 2 sess., House Rep., II, no. 2, pt. i, 83-88, 98-99; Charles Wright (Mountaineer, pseud.), The Prospect (Buffalo, 1862), 31 ff.; N. Y. Tribune, Jan. 14, 1862; Springfield (Mass.) Republican, Dec. 13, 25, 1861, July 5, 22, 1862; N. Y. Times, Feb. 6, 8, 1862; N. Y. Herald, April 18, 29, July 24, 1862;

The easiest fortunes seemed to be those made in supplying clothing and blankets for the soldiers. It was found that *"shoddy, a villainous compound, the refuse stuff and sweepings of the shop, pounded, rolled, glued, and smoothed,"* could be quickly and cheaply made in the semblance of cloth.[1] Uniforms of this material quickly disintegrated under exposure to the elements and a resentful public soon incorporated the word into its vocabulary as the very essence of shameful deception. A "shoddy" aristocracy was soon in evidence, its pretentious vulgarity proclaiming its ill-gotten gains. It was promptly joined by a *nouveau-riche* class of arms contractors, successful coal operators, railroad magnates and others who were all labeled in the public mind as "shoddy."

The careful budgeting of most American households, striving each to furnish its quota to meet the war's expenses, threw into sharp relief the extravagance of the first lady of the land, who, determined duly to impress a hostile and snobbish society circle which had previously revolved around Southern leadership, built up a wardrobe of silks and satins, ornaments and jewels that soon set the gossips talking of her disgraceful self-indulgence at a time when her sister-women were busy sewing, scraping lint and making bandages. Mrs. Lincoln, to be sure, discontinued state dinners and balls but this and certain petty economies seemed to her critics only a means of furthering her own selfish social program. The President must have noted the sensational newspaper accounts of the lavish bargains achieved on the frequent shopping trips to New York City but he seems

Leslie's Illustrated Newspaper (N. Y.), XVII, 66, 114, 178 (Oct. 24, Nov. 14, Dec. 12, 1863).

[1] Robert Tomes, "The Fortunes of War," *Harper's Mo.*, XXIX (1864), 227-228.

to have been unaware of the fact that his ambitious spouse was accumulating a debt of $70,000.[1]

But Mrs. Lincoln's indulgences were nothing to the vulgar ostentation which the "Sybarites of 'Shoddy'" were soon displaying in the great cities of the North. Even in military circles, declared Charles H. Van Wyck, chairman of a congressional investigating committee that first reported on December 17, 1861, the mania for graft extended "almost from the general to the drummer boy." It was a lurid story of "colonels, entrusted with the power of raising regiments, colluding with contractors, bartering away and dividing contracts for horses and other supplies to enrich personal favorites; purchasing articles and compelling false invoices to be given." [2] One fourth of the government's war expenditures were tainted with dishonesty before the orgy ended.[3]

As the federal armies penetrated the valley states of the Confederacy a new opportunity for corrupt profit was provided by the vast stores of cotton that were badly needed by Northern mill owners. It was not long before it seemed to many in the army that the deep-laid schemes of certain cotton speculators were determining factors in military policy. For example, even after such trade was licensed and regulated by the treasury department, Charles A. Dana, the journalist, who went South as a partner of Roscoe Conkling to purchase cotton under governmental authorization, was shocked to find

[1] W. A. Evans, *Mrs. Abraham Lincoln: A Study of Her Personality and Her Influence on Lincoln* (N. Y., 1932), 168-184. Mrs. Lincoln's exquisite toilet and social *savoir faire* surprised those who had prophesied a régime of Western boorishness but her bad judgment and sharp tongue in time alienated many who had at first been favorably impressed by her social charm.

[2] *Congressional Globe*, 37 Cong., 2 sess., 711.

[3] Rhodes, *History of the United States*, V, 216 ff.

that "the mania for sudden fortunes" had corrupted and demoralized the army, with "every colonel, captain or quartermaster . . . in secret partnership with some operator in cotton." [1] Nearly every treasury agent employed in this area was himself engaged in the nefarious business. [2]

Indeed, a member of a Senate investigating committee admitted with shame: "Under this permission to trade, supplies have not only gone in [to the Confederacy], but bullets and powder, instruments of death which our heroic soldiers have been compelled to face and meet on every field of battle." [3] A traffic of half a million dollars passed daily through the lines along the Mississippi. As the center of this trade Memphis proved to be virtually a "regular depot for rebel supplies," [4] being more valuable to the Confederates in federal hands than if they had effected its recapture. New Orleans was another busy headquarters of cotton speculators and other traders. The profits of this traffic made unimportant the reward to contractors who agreed to gather the cotton on abandoned farms for half the crop. [5]

The actual conduct of this "brothers' war" revealed the extent to which passion and hysteria came to domi-

[1] Dana in disgust abandoned the trade after a few weeks. C. J. Rosebault, *When Dana Was the Sun* (N. Y., 1931), 67-68.

[2] *Official Records of the Union and Confederate Navies in the War of the Rebellion* (Wash., 1894-1922), ser. 1, XXVI, 342.

[3] *Congressional Globe*, 38 Cong., 1 sess., III, 2823. See also "Trade with Rebellious States," 38 Cong., 2 sess., *House Rep.*, no. 24; "Purchase of Products in States in Insurrection," 38 Cong., 2 sess., *House Exec. Doc.*, no. 16, 2-3; *The War of the Rebellion: A Compilation of the Official Records of the Union and Confederate Armies* (Wash., 1880-1901), ser. 1, XVII, pt. ii, 522; E. M. Coulter, "Effects of Secession upon the Commerce of the Mississippi Valley," *Miss. Valley Hist. Rev.*, III, 275-300.

[4] *Official Records of Navies*, ser. 1, XXVI, 341. See also *N. Y. Times*, May 21, 1864, and *American Annual Cyclopedia*, IV (1864), 190.

[5] Livermore, *My Story of the War*, 351; T. W. Knox, *Camp-Fire and Cotton-Field* (N. Y., 1865), 307, 394-398.

nate public opinion on both sides. President Davis, the Confederate Congress, and generals in the field, as well as less official propagandists, repeatedly proclaimed the "savage ferocity" with which the Union forces conducted the conflict in utter disregard of the usages of civilized warfare and the dictates of humanity. Rape, rapine and plunder—"beauty and booty"—were declared the objects of the hosts of Attila, of the "ruthless Hessians of the North." [1] "Butler, the Beast," "Grant, the Butcher," "Sherman, the Brute," were pictured as "heaven-defying, monstrous specimens of humanity," leading the "Lincoln hordes" against the people of the South "to destroy their property, burn their houses, and murder their wives and children." [2] "What stealing of spoons and forks; what chopping of pianos; what burning of libraries, appropriating of pictures and wearing apparel; women taking shelter, cowering and shivering in the woods, with their homeless little ones, and looking out from their covert upon the blazing roof-trees of their houses." [3] "Their pathway is that of fiends and demons, not men," proclaimed a writer on "Yankee atrocities." "Tender women have been insulted, whipped, violated." [4] To complete the picture it was widely believed that a brutal blockading captain, besides participating in the supposedly popular pastime of Negro stealing, had ruthlessly thrown overboard a Negro infant. [5]

Champions of the Union cause found ample oppor-

[1] See "Documents" in Moore, *Rebellion Record*, I, 339; II, 356, 442; III, 406; VI, 292, 295; VII, 199; VIII, 278.

[2] *Atlanta Intelligencer*, cited in *N. Y. Tribune*, Aug. 3, 1864; Dicey, *Six Months in the Federal States*, II, 88-89.

[3] See *Richmond Examiner*, May 16, 1864, cited in A. O. Abbott, *Prison Life in the South* (N. Y., 1865), 35-36.

[4] *De Bow's Rev.*, XXXIV (1864), 104.

[5] W. W. Malet, *An Errand to the South in the Summer of 1862* (London, 1863), 126-127.

tunity to reply to Confederate charges with counter-
charges. Tales of rebel barbarities seemed almost from
the start to offer opportunities of "making falsehood
negotiable." [1] After Bull Run rumors began to circulate
of the mistreating of wounded federals, who were
bayoneted or shot or had their throats cut, and of
desecration of the dead whose heads were said to have
been cut off and kicked about and whose bodies were
alleged to have later suffered even greater indignities. [2]
The public was presently regaled with stories of Confederate Indians scalping their prisoners at Pea Ridge
and, in due time, of Indians bringing in a string of ears
cut from the Union dead. [3] Next came a thrill of horror
over robbery and murder by N. B. Forrest's troops at
Paducah and over their massacre of Negro soldiers and
their white officers at Fort Pillow. [4] President Lincoln
himself made a careful distinction between mere rumor
and actual knowledge and decided to postpone judgment
until the facts could be established. [5] Before this was
accomplished the burning of Chambersburg, Pennsylvania, by General John McCausland's cavalry force re-

[1] N. Y. Daily News, Aug. 9, 1861.

[2] N. Y. Times, July 25, 1861; anon., "Bayoneting Our Wounded,"
Harper's Wkly., V, 522-523, 525 (Aug. 17, 1861); anon., "Southern
Chivalry," same mag., VII, 87-89 (Feb. 7, 1863). See report of Senate
investigating committee, 37 Cong., 2 sess., Senate Rep., no. 41. A Confederate participant shortly told of "a general butchering. Like wild
beasts, the incensed soldiery fell upon their victims, hewing, stabbing and
slashing like madmen." Bela Estvàn, War Pictures from the South (N. Y.,
1863), 93. Cf. Russell, My Diary, 489; N. Y. Daily News, July 27,
30, 1861.

[3] Official Records of Armies, ser. 1, VIII, 194-195, 206-208, 235-236,
249-250; J. G. Nicolay and John Hay, Abraham Lincoln (N. Y., 1890),
V, 292-293; Chicago Tribune, March 7, 1863; J. H. Browne, Four
Years in Secessia (Hartford, 1865), 109-110.

[4] Official Records of Armies, ser. 1, XXXII, pt. iii, 367, 373; Philadelphia Inquirer, April 8, 16, 19, 1864; Columbus Gazette, April 1,
22, 1864; J. R. Bartlett (Percy Howard, pseud.), The Barbarities of the
Rebels, as Shown in Their Cruelty to the Federal Wounded and Prisoners
(Providence, R. I., 1863).

[5] Nicolay and Hay, Abraham Lincoln, VI, 477-478.

vived unpleasant memories of the earlier destruction of Morgan's raiders and of the sacking of Lawrence, Kansas, by Quantrell. Still later came stories of Confederate complicity in the efforts to put the torch to various Northern cities.[1]

Whatever the facts behind such atrocity tales Northern zealots showed a tendency to believe the worst. Instruments of slave torture were publicly exhibited or presented in illustration, including a Boston showing of a pronged iron collar which had supposedly rusted on the neck of its victim, an eighteen-year-old New Orleans octoroon.[2] A story circulated of how General Lee with his own hands had flogged a slave girl and put brine on her bleeding wounds. *Harper's Weekly* printed lurid tales and vivid illustrations of the unfortunate lot of Southern Unionists, their "outraged matrons and maidens, butchered children and sacked households."[3] It told of poisoned wells and lakes, of the wanton destruction of ambulances with their wounded, of rebels boiling the bodies of Union soldiers so as more readily to secure the bones, of the strangling and the hanging of Unionist victims before the eyes of aged parents. Others supplied stories of the crucifixion of deserters of Unionist sympathies and of Southern women drinking out of Yankee skulls or wearing rings made from the bones of Northern soldiers who fell at Bull Run.[4] After the cruel war was over, newspapers printed tales of a last des-

[1] E. A. Pollard, *Life of Jefferson Davis* (Phila., 1869), 407-408. For the work of Confederate emissaries in the North, see J. W. Du Bose, *Life and Times of William Lowndes Yancey* (Birmingham, 1892), 715.

[2] Livermore, *My Story of the War*, 238-239.

[3] Anon., "The Guerrillas in the West," *Harper's Wkly.*, VI, 555 (Aug. 30, 1862).

[4] Browne, *Four Years in Secessia*, 154-155; H. T. Tuckerman, *America and Her Commentators* (N. Y., 1864), 447; *N. Y. Tribune*, July 26, 1863; Adolf Douai, *Personen, Land und Zustände in Nord-Amerika* (Berlin, 1863), 288; *Philadelphia Inquirer*, April 8, 1862; *Philadelphia Press*, May 16, 1862.

perate effort to prolong the rebellion by the wanton introduction of yellow fever into New York.[1]

The horrors of prison life formed the chief stock in trade of the war propagandist. Southern prisons gorged with the heavy captures at Bull Run gave opportunity for tales of suffering that in their various versions produced anger in the North and protestation in the South.[2] The flood of prison literature thus begun appeared first in newspaper and magazine columns and then in book-length accounts that continued for half a century and more. In 1864, in addition to committee reports from both houses of Congress, a special committee of the United States Sanitary Commission brought out its findings with plenty of gruesome detail.[3] Through such channels an aroused public learned of the sufferings of shivering and starving heroes in the filth and squalor of prison and prison camp. It was led to believe that every prisoner was promptly robbed by his captors and subjected to more or less systematic abuse or indignity. The brutality of prison officials or of guards who delighted in shooting down their victims in cold blood was an essential part of the story. Little or nothing was said of generous acts of kindness to relieve suffering captives; nor was allowance made for the stern dictates of necessity in the face of inadequate prison facilities or of limited supplies of food, clothing and medicine. The horrors of Libby prison where thousands were packed

[1] *Cincinnati Daily Commercial*, May 4, 18, 1865.

[2] *N. Y. Times*, Sept. 30, Oct. 4, 5, 1861; Alfred Ely, *Journal* (Charles Lanman, ed., N. Y., 1862), 104.

[3] U. S. Sanitary Commission, *Narrative of Privations and Sufferings of United States Officers and Soldiers while Prisoners of War* (Phila., 1864), issued also as Loyal League, *Pamphlet*, no. 76. See comment in *Harper's Wkly.*, VIII, 691 (Oct. 29, 1864). The congressional reports are to be found in 38 Cong., 1 sess., *House Rep.*, I, no. 67; 40 Cong., 3 sess., *House Rep.*, IV, no. 45.

within the walls of an old tobacco warehouse, and of Andersonville where thirty thousand Union soldiers were confined within a roofless stockade that inclosed twenty-six and a half acres, were made to seem a true measure of the humanity of Dixie.[1]

There was a Southern counterpart to this picture; yet one who served the Confederacy contrasted the generosity of Union policy with the steady brutalizing of all classes at the South.[2] In the North prisoners were often transferred to more salubrious locations. There were occasional instances of amazing leniency toward them. Uniformed Confederates from Camp Chase were allowed to wander the streets of Columbus, Ohio, and to register at hotels as belonging to the "C. S. Army" until a reaction set in against such laxity. There was, of course, a deliberate policy of fraternizing with prisoners in the hope of inducing them to return to allegiance to the Union and become "galvanized Yankees." At times generous captors were given cards of thanks by appreciative prisoners from the South.[3] Early in 1864, however, the war department issued a "retaliatory order" reducing the prison ration to the Southern level. In some Northern prisons recourse now had to be made to drastic devices for supplementing the regular food allowance, the infesting rodents being levied upon to contribute "fresh meat and rat soup." [4] Of course, the amount of

[1] N. P. Chipman, *The Tragedy of Andersonville* (San Fran., 1911).

[2] Estvàn, *War Pictures from the South*, 169-170.

[3] *Official Records of Armies*, ser. 2, III, 498-500; Ohio Senate, *Journal for 1862*, app., 15, 155-156; N. Y. *Tribune*, July 14, 1862; *Columbus Crisis*, May 13, 1863. See also letters of "A Confederate Private at Fort Donelson, 1862," *Am. Hist. Rev.*, XXXI, 481-482.

[4] *Official Records of Armies*, ser. 2, VII, 73, 150-151; J. A. Wyeth, *With Sabre and Scalpel* (N. Y., 1914), 292, 294, 299; Randolph Abbott Shotwell, *Papers* (J. G. deR. Hamilton, ed., Raleigh, 1929-1931), II, 139-141, 159-160, 173-174, 177.

hardship on both sides was greatly increased as a result of the difficulties in the way of working out satisfactory arrangements for the exchange of prisoners.[1]

It was often promised that the federal government would retaliate in kind upon the rebels for all outrages.[2] Parson Brownlow, with screaming denunciation of the Confederacy, poured forth his narrative of the cruelties he underwent as a Union man and implored "frightful vengeance."[3] Out of such passions was born not only a greater zeal to save the Union and free the slaves but also a determination to visit upon the South "proper" punishment even to the point of its being "made a desert of, if need be."[4] On the other hand, tales of fiendish atrocities in prison, in camp or upon the battle-field occasionally involved a severe strain on the credulity. "After all," commented a Confederate war clerk, "I am inclined to think our papers have been lying about the barbarous conduct of the enemy."[5] In marked contrast with the cant, hypocrisy and bloodthirstiness that was to be found in the pulpit, in the press and around the tea table, there was actually little bitterness among the soldiers who waged the war. Both officers and men ordinarily spoke of their opponents with a conspicuous absence of ill feeling. Soldiers on picket duty

[1] See W. B. Hesseltine, *Civil War Prisons* (Columbus, 1930), chaps. ii, v, x.

[2] "Monthly Record of Current Events," *Harper's Mo.*, XXVII (1863), 559.

[3] Dicey, *Six Months in the Federal States*, II, 246-249; Higginson, *Letters and Journals*, 168. Supplementing his personal appeal, Parson Brownlow's "Book," formally titled *Sketches of the Rise, Progress and Decline of Secession* (Phila., 1862), had a wide vogue beginning with an advance sale of 100,000 copies. *Independent*, July 3, 1862.

[4] Franklin A. Buck, *A Yankee Trader in the Gold Rush* (Katherine A. White, ed., Boston, 1930), 194. George H. Hepworth, in his *Whip, Hoe, and Sword* (Boston, 1864), 84, suggested that "half our army [might have] to settle in the lands they have conquered."

[5] J. B. Jones, *A Rebel War Clerk's Diary* (Phila., 1866), II, 34. See also Browne, *Four Years in Secessia*, 132.

often engaged in friendly banter and even in a sly barter that ignored military orders forbidding fraternization.[1]

Yet there was no denying that, quite apart from war-time falsehoods, the conflict had its many horrors and that the South in particular experienced them to the full. Brave heroes suffered untold privation. In winter they shivered in the cold and the wet, floundered and wallowed in the mud of the roads and trenches, while in summer they sweated under torrid skies amid the stench of camp and battle-field and writhed with vermin that infested their bodies and clothes. Uncertain food supplies left the gnawing pangs of hunger or drove foraging parties to participate in raids that exceeded the bounds of authority, if not of decency. After a bloody contest the scarred and ravaged fields strewn with corpses and abandoned arms and equipment gave further testimony to man's inhumanity to man.[2] Only the photographs of Brady's field representatives can begin to reproduce this sight and they omit the terrible sounds of suffering that rent the air after gun and cannon had been silenced.[3]

Brave men, suffering the first agonies of their wounds, whined and shrieked like babies as they were carried to the ambulances. Meantime hardened veterans remained deaf to the cry of expiring comrades for a swallow of

[1] G. A. Sala, *My Diary in America in the Midst of War* (London, 1865), I, 321-326; anon., "The Army of the Potomac," *Harper's Wkly.*, VII, 93 (Feb. 7, 1863); VIII, 651 (Oct. 8, 1864); Moore, *Rebellion Record*, V, "Incidents," 33-34.

[2] The horrors of the battle-field may be glimpsed in Townsend, *Campaigns of a Non-Combatant*, 207, 270-272; Browne, *Four Years in Secessia*, 47, 53-54, 75, 76-77; M. W. Tyler, *Recollections of the Civil War* (N. Y., 1912), 195-196; Shotwell, *Papers*, I, 227, 289, 295-300, 430-431; Livermore, *My Story of the War*, 223-224; Wyeth, *With Sabre and Scalpel*, 247-248; W. W. Orme to Wife, Dec. 9, 1862, Ill. State Hist. Soc., *Journ.*, XXIII, 266-267.

[3] F. T. Miller, ed., *The Photographic History of the Civil War* (N. Y., 1912), esp. II, III, IX, *passim*.

water; elsewhere callous captors eagerly appropriated articles of clothing from their wounded prisoners. An armistice to allow for the burial of the dead removed from sight bloody corpses "with their eyes and noses carried away; their brains oozing from their crania; their mouths shot into horrible disfiguration," "heads off, arms off, legs off, and great swarms of flies and gnats buzzing around the open mouths, froth-lined and horrible," or perhaps "horses and men chopped into hash by the bullets, and appearing more like piles of jelly than the distinguishable forms of human life." Hogs overnight "mangled many of the bodies" or ghouls stripped them, leaving the naked forms all the more bloody and ghastly. Under the excessive Southern heat corpses swelled to twice their natural size and decomposed amidst the buzz of gyrating insects that attacked them. At the end of the war thousands of dead on both sides lay unburied in swamp and wilderness while whitening bones and skulls were visible from many a roadside.[1]

"The genius of destruction is let loose in war. Soldiers acquire a passion for destruction," lamented a Northern participant as he saw his comrades break up for firewood the mahogany chairs and rosewood piano of an abandoned Southern mansion.[2] Many a time did the federal troops, according to their own testimony, "drive to the rear every pony and mule, every ox and cow and sheep. They did not leave, on an average, two chickens to a plantation. Wherever they encamped, the fences served as beds and firewood." This was war with all its penalties and all its horrors, boasted a preacher aid-de-camp

---

[1] A. T. Volwiler, ed., "Letters from a Civil War Officer," *Miss. Valley Hist. Rev.*, XIV, 528-529.

[2] Livermore, *My Story of the War*, 659-660. For a case of similar "vandalism" by General W. T. Sherman, see his *Memoirs* (N. Y., 1875), II, 256.

to General N. P. Banks, betraying little sympathy for the helpless victims who cursed, whined or cried.[1] It was especially difficult to control the numerous stragglers, or "bummers," who concentrated upon spoils as they went about marauding and committing every sort of outrage.[2] A tender-hearted Yankee officer deplored "the desolation and misery, and poverty and woe, that fell upon the inhabitants of every town, village, hamlet, and homestead wherever this army moves." "Our train of confiscated Horses mules and negroes was nearly two miles long. . . . Now nothing remains but the occupied dwellings and negro shanties," wrote one of the participants in a fifty-mile raid "through the Garden of Miss [issippi]."[3] "I send out parties of cavalry here & there, and instruct men cooly to burn, kill and destroy," wrote an officer engaged in suppressing guerrilla warfare in Missouri.[4]

Early in the struggle federal generals were intent upon protecting civilians and private property and upon preventing plundering.[5] It soon seemed sound policy, however, to break the rebellion by a systematic appropriation of enemy property. On July 22, 1862, the war department authorized military commanders to seize and convert to their use any property belonging to inhabitants of the Confederacy.[6] Generals Pope, Grant and

[1] Hepworth, *Whip, Hoe, and Sword*, 99-100, 272.

[2] Sherman, *Memoirs*, II, 182; Townsend, *Campaigns of a Non-Combatant*, 80; Hepworth, *Whip, Hoe, and Sword*, 278-280.

[3] Shotwell, *Papers*, I, 319; II, 47, 75, 81. For other scruples against confiscation, see E. H. Frank to Catherine Varner, April 20, 1863, *N. D. Hist. Quar.*, IV, 191-192, and Higginson, *Letters and Journals*, 207.

[4] W. W. Orme to Wife, Oct. 20, 1862, 256, 304-305.

[5] Russell, *My Diary*, 414; H. V. Boynton, *Sherman's Historical Raid* (Cin., 1875), 23; Horace Greeley, *The American Conflict* (Hartford, 1866), II, 248; H. H. McGuire and G. L. Christian, *The Confederate Cause and Conduct in the War between the States* (Richmond, 1907), 74; Moore, *Rebellion Record*, III, "Documents," 2-3.

[6] J. D. Richardson, comp., *Messages and Papers of the Presidents, 1789-1897* (Wash., 1897), VI, 117-118. The Confederate retaliatory

Sherman pressed this policy until they became the most feared and hated of federal commanders.

The most elaborate application of this policy of systematic devastation was made by William T. Sherman. This Northern soldier had learned to know and love Dixie in various parts of which he had enjoyed several years of army life and of civilian hospitality. Indeed, on the eve of the war he was just deciding that in a quiet Southern college town "we will drive our tent pins and pick out a magnolia under which to sleep the long sleep." [1] But when the flaming sword of civil war beckoned him into the service of the Union, he prepared to apply a new brand of ruthless warfare to his former friends and neighbors. By 1863 he had come to "insist on war pure and simple, with no admixture of civil compromises." [2] When he planned his great march to the sea it was essential that his troops forage liberally on the country; but it seemed to him equally valid that rebels who had willed the war should be made to suffer for their sins. He even doubted whether the region could be trusted after being conquered unless it should later be "repopulated" with loyal stock. He accordingly warned the governor of Georgia of his determination, if necessary, to devastate "the State in its whole length and breadth." [3]

To "make old and young, rich and poor, feel the hard hand of war" Sherman's army left a path of destruction "thirty miles on either side of the line from Atlanta to Savannah." Most of his officers tried to keep

order did not include confiscation. See *Official Records of Armies*, ser. 2, IV, 836-837; Southern Hist. Soc., *Papers*, I (1876), 300-302.

[1] W. T. Sherman, *Home Letters* (M. A. DeWolfe Howe, ed., N. Y., 1909), 177. See also W. L. Fleming, ed., *General W. T. Sherman as College President* (Cleveland, 1912), 26 ff.

[2] Sherman, *Memoirs*, I, 342.

[3] Sherman, *Memoirs*, II, 175. See also 111, 138, 152, 157-158.

the work of devastation within the limits set. But there was often no restraining the rank and file and many an officer looked on sympathetically. As a result there were many scenes of indiscriminate pillage. "Everywhere," wrote a Yankee colonel to his wife, "the houses of the wealthy were pillaged, clothes torn up, beds torn to pieces, barns and gins and their contents given to the flames. . . . I have no doubt that fifty thousand dollars worth of silk dresses were found buried and were exhumed and torn to pieces by the men." [1] When Sherman's forces reached South Carolina the work of ruin attained its height. The whole army was "burning with an insatiable desire to wreak vengeance" upon the state that had led secession; its path was marked by the smoky clouds of burning towns and homes.[2] Meantime General "Phil" Sheridan was in his own way accomplishing the devastation of the Shenandoah Valley and rendering it untenable for a hostile army.[3] By such methods was the Confederacy finally brought to its knees.

Southerners have ever since pointed proudly to the contrasting scrupulous regard for private property shown by their invading forces. Lee's men knew that his " 'touch not, taste not, handle not' orders were something more than mere idle words." [4] Even the fact that Ben Butler's troops had looted and burned his ancestral

[1] Volwiler, "Letters from a Civil War Officer," 524. See also Sherman, *Memoirs*, II, 185-186, 207-208, 213, 227; J. D. Cox, *The March to the Sea* (Campaigns of the Civil War, X, N. Y., 1913), 24, 36; G. W. Pepper, *Personal Recollections of Sherman's Campaigns in Georgia and the Carolinas* (Zanesville, Ohio, 1866), 246-247, 275-276, 279, 306-320, 331; G. W. Nichols, *The Story of the Great March* (N. Y., 1865), 240.

[2] Sherman, *Memoirs*, II, 227-228, 254, 286-287.

[3] *Official Records of Armies*, ser. 1, XLIII, pt. i, 37, 43; "Domestic Intelligence," *Harper's Wkly.*, VIII, 675 (Oct. 22, 1864); Richard Taylor, *Destruction and Reconstruction* (N. Y., 1879), 46-47; Pollard, *Life of Jefferson Davis*, 401-402.

[4] Shotwell, *Papers*, I, 318-321, 348, 372-373, 493, 496; Pickett, *Soldier of the South*, 50.

homestead did not alter the fine regard of the gallant General Pickett for the amenities of civilized warfare, while that dashing raider "Jeb" Stuart took justifiable pride in his generous treatment of enemy civilians.[1] Yet it cannot be denied that there was frequent difficulty in restraining Southern cavalry forces from despoiling not only the enemy but also their own people.[2] War, the destroyer, loosed all his macabre forces in these four terrible years of fratricidal strife. Fifteen years later "the million dead . . . strewing the fields and woods and valleys and battlefields of the south" still troubled the conscience of the ex-war nurse Walt Whitman, whose pen recounted the tale of human destruction.[3]

The continued good health of the soldier was from the start menaced by crowded transportation in cattle cars and by filthy and unsanitary conditions in camp. Mud and stench seemed all pervasive; mosquitoes of apparently "secession sympathies" swarmed everywhere. It was not long before disease, from "camp fever" to smallpox, decimated the ranks. The former under the label of the "Chickahominy fever" was a serious factor in the final delay in the Peninsular campaign; its steady toll kept the twenty coffin makers working night and day at the specially improvised army shop.[4] After a year of fighting forty thousand Union troops were away on sick leave, and enlistment did not proceed fast enough "to compensate for the emasculation of the army by disease."[5] Of the total of over three hundred thousand

[1] Pickett, *Soldier of the South*, 10, 104-105; J. W. Thomason, jr., *Jeb Stuart* (N. Y., 1930), 266.

[2] Taylor, *Destruction and Reconstruction*, 60; R. N. Early, ed., *Lieutenant General Jubal Anderson Early, C. S. A.* (Phila., 1912), 401-404.

[3] Walt Whitman, *Complete Prose Works* (Phila., 1892), 79-80.

[4] Townsend, *Campaigns of a Non-Combatant*, 145-146; Trobriand, *Four Years with the Army of the Potomac*, 221 ff.

[5] Bigelow, *Retrospections of an Active Life*, I, 504, 521.

deaths in the Union army two men succumbed to disease for every one that died of wounds." [1]

Two hundred and thirty-three general army hospitals were established to take care of the sick and wounded, while Washington was described as "one vast hospital." In the battle area each bloody conflict caused the temporary conversion into hospitals of not only schools, churches and stately mansions but even "cow-houses, wagon-sheds, hay-barracks, hen coops, negro cabins, and barns." [2] In such shelters bare-armed surgeons with bloody instruments added steadily to the growing heaps of human fingers, feet, legs and arms. For months after a major battle like Gettysburg there were not enough "good Christian praying men" at the general hospital "to point the two thousand mangled and dying men still remaining to the Lamb of God who taketh away the sin of the world." [3]

More comforting, perhaps, were the tender ministrations of the nurses, especially the women recruited under the dauntless leadership of Dorothea L. Dix who labored untiringly despite her advancing years and shattered health. [4] So courageously did these angels of mercy face conditions that made many a hardened man wince that they promptly established their claims to control over the new profession. The United States Sanitary Commission, established in June, 1861, to coöperate with the army, used its income from private gifts and from

[1] Charles Smart, *The Medical and Surgical History of the War of the Republic* (Wash., 1888), pt. iii, I, 1 ff.

[2] Townsend, *Campaigns of a Non-Combatant*, 108, 229; Trobriand, *Four Years with the Army of the Potomac*, 208. On work of the ambulance corps, see esp. T. L. Livermore, *Days and Events, 1860-1866* (Boston, 1920), 226, and *passim*.

[3] See advertisement for four such "praying men" in *N. Y. Tribune*, Sept. 5, 1863.

[4] Francis Tiffany, *Life of Dorothea Lynde Dix* (Boston, 1890), 336-341; Livermore, *My Story of the War*, 246.

a series of great fairs to relieve sickness and suffering and to improve the sanitation of camp and hospital. It spurred on the official agencies but encountered numerous obstacles from governmental authorities. The Sanitary Commission set up depots for the collection of sanitary stores, supplied diet deficiencies and delicacies, established soldiers' lodges, and directed its criticism to the improvement of the medical department of the army. Not the least important of its contributions was its directory of the six hundred thousand men invalided in the numerous hospitals.[1]

Meanwhile various sectarian agencies, as well as the American Bible Society and the American Tract Society, concerned themselves with the spiritual needs of the soldiers. An Evangelical Alliance also entered the field, and representatives of the Y.M.C.A., which had suspended its regular annual convention, organized on November 15, 1861, the United States Christian Commission.[2] This agency coördinated the various field activities looking toward the religious welfare and physical comfort of the men under arms and worked zealously to justify its existence. The government designated as chaplains, with the rating of privates, certain preachers who volunteered their services. Though most of these won the respect and admiration of the men by their courage and industry, complaints were heard of hypocritical or indolent chaplains who gave little spiritual aid, even to the sick and dying, but lounged about and grew

[1] C. J. Stillé, *History of the United States Sanitary Commission* (Phila., 1866); J. S. Newberry, *United States Sanitary Commission in the Valley of the Mississippi* (Cleveland, 1871); F. L. Olmsted, *Books and Papers Relating to Concerns of the United States Sanitary Commission in the War of the Rebellion* (n. p., 1890); Livermore, *My Story of the War*, 133 ff.; Trobriand, *Four Years with the Army of the Potomac*, 244 ff.

[2] *N. Y. Tribune*, July 10, 1861; *N. Y. World*, Oct. 4, 23, 1861; *American Annual Cyclopedia*, IV (1864), 801-803; Lemuel Moss, *Annals of the United States Christian Commission* (Phila., 1868), 106 ff.

ridiculous mustaches. Some hoped to improve matters by raising chaplains to the rank of major and by the establishment of a military religious bureau under a chaplain general, with rigid supervision over the religious conduct of the soldiers.[1]

Despite a record of civilian war relief unmatched in any earlier conflict, public opinion in the North was far from unanimous in support of the war. As the passion of those who claimed a monopoly of patriotism rose, there was an increasing demand that all opposition be silenced. Where Union sentiment was strongest mob violence wreaked vengeance upon the "disloyal," newspaper offices were raided and the forces of destruction loosed. Besides the official ban in army camps, Copperhead journals were unofficially denied circulation in many quarters. A powerful demand arose for their general suppression. To this demand Lincoln, who maintained an admirably level head, gave little heed, although the same cannot be said of cabinet members who had reflected their share in the war psychosis by the arbitrary arrests of alleged disloyalists. A foreign visitor recorded his impression in the strong statement: "The Bill of Rights in America has been dishonoured and protested, and the Palladium of American liberty is of no more account than a cracked tin kettle."[2]

Although Copperhead riots broke out in various spots and there were frequent episodes like the daubing of the home of Henry Ward Beecher with petroleum and lamp black while he was giving a Thanksgiving welcome to a

[1] Sala, *My Diary in America*, I, 328; *Columbus Crisis*, Feb. 4, 1863; Lawrence Van Alstyne, *Diary of an Enlisted Man* (New Haven, 1910), 77; Townsend, *Campaigns of a Non-Combatant*, 203.

[2] Sala, *My Diary in America*, I, 22. See also Russell, *My Diary*, 63; J. G. Randall, *Constitutional Problems under Lincoln* (N. Y., 1926), chaps. vii, viii, xix; A. C. Cole, *The Era of the Civil War* (C. W. Alvord, ed., *The Centennial History of Illinois*, Springfield, 1918-1920, III), 300-305; J. A. Marshall, *The American Bastile* (Phila., 1869).

Maine regiment at his church, the most determined opposition to the war was generally driven underground.[1] In regions of especial pro-Confederate strength like southern Illinois, bushwhacking and guerrilla warfare attested a spirit of reprisal for outrages upon Copperheads, and lawless elements of all sorts availed themselves of the local disorders to rob and pillage. Meantime secret political societies, like the Knights of the Golden Circle, furnished the basis for unity of action by those antiwar forces that preferred more constructive organization under cover, while the Unionists organized a secret oath-bound society of their own known as the Union League.[2] As a further means of combating defeatist agitation some prominent New Yorkers early in 1863 organized a Loyal Publication Society for the purpose of distributing throughout the country tracts and papers in support of the national cause. A month later a group of Yankee literati independently formed a New England society which distributed broadsides that virtually determined the content of the editorials of administration papers throughout New England. These two agencies rendered an important service to the maintenance of Northern morale.

The problem of keeping a united public opinion behind the administration became more complex as the original purpose of the war broadened to include emancipation. The loyal border states, themselves slaveholding commonwealths, were averse to the new departure. Antislavery extremists, on the other hand, insisted that Lincoln was moving too slowly. They found allies in generals in the field, editors and politicians who had not long since boasted of their antiabolition sentiments.

[1] *N. Y. Times*, Dec. 1, 1862; edit., *Harper's Wkly.*, VII, 50-51 (Jan. 24, 1863).

[2] E. J. Benton, *The Movement for Peace without a Victory during the Civil War* (Western Reserve Hist. Soc., *Publs.*, no. 99).

When Lincoln, busy at the helm of the ship of state, tried to restrain them within the limits of what seemed to him sound policy, they came to doubt his wisdom and his statesmanship, if not his patriotism. Even when the emancipation proclamation of September 22, 1862, announced the new objective of the war, some of the Radicals, dissatisfied with the limited application of the proclamation, denounced the president's "quarter loaf" as wholly inadequate to the occasion.

Such critics organized the movement in opposition to Lincoln's renomination, at the extreme of which was the Wendell Phillips group of abolitionists who applauded the determination of their leader to "cut off both hands before doing anything to aid Abraham Lincoln." [1] The veteran apostles of freedom——reënforced by new recruits like the fiery Anna Dickinson, a mere girl ——kept up the attack from platform, pulpit and press. Notwithstanding their intemperate and uncharitable opposition the social and moral status of the abolitionists rose steadily in the North. Their cause, indeed, received triumphant vindication when the Republican platform of 1864 pledged the party to a constitutional amendment for the total abolition of slavery. An erstwhile critic admitted, "Now the scales have fallen from our eyes. We honor the Abolitionist and Reformer." [2] The eloquent Phillips could now proclaim the cause of human liberty to an eager audience in the national capital with the vice-president and other dignitaries as honor guests. To him and thousands of others John Brown now seemed "the most influential American in aiding our civilization." [3] If mobs still awaited abolition cru-

[1] Stanton, *Elizabeth Cady Stanton*, II, 100-101.

[2] *Newburyport Herald*, cited in *National Anti-slavery Standard* (N. Y.), April 1, 1865.

[3] Dicey, *Six Months in the Federal States*, I, 162; Carlos Martyn, *Wendell Phillips: The Agitator* (N. Y., 1890), 325.

saders in Northern strongholds of proslavery sentiment, untold thousands of marching men joyously chanted the refrain: "John Brown's body lies a mouldering in the grave—his soul goes marching on." [1]

Meanwhile the vast mass of slaves continued loyally to serve their masters and mistresses even after word came to them, by direct or devious channels, that the armies of "Abe Linkum" were penetrating the South, bringing to the Negro freedom from his bondage. [2] Though war-time uncertainties greatly undermined the value of the black chattel, there was considerable buying and selling of slaves within the Confederacy. [3] Some traders operated in the war zone of Virginia, "running off" Negroes to the South in chains to prevent their escape. [4] Many slave owners in exposed areas transferred their holdings to Texas where they hoped to find greater security. Prices in the slave market dropped rapidly until they were outrun by the rapidly depreciating Confederate paper. It was not long before they had only one fourth their prewar value.

Freedom under these conditions was no less precious to the many chattels who, chafing under their bonds, now found that the prospects of escape had become better than ever before. During the first year of the war, despite numerous preventive enactments, the border slave states lost at least fifty thousand slaves, two thirds of them the property of Virginians. [5] In the spring of

---

[1] Townsend, *Campaigns of a Non-Combatant*, 249.

[2] Malet, *Errand to the South*, 46-47, 56, 177, 213-214. Many a free Negro demonstrated in practice his loyalty to the Confederacy and his desire to share in its defense. L. P. Jackson, "Free Negroes of Petersburg, Virginia," *Journ. of Negro History*, XII, 387-388.

[3] A. J. Fremantle, *Three Months in the Confederate States* (N. Y., 1864), 179, 191; Malet, *Errand to the South*, 116-117, 292.

[4] *N. Y. Times*, Oct. 23, 1862.

[5] Cf. Joseph Segar, *Letter to a Friend in Virginia* (Wash., 1862), 29; *N. Y. Tribune*, July 21, 1862; *N. Y. Times*, Oct. 17, 1862.

1862 many Maryland slaves sought refuge in the District of Columbia, just as District slaveholders were carrying their property into Maryland to escape loss from the local emancipation scheme decreed by federal statute.[1] But safety from rendition as fugitive slaves was greater in more remote parts, a fact which caused Philadelphia, Detroit, Cleveland and the other cities to witness a new influx of Negroes, some of whom did not stop until they achieved genuine security in Canada. Distant Kansas, in which the slaveholder had never found adequate protection for his human property, also witnessed a sudden immigration of self-emancipated chattels.[2]

At the same time thousands of Negro chattels sought sanctuary within the easy reach of the federal lines. In the early months of the war General Butler at Fortress Monroe found himself deluged by such a flood and gave his self-assigned charges the designation of "contrabands," which recognized some obligations for their care. It was soon necessary to establish a number of camps in the Potomac area for their relief.[3] With the best of intentions on the part of the federal authorities, however, there was much hardship and suffering in the lot of these refugees. After Lincoln's emancipation policy went into force on January 1, 1863, the victorious Union armies proclaimed freedom to the slaves of invaded districts, and crowds of Negroes, welcoming the troops with joyful demonstrations, threw themselves upon their bounty.

The tendency to depend upon government rations,

[1] N. Y. Tribune, May 5, 16, 1862; Independent, May 22, 1862.

[2] Nearly 4000 reached Kansas by March, 1862. Independent, March 13, 27, 1862.

[3] C. G. Woodson, A Century of Negro Migration (Wash., 1918), 104 ff.; Livermore, My Story of the War, 257 ff.; [E. L. Pierce], "The Contrabands of Fortress Monroe," Atlantic Mo., VIII (1861), 628, 630, 632.

even if this meant the necessity of following the marching columns, was soon checked by efforts to get the freedmen to return to their homes and to agricultural labor. This was a fundamental lesson that was stressed by the various relief agencies that entered the field in the early months of the war. Workers of the American Missionary Association and similar bodies followed closely in the wake of the armies, establishing schools and administering to the physical as well as spiritual needs of the race. In the winter of 1861-1862 special Freedmen's Relief Associations were formed in Boston, New York and Philadelphia. The movement spread to every section of the North and West until hundreds of organizations were in the field with overlapping designations and much duplication of work. Efforts to federate these agencies did not bear satisfactory fruit until January 31, 1866, when the American Freedmen's Union Commission was created. Meantime the government experimented with various schemes for the administration of abandoned plantations upon which Negroes were placed as wage-earners or as lessees or in "freemen's home colonies." The most successful of these were the relief camps established in the lower Mississippi Valley by the Reverend John Eaton under an order from General Grant dated in early November, 1862.[1] On March 3, 1865, the government finally created a special freedmen's bureau to direct activities previously supervised alternately by the war and treasury departments.

In no accessible Northern state was there an unqualified welcome for Negroes, bond or free. Everywhere

[1] *Am. Ann. Cyc.*, IV (1864), 387-388; Hepworth, *Whip, Hoe, and Sword*, 26 ff.; Knox, *Camp-Fire and Cotton-Field*, 227-228, 307-322; L. P. Brockett, *Women's Work in the Civil War* (Phila., 1867), 76; John Eaton, *Grant, Lincoln and the Freedmen* (N. Y., 1907), 5, 28-31. Cf. *Official Records of Armies*, ser. 1, LII, pt. i, 301-302.

critics objected to their presence, usually on the ground that black labor would "steal the work and bread of the honest Irish and Germans" and that wages generally would drop disastrously as a result.[1] Various states tried to erect new barriers against them, while Illinois as late as 1862 reënacted her constitutional provision against the immigration of free Negroes. Almost at once, however, by arrangement between the secretary of war and the military commander at Cairo, contrabands began to pour into that town until the levees were "so dark with negroes that pedestrians found it difficult to peregrinate without lanterns."[2] From Cairo, which was under martial law and legally amenable to such a policy, the Illinois Central carried one or more carloads northward daily and distributed them over the state. Although farmers were urged to welcome this supply of cheap help and the mayor of Chicago was formally invited to co-operate in securing employment for Negro immigrants in that city, the latter supported by the city council refused to act in violation of the state law "to the great injustice of our laboring population." The influx, however, continued until the war department changed its policy and finally transferred the contraband camp at Cairo to Island Number 10 beyond the state borders. After Lincoln's emancipation proclamation there were many Illinoisians who hoped that the colored man would henceforth "shape his bearings and route by the Southern Cross instead of the North Star." Some Northern blacks did go South to rejoin their kith and kin, but

[1] *Congressional Globe*, 37 Cong., 2 sess., app., 84, 244-247; House of Representatives of Ohio, *Journal for 1862*, 106, 170, 213, 251, 253, 263, 278, 298, 333-335, 358; C. M. Knapp, *New Jersey Politics during the Period of the Civil War and Reconstruction* (Geneva, N. Y., 1924), 69, 92; "The Lounger," *Harper's Wkly.*, V, 802 (Dec. 21, 1861); VI, 530-531 (Aug. 23, 1862); *N. Y. Tribune*, July 11, 1862.

[2] *Cairo Gazette*, Aug. 19, 1862.

Illinois repeatedly found it necessary to invoke its law and sell for their fines Negroes illegally residing within the state.[1]

War-time idealism, in fact, broke down few of the barriers against the race. In the spring of 1862 Congress repealed the black code of the District of Columbia, but despite the tragic need for educating the freedmen in and about Washington they were denied access to the city's educational system and had to be content with the inadequate facilities of the makeshift schools set up by the various missionary and relief agencies.[2] Senator Sumner, backed by Secretary of the Treasury Chase, protested with little result against the color line drawn on the street cars of the capital. Ardent New York friends of the Negro proclaimed his right to "ride in the Eighth-avenue cars, to sit in the parlor of the New York Hotel, to hire the best pew in Grace Church, to run for Congress . . . and to be a candidate for the next presidency of the United States"; but most people shared with Lincoln "the ordinary American opinion" adverse to the possibility of black and white associating on terms of social equality.[3]

Some efforts were also made to secure the suffrage for the Afro-American in the Northern border states, which generally denied him any political rights. A special legislative committee in Ohio reported favorably in 1864, pointing out that the ignorance and degradation of the Negro was the inevitable result of past oppression, but the minority protested that the idea of suffrage was "suicidal madness" and the assembly withheld action.[4]

---

[1] Cole, *Era of the Civil War*, 333-335.

[2] *Boston Recorder*, cited in *National Intelligencer* (Wash.), Jan. 8, 1865.

[3] *Independent*, Oct. 1, 1863; Dicey, *Six Months in the Federal States*, I, 233.

[4] House of Representatives of Ohio, *Journal for 1864*, app., 56-62.

The services of the "degraded race," however, could be very useful in war time. Eight or ten thousand colored teamsters were soon hauling supplies for the Army of the Potomac. Five times that number of contrabands were put to work upon the fortifications guarding Washington. There was much difference of opinion as to whether the Negro should be allowed the privilege of sharing the dangers of the battle-field. Abolitionists warmly advocated giving him this starting point from which he might rise to a recognized place among men.[1] But their opponents wished to reserve for the "superior" race the right of defending the flag, and talked glibly, now of the Negro's inherent lack of courage, now of the danger of bloody servile insurrection. Lincoln himself actively advocated colonization of the Negro, hoping that therein would be found the ultimate solution of the race problem; but he was forced to recognize that there was a good deal of "itching to get niggers into our lines."[2] Congress voiced its share in this sentiment when in the second confiscation act on July 17, 1862, it authorized the enlistment of persons of African descent.

General David Hunter had already in the preceding May tried without success to organize a Negro regiment in South Carolina, an attempt abandoned after months of slow recruiting and drastic camp discipline. General Butler at New Orleans had reorganized as Union troops the regiment of "Native Guards, Colored," that the Confederate governor had previously recruited, but these were wealthy free mulattoes the darkest of whom was

[1] *Liberator*, Sept. 12, 1862. See also *Independent*, April 16, 1863.
[2] A. B. Hart, *Salmon Portland Chase* (J. T. Morse, jr., ed., *American Statesmen*; Boston, 1899), 259; Lincoln, *Complete Works*, VIII, 1-9, 97-98; W. L. Fleming, "Deportation and Colonization: An Attempted Solution of the Race Problem," J. W. Garner, ed., *Studies in Southern History and Politics* (N. Y., 1914), 8-30.

"about the complexion of the late Mr. Webster." [1] The first regular regiment of ex-slaves was the First South Carolina Volunteers recruited in the Sea Islands under federal control, followed soon by a similar Kansas regiment. [2] These were the first of a series of units which, together with colored regiments recruited in the Northern states, made a Negro contribution to the war of 186,017 soldiers. [3]

These black troops generally served under Negro non-commissioned officers with white superiors, and they were usually denied the full regular pay of white soldiers. [4] Some of their critics never abandoned the emotions that impelled a Broadway mob to attack Sergeant Prince Rivers, a jet-black six-foot trooper whose chevrons seemed a special invitation to an outburst of race prejudice. [5] But competent military authorities, former slaveholders on the one hand and abolitionists on the other, testified to their general competence, courage and at times conspicuous gallantry, and the principal problem was to get them in sufficient numbers. [6] Lincoln soon impressed this upon his military representatives in the

[1] T. W. Higginson, *Army Life in a Black Regiment* (Boston, 1870), 1; B. F. Butler, *Private and Official Correspondence during the Civil War Period* (Boston, 1917), II, 192, 209-211, 270-271; same author, *Autobiography and Reminiscences* (Boston, 1892), 491-493.

[2] Higginson, *Army Life in a Black Regiment*, 1-45, 269-272. See illustration in *Leslie's Illustrated Newspaper*, XV, 200-201 (Dec. 20, 1862).

[3] *Official Records of Armies*, ser. 3, V, 661; G. W. Williams, *A History of the Negro Troops in the War of the Rebellion, 1861-1865* (N. Y., 1888); Shannon, *Organization and Administration of the Union Army*, II, 160.

[4] Higginson, *Army Life in a Black Regiment*, 278-292; B. T. Washington, *Frederick Douglass* (Phila., 1906), 223, 232.

[5] Higginson, *Army Life in a Black Regiment*, 57.

[6] *Official Records of Armies*, ser. 1, XXIV, pt. i, 96, 106, 547. General Andrew J. Smith, "a former slaveholder," thanked the colored troops for their "conspicuous gallantry" at Tupelo. *Wisconsin State Journal* (Madison), Oct. 17, 1864. See also Bigelow, *Retrospections of an Active Life*, II, 278.

South, telling Governor Andrew Johnson of Tennessee that there was no greater specific need than that he, as a Southerner and a slaveholder, take up this work.[1] The *Corps d'Afrique* thus became a recognized and important adjunct of the federal forces, contributing to the success of the conflict for which the black man had unwittingly been so largely responsible.

[1] Lincoln, *Complete Works*, VIII, 233.

CHAPTER XIV

NORTHERN LIFE BEHIND THE LINES

NORTHERN life behind the military front was profoundly affected by the contest. The disruptive impact of civil war bore down at the start with cataclysmic force upon the industrial machine just recovering from the Panic of 1857. Business, paralyzed during the months of fearful waiting that preceded Sumter, next faced the chaos caused by the violent breaking of economic ties that had previously bound the nation.[1] Trade with the South came to an abrupt end. Property values, even in the case of real estate, dropped rapidly. Besides Southern debts on the books of Northern merchants and bankers, a considerable amount of the bonds of Southern states was held in the North. The paper currency of Western banks, issued upon such securities under the state free-banking laws, depreciated rapidly as those bonds declined in value. Panic swept the West as dozens of banks failed and the bonds held in security sold at auction at from sixty to seventy cents on the dollar.

The closing of the Mississippi by the Confederates threatened to be an even more serious blow, particularly to cities on the upper river and on the Ohio. Ruin threatened St. Louis especially, as its river trade stopped and the values of accumulated commodities collapsed. Even in central Illinois corn sold in the autumn at eight and ten cents a bushel and was often found more valuable for use as fuel. All land and water routes eastward were

[1] The number of failures in 1861 exceeded those of 1857 although less money was involved. *American Annual Cyclopedia*, V (1865), 349.

soon choked with traffic.[1] Prices declined as freight rates soared. It cost nearly as much to carry grain by water from Chicago to Buffalo as it did for the transoceanic freight to Liverpool.[2]

But after the first summer's hostilities the alluring spectacle of a general war-time prosperity appeared upon the horizon. A shrewd Northern financier read in the battle of Bull Run, with its promise of a long war and resulting expenditure and inflation, the signs of a fortune for every man in Wall Street "who is not a natural idiot." [3] Portents of a reanimation of all branches of industry and trade were soon in evidence in the large cities. Even in border towns like Cincinnati stringency was ended by the army contracts awarded to their citizens.[4] Despite the threat of heavy taxation a general rise in land values was only well under way when Lewis A. Cass found an undeveloped holding of three hundred acres in Detroit worth over four hundred thousand dollars.[5] In another year or two the cautious business leaders of 1861 could be reminded that the loss of Southern trade had not after all proved a vital blow to the national economy. New York revealed at every turn the full glory of the new prosperity. Travelers swarmed into the metropolis, crowding its hotels until beds were set up in billiard parlors and barrooms. Many of these were merchants from North, East and West in quest of goods to replenish their stocks. New York was "never

[1] *N. Y. World*, Oct. 10, 1861. See also *N. Y. Times*, March 22, 1863.

[2] Anthony Trollope, *North America* (N. Y., 1862), 148, 152; Edward Dicey, *Six Months in the Federal States* (London, 1863), II, 164; *Boston Eve. Transcript*, July 5, 1861.

[3] Anon., "Wall Street in War Time," *Harper's Mo.*, XXX (1865), 615.

[4] *Cleveland Leader*, Sept. 3, 6, 1861; *Am. Ann. Cyc.*, I (1861), 307.

[5] *N. Y. Wkly. Tribune*, Feb. 15, 1862. During the preceding eighteen months real property had depreciated one third in New York, if not generally in the North. *Independent*, April 10, 1862. See also issue of March 27, 1862.

more crowded, more brilliant, more extravagant." [1]
To Alexander T. Stewart, entrepreneur extraordinary,
was attributed the largest income in the country, if not
in the world; for 1864 he paid an income tax of two
hundred and fifty thousand dollars on a net of five
million. [2]

The full swing of prosperity was not evident until
the autumn of 1862. It took time to wipe out the lessons of the Panic of 1857 and the bad times of 1861. [3]
But the improvement in stocks noted in the first autumn
of the war proved only the harbinger of a general boom
market. Stock values rose an average of forty per cent in
1862; many popular shares more than tripled their prewar value. During 1863 transactions in the stock exchange totaled nearly a billion and a half dollars, and
in the two boom years stock operators were said to have
realized profits of a quarter of a billion. [4] By 1864 the
industrial profiteer was transferring his activities to the
stock market and to lead in an even greater rage for
speculation. "The city exchanges and their approaches
are already crowded with a frenzied throng of eager
speculators," reported a critic. [5]

> Streets are blocked up by a mass so frenzied by the
> general passion for gain that almost all regard for per-
> sonal safety and respect for personal propriety seems
> lost. . . . The number of brokers has more than

[1] N. Y. Herald, Jan. 1, 1863; N. Y. Times, May 22, 1863; N. Y.
Tribune, Sept. 25, 1863; John Bigelow, Retrospections of an Active Life
(N. Y., 1909-1913), II, 43-44.

[2] National Intelligencer (Wash.), Jan. 5, 1865. Contrast this to the
depression of his business in 1860-1861 with resulting discharge of
large numbers of his clerks. N. Y. Tribune, Jan. 9, 1860.

[3] Failures in 1861 more than doubled those of 1860 and involved
nearly three times the liabilities. Am. Ann. Cyc., V (1865), 349; N. Y.
Herald, Jan. 1, 1862.

[4] Am. Ann. Cyc., III (1863), 410.

[5] Robert Tomes, "The Fortunes of War," Harper's Mo., XXIX
(1864), 229.

quadrupled in a few months, such has been the enormous increase of stock-jobbing. Their aggregate business, in the city of New York alone, has arisen from twenty-five to more than a hundred millions a day.

The rapid appreciation in stocks was attended by a disposition to purchase and hold property for the inevitable rise. Metals and many articles of merchandise were the objects of such speculation. A "Washington party," a clique of politicians and bankers, were thought to secure advance inside information in regard to political and military developments and thus to harvest enormous profits.[1] Gold was a favorite investment and rose rapidly, with some interruptions resulting from treasury operations, until in the summer of 1864 it reached the figure of 285 and seemed likely to be forced by energetic operators to 300.[2]

These halcyon days of the speculator were in large part the result of a currency inflation only partly represented by the four hundred millions of legal-tender greenbacks placed in circulation by the federal government. The early collapse of the Western banks had forced new demands upon specie just as it was succumbing to further pressure from the currency issues of the government. In December, 1861, the New York banks suspended specie payment and the country went on a paper basis. As the flood of government greenbacks began to pour into all parts, it met a tide of paper money issued by Western banks with reckless prodigality. There was no longer the need of redeeming such issues in coin and the demand for more money seemed unlimited. Paper bills "circulated like fertilizing dew throughout the land, generating enterprise, facilitating industry, de-

[1] Jeremiah Best, "Wall Street in War Time," *Harper's Mo.*, XXX (1865), 615, 621.

[2] Bigelow, *Retrospections of an Active Life*, II, 229-230.

veloping internal trade." [1] The inevitable revulsion against this chaos came in the final years of the war when well-regulated national banks, organized in 1864 and 1865 under Chase's plan, signalized a growing popular feeling that the issues of state banks might well be done away with altogether.

Greenback inflation represented one phase of a policy of loan financiering to meet war-time needs, for the notes of the government constituted a sort of forced loan from its citizens. But from the very start there was an active realization of the importance of securing more direct help from the public in financing the cause. Edward Everett Hale wrote his earnest appeal, "Take the Loan," urging the people to open their purse strings at their country's call; it soon became one of the anthems of the great crusade.[2] Later when bank and counting-house failed to provide sufficient support Chase found more popular methods necessary. Jay Cooke, a Philadelphia banker who had developed a clientele among the masses, was made sole agent for the sale of the "five-twenties" authorized in February, 1862. His well-organized staff, with their paraphernalia of circular, handbill, editorial and newspaper advertisement, soon aroused the humble citizen to an awareness of his stake in the cause, with the result that gold treasure was lured from many an old sock or mattress to join the sums that large investors could be induced to lend.[3] The Union was vitally assisted by a new kind of mass action in its behalf.

The thrift and frugality of the average American home which responded with its contribution to the sinews of war contrasted strangely with the luxury

---

[1] Best, "Wall Street in War Time," 615.

[2] E. E. Hale, jr., *Life and Letters of Edward Everett Hale* (Boston, 1917), II, 327-328, 336.

[3] E. P. Oberholtzer, *Jay Cooke* (Phila., 1907), I, 218-220 ff.

which, led by the "Sybarites of 'shoddy'," stalked un-
ashamed through the great cities. Silks and satins, laces
and costly jewels, heads powdered with gold and silver
dust, were flaunted at opera and theater, in the parks
and on the streets, until at length the conscience of
some of the fair sex was pricked into organizing a "national covenant" to discourage lavish expenditure, particularly for imported luxuries.[1] Among their male companions, who buttoned their waistcoats with diamonds
of the first water, there was no corresponding movement for the abandonment of reckless indulgence at the
gaming table or in wines and spirits. For the wealthy
and especially the newly rich the war seemed a continual carnival of abundance and dissipation.

Meanwhile most branches of manufacturing responded
to the war-time prosperity, being assisted by protective
duties that far surpassed the rosiest dreams of a Clay
or a Webster.[2] The chief exception was the cotton-
spinning industry which, after two years of profitable
production based upon the surplus raw stocks of 1860,
was prostrated by the effects of the war-time shortage.
In its place, however, rose a new prosperity in the manufacture of woolens that quite balanced this loss. Under
the encouragement of actual or possible government
contracts factories multiplied their output, while new
companies were organized and new plants were erected
with incredible speed. At the same time, the making of
ready-made clothing expanded from a petty business
largely in the hands of German Jews in the Eastern
cities into a huge industry chiefly for the manufacture
of soldiers' uniforms, but the labor-saving operations

[1] *N. Y. Tribune*, May 9, 24, 1864; G. A. Sala, *My Diary in America
in the Midst of War* (London, 1865), II, 189-194; *Leslie's Illustrated
Newspaper* (N. Y.), XVIII, 162, 163 (June 4, 1864).
[2] E. D. Fite, *Social and Industrial Conditions in the North during the
Civil War* (N. Y., 1910), chap. iv.

of Elias Howe's invention, the sewing machine, did not as yet take the manufacture of clothing out of the home or the shop. The government was responsible for employing thousands of women who received five and three-quarter cents for making a pair of drawers.[1] Thanks to the ingenuity of L. R. Blake and Gordon McKay the machine was also adapted to the sewing of uppers to the soles of shoes. The result was the development of the modern shoe industry, concentrated, like the preceding handicraft, largely in eastern Massachusetts.

Other sources of new-found wealth were realized in sugar refining which became the ninth most important industry in the nation, in the making of whisky which was pushed to capacity on a speculative basis in anticipation of increased taxation, and especially in iron and steel manufacturing which, increasingly freed from foreign competition, found profitable markets in war-time railroad development and government needs. Nor did the government leave all its manufacturing to private enterprise. The federal armory at Springfield produced a standard rifle at nine dollars, less than one half of what contractors asked, and turned them out at a rate that contributed significantly to victory. During the war years the debate as to the relative merits of muzzle-loaders and breechloaders continued with the result that a decision recognizing the superior merits of the latter was not reached until the fighting was nearly finished. For a similar reason the Gatling gun played no important part in the war.[2] The government was not so slow in reaching a decision in favor of the ironclad battleship. In the case of the *Monitor*, designed by John Erics-

[1] *N. Y. Tribune*, Dec. 14, 1864.
[2] F. A. Shannon, *The Organization and Administration of the Union Army* (Cleveland, 1928), I, 128-148.

son, it effectively applied the distinctive feature of the revolving turret.[1]

War, with its insistent needs, spurred rather than retarded the mineral industries.[2] Newly discovered salt deposits along the Saginaw River in lower Michigan, together with the Syracuse wells in New York, relieved the North from a salt famine that might otherwise have followed the destruction of the Kanawha River works early in the war. The extensive use of coal in locomotives and in manufacturing establishments placed new demands on the anthracite fields of Pennsylvania. The bituminous deposits of other states like Illinois were now first extensively prospected and a number of new mines opened. Lake Superior iron and copper developed a new significance as the completion of the Sault Ste. Marie Canal and the Marquette Railroad simplified the problem of getting the ore to distant markets. Smelting operations in Cleveland and Ohio Valley towns marked the beginning of iron manufacturing in northeastern Ohio in competition with the established industry of Pennsylvania.

At the same time the significance of the petroleum deposits of western Pennsylvania and eastern Ohio was just being realized. In 1859 the first oil well had been sunk at Titusville, Pennsylvania, by Colonel Edwin L. Drake who proved his theory that the pools of surface petroleum indicated subterranean deposits that might be tapped. Soon after oil bubbled from the first well a forest of derricks sprang up and the little village grew into a boom town. The craze spread, the oil field grew and petroleum refining became an important indus-

---

[1] The first successful experiments with the revolving turret were made in England. J. P. Baxter, 3d, *The Introduction of the Ironclad Warship* (Cambridge, Mass., 1933), chaps. ix, xii.

[2] Fite, *Social and Industrial Conditions*, chap. ii.

try in near-by cities and New York. The new fuel proved more satisfactory as well as safer than camphine for illuminating purposes, and the kerosene lamp soon came into its own.[1] The industry grew so rapidly that for a time prices collapsed, but recovery in 1864 marked the beginning of a new era of profits and of a petroleum aristocracy which seemed to the *New York Herald* the fit successor of the shoddy aristocracy.[2]

The railroads also achieved a new prosperity out of war-time transportation needs, many a company apparently destined for collapse under normal circumstances finding an escape from financial embarrassment. At the start certain roads extended generous favors to volunteers using their accommodations. Others, however, exploited consistently all the advantages of the situation, as did especially the Camden and Amboy with its "grasping" monopoly of traffic from New York to Philadelphia. The Baltimore and Ohio at first tried to maintain and extend its trade with the inland Southern states to the point of being dubbed a "treasonable corporation," [3] but soon found its right of way the special object of destructive Confederate attack. The government, however, came to the rescue and sought with military protection to maintain the use of this important route into the interior.

Railroad consolidation was the order of the day.[4] The Pennsylvania rapidly extended its holdings at the expense of smaller lines. By absorbing a group of competing roads the Chicago and Northwestern prepared the

---

[1] *N. Y. Tribune*, March 9, July 21, 1861; anon., "Coal and Petroleum," *Harper's Mo.*, XXVII (1863), 259; J. S. Schooley, "The Petroleum Region of America," same mag., XXX (1865), 562-574.

[2] *N. Y. Herald*, Oct. 18, 1864. To some the essence of capitalism seemed to be highway robbery "in the new gospel of Saint Petroleum." O. W. Holmes, *The Poet at the Breakfast Table* (Boston, 1891), 40.

[3] *N. Y. Times*, June 19, 1861.

[4] *Hunt's Merchants' Mag.*, XLVIII (1863), 502.

way to becoming temporarily, with a mileage of 1152, the largest railway in the country. Meantime, the completion of a new trunk line, projected in the fifties, gave New York another connection with the Mississippi. This was the Atlantic and Great Western, a continuous broad-gauge line running from Salamanca, New York, on the Erie to Cincinnati and thence to St. Louis, and the longest piece of construction work accomplished during the war. New extensions, connecting links, double tracks, bridges and union depots proved to be important factors working for the economic unity of the North.

The spectacular development of the era was the inauguration of Pacific railroad building. The pressure of the westward movement which resulted from the gold and silver rushes of the early sixties, reënforced by the new military need, led Congress to give its approval in 1862 to the Union Pacific-Central Pacific project for a transcontinental road through the scattered settlements of Nebraska, Colorado, Utah and Nevada to California. Eastern financiers were lukewarm about this "wild dream," but a meeting at Chicago brought together a group of enthusiastic backers and assured the necessary capital.[1] That erratic genius George Francis Train, borrowing from a French model, shortly organized the Crédit Mobilier as a construction company for building the road. Ground was broken at the straggling town of Omaha on December 2, 1863, as Train grandiloquently proclaimed this the future population center of the United States and predicted the completion of the road by 1870.[2] Owing to promotional difficulties, however,

---

[1] *N. Y. Times*, Sept. 6, 1862; *N. Y. Tribune*, Sept. 6, 1862; *Hunt's Merchants' Mag.*, XLVII (1862), 313 ff.

[2] E. L. Sabin, *Building the Pacific Railway* (Phila., 1919), 86, 90, 94; G. F. Train, *My Life in Many States and in Foreign Lands* (N. Y., 1902), 283 ff. For the completion of the road, see Allan Nevins, *The Emergence of Modern America* (*A History of American Life*, VIII), 53-57, 188-190.

the first rail was not laid until July, 1865. Yet by that time the success of the road was fairly assured.

Renewed attention was given also to the problem of inland water transportation.[1] The closing of the Mississippi caused agitation for enlarging the Illinois and Michigan Canal, thus permitting an outlet for Western products by way of the Great Lakes; but Congress took no action. In 1863 Governor Richard Yates of Illinois, at the suggestion of Western business and farming interests, went so far as to send a commission to Canada to arrange for a Canadian route to the seaboard. Though the ship-canal fever led to a great national canal convention at Chicago on June 2 and 3, 1863, which indorsed a number of projects in the hope of securing the rights of the states of the Mississippi Valley to "national recognition as coequal sovereignties of the Great Republic," Congress withheld its necessary coöperation and no important progress was made.

Meanwhile, despite transportation handicaps and the drain on farm labor due to army recruitment, agriculture prospered, acreage increased and good crops were harvested. From the outset farmers were lured by the promise of "war prices."[2] Agricultural values soon reflected not only the new demand for foodstuffs to feed the Union armies but also, thanks to poor European harvests in 1860, 1861 and 1862, enlarged purchases by foreign countries. Indeed, the amount and value of grain exports increased many fold in 1861 and reached their height in 1863. During the war years Europe purchased a third of a billion dollars' worth of breadstuffs.[3] Such periods of extreme uncertainty in diplomatic relations as the *Trent* affair were used by grain buyers to force lower

[1] Fite, *Social and Industrial Conditions*, 48-54.
[2] *Ohio Farmer* (Cleveland), X (1861), 142, 150.
[3] U. S. Commissioner of Agriculture, *Report for 1865*, 83, 87.

prices.[1] On the other hand, the dependence of England upon the American crop was soon realized to be an important factor in foreign affairs. It was not long before sturdy champions of the West, declaring King Cotton dethroned, hailed a new sovereign—"Corn is King!"[2]

Northern resources in horses and cattle were considerably reduced by war demands, but the sheep and wool output reflected distinct gains at handsome prices and the hog crop was the particular pride of seven Western states. Especially in areas not favored by transportation facilities, local prices often made it wise to market the corn crop in the form of fat hogs. The peak of production was reached in 1862-1863 when over four million porkers were listed.[3] In the packing industry as well as in the grain and lumber market, the war accelerated the growing supremacy of Chicago, the new "porkopolis" of the sixties.[4]

Since the war cut off access to Southern staples efforts were made to find a Northern source of supply. Soon Indiana, Illinois and Missouri were the scenes of extensive experimentation with growing cotton. Individual successes led to a "cotton mania" in southern Illinois in which the "procottonists" worked with infectious zeal. As a result a seed problem arose and the federal gov-

[1] Anon., "Times in Iowa," *Home Missionary*, XXXIV (1862), 295.

[2] Bigelow, *Retrospections of an Active Life*, II, 256-259. A native-born Southerner and slaveholder pointed out that the grain and flour receipts of Chicago for 1861 were nearly double in weight the total cotton crop of the South. See also W. H. Russell, *My Diary North and South* (Boston, 1863), 358; Lorin Blodget, *The Commercial and Financial Strength of the United States* (Phila., 1864), 37; Fite, *Social and Industrial Conditions*, 19-21; L. B. Schmidt, "The Influence of Wheat and Cotton on Anglo-American Relations during the Civil War," *Iowa Journ. of History and Politics*, XVI, 400-439.

[3] U. S. Comnr. of Agr., *Rep. for 1865*, 70 ff.; *Hunt's Merchants' Mag.*, XLVIII (1863), 400-403; LIV (1866), 382-383.

[4] *N. Y. Times*, March 28, 1863; Auguste Laugel, *Les États-Unis pendant la Guerre* (Paris, 1866), 152-155; H. C. Hill, "The Development of Chicago as a Center of the Meat Packing Industry," *Miss. Valley Hist. Rev.*, X, 262-263.

ernment undertook to secure seed and distribute it through the offices of the state agricultural societies.[1] The resulting crops, harvested when prices had climbed to from sixty cents to $1.50 a pound, in large part took care of local needs, but failed to solve the fundamental problem raised by the war. Nor did outside sources of supply like South America afford much relief, while the increased production of flax availed little since linen could not be made with the existing machinery for cotton manufacture. The problem remained unsolved even after enterprising Yankees entered the field in the wake of the Union armies as lessees of Southern plantations.[2]

Advancing sugar prices invited similar efforts in raising saccharose crops to take the place of the Louisiana cane sugar. A slight increase in maple-sugar production resulted, but sorghum culture made far greater gains. Southern Illinois virtually doubled its output and a convention at Columbus in January, 1863, demonstrated successful efforts in the states from Ohio to Iowa. Repeated attempts to produce a satisfactory granulated sugar from Chinese cane ended in failure. Even such large-scale ventures as the Northwestern Chinese Sugar Manufacturing Company, incorporated in 1863, promptly collapsed. Interest in the possibility of beet-sugar production was aroused by the dissemination of information in regard to conditions in France and Germany. Soon ventures were launched in this field, but little was accomplished except to satisfy many of its advocates that the manufacture of sugar from beets could be made to pay.

One of the most remarkable features of the agricultural contribution to the war was the fact that so much

---

[1] A. C. Cole, *The Era of the Civil War* (C. W. Alvord, ed., *The Centennial History of Illinois*, Springfield, 1918-1920, III), 378-379; *Chicago Tribune*, March 4, 10, 1863; *Ohio Farmer*, XI (1862), 26, 46, 118.

[2] *N. Y. World*, Jan. 26, 1863; *N. Y. Tribune*, Jan. 12, 1864.

was achieved despite the reduced man power on the farm. From certain districts nine tenths of the young and able-bodied men promptly enlisted. The shortage of farm labor was soon reflected in increased wages and in appeals for help. Wages rose to $1.25, to $2.00 per day, and were then forced still higher by the depreciation of paper money. In some instances farmers turned their cattle into the grain fields rather than pay the rates required to harvest. In many cases women and children, in the pioneer spirit, took their places as farm hands, and a grown man at work in the fields came to be pronounced "a rare sight." [1] Reviving immigration offered some additional relief although the newcomer was often more interested in establishing his own farm upon the public domain.

Invisible labor units were added by the installation of agricultural machinery, especially the reaper which saved many a Western crop. Even conservative farmers were forced to replace and supplement man power by machines. Orders for reapers and other farm machines often consumed the entire output of factories. Midsummer made the upper prairie districts almost a continuous wheat field with hundreds of reapers harvesting the golden crop.[2] Oxen were found to be too slow for hauling expensive farm implements and, in spite of the scarcity and high price of horses, were steadily discarded.

The agricultural area of the North increased extensively as the government granted free homesteads under the act of 1862. By 1865 nearly two and a half million acres were parceled out. In addition, many purchases were made from the state governments and from private

[1] *Carthage* (Ill.) *Republican*, June 9, 1864.
[2] *Scientific American*, IX (1863), 9; Mary A. Livermore, *My Story of the War* (Hartford, 1889), 145-146; Frederick Merk, *Economic History of the Civil War Decade* (Hist. Soc. of Wis., *Studies*, I), 52-56, 145-146.

holdings. The Illinois Central Railroad made new records in its sales, dispensing virtually a quarter-million acres in both 1863 and 1864.[1] "Every day sees new settlers arriving and fresh lands subjected to the plough," testified an observer.[2] New England rural communities dwindled as their residents joined the foreign immigrant in the new westward movement. At the same time the thrifty pioneer farmer acted to clear his farm of mortgage or to reduce his indebtedness. In six months six hundred mortgages totaling some two hundred and forty thousand dollars were paid off in one Wisconsin county.[3]

A new sense of professional pride in husbandry evidenced itself in a tendency toward more effective organization. Agricultural leaders in Ohio held that the need of even greater attention to farming justified their not canceling the state fair in 1861.[4] County and state societies continued along established lines, but many new local farmers' clubs made their appearance. Agricultural organizations found fresh opportunities for practical service in directing the adjustment of farm economy to war conditions and in conducting the discussion of problems connected with the establishment of agricultural colleges under the Morrill land-grant act. The same sort of interest influenced the act for the creation of a federal commissioner of agriculture in 1862.

Not all Westerners were satisfied, however, that their section was duly appreciated and given its fair share in the national economy. Indeed, the lingering suspicion of

---

[1] *Chicago Tribune*, March 2, 1863; *Ohio Farmer*, XII (1863), 136; Auguste Laugel, *The United States during the War* (London, 1866), 146-147.

[2] G. T. Barrett, *Out West* (London, 1866), I, 154. See also E. D. Fite, "Industrial Development of the West," *Quar. Journ. of Econ.*, XX, 274-275.

[3] *Wisconsin State Journal* (Madison), Oct. 14, 1864.

[4] *Ohio Farmer*, X (1861), 150.

Eastern selfishness was sharpened by many war-time developments. If Western radicalism was scorned and feared by New England spokesmen, the farmers in the provinces were prone to see exploitation in the tariff and tax legislation sponsored by Eastern congressmen. "We pay every dollar, that is to be levied by this tax bill," protested Daniel W. Vorhees of Indiana against the measure of 1864.[1] It seemed unfair "that the young farmer just beginning on our prairies, has to pay just as much as the wealthy citizen in his luxurious New England home."[2] There were also those who pictured land grants to railroads as part of the process of making "the whole Northwest and the whole West but little more than a province of New York."[3] Throughout the war there were bitter expressions of resentment at the tendency of the East through its contractors and profiteers to make money out of the war while the West bore the brunt of the conflict. There was, moreover, a strong feeling of jealousy between the Eastern and Western armies.[4] For all these reasons, as well as because Westerners were impatient of compromise and anxious to force the issue of emancipation, disruptive influences operated in the West. Yet, as it was frequently remarked, the West filled its quotas and then kept on enlisting, while—so it was alleged—New England and New York stopped recruiting and took to praying instead.

One of the inevitable corollaries of the prosperity that spread from the industrial East to the Western

[1] *Congressional Globe,* 38 Cong., 1 sess., 304.

[2] Iowa State Agricultural Society, *Report for 1861-1862,* 8. "The mighty West has the bills to foot and the men to furnish to carry on the war, while the East is stealing, robbing and defrauding the Government every day of its existence," complained an ardent advocate of an aggressive war policy. James W. Hughes to Lyman Trumbull, Jan. 7, 1862 (Trumbull MSS., Library of Congress).

[3] Senator Howe in *Congressional Globe,* 37 Cong., 2 sess., 2626.

[4] U. S. Grant. *Personal Memoirs* (N. Y., 1885-1886), II. 460, 632.

prairies was a rise of prices to unprecedented levels. In the national capital with its war-time congestion food costs and house rents advanced to such exorbitant figures that several hundred government clerks decided to take up their residence in Baltimore and commute over the B. and O.[1] The cost of living generally increased, at first by fifty and eventually by over a hundred per cent.[2] But this represented commodity prices in a paper currency which in the later years of the war was worth only half its face value. There was some tendency on the part of wages to adjust themselves to the new price levels, if only because of the scarcity of workers with so much of the man power of the country in the army.[3] But wages did not keep pace with the rapidly mounting prices of food and clothing. Even in the later years of the war, when labor's greatest gains were made, there was a continued decline in real wages until they stood at about a third less than in 1860.

Labor therefore did not enjoy, along with industry and agriculture, its full share of the prevailing prosperity. Indeed, its standard of living declined materially, sometimes to the point where there was acute difficulty in making both ends meet. The shortage of labor that followed the hectic summer of 1861 was partly offset by labor-saving machines and by new recruits to the industrial army from the ranks of women, Negroes and immigrants. Seward utilized all the resources of the state department to induce unemployed workingmen in Eu-

[1] *N. Y. Tribune*, Sept. 14, 1863.

[2] See Aldrich report, 52 Cong., 2 sess., *Senate Rep.*, III, 176. See also U. S. Commissioner of Labor, *Annual Report for 1886*, 74; Mass. Bureau of Statistics of Labor, *Annual Report for 1872*, 516-520; F. W. Taussig, "Results of Recent Investigations on Prices in the United States," *Yale Rev.*, II (1893), 231-247.

[3] Under acts of December 21, 1861, and July 16, 1862, salaries of government employees were to be regulated according to the rates paid in other establishments.

rope to come to the "land of opportunity" where a great labor deficiency prevailed. The homestead act of 1862 opened the public domain to foreign settlers as well as to the native-born and, in addition, Lincoln recommended federal legislation for the direct encouragement of immigration. Congress responded with the act of July 4, 1864, which authorized the importation of wage-earners by contractors under supervision of a commissioner of immigration.

By this time immigration had already more than doubled the 1861 mark. The hungry surplus of Ireland had scored this gain a year earlier, and it was reasonably evident that concentrated efforts had been made to stimulate their coming, whether or not the methods included the direct and questionable efforts at military recruiting that were charged by Southern and British critics, including Foreign Secretary Lord John Russell.[1] It was not long before staid Bostonians were deploring the fact that their beloved city was overlaid by Celts from across the sea and that Catholics were beginning to occupy the historic strongholds of liberal Protestantism in America.[2] Meantime New Yorkers rejoiced that their metropolis had become the third largest German city in the world, and the nation generally took pride in the foreign contingent of over four hundred thousand which helped to fight the battles of the Union.[3]

The war came just as labor had begun to achieve a

---

[1] *London Morning Herald*, cited in *N. Y. Times*, May 23, 1863; Bigelow, *Retrospections of an Active Life*, II, 95; P. H. Bagenal, *The American Irish and Their Influence on Irish Politics* (London, 1882), 139-140 n.; J. B. McMaster, *A History of the People of the United States during Lincoln's Administration* (N. Y., 1927), 372-376. See Seward's explanation in 38 Cong., 1 sess., *Senate Exec. Doc.*, I, no. 54.

[2] H. T. Tuckerman, "A Village in Massachusetts," *Harper's Mo.*, XXXII (1865), 114.

[3] B. A. Gould, *Investigations in the Military and Anthropological Statistics of American Soldiers* (N. Y., 1869), 27.

certain amount of self-consciousness and self-expression. Certain leaders like William H. Sylvis, foreseeing the menace of war to their class as well as to the general welfare, had called a series of meetings terminating in a national workingman's convention at Philadelphia on February 22, 1861, which deplored the prevailing spirit of sectionalism and urged an adjustment by compromise.[1] They left little doubt, however, as to their devotion to the Union and when the war broke out they loyally rallied to the support of the government. Some labor unions enlisted to a man and adjourned their activities for the duration of the conflict. But in the face of the danger that the working classes might be ground between the upper and nether millstones of industry and agriculture there was a growing realization of the power of labor as well as a disposition to make use of it.

The warning went out that capital was trying to assume the right to own and control labor for its own greedy ends. As a result, with "self-preservation the first law of nature," the workers launched numerous local unions in all the Eastern states.[2] A number of new national bodies were also brought into existence, including the American Miners Association (1861), forerunner of the United Mine Workers' organization; the Brotherhood of Locomotive Engineers (1864), originally organized in Detroit as the Brotherhood of the Footboard (1863); the Cigar Makers' National Union (1864), which came into being just when Samuel Gompers, a young English immigrant, was joining a

[1] *National Intelligencer*, Jan. 15, 1861; *Philadelphia Inquirer*, Feb. 25, 1861; T. V. Powderly, *Thirty Years of Labor* (Columbus, 1890), 44-46; J. R. Commons and others, *History of Labour in the United States* (N. Y., 1918), 10-12.

[2] *Columbus* (Ohio) *Crisis*, April 8, 1863; Mass. Bur. of Stat. of Labor, *Ann. Rep. for 1870*, 100; Bur. of Labor Stat. of Ohio, *Ann. Rep. for 1877*, 31; Mary R. Beard, *A Short History of the American Labor Movement* (N. Y., 1920), 62-79.

New York local; the Iron Molders' International Union (1864), reflecting the indefatigable efforts of Sylvis; and the Bricklayers' and Masons' International Union (1865).

By the end of the war, trades' assemblies existed in every important city. They not only undertook to link together the local bodies and to encourage the formation of unions in unorganized trades, but assisted in the establishment of coöperative stores, in the creation of workingmen's libraries and reading rooms and in the development of a labor press.[1] They also made their existence felt in efforts to influence legislation, especially for an eight-hour day. In 1864, under the lead of Sylvis and the Iron Molders, an attempt was made to join these city federations into a national organization. But a convention at Louisville brought out only a small attendance and the meeting set for May, 1865, in Detroit never occurred.[2]

The organization of a union usually evidenced a determination to influence some adjustment of wages to prices. Employers therefore ordinarily found it wise to make some concession to stave off labor difficulties. Certain employers, however, were disposed to charge the economic problems of the day to the unreasonable demands of the unions[3] and showed a stubbornness that yielded only after a test of strength. As a result the number of strikes increased rapidly after 1863, totaling well over a hundred in the following year. In general, such disturbances were attended with little violence. Most serious passions were aroused when Negro strike

[1] Commons and others, *History of Labour*, II, 23-26.

[2] J. R. Commons and others, eds., *A Documentary History of American Industrial Society* (Cleveland, 1910-1911), IX, 118-125. For the later history of this effort, see Nevins, *Emergence of Modern America*, 72.

[3] *The War of the Rebellion: A Compilation of the Official Records of the Union and Confederate Armies* (Wash., 1880-1901), ser. 3, III, 1008, 1009.

breakers were employed to take the places of Irish workers. The Irish dock laborers especially resented such competition, with bloody affrays often the result.[1] Conditions in the industrial world in 1865 were still such as to make a militant reformer like Wendell Phillips feel that, now chattel slavery had been destroyed, it was the inevitable logic of events to transfer the attack to wage slavery.[2]

The distress of the working class was symptomatic of unsettled conditions that ramified in many different directions. As people looked about them in the large cities, they found much evidence to belie the dictum, "Peace enervates and corrupts society; war strengthens and purifies." [3] Aside from the abolition movement it was manifest that the strength of prewar idealism had withered before the hot breath of war. Humanitarian movements in general underwent a rapid decline, and reformers who did not throw their energies into the war found themselves isolated, if not discredited. This was the lot not only of the peace crusade but also of the temperance movement and the feminist cause.

Many, indeed, agreed with the New York board of metropolitan police that "a state of war is a school of violence and crime." [4] Newspapers chronicled with hor-

[1] *N. Y. Tribune,* July 11, 1862; Fite, *Social and Industrial Conditions,* 189, 203 ff.

[2] Wendell Phillips, *Speeches, Lectures, and Letters* (2d ser., Boston, 1905), 139; Carlos Martyn, *Wendell Phillips: The Agitator* (N. Y., 1890), 378 ff.

[3] Anon., "War as a Schoolmaster," *Harper's Wkly.,* V, 658 (Oct. 19, 1861). Religious leaders could look to war as "the restorer of national life," and this war as "destined to educate the nation to a loftier patriotism." Anon., "War as an Educator," *Independent,* April 18, 1861. See also *Monthly Religious Magazine,* XXV (1861), 378; XXVII (1862), 198 ff.; *Christian Examiner,* LXXI (1861), 114-115; *Boston Review,* I (1861), 252 ff.

[4] Commissioner of Statistics of Ohio, *Eighth Annual Report* (1864), 54; *N. Y. Times,* Jan. 5, 1865. See also issues of Aug. 23. 1861, May 11, 1862, June 29, July 15, 1865; *Rockford* (Ill.) *Register,* Aug. 12, 1865; *Nation,* II, 802 (June 26, 1866).

ror the growing prevalence of licentiousness and criminality.[1] Vice of every sort found safe refuge in the great cities and in communities that had large military establishments. Wrangling, profanity and intoxication were common among soldier and civilian population alike. Rowdiness and bloody brawls among the soldiers led at times to organized attacks upon persons and property. There was a marked tendency toward crimes of violence. What else could be expected, commented a contemporary, when men go about with arms in their hands?

Intemperance thrived upon war's numerous abnormalities. For the time the crusading John B. Gough turned into a lecturer upon "London Life" and "Eloquence and Orators," [2] while innocent youths in uniform who had previously known little of alcohol found increasing pleasure in its use. When efforts were made to curb drunkenness by the denial of liquor to common soldiers, they often found reason for resentment in seeing the confiscated gifts of well-wishers at home "staggering about afterwards with shoulder-straps on." [3] Apparently on the theory that important transactions of state were facilitated by the aid of alcoholic lubricants, liquor was served in the congressional refreshment room at the capitol, to the point where reformers began to conclude that there were too many drunkards in office.

[1] The number of convictions and commitments is not an adequate gauge of the situation since offenders were often allowed to enlist to avoid the penalty of their offense. Even the pardoning power was often exercised with amazing generosity. *N. Y. Times*, March 3, 1862; Gideon Haynes, *Pictures from Prison Life* (Boston, 1869), 107. Cf., however, Fite, *Social and Industrial Conditions*, 304-305.

[2] *Cleveland Herald*, Jan. 9, 1863; John B. Gough, *Autobiography and Personal Recollections* (Springfield, Mass., 1869), 526-528.

[3] Sala, *My Diary in America*, I, 288. See also F. A. Shannon, "The Life of the Common Soldier in the Union Army, 1861-1865," *Miss. Valley Hist. Rev.*, XIII, 481; *Norfolk Day Book*, March 21, 1862, cited in Frank Moore, ed., *The Rebellion Record* (N. Y., 1861-1868), IV, "Diary," 65.

Women came to Washington on various errands—to visit soldier relatives, to claim bodies of those who had been killed, to seek work—some with small funds, if any. In not a few cases the more comely of them were set upon by certain graceless petty officeholders offering to buy them for pleasure, the bargain being accepted as an alternative to destitution. Nor did politicians hesitate to put their mistresses into government clerkships. Moreover, the military segregation of healthy males who longed even for the sight of anything suggesting femininity invited the attention of female camp followers who flocked by the hundreds to the national capital and to the environs of military encampments. Fallen women were believed to constitute a quarter of the civilian population of Washington where a good Samaritan established a foundling hospital which saved many a despondent soul from suicide.[1]

Everywhere the "painted lady" seemed to ply her ancient calling with increasing patronage from soldier, profiteer and roué. Border cities on the Ohio declined to add to their swollen prostitute population in 1863 when the military authorities at Nashville planned to deport the three or four hundred female hangers-on who thronged that base. A scheme was therefore adopted by which the "ladies" were allowed to pursue their profession under a system of licensing and medical inspection. The arrangement, which was self-supporting, reduced materially the amount of venereal disease although it regularly increased with every fresh arrival of troops from the front or from the North.[2]

Nymphes du pavé, soliciting soldier patronage on the streets of Cincinnati, "nearly succeeded in elbowing all

[1] *Cincinnati Enquirer,* Jan. 2, 4, 8, 11, 15, 1864; *Springfield* (Mass.) *Republican,* May 7, 1864.

[2] *Am. Ann. Cyc.,* IV (1864), 769-770; *Leslie's Illustrated Newspaper,* XVII, 67 (Oct. 24, 1863).

decent women from the public promenade." The street corners and walks of Chicago became so infested by gay and flashing damsels, brazen-faced courtesans and their parasites that the newspapers—including the *Chicago Tribune,* with its estimate of two thousand lewd women —set up a cry of protest. Broadway boasted some two hundred supper and concert saloons with their "pretty waiter-girls," who represented the upper stratum of the twenty thousand prostitutes of that prosperous metropolis. Even Boston, home of the Puritans, "absolutely swarms with strumpets," a contemporary traveler announced. Matters came to a climax in 1865 when the soldiers were mustered out and paid. In New York and elsewhere "city sharpers" joined the women in the process of exploitation. The small capital city of Illinois was so "overrun with black legs, burglars, garroters, and harlots (male and female), who have congregated to rob the soldiers . . . of their hard earned wages," that General John Cook detailed two additional companies to act as a provost guard.[1]

In a quite different fashion the ever present fact of war colored the intellectual life of the times. The lyceum, adapting itself to the new conditions but catering to a dwindling public, added patriotic propaganda to its educational function. The schools were left to carry on largely from their own momentum although frontier states like Minnesota and Nevada found energy to organize their systems from the ground up. The annual sessions of various educational agencies, like the National Educational Association, were suspended during

[1] Cole, *Era of the Civil War,* 420-421. On Cincinnati, see *Cincinnati Enquirer,* Jan. 2, 1864; on Chicago, *Columbus Crisis,* March 2, 1864, and *Chicago Tribune,* July 22, 24, 1865; on New York, Dicey, *Six Months in the Federal States,* II, 17; Herbert Asbury, *Gangs of New York* (N. Y., 1928), 175; *N. Y. Times,* March 3, 1862; *Philadelphia Press,* April 4, 1863, Jan. 21, 1864; *Leslie's Illustrated Newspaper,* XX, 227 (July 1, 1865); on Boston, Sala, *My Diary in America,* II, 162.

the first two years of the war. The teacher was often prompt to volunteer his services upon the field of battle. Ohio alone sent to the front in 1861 over two thousand schoolmasters of whom some one hundred—topped by two brigadier generals and seven colonels—received commissions.[1] Those teachers who remained at their desks found their pupils at first inclined to desert their lessons to enjoy the excitement of military show and parade. Children who attended were taught songs and poems that excited their young heads and fired their young hearts. In the later years of the war the upper classrooms were quite bereft of their male contingent, for, in the absence of compulsory-attendance laws, boys found profitable employment waiting for them in many fields. The teachers sometimes shared in the adjustment of wages to soaring prices, if not in the general prosperity, but they often had to organize their request for increased pay.[2]

More serious was the invasion of the schools by wartime hysteria. Patriotic school boards sometimes forced the resignation of allegedly disloyal teachers and certain states such as Oregon, Kentucky and West Virginia required educators to take an oath of fidelity to the government.[3] There was a sudden plea for military instruction, especially since it was assumed that under impulse of the Civil War Americans would henceforth become to a greater extent "a military people."[4] A leading religious journal expressed sympathy with the notion of

[1] Commissioner of Common Schools of Ohio, *Eighth Annual Report* (1862), 6.

[2] *Cincinnati Enquirer*, Jan. 29, 1864.

[3] *Acts of Kentucky for 1861-1863*, 265; *N. Y. Times*, Sept. 1, 1862; Bessie L. Pierce, *Public Opinion and the Teaching of History* (N. Y., 1926), 29-34.

[4] Anson Smyth in Comnr. of Common Schools of Ohio, *Eighth Ann. Rep.*, 18. A later commissioner, E. E. White, concluded: "I am fully satisfied that, so far as our common schools are concerned, it is neither necessary, practicable nor desirable to attempt to include in them the

connecting drill with intellectual development and shared
the conviction "that the future of this country is to be
stamped with a more decidedly military character."[1]
Accordingly, many private schools added martial instruction to their curricula, a number of new military
schools were founded, and boards of education made
provision for drill.[2] It is significant of the times that
Elizabeth Cady Stanton shared in the contemporary
conversion of many pacifist reformers. Recognizing that
"the age of bullets has come again," she found the war
"music in my ears" and was anxious to prepare her son
Henry for a soldier's career with the aid of "a scientific
military education" at West Point.[3]

The field of higher education even more violently experienced all these new disturbing forces. In the first
flush of the war, college presidents hastened to offer their
services to the government. With equal fervor under-
graduates signed up for companies under the tutelage
of favorite professors turned soldier, or of drillmasters
who had had previous military training. In the four
years of the war, attendance at Yale, then the largest
institution, fell from 521 to 438, at Harvard from 443
to 385, at Dartmouth from 275 to 146, at Lafayette
from 87 to 51, and at Ohio Wesleyan from 157 to 119.[4]
For those who remained behind, military drill was added
to the usual round of studies.[5]

school of the soldier." Comnr. of Common Schools of Ohio, *Twelfth
Ann. Rep.*, 69-70.

[1] *Independent*, Aug. 7, 1862. See also *Round Table*, I, 148 (Feb. 20,
1864).

[2] During the first year of the war five Northern governors made favorable mention of this proposal in their messages. *N. Y. Tribune*, Dec. 31,
1861, July 3, 1862; *N. Y. Times*, March 8, 1862.

[3] Elizabeth C. Stanton, *Elizabeth Cady Stanton as Revealed in Her
Letters, Diary and Reminiscences* (Theodore Stanton and Harriot S.
Blatch, eds., N. Y., 1922), II, 88-89, 91.

[4] Fite, *Social and Industrial Conditions*, 237.

[5] M. W. Tyler, *Recollections of the Civil War* (N. Y., 1912), 8, 18;

It was not strange that a clause requiring offerings in military training insinuated itself into the Morrill act for land grants to agricultural and mechanical colleges. No protest was offered in Congress though there was grave doubt in the minds of many advocates of land-grant colleges as to the place of military training in a college curriculum. R. W. Taylor, auditor of state in Ohio, argued that the inclusion of military tactics would make the colleges "contain elements incongruous and destructive." "The teaching of agriculture and the mechanic arts, in a college where military science is also taught, would be almost as difficult as their peaceful pursuit in a country occupied by an army." [1]

In a different way the antagonism of war to education was brought home to Professor Oliver Wendell Holmes when he was reminded "that a ship of war costs as much to build and to keep as a college, and that every port-hole we could stop would give us a new professor." [2] Such considerations, however, inevitably yielded to sentimental ones, as when a crippled veteran returned to a Harvard commencement to become the hero of the day.[3] Still more serious was the threat to intellectual honesty and freedom when students were forbidden to wear Democratic badges, when Copperhead papers were banned from college libraries, when the faculty of Denison University refused to accept the "disloyal" oration of a senior on the suppression of civil liberties, and when the trustees of Dartmouth College, who had long acquiesced in the proslavery fulminations of their veteran president Dr. Nathan Lord, unwittingly forced his resignation in listening to the insistent ministerial

Henry James, *Charles W. Eliot* (Boston, 1930), I, 89; Andrew D. White, *Autobiography* (N. Y., 1905), I, 91.

[1] Auditor of State of Ohio, *Report for 1862*, 18.
[2] Caroline Ticknor, ed., *Dr. Holmes's Boston* (Boston, 1915), 58.
[3] Dicey, *Six Months in the Federal States*, II, 222.

declaration that the *"moral* and *religious* interests and material prosperity of Dartmouth College imperatively demand the removal of the presiding officer."[1] It was perhaps ominous of tendencies that the board of visitors of the University of Michigan found that certain valuable professors had resigned and that uneasiness prevailed among others because the regents had assumed the executive administration of the college which really belonged to the faculty.[2]

Despite these deterrent conditions the war did much to stimulate productive work, especially in applied science. Not only did scientific interest turn to the fabrication of ironclads, but experiments were carried on in the possibilities of submarine and aërial warfare and in other devices for strengthening and multiplying the sinews of war.[3] In 1863 a National Academy of Science was founded to make available to the government the contributions of leading American scientists. At the same time many students worked quietly in their laboratories with little reference to the national crisis.[4] In his *Methods of Study in Natural History* (1863) Louis Agassiz reached a wide popular audience, believing the time had come "when truth must cease to be the property of the few, when it must be woven into the common life of

[1] *Columbus Crisis*, July 15, 1863. See also Cole, *Era of the Civil War*, 431, and *N. Y. World*, Oct. 14, 1863. On October 15, 1863, Prof. Richard S. McCulloh was expelled from the faculty of Columbia College "for having abandoned his post and joined the rebels." He had meantime made discoveries concerning gunpowder which enabled him to secure a commission from the Confederate government to undertake the destruction of Northern war materials. *Independent*, Nov. 12, 1863; *Official Records of Armies*, ser. 4, III, 37-38, 1097; ser. 2, VIII, 567.

[2] *Independent*, Jan. 21, 1864. There was noted in "all colleges" a tendency "toward weakening the public force in favor of individual rights." W. H. Dixon, *New America* (London, 1867), 450.

[3] Shannon, *Organization and Administration of the Union Army*, I, 143-148.

[4] Scientific progress was annually summarized by D. A. Wells in the *Annual of Scientific Discovery*, published from 1850 to 1871.

the world." He also took the field in person and on a lecture tour in 1864 organized a Natural History Society at Chicago where nineteen persons promptly contributed forty-five hundred dollars toward a fund which in a year increased tenfold.[1] This, however, was as much a reflection of war prosperity as a proof of interest in pure science. Meanwhile John W. Draper, stepping out of his rôle of chemist and physiologist, boldly essayed an interpretation of history in which he blazed the trail for modern views in regard to the effects of climate upon human development. To a contemporary his product seemed an attempt "first, to absorb all physical science in theoretical materialism,—second, to absorb all history in physical science."[2] The work ran rapidly through many editions and exerted a profound influence for years.

As earlier, however, the newspaper formed the principal reading matter of the average American. For better or worse "the university was brought to every poor man's door in the newsboy's basket."[3] Under Greeley's leadership the Northern dailies entered the war with the cry, "On to Richmond!" But the editorial fraternity, assembled in force to witness a great Union victory, found their reward in the tragic spectacle of Bull Run. With people relying on newspapers as never before, the daily press increased in circulation and in power. The sales of the *New York Times* jumped forty thousand in the first two weeks of the war. The *Tribune's* forty thousand Illinois subscribers in 1864 represented an increase of over twice the prewar list. At the same time

---

[1] E. W. Emerson, *The Early Years of the Saturday Club, 1855-1870* (Boston, 1918), 337.

[2] Review of Draper's *A History of the Intellectual Development of Europe* (1863) in *Atlantic Mo.*, XIII (1864), 643.

[3] [Ralph Waldo Emerson], "American Civilization," *Atlantic Mo.*, IX (1862), 503.

the newspapers of Chicago, Cleveland and other inland cities had their first taste of real prosperity. With every important bit of news from the front "extras" were rushed through the press and promptly cried upon the streets.

The publication of military intelligence offered many problems if it were not to furnish the enemy with valuable information. At first a government censor inspected all news dispatches, with the result that sometimes only a few innocuous sentences were left of lengthy and vivid accounts, such as that which Henry J. Raymond wrote of Bull Run.[1] Later, correspondents were placed upon parole promising to transmit no information detrimental to the national cause. As to the policy of the war department Lincoln could jestingly refer to the danger, thanks to its "tight rein on the press," that he might "blab too much" in a public address.[2] There was the inevitable difficulty of striking a happy mean between a system which would suppress harmless news and one which would result in the publication of contraband information. This was complicated by the varying policies imposed by different generals within their respective jurisdictions. Some were disposed to order correspondents out of their lines, some required the approving initials of a young aid-de-camp, while others set up restrictions which led to the arrest of veteran journalists like Thomas W. Knox of the *Herald* as well as of striplings like the zealous George A. Townsend.[3]

Stirring events at Washington and in the field helped usher in the period of modern reportorial enterprise. The

[1] Elmer Davis, *History of the New York Times* (N. Y., 1921), 55-56.

[2] Abraham Lincoln, *Writings* (A. B. Lapsley, ed., N. Y., 1905-1906), VI, 56.

[3] T. W. Knox, *Camp-Fire and Cotton-Field* (N. Y., 1865), 254-258; G. A. Townsend, *Campaigns of a Non-Combatant* (N. Y., 1866), 91 ff.

Associated Press, after a dozen years of service, was found useful in forwarding news bulletins from Washington, and it transmitted much of the telegraphic news from the front. But a swarm of special war correspondents was soon in the field, led by the *Herald's* representatives with a tent and wagon for each army corps. The *Tribune* and the *World* also sent out well-known correspondents and Henry J. Raymond, editor of the *Times*, was himself often in the field. Yet some of the best accounts of battle, from the pens of Whitelaw Reid of the *Cincinnati Gazette* and Charles Carleton Coffin of the *Boston Journal*, appeared in less conspicuous prints.

Competition between such rivals was often fierce and jealousy intense. With little regard for lost lives and imperiled interests, for personal comfort or for public weal, they endured the fatigue and hardships of march and bivouac, the monotony and discomfort of camp and the heat of battle, in order to gather their "stories" and give them to the world in advance of their competitors. For inside news of the Confederacy many of them risked, or even permitted, capture when the field correspondent had no recognized war status. So successful were they in their labors that the president and the war department often received their earliest information concerning battles by way of New York or from correspondents who dropped in at Washington.[1]

With the literary talents of the nation stunned by the awful realities of war or enlisted in support of the national cause, American letters suffered a decline. Of "Eighteen Sixty-One" Walt Whitman wrote,

[1] Townsend, *Campaigns of a Non-Combatant*, 206; Knox, *Camp-Fire and Cotton-Field*, 484-492; J. H. Browne, *Four Years in Secessia* (Hartford, 1865), 15-17; Abraham Lincoln, *Complete Works* (J. G. Nicolay and John Hay, eds., N. Y., 1905), VII, 243; anon., "Gentlemen of the Press," *Harper's Mo.*, XXVI (1863), 367; [L. L. Crounse], "The Army Correspondent," same mag., XXVII (1863), 627-633.

Armed year—year of struggle,
No dainty rhymes or sentimental love verses for you,
    terrible year.

The news of a wounded brother summoned the poet to the front and to service in army hospitals, where war lost much of its heroics for the bearded two-hundred pounder who, by his own admission, came to resemble "a great wild buffalo." [1] His volume *Drum Taps* (1865) proclaimed, along with "the blast of the trumpet and the drum pounds," "the whirl and deafening din . . . the unprecedented anguish of wounded and suffering, the beautiful young men in wholesale death and agony, everything sometimes as if blood-color and dripping blood." [2]

Longfellow was shocked by hearing the pulpit thunder war sermons with glorified unction. Whittier's doubts concerning the righteousness of "this terrible war" were not resolved when he learned that his antislavery poem, set to the music of Luther's famous hymn, had been banned from the Army of the Potomac. [3] From the pen of Whittier came some slight contribution to the small quantity of good poetry that the war evoked, but much of his *In War Time and Other Poems* (1864) and of his *National Lyrics* (1865) reflected his passionate desire to find in the unfortunate cataclysm the way of destruction for chattel slavery.

Heading the popular poets of the day was Henry H. Brownell who shortly admitted that his *War Lyrics,* which first appeared in the daily papers, were "but

[1] G. R. Carpenter, *Walt Whitman* (N. Y., 1909), 89-96; Walt Whitman, *Autobiographia* (N. Y., 1892), 48 ff.; Bliss Perry, *Walt Whitman, His Life and Work* (Boston, 1906), 132-157.

[2] Perry, *Walt Whitman,* 150-151.

[3] *N. Y. Tribune,* Feb. 3, 1862; S. T. Pickard, ed., *Life and Letters of John Greenleaf Whittier* (Boston, 1894), II, 467-468.

ephemeral expressions . . . of the great national passion." [1] Esteeming the historical, if not literary, value of such effusions, the journalist Frank Moore culled them for republication in his *Rebellion Record* (twelve volumes, 1861-1868), which appeared in weekly installments from the very beginning of the struggle. His catholicity of interest was strikingly revealed in his special collections of *Lyrics of Loyalty* and of *Confederate Rhymes and Rhapsodies,* both published in 1864.

Much literary talent turned even more frankly to the business of propaganda. Charles Eliot Norton edited the *Papers* of the Loyal Publication Society and flooded the North with compelling arguments for the Union cause. In 1864 Norton and James Russell Lowell assumed editorial control of the *North American Review* and infused new life into that aging quarterly so that it might take a place alongside the *Atlantic* in proclaiming the cause of human rights. At the very end of the war the *Nation* was launched under the editorial direction of Edwin L. Godkin as a critical weekly devoted to the same ideals. The *Nation* proved a fatal challenge to the *Round Table,* another journal of opinion which had made its appearance in the very heart of the conflict. This "weekly record of the notable, the useful and the tasteful" gave space generously to literature and the arts, but in politics refused to take sides on the issues of the day.[2] Meantime the new régime at the Library of Congress, terminating a period of Southern domination, repaired the omission from the collections of that institution of such periodicals as the *Atlantic* and the *Knicker-*

---

[1] H. H. Brownell, *War Lyrics and Other Poems* (Boston, 1866); Emerson, *Early Years of the Saturday Club,* 399.

[2] *Round Table,* I, 1-3 (Dec. 19, 1863); Sala (*My Diary in America,* II, 161) estimated the *Round Table* as "a very fair American substitute for our *Saturday Review."*

bocker and such journals as the *New York Tribune* and the *New York Times*.[1]

By the third year of the war the printing press had recovered from its initial paralysis. Despite the high cost of paper and of bookmaking the literary output exceeded that of any previous year. In the deluge came a number of volumes on military science. Historical works referred largely to the existing war or to phases of the struggle as did also the large crop of biographies. Numerous essays and treatises in political science reflected the extensive field of controversy engendered by the war.[2] War novels also multiplied, few of which survived that era of blood and strife. A callous world soon forgot the moral of Henry Morford's sensational *The Days of Shoddy. A Novel of the Great Rebellion of 1861* (1863),[3] as it did such romances as Mrs. Victor's *The Unionist's Daughter,* Hearton Drille's *Tactics; or Cupid in Shoulder Straps* and the hundreds of dime thrillers that five publishing companies spawned in countless editions. But Lincoln, Seward and even Beecher found recreation in reading these novels and they went by the millions to the soldiers in camp.

Nickel and dime joke books also found new favor perhaps as an escape from war-time horrors. Petroleum V. Nasby, Private O'Reilly and Mrs. Partington were loved for their pungent sallies, and Lowell revived his erstwhile pacifist Hosea Biglow, dedicating his homely philosophy to the winning of a "righteous" war. But it was Artemus Ward whose lectures and articles in *Vanity Fair* supplied society with its best sayings; [4] Abraham

---

[1] Ralph Waldo Emerson, *Journals* (E. W. Emerson and W. E. Forbes, eds., Boston, 1909-1914), IX, 395-396.

[2] *Am. Ann. Cyc.,* III (1863), 573-584.

[3] Morford was also author of the popular *Shoulder Straps. A Novel of New York and the Army, 1862* (Phila., 1863).

[4] *N. Y. World,* Oct. 8, 1863.

Lincoln found him a homespun champion of the administration as well as an unofficial dispenser of mirth at the White House. All of this, indeed, was good tonic for war-time hypochondria; democracy had need of laughter.

Lincoln also found in the theater a cherished means of relaxation. He was often in the presidential box at Ford's Theatre, following the lines of some favorite Shakespearean play or enjoying the homely virtues of a piece like "Our American Cousin," which the sympathetic delineation of Laura Keene carried through something like a thousand performances.[1] At the same time Lord Lyons, the British ambassador, sought to enliven with private theatricals the usual "ineffable dullness" of the capital. In contrast New York, as it recovered from the first blows of the war, became a busy center of stage activity; its theater prospered with the mounting fortunes that war placed in the laps of the anointed. In the spirit of the hour new war-time themes appeared upon the boards. "The Ticket-of-Leave Man" was a popular offering with an excellent moral. "The National Guard," in which the Goddess of Liberty essayed the singing of "The Star Spangled Banner," was a favorite musical drama. At times military companies attended in a body a performance like that of "The Union Boys of '62." Meantime "Uncle Tom's Cabin" reappeared after six years' absence from New York and a great revival of the tragic tale swept the country.[2]

[1] Laugel, *United States during the War*, 277-278. The advertisement of the performance of "Our American Cousin," at which Lincoln was shot, claimed a run of "upwards of a thousand nights." John Creahan, *The Life of Laura Keene* (Phila., 1897), 23, 26.

[2] From that time until 1929 "Uncle Tom's Cabin" was a regular part of the theatrical fare of some part of the American people. G. C. D. Odell, *Annals of the New York Stage* (N. Y., 1927-1931), VII, 392. *N. Y. Tribune*, Feb. 24, 1862; J. F. Campbell, *A Short American Tramp in the Fall of 1864* (Edinburgh, 1865), 286. See also A. M.

But in the unexampled theatrical prosperity that began in 1862 entertainment of all sorts—Shakespearean tragedy, "sensation, or heavy melodrama, rich old comedy" and "creamy new burlesque"—were devoured with equal avidity. A people at war craved varying sensations to aid in forgetting "the harassing cares of the times." Alexander Herrmann, the "prestidigitator," was greeted by audiences of four thousand when he made his first American appearance at the Academy of Music in the fall of 1861. His sleight-of-hand tricks were also acclaimed at the national capital and in many an army camp. Well might his manager, the impresario Ullman, rejoice that he had left the field of opera to offer "a new and sharp sensation" such as the hour seemed to demand.[1] New York audiences, "proverbially the most indulgent in the world," accepted even the most shabby efforts. Thus by the midsummer of 1864 the city was "given up to the leg drama" where "legs, physical and of unpadded proportion," delighted audiences and managers alike.[2]

For some time grand opera, which could make little concession to the times, languished. The initial blow was the loss in the patronage of autumnal visitors returning from mountain and seaside resorts. Soon, perforce, famous European prima donnas yielded to a crop "of New York manufacture" with names "like Kellogg and Hinkley." [3] After 1863, however, the glories of war-

Schlesinger, *The Rise of the City* (*A History of American Life*, X), 291, 296.

[1] "The Lounger," *Harper's Wkly.*, V, 611, 643 (Sept. 28, Oct. 12, 1861).

[2] *Leslie's Illustrated Newspaper*, XV, 119 (Nov. 15, 1862); XVIII, 163, 179, 195, 290, 322 (June 4, 11, 18, July 30, Aug. 13, 1864). See also "Crowded Theatres and Poor Plays," *Round Table*, I, 169 (Feb. 27, 1864).

[3] "The Lounger," *Harper's Wkly.*, V, 674 (Oct. 26, 1861); VII, 34 (Jan. 17, 1863); *N. Y. Tribune*, Feb. 3, 1862; edit., *Harper's Mo.*, XXVI (1863), 853.

time prosperity were reflected in brilliant seasons of Italian, and even German, opera in Eastern cities. Meantime in 1864 the American composer W. H. Fry died in the year that his "Notre Dame de Paris" was produced in Philadelphia. So aloof did music in the grand manner seem from the proper business of Americans that many a fevered patriot felt with Emerson: "Politics, bankruptcy, frost, famine, war,—nothing concerns them but a scraping on a catgut, or tooting on a bass French horn." [1]

Music for the masses found expression largely in the patriotic songs and martial tunes that filled the air, belying the rumor that Congress was considering banning military bands and leaving the soldiers to find inspiration in whisky rather than in song.[2] Over a third of a million copies were sold of *Beadle's Dime Song Book,* the most popular collection. Two thousand songs were published during the first year of fighting and the musical deluge continued. Twelve hundred entries were considered by a national-anthem committee which conducted a five-hundred-dollar prize contest but made no award.[3] "Dixie" retained much of its earlier favor, and the tune was said to be as popular in New York as in Richmond.[4] It was not long, however, before the great Northern marching song, "John Brown's Body," was being "hummed and whistled and ground and played all over the loyal land." [5] The melody was that of a popular

[1] Emerson, *Journals,* VIII, 449.

[2] *N. Y. Tribune,* Feb. 1, 1862. Not only did the German troops continue the traditions of the *Männerchor,* but the Yankee choirmaster and singing teacher helped the New England troops beguile many an otherwise tedious evening. Moore, *Rebellion Record,* IV, "Incidents," 49. See also J. T. Howard, *Our American Music* (N. Y., 1931), chap. ix.

[3] "The Lounger," *Harper's Wkly.,* V, 722-723 (Nov. 16, 1861); R. G. White, *National Hymns* (N. Y., 1861).

[4] *Cleveland Leader,* May 9, 1861; [Catherine C. Hopley], *Life in the South* (London, 1863), I, 352.

[5] "The Lounger," *Harper's Wkly.,* VI, 787 (Dec. 13, 1862). See

hymn by a Southern composer William Steffe; to it were set in due time the words of Julia Ward Howe's "Battle Hymn of the Republic," which also achieved an immediate popularity. The later years of the war brought intensely partisan songs like "Marching through Georgia" and those of a more sad and mournful note like "Just before the Battle, Mother."

The graphic arts supplemented the appeal of music to both the gentler and the harsher emotions of war time. The photographic record of the proud recruit in his gay martial uniform and the crude tintype of the now whiskered soldier in the field accentuated a "photomania" that was sweeping the country when hostilities began. Indeed, the photograph album, with its *cartes des visites* not only of friends and relatives but also of celebrities and its "album gems" of French art beauties, was already promising to become an American institution. These were busy days not only for the local photographer—who sometimes furnished free pictures to new recruits—but for the photographic establishment on wheels which was set up in the neighborhood of every camp. Brady's large portraits of popular generals and views of incidents of the war formed alluring displays in shop windows.[1] Similar influences stimulated the development of frank commercialism in portrait painting. This began with pictures of war heroes and soon spread to the new plutocracy that was born of the war.

Only seldom was the true artist revealed, as in the case of Winslow Homer who followed his lithographs

also *U. S. Service Mag.*, I (1864), 48; Townsend, *Campaigns of a Non-Combatant*, 249; *Independent*, Aug. 29, 1861; *N. Y. Tribune*, Feb. 10, 1862; *Leslie's Illustrated Newspaper*, XX, 163 (June 3, 1865).

[1] *N. Y. Times*, Sept. 26, 1862; Trollope, *North America*, 421; Shannon, *Organization and Administration of the Union Army*, I, 248-249.

and military sketches with oil paintings on war subjects. His "Prisoners from the Front" (1864) had genuine merit and serves as a valuable record of Union and Confederate types.[1] So, too, the brush of Eastman Johnson reflected the incidents of the conflict as he painted such studies as "Knitting for Soldiers." Few, however, stood ready to carry on the tradition of Emanuel Leutze whose last years were busy with government commissions—like his "Westward Ho!" for the national capitol—and whose dying hand made the cartoon for a symbolic painting of "The Emancipation" of the slaves.

If hero and battle-field provided material for brush and palette, so too did the deeper meaning of the struggle offer inspiration to the sculptor's chisel. Randolph Rogers achieved excellent group effects with his "Slave Auction" (1860) and with his later war groups, as did Erastus D. Palmer, who followed his magnificent statue of the "White Captive" with his piece of plastic poetry, "Peace in Bondage" (1863). Indeed, the war showed the definite beginning of a national character in sculpture.[2] War-time nationalism could claim in various ways constructive cultural contributions to offset its many debasing influences.

[1] W. H. Downes, The Life and Works of Winslow Homer (Boston, 1911), 39-52.

[2] Lorado Taft, The History of American Sculpture (J. C. Van Dyke ed., The History of American Art, I, N. Y., 1903), 131, 138-139, 183-184; Sala, My Diary in America, II, 222; F. J. Mather, The American Spirit in Art (R. H. Gabriel, ed., The Pageant of America, New Haven, 1925-1929, XII), 184, 187. On the importance of nationality in art, see Julia H. Layton, "American Art," Knickerbocker, LVIII (1861), 48-52.

CHAPTER XV

THE BELEAGUERED CONFEDERACY

GRADUALLY hemmed in by the serried battalions of the North and by the vessels of the blockading squadrons, the people of Dixie struggled for independence against overwhelming odds. The conflict had begun in an atmosphere of enthusiasm and confidence. But as the fight dragged slowly on and defenses were penetrated or pushed back, hope yielded to a despair which by the fall of 1864 was writing the epitaph of the Confederate States of America. Proclaiming the supremacy of King Cotton, Southerners at the outset had urged a cotton embargo which they believed would compel an acknowledgment of their independence, either because of the resulting economic breakdown of the North or because of intervention by foreign countries to prevent the bankruptcy of their own textile interests. The federal blockade threatened more isolation than was desired, but few planters thought it would long persist; they and the factors at the start agreed to the policy of keeping the cotton crop on the plantations until the blockade was abandoned, a policy which state legislatures and executives warmly supported and which found favor with the Confederate Congress.[1]

Along with the embargo, which was gradually relaxed after a year's trial, went a policy of crop curtail-

[1] F. L. Owsley, "The Confederacy and King Cotton," *N. C. Hist. Rev.*, VI, 371-397. See also W. C. Corsan (An English Merchant, pseud.), *Two Months in the Confederate States* (London, 1863), 113-114, 130-131.

ment. Only about a million and a half bales were produced in 1862, one third of the crop of the previous year, while the combined crops of 1863 and 1864 fell to only half that amount. Meantime hundreds of thousands of bales had been put to the torch partly to increase the leverage upon England and France and partly to keep cotton from capture by the enemy. The amount, however, was greatly exaggerated in the Confederate propagandist statements, although, as the war progressed, probably two and a half million bales were destroyed before the advancing federals.

Many cotton lands were meantime sown to corn, wheat and other foodstuffs. Some of the largest planters of the Gulf states met in convention during the first winter of the war and agreed to set the example of greater food production. A year later the governors of Georgia and North Carolina urged this policy even more insistently. The more enthusiastic were not averse to a policy of mild coercion. Committees of safety waited upon their neighbors to urge coöperation. It was rarely, indeed, that a planter defied such pressure with the determination that General Robert Toombs put into a telegram from Richmond: "I refuse a single hand. . . . You may rob me in my absence, but you cannot intimidate me." [1]

Champions of Southern independence found the food problem an argument for curtailed production of alcoholic beverages. Whether or not as a result, within a year whisky mounted to five times its prewar price. It was a regular component of the navy ration except for a period of some months beginning late in 1863 when the navy department was unable to obtain the needed

---

[1] Robert Toombs, Alexander H. Stephens and Howell Cobb, *Correspondence* (U. B. Phillips, ed., Am. Hist. Assoc., *Ann. Rep. for 1911*, II), 595; U. B. Phillips, *The Life of Robert Toombs* (N. Y., 1913), 247.

supply. Soldiers in the field were issued whisky only under circumstances of great exposure and protracted fatigue. In view of the increasing deficiency of the meat ration, however, General Joseph E. Johnston ordered a regular issue of whisky to the Army of the Tennessee as it stood off the federal invasion of Georgia. Efforts were made generally, however, to keep strong drink from demoralizing the soldier in camp. The Confederate Congress twice passed acts to discourage drunkenness in the army, while several state prohibitory laws, intended primarily to safeguard the grain supply, were enacted after 1862.[1]

Under these statutes the state authorities even protested Confederate contracts for quantities of distilled liquor for the public services, and redoubtable Southern governors interposed their authority against local contractors who tried to make deliveries. It is probable that the grain used was largely weevily "tithe corn"—paid to the government as part of the tax in kind—which was hardly fit for breadstuffs or even stock feed. The Confederate military and naval authorities were finally forced to set up their own distilleries. These were most successfully operated in the Carolinas. In contrast, local authorities of other states, like Virginia, at times seized the government plants and their stocks of grain and defied the war department, creating delicate problems of federal relations. Strong drink became more and more a luxury. When Virginia's belated ban upon licensed retailing went into force on May 1, 1864, liquor prices of one hundred dollars a gallon and four dollars a "smile" had pretty well put an end to promiscuous barroom drinking. The tippling shops were promptly converted into groceries and cafés and more to eat was in evidence

[1] J. F. Rhodes, *History of the United States* (N. Y., 1892-1919), V. 372, 428-429.

at a slight reduction in price. None the less the insistent drinker found solace in an era of the green bottle and the solitary tumbler.[1]

The federal blockade added considerably to the difficulties of the beleaguered South, especially in 1862 when it achieved a relative effectiveness. From that time blockade running became an art practised by daring skippers in dull gray steamers of light draft and great speed. Their prototype was the *Colonel Lamb,* a vessel of fifteen hundred tons' burden commanded by Captain T. J. Lockwood, who at the time he assumed charge had successfully run the blockade thirty times in the *Kate* and was known as the "father of the trade." [2] Some two hundred runners were engaged in the traffic from Nassau and other West India ports to the Confederate coast, with Charleston, Georgetown and Wilmington the favorite Atlantic ports of entry.[3] In spite of the losses by capture blockade running was one of the principal sources of supply for Lee's army, bringing much-needed munitions, medicines, shoes and bacon as well as other commodities. The profits of the trade were sufficiently great not only to attract considerable British capital but even to invite extensive collusion by Northern merchants and shippers.[4] The Confederate government itself par-

[1] *Richmond* (Va.) *Examiner,* April 21, 30, May 3, 5, 1864.

[2] *Charleston Courier,* Oct. 28, 1864; F. B. C. Bradlee, *Blockade Running during the Civil War* (Salem, 1925), 116-117. See also J. R. Soley, *Blockade and the Cruisers* (N. Y., 1890), 156-157, and T. E. Taylor, *Running the Blockade* (London, 1896), 29, 34.

[3] The arrivals and departures of these vessels were regularly noted in the Charleston papers. Thurlow Weed complained in June, 1863, that a line of steamers from Nassau to Charleston had lost only thirteen out of 140 trips. John Bigelow, *Retrospections of an Active Life* (N. Y., 1909-1913), II, 22. See also Charles Cowley, *Leaves from a Lawyer's Life Afloat and Ashore* (Lowell, Mass., 1879), 112; D. D. Porter, *Naval History of the Civil War* (N. Y., 1888), 685; A. C. Hobart (Captain Roberts, *pseud.*), *Never Caught* (N. Y., 1867), 2.

[4] Cowley, *Leaves from a Lawyer's Life,* 112-113; Bradlee, *Blockade Running,* 64; *Official Records of the Union and Confederate Navies in*

ticipated in some of these operations, partly to insure a proper emphasis upon the importation of war supplies rather than of luxuries.

The South was not at any time ready to concede the real soundness of Lincoln's blockade strategy. The *Richmond Enquirer*, April 15, 1864, firmly denied that the blockade, despite its success in closing Southern ports, had "effected the [starvation] ends of the enemy." It believed moreover that, because of its expense, "operations on the water have . . . been as injurious to the enemy as to ourselves." [1] This optimistic statement probably also took into account the depredations of commerce raiders like the *Sumter*, the *Florida*, the *Alabama* and the *Shenandoah*, and of the Confederate privateers— "pirates," the North called them—which did "the fame of the Dane revive again." [2] But these spirited sea rovers with all their captures added little to the material resources of the Confederacy.

Cut off from new sources of supply, Southern merchants experienced in the early days of the war a flush of prosperity based on the sales of their rapidly ebbing stocks. Some made haste to acquire the goods of the stores of smaller interior towns to resell at enormous profits. Soon many had sold out their wares and closed their doors. Jewish traders made their appearance, however, scouring the country in all directions and setting their purchases at prices that often aroused bitter criticism. High charges, abetted by the redundant currency, only accentuated the misfortunes of the widows and orphans, the unemployed, and the thousands from the devastated regions who fled to Richmond. The

the *War of the Rebellion* (Wash., 1894-1922), ser. 1, VI, 111; *Philadelphia Inquirer*, Jan. 4, 1864.

[1] Cited in *N. Y. Times*, April 26, 1864.

[2] W. M. Robinson, *The Confederate Privateers* (New Haven, 1928), title page. See also *American Annual Cyclopedia*, I (1861), 586.

Y.M.C.A. and other relief agencies wrestled with these problems; the city government set up depots for the sale of goods at cost and dispensed poor relief with a necessary caution. There was much squalor and suffering in the cities of the beleaguered Confederacy.[1]

The morale of the South was increasingly undermined by the fear of starvation. On the very eve of the war Southern emissaries were actually soliciting Northern corn for the victims of the drought of 1860.[2] The food problem early became pressing in the Virginia area which, in the absence of proper transportation for outside supplies, had to assume the chief burden of feeding Lee's army, meantime watching while Northern troops consumed or destroyed much of the crop yield. Elsewhere supplies were generally adequate. The parched summer of 1862 aroused many fears; but the large surplus of corn and bacon from the yeoman farms of North Carolina helped relieve the acute shortage in the following spring when, with the railroads and river boats choked by the transport of troops, Confederate soldiers were on half rations and famishing women led bread riots in Richmond and other cities.[3] The crops of 1863 and 1864 were good enough to terminate the threat of famine, but there was always the serious problem of adequate transportation and of its efficient use while hungry mouths anxiously waited to be fed.

The food problem was aggravated by the difficulty of obtaining a store of salt adequate for the preservation

[1] Rhodes, *History of the United States*, V, 368-371.

[2] *Illinois State Journal* (Springfield), Feb. 14, March 20, 1861.

[3] Randolph Abbott Shotwell, *Papers* (J. G. deR. Hamilton, ed., Raleigh, 1929-1931), I, 468; J. L. M. Curry, *Civil History of the Government of the Confederate States* (Richmond, 1901), 159-160, 165; Corsan, *Two Months in the Confederate States*, 68; Rhodes, *History of the United States*, V, 363-366. See also J. D. Richardson, comp., *A Compilation of the Messages and Papers of the Confederacy* (Nashville, 1906), I, 331-335.

of the meat that had to be held in readiness for the insistent demands of the army. The average Southerner
seemed to care little for fresh meat when salt pork or
bacon was available.[1] Previously dependent upon a
Northern or foreign supply, the South made significant
headway under difficulties; by desperate efforts the states
contracted for supplies which, however, it was necessary
to distribute under careful regulation.[2] Ice, a luxury in
the *ante-bellum* South despite the huge shipments regularly floated down the Mississippi, was no longer available at any price, even to chill the fiery beverages of the
gentry.

Items in the newspapers bore quiet testimony to war-
time sacrifices. Editors generally lent ready aid to the
cause. Many of them abandoned their desks and went
to war in person. Those who remained found it necessary, on account of paper scarcity and high costs, to
reduce the size of their sheets and to raise their price,
with a resulting decline in circulation. Some papers soon
gave up publication while others were eliminated by
mergers. But the services rendered, even by the crude
half-sized sheets printed on a single side, were deemed
sufficient to warrant the exemption of newspapermen
from the draft. News, of course, was highly colored to
favor the Confederate cause. Items from the North were
published under the heading, "Foreign Intelligence."
Wide scope was left for journalistic dissent. A frankly
Union paper like Brownlow's *Knoxville Whig* was duly
suppressed, yet a moderate amount of freedom of the
press remained as an official ideal. When Georgia troops
sacked the office of W. W. Holden's antisecessionist
Raleigh *Standard* and provoked a mob to retaliate

---

[1] Corsan, *Two Months in the Confederate States*, 66, 67.
[2] J. L. Sellers, The Co-Relation of the Salt and Flood Supplies of the
Confederacy (unpublished article).

against the *State Journal,* an administration paper, Governor Z. B. Vance demanded of President Davis the punishment of the officers of the Georgia brigade.[1]

Since the regular prints offered little literary pabulum apart from the humorous skits of "Bill Arp" (C. H. Smith) on "Abe Linkhorn" and his generals, a *Southern Illustrated News* was launched at Richmond early in the war, and a weekly *Record of News, History, and Literature* made its appearance there just before Gettysburg, only to expire before the end of the year. Another short-lived venture was the *Southern Punch,* replete with humorous woodcuts. Few books were published, if only because of the paper shortage. Some English and French novels were reprinted by firms in Richmond and Mobile, but the local products like the Reverend E. W. Watson's novelette *Nellie Norton or Southern Slavery and the Bible* and "the great Southern novel," *Macaria or, Altars of Sacrifice,* by Augusta J. Evans were frank proslavery appeals. In the same cause, but in a spirit critical of the Davis administration, the opinionated Edward A. Pollard, editor of the *Richmond Examiner,* undertook in a series of volumes to interpret the developments of the war from a Southern standpoint.

As in the North, the schools were expected to reflect a sectionally patriotic outlook. The traditional demand for Yankee textbooks was laughed to scorn. The Methodist Book Concern at Nashville promptly issued an edition of McGuffey's *Readers,* the compiler of which could now be claimed as a Southerner by adoption. New texts purged of Yankee ideas were put out in "Confederate" or "Dixie" series. Illustrative material was taken from Southern life or, in arithmetic books, from comparisons greatly to the disadvantage of the North and its soldiers. Mrs. Marinda Branson Moore's *Primary*

---

[1] Rhodes, *History of the United States,* V, 449-452.

Geography admitted that the people of the "hellish Yankee nation" were "refined and intelligent on all subjects but that of negro slavery" upon which they were "mad." [1]

In further protest against the prevailing vice of "Yankeeism" in education, arguments were advanced for encouraging Southern women in the teaching profession.[2] Partly for this reason many girls' seminaries carried on successfully during the war. The Central Female Institute of Clinton, Mississippi, never closed its doors a single day in spite of successive Union and Confederate occupation of the town. When teachers were accorded exemption from conscription, male recruits readily offered themselves even for country schools in the remoter districts. Widespread complaint arose, however, when the pedagogue tried to adjust his tuition charges to the enhanced prices that he had to pay for commodities.[3]

It was inevitable that education should be sacrificed to war-time conditions. "Literary funds" were frequently diverted to military defense. The lower schools suffered least, for it was logical, as the *Charlotte Democrat* pointed out, that children should "be taught to read and write, war or no war." [4] North Carolina authorities therefore struggled desperately to maintain and even to improve the nascent educational system of that commonwealth. But the Southern youth, like his mentors, promptly deserted books and the classroom for the adventures of camp and battle-field. Some academies and

[1] A. B. Moore, *History of Alabama and Her People* (Chicago, 1927), I, 559; edit., *De Bow's Rev.*, XXXII (1862), 164.

[2] Anon., "Education of Southern Women," *De Bow's Rev.*, XXXI (1861), 381-390.

[3] *Charleston Courier*, Sept. 17, 1864; G. C. Eggleston, *A Rebel's Recollections* (N. Y., 1875), 106.

[4] E. W. Knight, *Public School Education in North Carolina* (Boston, 1916), 184.

colleges were closed for lack of patronage. Enrollment at the University of Virginia dropped from six hundred in 1861 to less than forty two years later. What students remained were usually mere boys not yet arrived at military age, joined later on by wounded soldiers incapacitated for further service, who were sometimes tendered free tuition.[1] Many college buildings were converted into hospitals. If invading armies found them convenient and necessary for military quarters, only occasionally did they visit upon them the wrath of the conqueror.

Religion and its houses of worship also suffered from the ravages of war. Promptly after secession Southern Christians completed the dissolution of ecclesiastical relations with their brethren of the North. As has been said, Protestant denominations generally achieved their own independent organization within the Confederacy. The organ of the Roman Catholics of New Orleans, announcing a boycott of Yankee schools and colleges, departed so far from the spirit of the Church Universal as to declare, "The social bonds between us and the Catholics at the North have been severed by them."[2] With the advance of the Northern armies, however, many of the Protestant clergy were suspended from their functions and the churches turned over to the ecclesiastical control of Northern bodies.[3]

Meanwhile the pulpit did all in its power to glorify the cause of the Confederacy. Prayers were offered for

[1] C. E. Jones, *Education in Georgia* (H. B. Adams, ed., *Contribs. to Am. Educational History*, no. 5, Wash., 1889), 65-66; Rhodes, *History of the United States*, V, 469.

[2] *Catholic Standard* (New Orleans), cited in Edward McPherson, *The Political History of the United States of America during the Great Rebellion* (Wash., 1865), 516-517.

[3] *N. Y. World*, March 23, 1864; W. L. Fleming, "The Churches of Alabama during the Civil War," *Gulf States Hist. Mag.*, I (1902), 110; McPherson, *Political History of United States*, 523-524.

the success of the army and collection plates were passed for its support. Hundreds of preachers served gallantly in the ranks; a few recruited companies of their own. "We fight," proclaimed Bishop Leonidas Polk of Louisiana, now a dashing major general, "for our hearth stones and our altars; above all we fight for a race that has been by Divine Providence entrusted to our most sacred keeping." [1] In this cause another Louisiana clergyman, one of five in a single company, announced his willingness to slay any Northern minister who accompanied an invading army "with as hearty a good-will, and with as clear a conscience, as I would the midnight assassin." [2]

While some thought that churchmen in general could do more good on the battle-field than "in preaching to empty meeting houses and old maids and grannies," others were of the opinion that "the minister and the priest [should] remain at the altars; [and] continue their warfare against the Devil (who is perhaps the strongest ally of the Yankees)." [3] If his satanic majesty was really "stalking at large in every village and city in the Confederacy," it soon became easy to enlist recruits to attempt his rout. After a year of fighting a wave of religious emotionalism swept through the South. The churches were aglow with revivals. "The force of example, and the contagion of ungovernable emotions" brought thousands of converts. [4] Hardened veterans in the camps also sought comfort in prayer and worship. Under the inspiration of leaders like Generals Polk and

1 McPherson, *Political History of United States*, 515 *n*.
2 Frank Moore, ed., *The Rebellion Record* (N. Y., 1861-1868), III, "Incidents," 13.
3 A. B. Moore, *Conscription and Conflict in the Confederacy* (N. Y., 1924), 58 *n*., 59.
4 J. B. Jones, *A Rebel War Clerk's Diary* (Phila., 1866), II, 64.

"Stonewall" Jackson rest periods often became huge
camp meetings. Evidence came to Lincoln that "the
rebel soldiers are praying with a great deal more earnest-
ness . . . than our own troops."[1] Soon, despite rather
uncertain evidence of Divine aid on the battle-field, perhaps as many as fifty thousand professed to have found
salvation in Christ.[2]

If religious faith gave courage to many, all were
stirred by the martial airs that voiced the national spirit
of the Confederacy. "Yankee Doodle," hissed and forbidden at Southern theaters, was promptly abandoned
for the throbbing strains of "Dixie." Soon the inspired
words of James R. Randall's impassioned lyric, "Maryland, my Maryland," made it the "Marseillaise of the
Confederacy," rivaled only by Henry McCarthy's "The
Bonny Blue Flag." In the cities one popular air after
another—a "Beauregard's" and a "President's" march,
a "Palmetto" and a "Jeff Davis" waltz—followed in
quick succession. The new tunes spread to the army, but
the military bands—and the marching columns—often
preferred the sentimental strains of "Nellie Gray,"
"Annie Laurie," "Alice, Where Art Thou?" "Swanee
River" and "Home Sweet Home."[3] Such songs of home
and sweetheart formed a strange contrast to the "rebel

[1] Abraham Lincoln, Complete Works (J. G. Nicolay and John Hay,
eds., N. Y., 1905), VIII, 29-30.

[2] Curry, Civil History of the Confederate States, 177, 178; J. A. C.
Chandler and others, The South in the Building of the Nation (Richmond, 1909-1910), X, 513; J. W. Jones, Christ in the Camp
(Richmond, 1887); Shotwell, Papers, I, 275-276, 385. An inter-
denominational Evangelical Tract Society distributed religious literature
among the soldiers to the point that, after the second battle of Bull Run,
the ground was "covered with leaves of tracts and bibles." Edward Dicey,
Six Months in the Federal States (London, 1863), II, 27.

[3] [Catherine C. Hopley], Life in the South (London, 1863), I, 172,
194, 351, 405; II, 104; G. E. Pickett, Soldier of the South: War Letters
to His Wife (A. C. Inman, ed., Boston, 1928), 48, 100. See also W. L.
Fagan, Southern War Songs (N. Y., 1890), and Frank Moore, ed., Songs
and Ballads of the Southern People, 1861-1865 (N. Y., 1886).

yell" of victory or defiance that shrieked the determination of the warriors in gray.[1]

With fiery enthusiasm Southern maid and matron spurred on husband and brother to do or die for fireside and country. Some patriots in crinoline not only donned "secession bonnets" and blue revolutionary badges, but organized target practice with pistols, "vowing to shoot the first 'Yankee' who came within sight of their homes."[2] Some volunteered for cartridge making and for filling shells and fuses. Some like the reckless young spy Belle Boyd undertook at the risk of their lives to supply the Confederacy with important military intelligence.[3] Some languished for a time in federal prisons in penalty for their active "treason." But others, more in keeping with the traditions of Southern womanhood, contented themselves with carding lint and preparing bandages. Many gladly contributed their money, plate and jewelry to the "Ladies' Gunboat Fund." Most of them accepted new domestic burdens—managing farms and gardens and developing substitutes for imported articles—and answered the call to service in soldiers' aid societies or in other relief work. But while the grand dame and her younger sisters were glorifying the Confederacy and its militant legions, in many a humble Southern home wives and mothers refused to reconcile themselves to the ruthless sacrifices of war and even refused to believe that the cause for which their men were fighting was more glorious than that of the Union which it challenged.[4]

[1] Fitzgerald Ross, *A Visit to the Cities and Camps of the Confederate States* (London, 1865), 40.

[2] [Hopley], *Life in the South*, I, 137, 139, 273; J. W. Thomason, jr., *Jeb Stuart* (N. Y., 1930), 45.

[3] Belle Boyd, *Belle Boyd in Camp and Prison* (London, 1865).

[4] A collection of letters to prisoners in Camp Chase, Columbus, Ohio, formerly on file in the Ohio State Library, revealed a lack of feminine en-

396   THE IRREPRESSIBLE CONFLICT

The sublimated emotions of Southern womanhood
revealed themselves most clearly in bitterness toward the
Yankee invader.[1] The gentler sex seemed to burn with
an unquenchable thirst for revenge and victory. Hardened veterans shrank before the abusive expressions by
which the ladies of Dixie revealed their loathing of the
hated Yankee. The federal authorities sometimes excluded them from military hospitals because of barbed
insults hurled at the wounded. Union prisoners were
often subjected to bitter taunts as they marched in humiliation through the streets of Southern towns. The
women seemed ready to believe all tales of outrages inflicted upon their section and especially of insults to
their own sex. Yet many a proud matron testified to
the humane and courteous treatment extended to them
in their hour of trial, and generous acts in return were
not uncommon.[2]

The bitter and haughty pride of the women of New
Orleans called forth all the ungraciousness of the erratic
general who commanded the army of occupation in that
area. Their taunts and defiance—dramatized by the lift-
ing of skirts in the presence of the federal uniform and
by petty acts of reprisal—led General B. F. Butler to
regard them as "she-adders," "the insulting enemies of
my army and my country." In retaliation he issued his

thusiasm for the Southern cause; wives not only deplored this "awful war"
but even indulged in elaborate denunciation of the alleged right of secession.

[1] To one observer it seemed that "all the men were gone to the war and
all the women were she-devils." Dicey, *Six Months in the Federal States*,
II, 78. See also W. H. Russell, *My Diary North and South* (Boston,
1863), 225, 229; Corsan, *Two Months in the Confederate States*, 28,
29-30, 192; Mary A. Livermore, *My Story of the War* (Hartford,
1889), 291, 292, 293.

[2] Judith W. McGuire, *Diary of a Southern Refugee* (Richmond, 1889),
279-280, 349; Sara A. Pryor, *Reminiscences of Peace and War* (N. Y.,
1904), 288-289, 365-371. *Cf.* Mary B. Chesnut, *A Diary from Dixie*
(London, 1905), 107, 385 ff.

famous "Women's Order," decreeing that "any female" who "by word, gesture or movement" should "insult or show contempt for any officer or soldier of the United States" should "be regarded and held liable to be treated as a woman of the town plying her avocation." While the order involved nothing more than that the woman in question should be lodged in the common jail, it was widely misinterpreted and bitterly resented. "Beast Butler," as the general was promptly dubbed, was held up as the epitome of Yankee brutality.[1] The order was effective in terminating direct insults to wearers of the blue, but Southern women in occupied areas found that they could still express their defiance by abstaining from wearing hoops or crinolines and by social ostracism.[2]

It was the proud boast of many a Southern family that it had throughout the war consistently declined any social acquaintance or intimacies with the "dam' Yankees."[3] On the other hand, young women who were ardent and unrepentant partisans by day often promenaded by night under a Southern moon arm in arm with dashing lieutenants and captains who found that "treason somehow heightened their beauty."[4] As a result, "many a New Orleans or Vicksburg lassie . . . surrendered before the courageous assaults of some adoring hero from the hated hills and valleys of New England."[5]

[1] Julia Le Grand, *Journal* (Kate M. Rowland and Agnes E. Croxall, eds., Richmond, 1911), 40-41, 284; Chesnut, *Diary from Dixie*, 164-165, 183; Eggleston, *A Rebel's Recollections*, 65-66; B. F. Butler, *Butler's Book* (Boston, 1892), 421; James Parton, *General Butler in New Orleans* (N. Y., 1864), 327 ff.

[2] *Leslie's Illustrated Newspaper* (N. Y.), XVII, 131 (Nov. 21, 1863).

[3] Corsan, *Two Months in the Confederate States*, 28.

[4] G. A. Townsend, *Campaigns of a Non-Combatant* (N. Y., 1866), 227.

[5] Edit., "Mars and Matrimony," *Round Table*, I, 308 (April 30, 1864).

Life at the Confederate capital presented many contrasts and anomalies. Varina Howell Davis, the competent and intellectual first lady, was vivacious and charming, yet something of an outsider in a community where the social graces had for generations been dictated by the grand dames of the Carters, Byrds and Lees. Mrs. Davis could not but sense their aloofness and incur their criticisms. Official society, however, included other newcomers, representatives of the great families of the plantation aristocracy. After the first shock of war, when the mere mention of gayety seemed sacrilege, Richmond offered a brilliant spectacle. Those who labored in anguish by day tried to forget at night in a round of balls, receptions and private and public theatricals. The *Southern Illustrated News,* January 2, 1864, rejoiced that certain Southern managers had "done all in their power to raise the Drama from the mire into which the libertines and demireps of the land of *isms* had plunged it." [1] Moreover there was still old wine in the cellars and brilliant silks and satins appeared despite the declining stocks of the local shops. Dashing heroes with gold braid to brighten their somber gray uniforms paid court, and a "Jeb" Stuart's golden cavalry sash with tasseled ends and scarlet-lined cloak colored many a social gathering under the crystal chandeliers of an old Virginia homestead.

The third winter of the conflict was a season of "giddy gaiety" in which Richmond merely took the lead. Everything seemed to go as "merry as a marriage bell." "Five balls advertised, and flour 125 dollars per barrel!" protested Pollard in his *Examiner.* "Who

---

[1] *Southern Illustrated News* (Richmond, Va.), III, 4 (Jan. 2, 1864). See also same mag., III, 112 (April 9, 1864), and on Ella Wren's successful engagements in Savannah and Macon, same mag., III, 56, 104 (Feb. 20, April 2, 1864).

prates of famine and want?" [1] The next season brought fresh revels. "Starvation parties," in which good cheer was proclaimed without the stimulus of food and drink, were eclipsed by the lavish indulgence of the selfish. "While battle and famine encompass us on every hand," complained the *Richmond Whig*, ". . . upper-tendum is as gay as though peace and plenty blessed the land." [2] The president's suppers revealed to the end luxuries that made his guests marvel and his critics shake their heads in disapproval. [3]

But the grim fact of war could seldom be completely forgotten. Trembling from the beat of marching feet, the rumble of the transport of the commissariat and the rush of ambulances, the ground of Richmond was shaken at times by cannon fire from the enemy at the very portals. In the spring of 1862 the authorities sent women and children to safer places and prepared, if necessary, to evacuate the city. From time to time the midnight fire alarm broke the night's rest. The fires were often of incendiary origin—some perhaps the work of vicious youths in search of excitement—but by good fortune they seldom proved serious. [4] For hours on a day in early May, 1864, the same deep-toned bells sounded the tocsin, but this time it was to summon every able-bodied male to the trenches to repel the invader with whatever weapon he could procure. Boys of tender years, anæmic clerks, dapper dandies, stout burghers and pompous old gentlemen rallied to meet the enemy. The danger did not end until this motley band of de-

[1] *Richmond Examiner*, Nov. 24, 1863, May 3, 1864. See also *Leslie's Illustrated Newspaper* (N. Y.), XVII, 178 (Dec. 12, 1863).

[2] Cited in *Philadelphia Inquirer*, Jan. 9, 1865. See also McGuire, *Diary of a Southern Refugee*, 328.

[3] Chesnut, *Diary from Dixie*, 252-303; Pryor, *Reminiscences of Peace and War*, 263-264; Pickett, *Soldier of the South*, 122-123.

[4] *Richmond Examiner*, March 21, April 25, 1864; *Charleston Courier*, Sept. 28, 1864.

fenders had smelled powder and the "Departmental Battalion" of governmental clerks had stood their ground against the attack of the blue-coated cavalry.[1]

As hardship and suffering increased and the prospects of victory faded, confidence in those at the helm of the Confederacy underwent a steady decline. A disintegrating morale was revealed in the political undercurrents that ebbed and flowed. In the name of state rights and civil liberties public officials and their supporters challenged military rule and its expedients of conscription, impressment and martial law. Men in arms resented the exemption of thousands of the able-bodied who lived comfortably at home under the plea of holding some petty office, and were disposed to welcome an extension of military authority.[2] Some restive spirits openly proposed a dictatorship; others complained that the aloof president—who was merely conserving the health and strength of a nervous dyspeptic—had assumed the dignity of a satrap and surrounded himself with courtiers "in all the bravery of gold lace and feathers." Critics denounced his secretive tactics and "his astonishing prejudices and adherence to weak favorites,"[3] and added that Mrs. Davis was the power behind the throne, influencing promotions for dandyish young men over

[1] In the first winter of the war the business section of Charleston had experienced a devastating fire which had called forth sympathy and financial aid from the entire Confederacy. A little later the people of that city, who lived in constant fear of the attack which Northerners urged upon "that nest of treason," withdrew to the interior, leaving most of the fine old residences closed or in the care of servants.

[2] But such an advocate of military control condemned the way in which General J. H. Winder ruled Richmond like a military camp, complaining that the general permitted the city "to be over-run by rogues, spies, speculators, foreigners, blockaderunners, and fellows of that ilk." Shotwell, Papers, I, 383, 470-471.

[3] Shotwell, Papers, I, 370; E. A. Pollard, The Life of Jefferson Davis (Phila., 1869), 204 ff., 317-318; Toombs, Stephens and Cobb, Correspondence, 580 ff.

tested veterans because the former were "willing to pay court and smirk and dance attendance" upon her.[1]

Rumors of administrative inefficiency and of corruption added to the widely prevailing state of disaffection. The quartermasters and commissary departments often failed to conserve transportation by utilizing supplies near at hand. The prevalence of corruption and peculation led to a Confederate statute to prevent frauds in these departments.[2] It was common talk everywhere that the war department had connived at illegal trade with the enemy, in which cotton and tobacco had been exchanged for "Yankee notions," a rumor which strengthened the conviction that Secretary Judah P. Benjamin, the "Disraeli of the Confederacy," had only lived up to the unfortunate reputation which prejudice had fastened upon his race. There was an even more disturbing story that General J. C. Pemberton had himself participated in this traffic.[3] Almost every newspaper, it was complained, instanced graft by those occupying official positions.

Distrust bred by these apprehensions now added to the growing hunger of the townspeople and the increasing burdens upon the yeomanry. It was not strange that the spirit of unrest increased. The poorer classes proclaimed more boldly their resentment of the slaveholder and his "ill-gotten power," which denied them political and social equality. Many who had in 1861 reluctantly acquiesced in secession began to talk of peace. Leaders like W. W. Holden, editor of the Raleigh *Standard*, openly voiced the discontent of the "commoner." Peace meetings and peace societies, the latter widely prevalent

[1] Shotwell, *Papers*, I, 371.

[2] William Watson, *Life in the Confederate Army* (N. Y., 1888), 163-166. See also Rhodes, *History of the United States*, V, 429-431.

[3] Shotwell, *Papers*, I, 376, 391.

from Alabama to Virginia as secret ritualistic organizations, set up a demand that the fruitless struggle be
brought to an end. Holden, running for governor in
1864 on a peace platform, was beaten by Governor
Vance only because the latter had himself often acted
counter to Confederate policy almost to its nullification.[1]

"Peace alone can prevent starvation!" declared the
Raleigh Progress, December 22, 1863. "It is folly to
talk to us about there being enough supplies in the country." [2] Without adequate transport for what food there
was, hunger sapped the martial zeal of many a locality.
When defeatist talk was proclaimed seditious by the
leaders of the Confederacy and the president was given
power to suppress it by suspending the writ of habeas
corpus, opponents of the administration denounced
such measures as extinguishing the liberties of the people. On December 24, 1864, Henry S. Foote, a prominent opposition member of the Confederate Congress,
resigned his seat in protest. The military authorities arrested him at Fredericksburg on his way to the Union
lines, but, presently released, he opened communications
with Lincoln and Seward looking to peace.[3]

By this time the Confederacy was rapidly crumbling
under the onslaughts of the Union armies. Atlanta had
fallen into the hands of Sherman's triumphant forces,
thus opening the way for the drive to Savannah and the
coast. That hapless city, which Sherman presented to
Lincoln "as a Christmas gift," was thrown upon the
mercy of a bountiful North. Seven weeks later Charleston, the last remaining harbor of the Confederacy, sur-

[1] A. S. Roberts, "The Peace Movement in North Carolina," Miss.
Valley Hist. Rev., XI, 190-199.
[2] Cited in N. Y. Tribune, Jan. 18, 1864.
[3] Philadelphia Inquirer, Jan. 16, 1865; E. C. Kirkland, The Peace-
makers of 1864 (N. Y., 1927), 218-220, 236.

rendered to the federals—a scarred, mutilated city containing only a fraction of its prewar population. A like fate awaited other towns that had not already succumbed to the invader. When Lee finally evacuated the capital of the Confederacy, the torch was applied to the arsenals and public buildings and the burning fragments thrown into the air in a succession of deafening explosions set fire to much of the city, including the best residential district. Only the arduous efforts of the federal soldiers, who entered close upon the heels of the retiring Confederates, at length checked the spreading flames.

Ere the final collapse before Grant's armies, the Confederacy had decided upon a desperate expedient, the arming of the slaves. By their agricultural labors these patient servitors, knowing little of the issues of the war, had contributed substantially to the fighting resources of the white population, and their work upon fortifications and in other noncombatant fields had added even more directly to Southern military strength. Now Robert E. Lee became one of the strongest advocates of their enlistment for active service, believing that the slaves could "with proper regulations . . . be made efficient soldiers." [1] Besides giving such recruits immediate freedom, he further favored "a well digested plan of gradual and general emancipation."

In the face of the serious disintegration of their armies the Confederate authorities on March 13, 1865, enacted a law authorizing the employment in military services of as many as three hundred thousand slaves. The revolutionary character of this decision may be judged from the argument of Howell Cobb: "The day you make soldiers of them is the beginning of the end of the revolu-

---

[1] *The War of the Rebellion: A Compilation of the Official Records of the Union and Confederate Armies* (Wash., 1880-1901), ser. 4, III, 1013.

tion. If slaves will make good soldiers our whole theory
of slavery is wrong." But he added, "they won't make
soldiers." [1] The arming of the slaves was the last expedient of despair. By it possibly, just possibly, might
the South evade the conqueror's heel. Defeat, proclaimed Congress in a final appeal, with no thought of
anticlimax, meant having to "drink the cup of humiliation even to the bitter dregs of having the history of
our struggle written by New England historians!" [2]

The South had given generously of its blood and
treasure to the fight for independence. Careful calcula-
tion reveals that the equivalent of well over a half-bil-
lion gold dollars, nearly a sixth of the true wealth of
the South in 1860, not counting slave property, was
cast into the fiery furnace of civil strife. A section which
had an economic strength less than a third of that of
the North made material sacrifices more than half as
great as those which carried the Union arms to victory.
When peace at length settled upon the weary land with
its charred ruins of rural homesteads and of wrecked
towns and cities, the remaining personal property in
the South—only one fourth that of 1860—revealed
losses equal to the entire official expenditures for the
struggle. Aside from the confiscation of slave property
the total wealth of Dixie had shrunk to less than one
third of that upon which Southerners had hoped to lay
the foundations of a separate nation. And yet the full
story is not quite told. The defeated had still to assume
their proportionate share of the federal war debt which,
augmented by pensions to veterans of the successful
armies, totaled fully a billion dollars. The per-capita
cost of the war eventually fell thrice as heavily upon

[1] *Official Records of Armies*, ser. 4, III, 1009.
[2] *Am. Ann. Cyc.*, V (1865), 198.

the vanquished Southerners as upon the prosperous victors.[1]

The news of the collapse of the Confederacy, marked by the surrender of General Lee, was celebrated in the North amid the wildest enthusiasm—with no hint of the national tragedy that lay just ahead. In the language of a contemporary journalist,

> there was a smile on every face—happiness in every heart. Booming guns, clanging bells, streaming banners, and the tumultuous cheers of a happy populace told the public joy and proclaimed it to the world. But in a few short hours all this was changed. The people went about the streets mournfully, the bells tolled, the flag of the Republic was hung at half mast, and the hope of immediate Peace, which made the country glad, vanished like a beautiful vision of the night—for ABRAHAM LINCOLN, who in the days of his triumph had become the champion of the pacification of the South by conciliation, had fallen under the hand of an assassin, just as he was about to accomplish the grandest and most solemn problem of statesmanship in the world.[2]

With Lincoln, indeed, passed the hope that the South could be dealt with generously in defeat. Assassination seemed "the crowning fruit of slavery," according to the mixed metaphor of a young New England intellectual who was basking under the sunny skies of an Italian spring: "In our admiration of the soldierly virtues of Lee and his army, we felt like embracing our enemies and welcoming them back to Peace and Country. But here is the most dastardly of crimes thrown across the path of conciliation. It is the last proof that our struggle

[1] J. L. Sellers, "Civil War Finance," *Am. Hist. Rev.*, XXX, 287-297.
[2] *Cairo* (Ill.) *News*, April 20, 1865.

is a struggle of humanity against barbarism, but how shall we redeem or get rid of the barbarians." [1]

After four years of armed strife neither victor nor vanquished was in a mood to view in perspective the bloody struggle and assess the forces that had produced it. The South, its fields ravaged, its homes in smoking ruins, nursed a "lost cause," and mourned that righteousness had fallen before brute strength. Nor had war, "the avenger," satisfied the holy indignation of the North, for "treason" not only had struck at the foundations of the Union, but had loosed the assassin's knife in the final hour of its triumph. It was difficult to recall that but a decade and a half before Northerners and Southerners had proudly formed parts of the same great people, lying on opposite sides of the boundary between freedom and slavery. Both groups had found it wise to court or pacify the maturing West, but, as the frontier moved ever onward, the free North found it easier to assimilate the Western provinces and, at the same time, to make necessary concessions to their demands. The spirit of democracy and the cause of free land spread their influence over the industrial North. The railroad pushed its iron bands across the country binding together the young commonwealths and the old. The fruits of a new and glowing prosperity were tasted in the great agricultural empire as well as in the Eastern marts of trade and manufacture. The throbbing forces of enlightenment, culture and humanitarian reform spread over the North, while free labor, girding its loins, began to feel its power.

South of the Ohio's murky waters a plantation oligarchy basked contentedly in the waning sun of prosperity. For the few, life was easy and pleasant; culture

[1] Charles W. Eliot to his mother. Henry James, *Charles W. Eliot, President of Harvard University, 1869-1909* (Boston, 1930), I, 140.

—measured in terms of a passive leisure-class enjoyment and not in science and the creative arts—was within ready reach. An army of Negro vassals and a dependent white class made obeisance to planter rule, though the white yeomanry stirred restlessly as its opportunities of rising to a share in the plantation régime steadily declined and slave labor threatened to become a fatal incubus upon the back of Dixie. The revolutionary victory in 1860 of the forces that challenged the social institutions of the South severed the last bonds that held the cotton kingdom within the Union. Since the North and the administration that represented it refused to "allow the erring sisters to depart in peace," the issue was staked upon the arbitrament of arms. Workshop, farm, drawing-room, press and pulpit—all the gentle arts of peace were dedicated to the shrine of Mars. In the fiery furnace of war and the crushing defeat of the South the permanence of the Union was welded. Yet dislike, suspicion, fear, remained; the gaping wound lingered. Only when it could be bound up and healed could real peace and happiness come to the nation. Then emerged at length the glories of a modern America.

CHAPTER XVI

CRITICAL ESSAY ON AUTHORITIES

PHYSICAL SURVIVALS

THE state museums and the state historical societies of the trans-Mississippi region generally include valuable exhibits upon the population movements into that area and upon the Indian life and pioneer conditions there. Hundreds of active local and county historical societies in that section and elsewhere have assembled farm equipment, field and industrial implements, kitchen and household furnishings and the like. The Working Museum of History of the Northern Illinois State Teachers College at DeKalb has systematically brought together such materials for teaching purposes. These and museum collections generally are listed in the valuable *Handbook of American Museums* (Wash., 1932) issued by the American Association of Museums.

The costumes of this period are illustrated in various collections, notably those of the Plymouth (Massachusetts) Antiquarian Society, the Framingham (Massachusetts) Historical and Natural History Society and the Buffalo Historical Society. The Minnesota Historical Society at St. Paul exhibits a full-sized log cabin illustrating frontier life in the fifties. The Norwegian-American Historical Museum at Luther College, Decorah, Iowa, includes historic cabins and houses of the Norwegian pioneers of the fifties, as well as exhibits of Norwegian pioneer life and art. The Old Pawnee capital of Kansas, built in 1855, has been restored and opened to the public at Fort Riley Military Reservation. Objects relating to the early history of Salt Lake City and the Mormons may be seen at the Latter-Day Saints Church Museum and in the Relic Hall of the state capitol, Salt Lake City.

A special collection of the tools, implements and guns of the California pioneers may be found at the museum of the Claremont (California) Colleges. The first theater in California, an adobe structure built at Monterey in 1844, is preserved as a museum housing early Californiana. Sutter's Fort at Sacramento has similarly been converted by the state into an historical museum.

Illustrative materials on agriculture, industry and invention in the fifties and sixties are widely scattered. The reaper inventions of Cyrus H. McCormick are on exhibition in the Virginia State Museum at Richmond, while in the Chicago offices of the International Harvester Company may be found drawings, lithographs, photographs and models illustrating the development of the reaper. Similarly Armour and Company and Swift and Company have brought together photographs, plans, sketches and similar materials which depict the growth of the livestock and packing industries. Early problems of fencing the prairies are suggested in the collection on the history of barbed wire in the museum maintained by the American Steel and Wire Company in Worcester, Massachusetts.

The United States National Museum in Washington contains extensive collections revealing scientific and industrial development, as well as objects of military, naval, numismatic and philatelic interest. Early cotton textile machinery and other objects pertinent to cotton manufacturing are displayed in the National Textile Museum at Pawtucket, Rhode Island. Another collection on the early textile industry in New Hampshire may be found in the museum of the Manchester Historical Association. The United Shoe Machinery Corporation maintains in Boston an exhibit of shoes and shoemaking tools and machines. A valuable collection of early presses and implements of typography and type founding is kept in the Typographic Library and Museum of the American Type Founders Company at Jersey City. The development of watches and watch production may be studied with the aid of the James Arthur Collection of Timepieces at the Gould Memorial Library in New York City. The museum of Crane and Company, Inc., at Dalton,

Massachusetts, exhibits historical materials on paper and its production. A collection relating to the origins and development of the oil industry and oil illumination is preserved in the Drake Memorial Museum at Titusville, Pennsylvania. The General Electric Lighting Institute at Nela Park, Cleveland, Ohio, specializes in exhibits on the history of lighting; the Ellsworth collection at the Western Reserve Academy, Hudson, Ohio, has a similar scope. The Bell System Historical Museum in New York City displays instruments, models and photographs illustrating the important steps in the development of the electrical communicating art. The Edison Institute of Technology has extensive collections on the history of American industry and life in its museum at Dearborn, Michigan, and in the adjoining Greenfield Village. The Museum of Science and Industry, founded by Julius Rosenwald in Chicago, will doubtless develop into one of the most important collections in this field.

The Studebaker Museum of Transportation at South Bend, Indiana, exhibits collections showing the historical development of wheeled vehicles. The Transportation Exposition of the New York Central Lines in the Grand Central Terminal includes models, pictures and displays of actual railroad equipment. A large collection of patent models with emphasis on railroad apparatus is preserved in the Washington office of the Eastern Railroad Association. The Railway Museum of Purdue University includes locomotives used in the early days of railroading. The Railway and Locomotive Historical Society at the Harvard Business School in Boston has models, photographs, time-tables, posters and notices, equipment and personalia. The Commercial Museum at Philadelphia has a splendid collection of maps, charts, samples and models relating to the history of commerce. Other collections pertaining to the days of wood and sail on the seas, especially the clipper ships, may be found in the Marine Museum of Boston, in the Nautical Museum of the Massachusetts Institute of Technology (Cambridge), in the Municipal Museum of Baltimore and at the Naval Academy Museum in Annapolis, which has the significant offering of the original yacht *America*. The Cape Ann Scientific Library and Historical Society of Gloucester, Massachusetts, displays model fisheries and other exhibits on the life of that fishing town. The Old Dartmouth Historical Society and Whaling Museum at New Bedford, Massachusetts, has models of whaling barks, replicas of old-time sloops, old prints and pictures of the whaling industry. The Peabody Museum of Salem, Massachusetts, is noted for objects of the whaling industry, ship models and nautical instruments, while Whaling Enshrined, Inc., of South Dartmouth, Massachusetts, displays a full-rigged whaler restored to the condition that prevailed before 1867.

The homes of certain American authors have been restored as museums with the original furnishings and with personalia or memorabilia of the former occupants. Among others may be mentioned the John Greenleaf Whittier Homestead at Haverhill, and the Longfellow House at Cambridge, Massachusetts. The Brander Matthews Dramatic Museum of Columbia University includes models of early theaters and stage sets, posters, play bills, programs, etc. The Museum of the City of New York has a similar collection relating to the history of the theater in the metropolis. Originals or reproductions of American portraits and paintings of this period appear in many art galleries. Examples of the Hudson River School and of other early efforts are exhibited in the Berkshire Museum at Pittsfield, Massachusetts. The monuments of Washington and of Baltimore—the latter known in the Civil War period as "the City of Monuments"—reveal some of the early American efforts at sculpture.

Significant in the annals of the antislavery crusade, the John Brown Cottage at North Elba, New York, near which Brown was buried, is preserved as a museum. Other collections of John Brown materials will be found in the Ohio Archeological and Historical Society in Columbus and the Cumberland County Historical Association of Carlisle, Pennsylvania. The Storer College Museum at Harper's Ferry displays a significant Civil War collection in the historic John Brown fort. Ford's Theatre, the building in which Lincoln was assassinated, is now a public museum housing the Oldroyd collection of Lincolniana, replacing the older Lincoln museum at the Peterson House which has been restored to the original lodging house of 1865. Other important Lincoln collections are found in the museums of the Chicago Historical Society, the Illinois State Historical Society at Springfield, and the Lincoln Historical Research Foundation at Fort Wayne, Indiana. Personalia of Judge Roger B. Taney are preserved in the Taney Home at Frederick, Maryland.

Nearly every historical museum includes a Civil War collection; official or quasiofficial state exhibits are generally the best. The Jennie Wade Museum at Gettysburg, Pennsylvania, displays objects relating to the great battle there. The Barbara Fritchie House at Frederick, Maryland, has its special collection. The National Battlefield Museum at Fredericksburg, Virginia, displays materials from all the battle-fields of the war; the Crater Battlefield Museum at Petersburg is more definitely local in its appeal. The Springfield (Massachusetts) Armory and the Rock Island (Illinois) Arsenal have collections of small arms, machine guns and artillery, while the John Woodman Higgins Armory at Worcester displays sheet steel armament and products of all ages. The Confederate Museum at Richmond and the corresponding institutions at Charleston, South Carolina, and Austin, Texas, include portraits, furniture, costumes and personal belongings of distinguished contemporaries as well as the customary war displays. Another extensive collection is in the possession of the Louisiana Historical Association at New Orleans. The first White House of the Confederacy at Montgomery, Alabama, is a public museum and exhibits, besides war material, furniture and personalia of Jefferson Davis. The old Robert E. Lee mansion at Arlington, Virginia, preserves in itself and with the aid of period furnishings some of the flavor of the Old South.

Many of the thousands of excellent Civil War photographs taken by Matthew B. Brady, along with the works of other field photographers, are made available in the ten-volume *Photographic History of the Civil War* (N. Y., 1912), edited by Francis T. Miller. The originals, not including those scattered over the country in historical societies, libraries and government bureaus, and in the hands of private collectors, were brought together by Edward Bailey Eaton, of Hartford, Connecticut. For the Civil War as well as other aspects of the life of the period the photographic record reproduced in R. H. Gabriel, ed., *The Pageant of America* (15 vols., New Haven, 1926-1929), is also of value.

DOCUMENTARY SOURCES

The *Congressional Globe* and the Senate and House *Reports* and *Documents* include materials which throw important light on various phases of social history. The seventh and eighth census reports supply indispensable statistical materials. Valuable items are often found in J. D. Richardson, comp., *A Compilation of the Messages and Papers of the Presidents* (10 vols., Wash., 1896-1899), and in his *Messages and Papers of the Confederacy* (2 vols., Nashville, 1905). For the period of the Civil War, *The War of the Rebellion: A Compilation of the Official Records of the Union and Confederate Armies* (128 vols., Wash., 1880-1901) and *Official Records of the Union and Confederate Navies in the War of the Rebellion* (30 vols., Wash., 1894-1922, and index, 1927) are indispensable storehouses of informal personal records as well as of documentary evidence. Frank Moore, ed., *The Rebellion Record* (11 vols., N. Y., 1861-1868), presents a medley of ephemeral materials such as newspaper clippings, poems, bits of pamphlets and the like. The *American Annual Cyclopedia* (1st ser., 15 vols., N. Y., 1862-1876) is an alphabetically arranged collection of items analyzing the chief events and developments of each year largely from the current newspaper sources; its articles illumine many obscure points in social history. On the published and archival materials of the several states, see the discussion in C. R. Fish, *The Rise of the Common Man* (*A History of American Life*, VI), 342-343.

PERIODICAL LITERATURE

This was a period of extensive journalistic experimentation, in which worthy as well as shabby ventures often came to untimely ends. The gap left by the suspension of *Niles' Weekly Register* (Balt., 1811-1849) was not adequately filled for some time; hence the fifties lacked a general weekly of national importance. Meantime useful items appeared occasionally in the *North American Review* (Boston, 1815-1877; N. Y., from 1878) and in the *Southern Literary Messenger* (Richmond, 1838-1864), and valuable materials on the economic side in *Hunt's Merchants' Magazine* (N. Y., 1839-1870) and in *De Bow's Commercial Review of the South and West* (New Orleans, 1846-1870). *Harper's New Monthly Magazine* (N. Y., from 1850) achieved sufficient success to encourage other undertakings, notably the *Atlantic Monthly* (Boston, from 1857), which mirrored the reform aspirations of the New England *intelligentsia*. The taste of the masses was reflected in the very successful *New York Ledger* (N. Y., 1844-1898), the weekly newspaper of Robert Bonner; and in the *National Police Gazette* (N. Y., from 1845). Soon new and better weeklies, *Frank Leslie's Illustrated Weekly* (N. Y., 1855-1922) and *Harper's Weekly* (N. Y., 1857-1916), took their place alongside the flourishing religious weeklies, of which the *Independent* (N. Y., 1848-1928, when it was merged with the *Outlook*) was the most successful.

The daily newspapers were beginning to take on an essentially modern character, and offer interesting cross sections of American life, the metropolitan press being of particular importance, especially the leading journals of New York, Philadelphia, Boston and Washington. Local papers scattered throughout the nation reflect conditions in their respective communities. The *Chicago Tribune* (from 1847), *Missouri Democrat* (St. Louis, from 1852), *New Orleans Picayune* (from 1837), *Charleston News and Courier* (from 1803), *Richmond Enquirer* (from 1804), *Cincinnati Enquirer* (from 1842) and *Cleveland Leader* (1854-1885) are typical of the provincial papers which, in most cases, merit special individual study.

TRAVEL ACCOUNTS

The descriptive accounts of travelers have especial value for social history. An extensive list of books by English visitors appears in Allan Nevins, ed., *American Social History as Recorded by British Travellers* (rev. edn., N. Y., 1931). The works of many of those who penetrated well into the interior of the continent are listed in S. J. Buck, *Travel and Description, 1765-1865* (Ill. State Hist. Library, *Colls.*, IX, 1914). Professor Buck is chairman of a committee of the American Historical Association that is engaged in the preparation of a complete bibliography of American travel. H. T. Tuckerman, *America and Her Commentators* (N. Y., 1864), is an interesting compilation for this period; so also is a recent collection of local materials in Bessie L. Pierce, ed., *As Others See Chicago: Impressions of Visitors, 1673-1933* (Chicago, 1933). The author of this volume has found especially useful: J. J. Ampère, *Promenade en Amérique* (2 vols., Paris, 1855); *Atlantische Studien: Von Deutschen in Amerika* (8 vols. in 2, Göttingen, 1853-1857); W. E. Baxter, *America and the Americans* (London, 1855); [Isabella L. (Bird) Bishop], *The Englishwoman in America* (London, 1856); William Chambers, *Things as They Are in America* (N. Y., 1854); Edward Dicey, *Six Months in the Federal States* (2 vols., London, 1863); Adolf Douai, *Land und Leute in der Union* (Berlin, 1864); Julius Fröbel, *Aus Amerika: Erfahrungen, Reisen, und Studien* (2 vols., Leipzig, 1857-1858); Agénor de Gasparin, *The Uprising of a Great People* (Mary L. Booth, tr., N. Y., 1861); T. C. Grattan, *Civilized America* (2 vols., London, 1859); Theodor Griesinger, *Lebende Bilder aus Amerika* (Stuttgart, 1858); J. G. Kohl, *Travels in Canada, and through the States of New York and Pennsylvania* (Mrs. Percy Sinnett, tr., 2 vols., London, 1861); Auguste Laugel, *The United States during the War* (London, 1866); Charles Mackay, *Life and Liberty in America* (N. Y., 1859); J. W. Massie, *America: The Origin of Her Present Conflict* (London, 1864); D. W. Mitchell, *Ten Years Residence in the United States* (London, 1862); Amelia M. Murray, *Letters from the United States, Cuba and Canada* (2 vols., London, 1856); Francis and Theresa Pulszky, *White, Red, Black: Sketches of American Society in the United States* (2 vols., London, 1853); Karl Quentin, *Reisebilder und Studien aus dem Norden des Vereinigten Staaten von Amerika* (Arnsberg, 1851); W. H. Russell, *My Diary North and South* (Boston, 1863); G. A. Sala, *My Diary in America in the Midst of War* (2 vols., London, 1865); and Anthony Trollope, *North America* (N. Y., 1862).

GENERAL TREATMENTS

Earlier general works have not altogether neglected the social history of this period. Especially rich in such materials is the last volume of J. B. McMaster, *A History of the People of the United States* (8 vols., N. Y., 1883-1913), and his continuation of the narrative in *A History of the People of the United States during Lincoln's Administration* (N. Y., 1927). Important contributions to social history may also be found in J. F. Rhodes, *History of the United States from the Compromise of 1850* (7 vols., N. Y., 1893-1906), and to a lesser degree in the sixth volume of Edward Channing, *History of the United States* (6 vols., N. Y., 1909-1929). There are suggestive chapters in volumes XVIII-XXI of A. B. Hart, ed., *The American Nation: A History* (26 vols., N. Y., 1904-1908), and salient phases are treated in certain volumes of Allen Johnson, ed., *The Chronicles of America Series* (50 vols., New Haven, 1918-1921). C. A. and Mary R. Beard, *The Rise of American Civilization* (2 vols., N. Y., 1927), is brief but useful for this period. C. A. Beard, ed., *A Century of Progress* (N. Y., 1933), is a coöperative survey of American social and economic history of the last century in essays of varying merit.

BIOGRAPHY

Significant material for social history may often be found in the standard biographies of political leaders. Special series have been published to appraise leadership in other fields, notably M. A. DeW. Howe, ed., *The Beacon Biographies* (31 vols., Boston, 1899-1910), including authors, inventors and actors; C. D. Warner, ed., *American Men of Letters* (Boston, 1881-1906); Carlos Martyn, ed., *American Reformers* (N. Y., 1890-1896); and Laurence Hutton, ed., *American Actor Series* (Boston, 1881-1882). These include but a fraction of such biographical items, some of which will be cited later under appropriate headings. The brief sketches by competent writers in the *Dictionary of American Biography* (20 vols., N. Y., 1928, in progress), edited by Allen Johnson and Dumas Malone, are valuable for their contents and their accompanying bibliographies. Most of the personal items listed in Fish, *Rise of the Common Man* (cited earlier), 343-344, apply equally to the Civil War period.

THE OLD SOUTH

An extensive coöperative work in twelve volumes by J. A. C. Chandler and others undertakes to appraise Southern history under the title *The South in the Building of the Nation* (Richmond, 1909-1910). W. E. Dodd, *The Cotton Kingdom* (*Chronicles of America Series*, XXVII), is an excellent work in the briefest compass. Of recent studies, U. B. Phillips, *Life and Labor in the Old South* (Boston, 1929), is of outstanding importance. Other significant contributions are Susan D. Smedes, *Memorials of a Southern Planter* (Balt., 1883); F. P. Gaines, *The Southern Plantation* (Columbia Univ., *Studies in English*, 1924); and J. S. Bassett, ed., *The Southern Plantation Overseer as Revealed in His Letters* (Smith College, *Fiftieth Anniversary Publs.*, V, 1925). Less valuable are R. Q. Mallard, *Plantation Life before Emancipation* (Richmond, 1892), and Nancy B. De Saussure, *Old Plantation Days* (N. Y., 1909).

The best account of the slave system is U. B. Phillips, *American Negro Slavery* (N. Y., 1918). A recent local study emphasizing the *ante-bellum* period is R. H. Taylor, *Slaveholding in North Carolina: An Economic View* (Univ. of N. C., *James Sprunt Hist. Publs.*, XVIII, nos. 1-2, 1926).

An invaluable contribution is Frederic Bancroft, *Slave-Trading in the Old South* (Balt., 1931). The best study of Southern agriculture is L. C. Gray, *History of Agriculture in the Southern United States to 1860* (2 vols., Carnegie Inst., *Contribs. to Am. Econ. History;* Wash., 1933). Other useful monographs in this field include M. B. Hammond, *The Cotton Industry* (Am. Econ. Assoc., *Publs.,* new ser., I, 1897), and A. O. Craven, *Soil Exhaustion as a Factor in the Agricultural History of Virginia and Maryland, 1606-1860* (Univ. of Ill., *Studies,* XIII, no. 1, 1925). Avery Craven, *Edmund Ruffin, Southerner* (N. Y., 1932), is an excellent biography in the same field. Local studies include G. G. Johnson, *A Social History of the Sea Islands* (Chapel Hill, 1930); Caroline C. Lovell, *The Golden Islands of Georgia* (Boston, 1932); T. P. Abernethy, *From Frontier to Plantation in Tennessee* (Chapel Hill, 1932); and Minnie C. Boyd, *Alabama in the Fifties* (N. Y., 1931). Valuable contemporary discussions of Southern social conditions include George Fitzhugh, *Sociology for the South* (Richmond, 1854); D. R. Hundley, *Social Relations in Our Southern States* (N. Y., 1860); and G. M. Weston, *The Progress of Slavery in the United States* (Wash., 1857). U. B. Phillips, ed., *The Plantation and Frontier* (J. R. Commons and others, eds., *A Documentary History of American Industrial Society,* Cleveland, 1910-1911, I-II), and U. B. Phillips and J. D. Glunt, eds., *Florida Plantation Records: From the Papers of George Noble Jones* (St. Louis, 1927), are important source collections. The files of various agricultural journals are rich in offerings, notably the *Southern Cultivator* (Athens, Atlanta, Ga., from 1843) and the *American Cotton Planter* (Montgomery, Ala., 1853-1856).

Outstanding monographs on economic conditions include R. R. Russel, *Economic Aspects of Southern Sectionalism, 1840-1861* (Univ. of Ill., *Studies,* XI, nos. 1-2, 1923); J. G. Van Deusen, *Economic Bases of Disunion in South Carolina* (Columbia Univ., *Studies,* no. 305, 1928); same author, *The Ante-Bellum Southern Commercial Conventions* (Trinity Col. Hist. Soc., *Papers,* XVI, 1926); and Herbert Wender, *Southern Commercial Conventions, 1837-*

1859 (Johns Hopkins Univ., *Studies*, XLVIII, no. 4, 1930). Kathleen Bruce, *Virginia Iron Manufactures in the Slave Era* (N. Y., 1931), is a significant contribution. Special aspects of Southern transportation are treated in U. B. Phillips, *Transportation in the Eastern Cotton Belt to 1860* (N. Y., 1908); S. M. Derrick, *Centennial History of South Carolina Railroad* (Columbia, 1930); and T. J. Wertenbaker, *Norfolk: Historic Southern Port* (Durham, 1931). Important economic materials appear in J. D. B. De Bow, *The Industrial Resources, etc., of the Southern and Western States* (3 vols., New Orleans, 1852-1853). This reprints materials previously published in *De Bow's Review* (already mentioned), an indispensable periodical source. The *Southern Business Directory and General Commercial Advertiser* (Charleston, 1854) is useful. Contemporary statistical studies that must be utilized with caution include T. P. Kettell, *Southern Wealth and Northern Profits* (N. Y., 1860); Henry Chase and C. W. Sanborn, *The North and the South* (Boston, 1856); and C. J. Stillé, *Northern Interests and Southern Independence* (Phila., 1863).

THE EXPANDING WEST

The westward movement is carefully analyzed in such treatises as F. L. Paxson, *History of the American Frontier, 1763-1893* (Boston, 1924); E. D. Branch, *Westward: The Romance of the American Frontier* (N. Y., 1930); and R. E. Riegel, *America Moves West* (N. Y., 1930). R. H. Gabriel, *The Lure of the Frontier* (R. H. Gabriel, ed., *The Pageant of America*, New Haven, 1926-1929, II), supplies valuable illustrative material. F. J. Turner, *The Significance of Sections in American History* (N. Y., 1932), offers stimulating interpretations of American sectionalism. Significant contributions are to be found in J. F. Willard and C. B. Goodykoontz, eds., *The Trans-Mississippi West: Papers Read at a Conference Held at the University of Colorado, June 18-June 21, 1929* (Boulder, 1930). S. K. Humphrey, *Following the Prairie Frontier* (Minneapolis, 1931), and Dorothy A. Dondore, *The Prairie and the Making of Middle Amer-*

ica (Cedar Rapids, Iowa, 1926), are stimulating monographs. The keenest interpretation of the forces that influenced the region beyond the prairies is W. P. Webb, *The Great Plains* (Boston, 1931). F. L. Paxson, *The Last American Frontier* (N. Y., 1910), Cardinal Goodwin, *The Trans-Mississippi West* (N. Y., 1922), Katherine Coman, *Economic Beginnings of the Far West* (2 vols., N. Y., 1912), and R. McN. McElroy, *The Winning of the Far West* (N. Y., 1914), carry the narrative across the mountains to the Pacific. G. W. Fuller, *A History of the Pacific Northwest* (N. Y., 1931), is a valuable appraisal of the Oregon-Washington region.

Recent accounts of early days in Iowa include T. H. Macbride, *In Cabins and Sod Houses* (Iowa City, 1928), and Irving Richman, *Ioway to Iowa* (Iowa City, 1931). W. W. Folwell, *A History of Minnesota* (4 vols., St. Paul, 1921-1930), fills an important need for the extreme upper Mississippi area. It can well be supplemented by studies like W. P. Shortridge, *The Transition of a Typical Frontier with Illustrations from the Life of Henry Hastings Sibley* (Menasha, Wis., 1922). The most recent general contribution to the extensive Kansas literature (summed up in a pamphlet prepared by the Kansas Historical Society) is W. E. Connelley, *History of Kansas, State and People* (5 vols., N. Y., 1928). W. C. Holden, *Alkali Trails, or Social and Economic Movements of Texas Frontier, 1846-1900* (Dallas, 1930), illuminates the social history of the Southwest. R. P. Bieber, ed., *The Southwest Historical Series* (Glendale, Calif., 1931, in progress), is a twelve-volume project for bringing out important source material on social and economic conditions in this area.

The best account of life on the California trails is A. B. Hulbert, *Forty-Niners: The Chronicle of the California Trail* (Boston, 1932). Another significant study is Charles Kelly, *Salt Desert Trails: A History of the Hastings Cutoff, and Other Early Trails Which Crossed the Great Salt Desert Seeking a Shorter Route to California* (Salt Lake City, 1930). Recently published source items on the gold rush and its incidents include Georgia W. Read, ed., *A Pioneer of*

1850: George Willis Read, 1819-1880 (Boston, 1927);
Lucius Fairchild, *California Letters* (Joseph Schafer, ed.;
Wis. Hist. Publs., Colls., XXXI, 1931); Albert Jerome
Dickson, *Covered Wagon Days: A Journey across the Plains
in the Sixties, and Pioneer Days in the Northwest* (A. J.
Dickson, ed., Cleveland, 1929); G. D. Lyman, *John Marsh,
Pioneer: The Life Story of a Trail-Blazer on Six Frontiers*
(N. Y., 1930); Harris Newmark, *Sixty Years in Southern
California, 1853-1913* (M. H. and M. R. Newmark, eds.,
Boston, 1930); William H. Brewer, *Up and Down Cali-
fornia in 1860-1864* (F. P. Farquhar, ed., New Haven,
1930); Horace Bell, *On the Old West Coast: Being Further
Reminiscences of a Ranger* (Lanier Bartlett, ed., N. Y.,
1930); and the especially valuable and sparkling material
in Franklin A. Buck, *A Yankee Trader in the Gold Rush*
(Katherine A. White, comp., Boston, 1930). Earlier travel
items are largely listed in H. G. Wagner, comp., *The Plains
and the Rockies: A Bibliography of Original Narratives of
Travel and Adventure, 1800-1865* (San Fran., 1921).
More recent state histories include R. G. Cleland, *A History
of California: The American Period* (Cleveland, 1922),
and two volumes in the *California* series, edited by J. R.
McCarthy: O. C. Coy, *Gold Days* (Los Angeles, 1929),
and R. G. Cleland and Osgood Hardy, *March of Industry*
(Los Angeles, 1929). The standard account of the Mormon
development in Utah is still W. A. Linn, *The Story of the
Mormons* (N. Y., 1902). L. R. Hafen, *Colorado: The
Story of a Western Commonwealth* (Denver, 1933), is a
valuable recent item.

The mining frontier is treated in such monographs and
treatises as W. J. Trimble, *The Mining Advance into the
Inland Empire* (Univ. of Wis., *Bull.,* no. 638, 1914); C. H.
Shinn, *The Story of the Mine* (Ripley Hitchcock, ed., *The
Story of the West Series;* N. Y., 1896); E. S. Mead, *The
Story of Gold* (N. Y., 1908); G. F. Willison, *Here They
Dug the Gold* (N. Y., 1931); C. B. Glasscock, *The Big
Bonanza: The Story of the Comstock Lode* (Indianapolis,
1931); and T. A. Rickard, *A History of American Mining*
(N. Y., 1932). The problem of maintaining order is treated

in Emerson Hough, *The Story of the Outlaw* (N. Y., 1907), and in Mary F. Williams, *History of the Committee of Vigilance of 1851* (Univ. of Calif., *Publs.*, XII, 1921). Indian policy and relations are effectively surveyed in W. C. McLeod, *The American Indian Frontier* (N. Y., 1928), and J. C. Malin, *Indian Policy and Westward Expansion* (Univ. of Kansas, *Humanistic Studies*, II, no. 3, 1921), which are followed chronologically by G. B. Grinnell, *Two Great Scouts and Their Pawnee Battalion* (Cleveland, 1928); Grace R. Hebard and E. A. Brisinstool, *The Bozeman Trail;. Historical Accounts of the Blazing of the Overland Routes into the Northwest, and the Fights with Red Cloud's Warriors* (2 vols., Cleveland, 1922); and Grace R. Hebard, *Washakie: An Account of Indian Resistance of the Covered Wagon and Union Pacific Railroad Invasions of Their Territory* (Cleveland, 1930); and by the monographs of Annie H. Abel, especially *The American Indian as Participant in the Civil War* (Cleveland, 1919).

AGRICULTURE AND LAND

The standard work on Northern agriculture in the mid-century is P. W. Bidwell and J. I. Falconer, *History of Agriculture in the Northern United States, 1620-1860* (Carnegie Inst., *Contribs. to Am. Econ. History;* Wash., 1925). The Civil War period remains an open field for intensive study and appraisal. Perhaps the best summary is B. P. Poore, "History of Agriculture in the United States," Comnr. of Agr., *Ann. Rep. for 1866*, 498-527. An excellent local study is Joseph Schafer, *A History of Agriculture in Wisconsin*, the introductory *Wisconsin Domesday Book* (*General Studies*, I, Madison, 1922), which is followed by *Four Wisconsin Counties; Prairie and Forest* (*General Studies*, II, 1927). Agriculture occupies a prominent place in Frederick Merk, *Economic History of Wisconsin during the Civil War Decade* (Wis. Hist. Soc., *Studies*, I, 1916). The development of farming on the Minnesota frontier is traced in E. V. D. Robinson, *Early Economic Conditions and the Development of Agriculture in Minnesota* (Univ. of

Minn., *Studies,* no. 3, 1915); Henrietta M. Larson, *The Wheat Market and the Farmer in Minnesota, 1858-1900* (Columbia Univ., *Studies,* CXXII, no. 2, 1926); and Mildred L. Hartsough, *The Twin Cities as a Metropolitan Market* (Univ. of Minn., *Studies,* no. 18, 1925). W. T. Hutchinson, *Cyrus Hall McCormick: Seed-Time, 1809-1856* (N. Y., 1930), reveals forces at work in the agricultural world. There are valuable observations upon prairie husbandry in James Caird, *Prairie Farming in America* (N. Y., 1850); Charles Casey, *Two Years on the Farm of Uncle Sam* (London, 1852); and Parker Gillmore, *Prairie Farms and Prairie Folk* (2 vols., London, 1872). The most important collection of source materials on agricultural history is probably that in the McCormick Agricultural Library in Chicago. Public land policy has been studied in works like B. H. Hibbard, *A History of Public Land Policies* (N. Y., 1924), and G. M. Stephenson, *The Political History of the Public Lands from 1840 to 1862* (Boston, 1917). Few works have reached out into the field of the social history of land; A. M. Sakolski, *The Great American Land Bubble* (N. Y., 1932), is a promising effort in this direction.

TRANSPORTATION AND COMMUNICATION

The most thorough analysis of the earlier phases of American transportation is Caroline E. MacGill, *History of Transportation in the United States before 1860* (Carnegie Inst., *Contribs. to Am. Econ. History;* Wash., 1917). Seymour Dunbar, *A History of Travel in America* (4 vols., Indianapolis, 1915), treats more amply human experiences and changing social conditions. Stagecoach and tavern days are effectively portrayed in George Estes, *The Stage Coach: A History* (Portland, Ore., 1926); M. M. Quaife, *Chicago's Highways, Old and New* (Chicago, 1923); H. E. Cole, *Stagecoach and Tavern Tales of the Old Northwest* (Cleveland, 1930); and F. A. Root, *Overland Stage to California* (Topeka, 1901). Commercial aspects of the open road are portrayed in Richardson Wright, *Hawkers and Walkers in*

Early America (Phila., 1927). Good general accounts of railroad development are included in Slason Thompson, *A Short History of American Railways* (Chicago, 1925); A.T. Hadley, *Railroad Transportation: Its History and Its Laws* (N. Y., 1885); and C. F. Carter, *When Railroads Were New* (N. Y., 1909). Two comprehensive contemporary compilations are W. P. Smith, *The Book of the Great Railway Celebrations of 1857* (N. Y., 1858), and H. M. Flint, *Railroads of the United States* (Phila., 1868). More specific and valuable for their respective sections are R. E. Riegel, *The Story of the Western Railroads* (N. Y., 1926); W. F. Gephart, *Transportation and Industrial Development in the Middle West* (Columbia Univ., *Studies*, XXXIV, no. 1, 1909); and Phillips, *Transportation in the Eastern Cotton Belt* (already mentioned). Federal aid is studied in L. H. Haney, *A Congressional History of Railways in the United States, 1850-1887* (Univ. of Wis., *Bull.*, no. 342, 1910). Joseph Husband, *The Story of the Pullman Car* (Chicago, 1917), throws light on conditions of early travel.

Histories of individual railroads include F. C. Hicks, ed., *High Finance of the Sixties: Chapters from the Early History of the Erie Railroad* (New Haven, 1929); E. H. Mott, *Between the Ocean and the Lakes: The Story of the Erie* (N. Y., 1902); James Dredge, *The Pennsylvania Railroad: Its Organization, Construction and Management* (London, 1879); W. B. Wilson, *Pennsylvania Railroad Company* (2 vols., Phila., 1899); Milton Reizenstein, *The Economic History of the Baltimore and Ohio Railroad* (Johns Hopkins Univ., *Studies*, XV, 1897); H. G. Brownson, *The History of the Illinois Central Railroad to 1870* (Univ. of Ill., *Studies*, IV, 1915); W. H. Stennett, *History of the Chicago and Northwestern Railway System* (Chicago, 1910); Derrick, *Centennial History of South Carolina Railroad* (cited earlier); and J. P. Davis, *The Union Pacific* (N. Y., 1894). On the railroads in war time two articles of high order are C. R. Fish, "The Northern Railroads, April, 1861," *Am. Hist. Rev.*, XXII, 778-793, and R. S. Cotterill, "The Louisville and Nashville Railroad, 1861-1865," same mag., XXIX, 700-715. More general is J. W. Starr, jr., *Lincoln and the Railroads* (N. Y., 1927). A thrilling war tale is narrated in William Pittenger, *Capturing a Locomotive: A History of Secret Service in the Late War* (Wash., 1905).

Postal developments in general are surveyed in A. F. Harlow, *Old Post Bags* (N. Y., 1928), and Clyde Kelly, *United States Postal Policy* (N. Y., 1931). Transcontinental communications are discussed in L. R. Hafen, *The Overland Mail, 1849-1869* (Cleveland, 1926); G. D. Bradley, *The Story of the Pony Express* (Chicago, 1913); and W. L. Visscher, *The Pony Express* (Chicago, 1924). A war-time mail problem is treated in M. M. Quaife, ed., *Absalom Grimes, Confederate Mail Runner* (New Haven, 1926). The closely related express service receives attention in P. A. Stimson, *History of the Express Business* (N. Y., 1881). Telegraphic communication forms the theme of C. F. Briggs and Augustus Maverick, *The Story of the Telegraph and a History of the Great Atlantic Cable* (N. Y., 1858); the wartime phase is treated in W. R. Plum, *The Military Telegraph during the Civil War* (2 vols., Chicago, 1882).

The standard work on American commerce, E. R. Johnson and others, *History of Domestic and Foreign Commerce of the United States* (Carnegie Inst., *Contribs. to Am. Econ. History;* 2 vols., Wash., 1915), contains an invaluable bibliography. Briefer surveys include Malcolm Keir, *The March of Commerce* (*Pageant of America,* IV), and J. H. Frederick, *The Development of American Commerce* (N. Y., 1932). This heyday of the American marine is stressed in W. W. Bates, *American Marine* (Boston, 1897); W. L. Marvin, *The American Merchant Marine* (N. Y., 1902); and J. R. Spears, *The Story of the American Merchant Marine* (N. Y., 1910). A. H. Clark, *The Clipper Ship Era, 1843-1869* (N. Y., 1911), and S. E. Morison, *Maritime History of Massachusetts, 1783-1860* (Boston, 1921), have unique value. Mary M. Bray, *A Sea Trip in Clipper Ship Days* (Boston, 1920), presents colorful material from an original diary. E. P. Hohman, *The American Whaleman* (N. Y., 1928), stressing labor conditions, comes as the latest of a long list of histories of this industry.

The story of the passing canal era is popularly told in

A. F. Harlow, *Old Towpaths* (N. Y., 1926). Inland river navigation is analyzed in important new monographs like C. H. Ambler, *A History of Transportation in the Ohio Valley* (Glendale, Calif., 1932); C. E. Russell, *A-Rafting on the Mississippi* (N. Y., 1929); W. A. Blair, *A Raft Pilot's Log: A History of the Great Rafting Industry on the Upper Mississippi, 1840-1915* (Cleveland, 1930); and Herbert and Edward Quick, *Mississippi Steamboatin': A History of Steamboating on the Mississippi and Its Tributaries* (N. Y., 1926). G. B. Merrick, *Old Times on the Upper Mississippi* (Cleveland, 1909), offers the recollections of a steamboat pilot of this period; S. L. Clemens (Mark Twain, pseud.), *Life on the Mississippi* (Boston, 1883), is a classic source on this subject.

INDUSTRY, FINANCE AND INVENTION

Among the numerous brief manuals on American economic development special mention should be made of H. U. Faulkner, *American Economic History* (G. S. Ford, ed., *Harper's Historical Series;* N. Y., 1924), and E. C. Kirkland, *A History of American Economic Life* (N. Y., 1932). E. D. Fite, *Social and Industrial Conditions in the North during the Civil War* (N. Y., 1910), is a contribution of unique importance. Felix Flügel and H. U. Faulkner, eds., *Readings in the Economic and Social History of the United States* (N. Y., 1929), is a handy compilation of source material. *Statistical View of the United States* (*U. S. Seventh Census,* 1850) presents valuable data. A useful contemporary summary may be found in C. L. Flint and others, *Eighty Years Progress of the United States* (Hartford, 1866). The best study of industrial beginnings is V. S. Clark, *History of Manufactures in the United States, 1607-1860* (Carnegie Inst., *Contribs. to Am. Econ. History;* Wash., 1916). The same ground is covered in an older work: J. L. Bishop, *A History of American Manufactures from 1608 to 1860* (3 vols., Phila., 1866). Important special studies include R. M. Tryon, *Household Manufactures in the United States, 1640-1860* (Chicago, 1917); Isaac Lippincott, *A History of Manufactures in the Ohio Valley to the Year 1860* (Chicago, 1914) ; A. H. Cole, *The American Wool Manufacture* (2 vols., Cambridge, Mass., 1926) ; H. N. Casson, *The Romance of Steel* (N. Y., 1907) ; and F. J. Allen, *The Shoe Industry* (N. Y., 1916).

Banking and financial development is summarized in a number of manuals of which the outstanding are D. R. Dewey, *Financial History of the United States* (A. B. Hart, ed., *American Citizen Series;* N. Y., 1903) ; W. O. Scroggs, *A Century of Banking Progress* (N. Y., 1924) ; and A. S. Bolles, *Financial History of the United States* (3 vols., N. Y., 1894-1896). Monographic studies include W. L. Royall, *A History of Virginia Banks and Banking prior to 1860* (Columbia, S. C., 1922). G. F. Redmond, *Financial Giants of America* (2 vols., Boston, 1922), and Gustavus Myers, *History of the Great American Fortunes* (3 vols., Chicago, 1907-1910), present contrasting views as regards the tendency toward concentration of wealth. J. K. Winkler, *Morgan the Magnificent* (N. Y., 1930), discloses the origins of one great American fortune. W. O. Scroggs, *Filibusters and Financiers* (N. Y., 1916), reveals the economic forces back of William Walker in Nicaragua. Information on Civil War finance will be found in the inadequate biographies of Salmon P. Chase and in E. P. Oberholtzer's excellent *Jay Cooke, Financier of the Civil War* (2 vols., Phila., 1907). J. L. Sellers, "An Interpretation of Civil War Finance," *Am. Hist. Rev.*, XXX, 282-297, illuminates the broader economic implications of the war. A strong contemporary argument for the war-time prosperity of the North is found in Lorin Blodget, *The Commercial and Financial Strength of the United States* (Phila., 1864). Notable contributions in regard to internal commercial relations appear in two articles by E. M. Coulter: "Effects of Secession upon the Commerce of the Mississippi Valley," *Miss. Valley Hist. Rev.*, III, 275-300, and "Commercial Intercourse with the Confederacy in the Mississippi Valley," same mag., V, 377-395. A contemporary exposure of war-time corruption is found in Edward Bacon, *Among the Cotton Thieves* (Detroit, 1867). Invention and its bearings upon industry are discussed in

E. W. Byrn, *The Progress of Invention in the Nineteenth Century* (N. Y., 1900); George Iles, *Leading American Inventors* (N. Y., 1912); Holland Thompson, *The Age of Invention* (*Chronicles of America Series*, XXXVII); and Waldemar Kaempffert, ed., *A Popular History of American Invention* (2 vols., N. Y., 1924). Inventions in special fields are treated in M. F. Miller, *Evolution in Reaping Machines* (U. S. Experiment Station Office, *Bull.*, no. 103, 1902); Robert Hoe, *A Short History of the Printing Press* (N. Y., 1902); Charles Goodyear, *Gum Elastic and Its Varieties* (N. Y., 1853); Joseph Torey and A. S. Manders, *The Rubber Industry* (International Rubber Congress, *Rep. for 1911*); J. V. Woodworth, *American Tool Making and Interchangeable Manufacturing* (N. Y., 1911); J. W. Roe, *English and American Tool Builders* (New Haven, 1916); and R. H. Thurston, *The Messrs. Stevens, of Hoboken, as Engineers, Naval Architects and Philanthropists* (Phila., 1874).

LABOR

The labor movement of the period is thoroughly discussed in the coöperative *History of Labour in the United States* (2 vols., N. Y., 1918) by J. R. Commons and others. Brief treatises of merit include Mary R. Beard, *A Short History of the American Labor Movement* (N. Y., 1920); F. T. Carleton, *History and Problems of Organized Labor* (N. Y., 1920); S. P. Orth, *The Armies of Labor* (*Chronicles of America Series*, XL); G. G. Groat, *An Introduction to the Study of Organized Labor in America* (rev. edn., N. Y., 1926); and Selig Perlman, *A History of Trade Unionism in the United States* (N. Y., 1922). N. J. Ware followed his excellent monograph on *The Industrial Worker, 1840-1860* (Boston, 1924) with another on *The Labor Movement in the United States, 1860-1895* (N. Y., 1929). C. D. Wright, "The Course of Wages in the United States since 1840," Am. Stat. Assoc., *Publs.*, III (1893), 496-500, is useful when used with a study like F. W. Taussig, "Results of Recent Investigations on Prices in the United States," *Yale Review*, II (1893), 231-247. J. D. Burns, *The Working*

Classes in the United States during the War (London, 1865),
and an anonymous work, *Three Years among the Working
Classes in the United States during the War* (London, 1865),
present important materials, while the seventh, eighth and
ninth volumes of J. R. Commons and others, eds., *A Documentary History of American Industrial Society* (Cleveland,
1910), make available otherwise elusive source items. The
first annual reports of the several state bureaus of labor
statistics, set up in the eighties, generally summarize earlier
developments in the labor world.

IMMIGRATION AND RACE RELATIONS

THE IMMIGRANT: Among sociological studies of immi-
gration useful for social history are J. R. Commons, *Races
and Immigrants in America* (N. Y., 1920) ; L. G. Brown,
Immigration (N. Y., 1933) ; H. P. Fairchild, *Immigration*
(rev. edn., N. Y., 1924) ; P. F. Hall, *Immigration and Its
Effects upon the United States* (N. Y., 1906) ; F. J. Warne,
The Tide of Immigration (N. Y., 1916) ; and R. L. Garis,
Immigration Restriction (N. Y., 1927). The historical
approach is more apparent in S. P. Orth, *Our Foreigners*
(*Chronicles of America Series,* XXXV), and G. M. Stephenson, *A History of American Immigration* (N. Y., 1926).
A valuable documentary collection is Edith Abbott, ed., *Historical Aspects of the Immigration Problem* (Chicago,
1926). In addition to scattered federal documents, important statistical materials are available in the reports of the
commissioners of emigration of the state of New York,
which were collected and published in 1861 and later summarized in Friedrich Kapp, *Immigration, and the Commissioners of Emigration of the State of New York* (N. Y.,
1870).

The distinctive influence of various racial stocks has been
increasingly a subject of investigation. The British contribution is considered by S. C. Johnson, *A History of Emigration from the United Kingdom to North America, 1763-
1912* (N. Y., 1914). Studies of the Irish and their influence
are few and disappointing. A significant contemporary item

is J. F. Maguire, *The Irish in America* (London, 1868), a critique of which appeared in John White, *Sketches from America* (London, 1870). Jeremiah O'Donovan, *A Brief Account of the Author's Interview with His Countrymen, and of the Parts of the Emerald Isle Whence They Emigrated* (Pittsburgh, 1864), is the intimate account of an Irish author who undertook to sell his book to his fellow countrymen. D. P. Conyngham, *The Irish Brigade and Its Campaigns with Some Accounts of the Corcoran Legion* (Boston, 1869), suggests something of the war-time contribution of the Irish, as does also Michael Cavanagh, *Memoirs of Gen. Thomas Francis Meagher* (Worcester, 1894).

On the Germans the standard work is A. B. Faust, *The German Element in the United States* (2 vols., Boston, 1909). Less extensive is F. F. Schrader, *The Germans in the Making of America* (Boston, 1924), which, like J. B. Rosengarten, *The German Soldier in the Wars of the United States* (Phila., 1886), discusses the Teutonic rôle in the Civil War. Contemporary pictures of the German element will be found in Philip Schaff, *Amerika: Die Politischen, Socialen und Kirchlick-Religiösen Zustände der Vereinigten Staaten von Nordamerika* (Berlin, 1854); Friedrich Kapp, *Geschichte der Deutschen Einwanderung in Amerika* (N. Y., 1867); E. Schlaeger, *Die Sociale und Politische Stellung der Deutschen in den Vereinigten Staaten* (Berlin, 1874); and Adalbert Baudissin, *Zustände in Amerika* (Altona, 1862). Special studies of local German groups include J. L. Rosenberger, *The Pennsylvania Germans* (Chicago, 1923); R. L. Biesele, *The History of the German Settlements in Texas, 1831-1861* (Austin, 1930); Bertha M. H. Shambaugh, *Amana That Was and Amana That Is* (Iowa City, 1932); and Ernest Bruncken, *The Political Activity of Wisconsin Germans, 1854-1860* (Madison, 1906). Additional materials will be found in the biographical and autobiographical works on Carl Schurz, Gustave Koerner, Henry Villard and others. Josephine C. Goldmark, *Pilgrims of '48: One Man's Part in the Austrian Revolution of 1848 and a Family Migration to America* (New Haven, 1930), suggests further possibilities in the biographical field. Important contributions are often published in the *German-American Annals* (Phila., 1903-1919) and in the Deutsch-Amerikanische Historische Gesellschaft von Illinois, *Jahrbuch* (Chicago, from 1901).

The Jewish contribution is summarized in M. C. Peters, *The Jews in America* (Phila., 1905); Simon Wolf, *The American Jew as Patriot, Soldier and Citizen* (Phila., 1895); and George Cohen, *The Jews in the Making of America* (Boston, 1924). The Scandinavian migration is analyzed in K. C. Babcock, *The Scandinavian Element in the United States* (Univ. of Ill., *Studies*, III, no. 3, 1914), and more intensively in G. T. Flom, *A History of Norwegian Immigration to the United States* (Iowa City, 1909); T. C. Blegen, *Norwegian Migration to America, 1825-1860* (Northfield, Minn., 1931), a model study; Amandus Johnson, *The Swedes in America, 1638-1900* (Phila., 1914); J. S. Lindberg, *The Background of Swedish Emigration to the United States* (Minneapolis, 1930); and T. P. Christensen, *Dansk Amerikansk Historie* (Cedar Falls, Iowa, 1927). The religious forces involved are considered in J. M. Rohne, *Norwegian-American Lutheranism up to 1872* (N. Y., 1926), and G. M. Stephenson, *The Religious Aspects of Scandinavian Immigration* (Minneapolis, 1932). Other phases are treated in monographs published in the *American-Scandinavian Review* (N. Y., from 1913), the *Studies and Records* of the Norwegian-American Historical Association and the *Yearbook* of the Swedish Historical Society of America. Certain other elements are specifically studied in Ruth Putnam, "The Dutch Element in the United States," Am. Hist. Assoc., *Ann. Rep. for 1909*, 205-218; A. J. Pieters, *A Dutch Settlement in Michigan* (Grand Rapids, 1923); Eugene Piványy, *Hungarians in the American Civil War* (Cleveland, 1913); and Mary R. Coolidge, *Chinese Immigration* (N. Y., 1909).

The student of Know Nothingism should begin with R. A. Billington, comp., "Tentative Bibliography of Anti-Catholic Propaganda in the United States (1800-1860)," *Catholic Hist. Rev.*, XVIII, 492-513. The movement in two of its chief centers is described in L. D. Scisco, *Political Nativism in New York State* (Columbia Univ., *Studies*, XIII, no. 2, 1901), and L. F. Schmeckebier, *History of the Know Nothing Party in Maryland* (Johns Hopkins Univ., *Studies*, XVII, 1899). Contemporary defenses of the Know Nothing party include anon., *The Sons of the Sires: A History of the Rise, Progress, and Destiny of the American Party* (Phila., 1855); T. R. Whitney, *A Defense of the American Policy* (N. Y., 1856); and the more subtle annotated argument for nativism in J. P. Sanderson, *Republican Landmarks: The Views and Opinions of American Statesmen on Foreign Immigration* (Phila., 1856).

THE NEGRO: The most comprehensive bibliography is M. N. Work, comp., *A Bibliography of the Negro in Africa and America* (N. Y., 1928). Among more recent important items is E. F. Frazier, *The Free Negro Family: A Study of Family Origins before the Civil War* (Nashville, 1932). A number of ex-slave narratives played an important part in antislavery propaganda, including Frederick Douglass, *My Bondage, and My Freedom* (N. Y., 1855); T. H. Jones, *The Experience of Thomas Jones Who Was a Slave for Forty-three Years* (Boston, 1850); Austin Steward, *Twenty-Two Years a Slave and Forty Years a Freeman* (Rochester, 1857); J. W. Loguen, *As a Slave and as a Freeman* (Syracuse, 1859); Solomon Northup, *Twelve Years a Slave* (N. Y., 1855); and L. Maria Child, ed., *Incidents in the Life of a Slave Girl* (Boston, 1861). On the war-time problems of freedmen are available such works as Elizabeth H. Botume, *First Days amongst the Contrabands* (Boston, 1893); Mrs. A. M. French, *Slavery in South Carolina and Ex-Slaves: or the Port Royal Mission* (N. Y., 1862); Charles Nordoff, *The Freedmen of South Carolina* (N. Y., 1863); and John Eaton, *Grant, Lincoln and the Freedman* (N. Y., 1907). On the question of arming the slaves important works are G. W. Williams, *History of the Negro Troops in the War of the Rebellion* (N. Y., 1888), and T. W. Higginson, *Army Life in a Black Regiment* (Boston, 1870), the latter recounting the experiences of a young New England idealist.

RELIGION

The coöperative work edited by Philip Schaff and others, *The American Church History Series* (13 vols., N. Y., 1893-1897), reviews the history of leading denominations and sects, with an attempt at broader synthesis in the first volume, *The Religious Forces of the United States*, by H. H. Carroll and in the last, *A History of American Christianity*, by L. W. Bacon. Other works aiming at breadth of interpretation include H. K. Rowe, *The History of Religion in the United States* (N. Y., 1924), and W. W. Sweet's excellent factual summary entitled *The Story of Religions in America* (N. Y., 1930). The broader forces of American idealism are considered in L. A. Weigle, *American Idealism* (*Pageant of America*, X), and in Gustavus Myers, *The History of American Idealism* (N. Y., 1925). J. H. Denison, *Emotional Currents in American History* (N. Y., 1932), is a pseudopsychological but provocative effort at interpretation.

Besides the formal source materials like published proceedings of national church gatherings, there are numerous memoirs of early preachers and religious leaders, as well as contemporary appraisals of the religious situation, such as are found in Joseph Belcher, *Religious Denominations in the United States* (Phila., 1854); Georges Fisch, *Nine Months in the United States during the Crisis* (London, 1863); William Rey, *L'Amérique Protestante* (Paris, 1857); Hermann Wimmer, *Die Kirche und Schule in Nord-Amerika* (Leipzig, 1853); and Philip Schaff, *America* (N. Y., 1855). Many of the intradenominational controversies of the day can be traced only in the religious press, which reached its height in this period.

The rapid expansion of the Catholic Church is traced in the last volume of J. G. Shea, *The Catholic Church in the United States* (4 vols., N. Y., 1886-1892), and in Gerald Shaughnessy, *Has the Immigrant Kept the Faith?* (N. Y., 1925). The note of revolt is sounded in Father Chiniquy, *Fifty Years in the Church of Rome* (Chicago, 1886). A suggestive local study is John Rothensteiner, *History of the*

Archdiocese of St. Louis (2 vols., St. Louis, 1928). In the history of the leading Protestant denomination a recent popular survey of decided merit is H. E. Luccock and Paul Hutchinson, *The Story of Methodism* (N. Y., 1926). The development of Sunday schools is surveyed in Marianna C. Brown, *Sunday School Movements in America* (N. Y., 1901), and Addie G. Wardle, *History of the Sunday School Movement in the Methodist Episcopal Church* (N. Y., 1918). Missionary activities and controversies are followed in Lewis Tappan, *History of the American Missionary Association* (N. Y., 1855), and W. E. Strong, *The Story of the American Board* (Boston, 1901).

The war-time rôle of Northern religious agencies is summed up in H. B. Hockett, *Christian Memorials of the War* (Boston, 1864); *Christ in the Army: A Selection of Sketches of the Work of the U. S. Christian Commission* (Phila., 1865), by various writers; Lemuel Moss, *Annals of the United States Christian Commission* (Phila., 1868); and E. P. Smith, *Incidents of the United States Christian Commission* (Phila., 1869). Corresponding developments in the Confederacy are chronicled in J. W. Jones, *Christ in the Camp; or, Religion in Lee's Army* (Richmond, 1887); Joseph Cross, *Camp and Field: Papers from the Portfolio of an Army Chaplain* (Columbia, S. C., 1864); and W. W. Bennett, *A Narrative of the Great Revival Which Prevailed in the Southern Armies during the Late Civil War* (Phila., 1877). Biographical material includes W. M. Polk, *Leonidas Polk, Bishop and General* (2 vols., N. Y., 1915); J. B. Cheshire, *Confederate Atkinson and the Church in the Confederacy* (Raleigh, 1909); W. B. Capers, *The Soldier Bishop, Ellison Capers* (N. Y., 1912); and T. C. Johnson, *The Life and Letters of Benjamin Morgan Palmer* (Richmond, 1906), the last an ardent pulpit champion of secession and Southern rights.

HUMANITARIAN STRIVING

ANTISLAVERY: The abolition movement of the fifties has been somewhat neglected because of its intransigence. Recent special contributions include L. D. Turner, *Anti-Slavery Sentiment in American Literature prior to 1865* (Wash., 1929); A. W. Crandall, *The Early History of the Republican Party, 1854-1856* (Boston, 1930); and Annie H. Abel and F. J. Klingberg, *A Side Light on Anglo-American Relations, 1839-1858, Furnished by the Correspondence of Lewis Tappan and Others with the British and Foreign Anti-Slavery Society* (Wash., 1927). W. H. Siebert, *The Underground Railroad from Slavery to Freedom* (N. Y., 1898), is important for this period; J. R. Shipherd, *History of the Oberlin-Wellington Rescue* (Boston, 1859), is a significant contemporary item in the same field. The biographies and memoirs of leading agitators are of decided importance, notably those of Henry Ward Beecher, John Brown, Salmon P. Chase, James Freeman Clarke, William Lloyd Garrison, Sallie Holley, Samuel J. May, Wendell Phillips, Parker Pillsbury, Alexander M. Ross, Gerrit Smith, Harriet Beecher Stowe, Charles Sumner and Henry Wilson. D. W. Bartlett, *Modern Agitators; or Pen Portraits of Living American Reformers* (N. Y., 1855), is a brief contemporary introduction to this group.

PEACE: Excellent studies of the peace movement are to be found in A. C. F. Beales, *The History of Peace* (N. Y., 1931); E. L. Whitney, *The American Peace Society: A Centennial History* (Wash., 1928); M. E. Curti, *The American Peace Crusade, 1815-1860* (Durham, 1929); Christina Phelps, *The Anglo-American Peace Movement in the Mid-Nineteenth Century* (Columbia Univ., *Studies*, no. 330, 1930); and E. N. Wright, *Conscientious Objectors in the Civil War* (Phila., 1931).

WOMAN'S RIGHTS: The changing status of women can be traced in A. W. Calhoun, *Social History of the American Family* (3 vols., Cleveland, 1917-1919), which includes a valuable bibliography. The movement for civil and political rights is authoritatively presented in Elizabeth Cady Stanton, Susan B. Anthony and others, *The History of Woman Suffrage* (4 vols., N. Y., 1881-1902). Elizabeth Cady Stanton, *Elizabeth Cady Stanton as Revealed in Her Letters, Diary and Reminiscences* (Theodore Stanton and Harriot

S. Blatch, eds., 2 vols., N. Y. 1922), supplements this more general work, as does Alice Stone Blackwell, *Lucy Stone: Pioneer of Woman's Rights* (Boston, 1930). Caroline H. Dall, *The College, the Market, and the Court* (Boston, 1867), is a contemporary appeal for a wider employment of women. The concern of women leaders for the health and education of their sex may be glimpsed in Catharine E. Beecher, *Educational Reminiscences and Suggestions* (N. Y., 1874), and Mae E. Harveson, *Catharine Esther Beecher, Pioneer Educator* (Phila., 1932).

MORALS, TEMPERANCE AND OTHER REFORMS: A sketch of morals may be found in Leo Markun, *Mrs. Grundy: A History of Four Centuries of Morals in Great Britain and the United States* (N. Y., 1930). This period brought the first intensive study of prostitution in W. W. Sanger, *History of Prostitution* (N. Y., 1858). Developing urban problems are revealed in C. L. Brace, *The Dangerous Classes of New York* (N. Y., 1872), and Herbert Asbury, *The Gangs of New York* (N. Y., 1928). A Western problem is illustrated by G. H. Devol, *Forty Years a Gambler on the Mississippi* (Cin., 1887). The last days of the duel are covered in Lorenzo Sabine, *Notes on Duels and Duelling* (Boston, 1855), and D. C. Seitz, *Famous American Duels* (N. Y., 1929). Its lingering popularity in the South is shown in J. L. Wilson, *The Code of Honor; or, Rules for the Government of Principals and Seconds in Duelling* (Charleston, S. C., 1858). The temperance movement is reviewed in works like J. G. Woolley and W. E. Johnson, *Temperance Progress of the Century* (*The Nineteenth Century Series*, XXIV, Phila., 1903); E. H. Cherrington, *The Evolution of Prohibition in the United States* (Westerville, Ohio, 1920); and Ernest Gordon, *The Maine Law* (N. Y., 1919). J. B. Gough, *Autobiography and Personal Recollections* (Phila., 1870), gives the experiences of a leading temperance worker.

EDUCATION

Educational progress is sketched in the standard manuals, notably E. P. Cubberley, *Public Education in the United*

States (Boston, 1919), and E. G. Dexter, *History of Education in the United States* (N. Y., 1904). Contemporary accounts appeared in the *American Journal of Education* (Henry Barnard, ed., Hartford, 1855-1870). Meantime a number of state teachers' publications made their appearance: *Massachusetts Teacher* (Boston, 1848-1874); *Connecticut Common School Journal* (Hartford, 1838-1866); *New York Teacher* (Albany, 1852-1867); *Ohio Journal of Education* (Columbus, from 1852); *New Hampshire Journal of Education* (Concord, 1857-1862); *Indiana School Journal* (Indianapolis, 1856-1900); and *Illinois Teacher* (Peoria, 1855-1872). The annual reports of state commissioners of education contain valuable statistical material. A. D. Mayo has compiled significant special articles on the situation in the South in "The Organization and Development of the American Common School in the Atlantic and Central States of the South," U. S. Comnr. of Educ., *Rep for 1899-1900*, I, 427-561, and "The Common School in the Southern States beyond the Mississippi River from 1830 to 1860," *Rep. for 1900-1901*, I, 357-401. A recent excellent survey is E. W. Knight, *Public Education in the South* (Boston, 1922); his *Public School Education in North Carolina* (Boston, 1916) is now paralleled by M. C. S. Noble, *A History of the Public Schools of North Carolina* (Chapel Hill, 1930). Other state histories include J. P. Wickersham, *A History of Education in Pennsylvania* (Lancaster, 1886); E. E. White and T. W. Harvey, eds., *A History of Education in the State of Ohio* (Columbus, 1876); and R. G. Boone, *History of Education in Indiana* (N. Y., 1892).

Important documents on the early struggle for free public schools in the cities may be found in J. M. Wightman, comp., *Annals of the Boston Primary School Committee, 1818-1855* (Boston, 1860); W. A. Bourne, *History of the Public School Society of the City of New York* (N. Y., 1870); and School Committee of Providence, R. I., *Centennial Report for 1899-1900*. More formal surveys include Thomas Boese, *Public Education in the City of New York* (N. Y., 1869); Edward Smith, *A History of the Schools of Syracuse from Its Early Settlement to January 1, 1893*

(Syracuse, 1893); and W. J. Akers, *Cleveland Schools in the Nineteenth Century* (Cleveland, 1901). Less formal aspects of educational history are treated in Clifton Johnson, *Old-Time Schools and School Books* (N. Y., 1904); R. R. Reeder, *The Historical Development of School Readers and Methods of Teaching Reading* (Columbia Univ., *Contribs. to Phil., Psych. and Educ.*, VIII, no. 2, 1900); and A. H. Nelson, "The Little Red Schoolhouse," *Educational Rev.*, XXIII, 304-315. The shift from academies to high schools is noted in E. E. Brown, *The Making of Our Middle Schools* (N. Y., 1903); G. F. Miller, *The Academy System of the State of New York* (Albany, 1922); and E. D. Grizzell, *Origin and Development of the High School in New England before 1865* (N. Y., 1923).

Developments in college and university education are summarized in C. F. Thwing, *A History of Higher Education in America* (N. Y., 1906). The volumes in G. P. Krapp, ed., *The American College and University Series* (N. Y., 1914-1920), are brief but useful studies of individual institutions. J. H. Fairchild, *Oberlin: The Colony and the College* (Oberlin, 1883), should be supplemented by R. S. Fletcher's forthcoming *The Early History of Oberlin, 1833-1866*. J. M. Taylor, *Before Vassar Opened* (Boston, 1914); C. H. Rammelkamp, *Illinois College: A Centennial History, 1829-1929* (New Haven, 1928); and Ellsworth Eliot, jr., *Yale in the Civil War* (New Haven, 1932), are especially valuable for this period. Andrew D. White, *Autobiography* (2 vols., N. Y., 1905); Henry James, *Charles W. Eliot, President of Harvard, 1867-1909* (2 vols., Boston, 1930); Mary Mann, ed., *Life and Works of Horace Mann* (5 vols., Boston, 1865-1868); and Timothy Dwight, *Memories of Yale Life and Men, 1845-1899* (N. Y., 1903), throw light on various aspects of college life in the fifties and sixties.

SCIENCE

Scientific progress before and during the Civil War is reflected in the works listed in Max Meisel, comp., *A Bib-*

liography of American Natural History: The Pioneer Century, 1769-1865 (3 vols., Brooklyn, 1924-1929). A good general outline is found in E. S. Dana and others, *A Century of Science in America* (New Haven, 1918). More specific are works like R. T. Young, *Biology in America* (Boston, 1922); G. P. Merrill, *The First Hundred Years of American Geology* (New Haven, 1924); E. F. Smith, *Chemistry in America* (N. Y., 1914); and A. S. Packard, jr., "A Century's Progress in American Zoology," *Am. Naturalist,* X (1876), 591-598. The work of the leading American scientific institution is chronicled in G. B. Goode, *The Smithsonian Institution, 1846-1896* (Wash., 1897), and in W. J. Rhees, *An Account of the Smithsonian Institution* (Phila., 1896), with illustrative source material in W. J. Rhees, *Smithsonian Institution: Documents Relative to Its Origin and History, 1835-1899* (2 vols., Wash., 1901). Much of the current scientific advance is recorded in D. A. Wells, ed., *Annual of Scientific Discovery, or Yearbook of Facts in Science and Art* (21 vols., Boston, 1850-1871), and in the issues of the *Scientific American* (N. Y., from 1859).

Developments in the field of medicine are summarized in E. H. Clarke and others, *A Century of American Medicine, 1776-1876* (Phila., 1876), and N. S. Davis, *Contributions to the History of Medical Education and Medical Institutions in the United States, 1776-1876* (Wash., 1877). Localized studies include P. M. Hamer, *The Centennial History of the Tennessee State Medical Association, 1830-1930* (Nashville, 1930); W. T. Howard, ed., *Public Health and Administration and the Natural History of Disease in Baltimore, Maryland, 1797-1920* (Wash., 1924); and R. C. Holcomb, *A Century with Norfolk Naval Hospital, 1830-1930* (Portsmouth, Va., 1930). One of the earliest studies of Amercian hospitals is W. G. Wylie, *Hospitals: Their History, Organization and Construction* (N. Y., 1877). The earlier stages of the controversy over the Darwinian theory of evolution are treated in Asa Gray, *Darwinism* (Boston, 1878), and Elizabeth F. Agassiz, *Agassiz, His Life and Correspondence* (Boston, 1885).

LITERATURE AND JOURNALISM

LITERATURE: W. P. Trent and others, eds., *The Cambridge History of American Literature* (4 vols., N. Y., 1917-1921), is broad and authoritative in content and in its bibliographical information. It is usefully supplemented by V. L. Parrington's brilliant *Main Currents in American Thought* (3 vols., 1927-1930). Southern literature has been appraised in J. W. Davidson, *The Living Writers of the South* (N. Y., 1869); W. M. Baskervill, *Southern Writers* (2 vols., Nashville, 1898-1903); Carl Holliday, *A History of Southern Literature* (N. Y., 1906); and M. J. Moses, *The Literature of the South* (N. Y., 1910). Special information on Southern cultural development may be found in B. B. Minor, *The Southern Literary Messenger, 1834-1864* (N. Y., 1905), and in J. D. Wade, *Augustus Baldwin Longstreet* (N. Y., 1924). Studies of Western literary movements include W. T. Coggeshall, *Poets and Poetry of the West* (N. Y., 1864); W. H. Venable, *The Beginnings of Literary Culture in the Ohio Valley* (Cin., 1891); and Dondore, *The Prairie and the Making of Middle America* (cited earlier). Popular literary forces are portrayed in Jennette Tandy, *Crackerbox Philosophers in American Humor and Satire* (N. Y., 1925); Cyril Clemens, *Josh Billings, Yankee Humorist* (Webster Groves, Mo., 1932); and Edmund Pearson, *Dime Novels* (Boston, 1929).

Indispensable for the appraisal of literary currents are the biographies and memoirs, as well as the works of such writers as John Bigelow, Henry H. Brownell, William Cullen Bryant, Ralph Waldo Emerson, Thomas Wentworth Higginson, Oliver Wendell Holmes, Henry Wadsworth Longfellow, James Russell Lowell, Charles Eliot Norton, Richard H. Stoddard, Henry D. Thoreau, George Ticknor, John T. Trowbridge and John Greenleaf Whittier. A useful supplement may be found in E. W. Emerson, *The Early Years of the Saturday Club, 1855-1870* (Boston, 1918). The important cultural influence of the publishing field is revealed in memoirs like J. C. Derby, *Fifty Years among Authors, Books and Publishers* (N. Y., 1886), and also in special studies like Lea Brothers and Company, *One Hundred Years of Publishing, 1785-1885* (Phila., 1885); J. H. Harper, *The House of Harper* (N. Y., 1912); and E. L. Bradsher, *Mathew Carey, Editor, Author and Publisher* (N. Y., 1912).

JOURNALISM: Algernon Tassin, *The Magazine in America* (N. Y., 1916), the only general manual, needs to be supplemented by more studies like M. A. DeW. Howe, *The Atlantic Monthly and Its Makers* (Boston, 1919). Everyday journalism is surveyed in J. M. Lee, *History of American Journalism* (rev. edn., Boston, 1923); G. H. Payne, *History of Journalism in the United States* (N. Y., 1920); and W. G. Bleyer, *Main Currents in the History of American Journalism* (Boston, 1927). Frederic Hudson, *Journalism in the United States* (N. Y., 1873), has a value as source material for this period, as have Augustus Maverick, *Henry J. Raymond and the New York Press for Thirty Years* (Hartford, 1870), and W. L. King, *The Newspaper Press of Charleston* (Charleston, S. C., 1872). Walt Whitman, *I Sit and Look Out* (Emory Holloway and Vernolian Schwarz, eds., N. Y., 1932), reproduces some of the early editorial efforts of the "gray poet." Allan Nevins, *The Evening Post* (N. Y., 1922); F. M. O'Brien, *The Story of the Sun* (N. Y., 1918); Elmer Davis, *History of the New York Times* (N. Y., 1921); Royal Cortissoz, *The New York Tribune* (N. Y., 1923); and Richard Hooker, *The Story of an Independent Newspaper* (N. Y., 1924), treating the *Springfield Republican,* are among the best newspaper biographies. The reminiscences and lives of James Gordon Bennett, Samuel Bowles, Charles A. Dana and Horace Greeley are of value, as are war-time experiences of such journalists as T. W. Knox, *Camp-Fire and Cotton-Field* (N. Y., 1865); G. A. Townsend, *Campaigns of a Non-Combatant* (N. Y., 1866); and Ida M. Tarbell, *A Reporter for Lincoln: Story of Henry E. Wing, Soldier and Newspaperman* (N. Y., 1927). Recent biographical items of value include

D. C. Seitz, *The James Gordon Bennetts; Father and Son* (Indianapolis, 1928), and C. J. Rosebault, *When Dana Was the Sun* (N. Y., 1931).

THE FINE ARTS

PAINTING, SCULPTURE AND MUSIC: The standard histories of American painting appraise the developments of this period: Sadakichi Hartmann, *A History of American Art* (2 vols., Boston, 1901); Samuel Isham, *The History of American Painting* (J. C. Van Dyke, ed., *The History of American Art*, III, N. Y., 1905); C. H. Caffin, *The Story of American Painting* (N. Y., 1907); and Eugen Neuhaus, *The History and Ideals of American Art* (Stanford, 1931). The recent vogue of Currier and Ives lithographs has led to the publication of W. A. Weaver, *Lithographs of N. Currier and Currier & Ives* (3 vols., N. Y., 1925-1926), and Russel Crouse, *Mr. Currier and Mr. Ives: A Note on Their Lives and Times* (N. Y., 1931). The beginnings of an American sculpture are appraised in Lorado Taft, *The History of American Sculpture* (*History of American Art*, I, rev. edn., N. Y., 1924), and W. H. Downes, *The Life and Works of Winslow Homer* (Boston, 1911). L. C. Elson, *The History of American Music* (*History of American Art*, II, rev. edn., N. Y., 1925), and J. T. Howard, *Our American Music* (N. Y., 1931), are the most useful surveys; they may be supplemented by H. C. Lahee, *Annals of Music in America* (Boston, 1922), and O. G. Sonneck, *Early Opera in America* (N. Y., 1915).

THE THEATER: The history of the American stage is effectively presented in O. S. Coad and Edward Mims, jr., *The American Stage* (*Pageant of America*, XIV). Other surveys include Mary C. Crawford, *The Romance of the American Stage* (rev. edn., Boston, 1926); and Arthur Hornblow, *A History of the Theatre in America* (2 vols., Phila., 1919). T. A. Brown, *History of the American Stage* (N. Y., 1870), has many faults, but gives a biographical sketch of nearly every early actor. A. H. Quinn, *A History of the American Drama from the Beginning to the Civil War*

(N. Y., 1923), is a scholarly analysis, and M. J. Moses, *The American Dramatist* (rev. edn., Boston, 1926), a popular survey of early American efforts at playwrighting. The origins of the American minstrel show are traced in Carl Wittke, *Tambo and Bones: A History of the American Minstrel Stage* (Durham, 1930). In the field of popular amusement E. C. May, *The Circus from Rome to Ringling* (N. Y., 1932), is a poorly organized work which presents some valuable materials, as does Gil Robinson, *Old Wagon Show Days* (Cin., 1925). Of the many local studies of the stage, the most recent and scholarly is G. C. D. Odell, *Annals of the New York Stage* (7 vols., N. Y., 1927-1931), of which V and VI deal with this period. Eugene Tompkins, *The History of the Boston Theatre* (Boston, 1908), is rich in material. There is an extensive array of biographical and reminiscent literature about stage celebrities of the Civil War era. Leota S. Driver, *Fanny Kemble* (Chapel Hill, 1933), is a valuable recent item.

SOCIAL CUSTOMS AND SPORTS

Domestic relations are surveyed in Calhoun, *A Social History of the American Family* (already cited). Some of the proprieties of the numerous *ante-bellum* etiquette books have been excerpted and brought together in C. J. Furness, ed., *The Genteel Female* (Bernard De Voto, ed., *Americana Deserta;* N. Y., 1931). The currents of American fashions in correct dress are revealed, with numerous illustrations, in Elizabeth McClellan, *Historic Dress in America, 1800-1870* (Phila., 1910). Some of the dominant forces in society life are suggested in Mrs. Clement C. Clay, *A Belle of the Fifties* (Ada Sterling, ed., N. Y., 1904); Elizabeth F. Ellet, *Queens of American Society* (N. Y., 1867), and *Court Circles of the Republic* (N. Y., 1869); T. C. De Leon, *Belles, Beaux and Brains of the 60's* (N. Y., 1909); and Mrs. John K. Van Rensselaer, *The Social Ladder* (N. Y., 1924), and *Newport, Our Social Capital* (Phila., 1905). The foibles of "our best society" are revealed in bold outlines in G. W. Curtis, *The Potiphar Papers* (N. Y., 1860).

The origins of modern American sports are surveyed in two very useful works: J. A. Krout, *Annals of American Sport* (*Pageant of America*, XV), and Herbert Manchester, *Four Centuries of Sport in America, 1490-1890* (N. Y., 1931). Additional material may be found in F. W. Janssen, *History of American Amateur Athletics and Aquatics* (N. Y., 1887); Henry Hall, ed., *The Tribune Book of Open-Air Sports* (N. Y., 1887); and H. C. Palmer, *Amateur Sports in America* (Phila., 1889). Field sports are described by contemporaries in the following works: William Elliott, *Carolina Sports by Land and Water* (N. Y., 1859); Captain Flack, *A Hunter's Experiences in the Southern States of America* (London, 1866), and *The Texas Rifle-Hunter, or Field Sports on the Prairie* (London, 1866); S. H. Hammond, *Wild Northern Scenes: Sporting Adventures with Rifle and Rod* (Phila., 1863); C. B. Hartley, *Hunting Sports in the West* (Phila., 1859); John Paliser, *The Solitary Hunter, or Sporting Adventures in the Prairies* (London, 1857); G. F. Berkeley, *The English Sportsman in the Western Prairies* (London, 1861); and W. E. Webb, *Buffalo Land* (Cin., 1872). Special studies covering individual sports include W. P. Stephens, *American Yachting* (N. Y., 1904); T. S. Andrews, *Ring Battles of Centuries* (Milwaukee, 1924); Hiram Woodruff, *The Trotting Horse in America* (N. Y., 1868); A. G. Spalding, *America's National Game* (N. Y., 1911); and F. C. Richter, *Richter's History and Records of Baseball* (Phila., 1914).

ARMY LIFE

A comprehensive study of the experiences of the Union soldier is given in F. A. Shannon, *The Organization and Administration of the Union Army, 1861-1865* (2 vols., Cleveland, 1928). This is supplemented by the valuable monograph of Ella M. Lonn, *Desertion during the Civil War* (N. Y., 1928). Back of such studies lie hundreds of memoirs and biographies and collections of letters which recount the experiences of participants. A number of these are listed by Shannon and in other Civil War studies. Some of the more recent of such accounts include H. M. Calvert, *Reminiscences of a Boy in Blue, 1862-1865* (N. Y., 1920); John Gibbon, *Personal Recollections of the Civil War* (N. Y., 1928); John Chipman Gray and John Codman Ropes, *War Letters, 1862-1865* (Boston, 1927); Henry Hitchcock, *Marching with Sherman* (M. A. DeW. Howe, ed., New Haven, 1927); Oscar L. Jackson, *The Colonel's Diary: Journals Kept before and during the Civil War* (D. P. Jackson, ed., Sharon, Pa., 1922); Theodore Lyman, *Meade's Headquarters, 1863-1865* (G. R. Agassiz, ed., Boston, 1922); E. P. McKinney, *Life in Tent and Field, 1861-1865* (Boston, 1922); A. Piatt Andrew, *Some Civil War Letters* (Gloucester, Mass., 1925); G. H. Putnam, *Some Memories of the Civil War* (N. Y., 1924); Leander Stillwell, *The Story of a Common Soldier of Army Life in the Civil War, 1861-1865* (2d edn., Erie, Kan., 1920); and Samuel Edmund Nicholas, *"Your Soldier Boy Samuel": Civil War Letters* (C. S. Underhill, ed., Buffalo, 1929). Thousands of other narratives have appeared in the various general and special historical periodicals. C. A. Ingraham, *Elmer E. Ellsworth and the Zouaves of '61* (Chicago, 1925), and O. D. Morrison, "Indiana's Care for Her Soldiers in the Field," *Studies in American History Inscribed to James Albert Woodburn* (Indiana Univ., *Studies*, XII, nos. 66-68, 1926), 277-302, throw valuable light on federal army life.

One of the finest glimpses into the idealism of Southern military leaders may be found in G. E. Pickett, *Soldier of the South: War Letters to His Wife* (A. C. Inman, ed., Boston, 1928). The colorful figure of a popular Confederate cavalry leader is revealed in A. N. Lytle, *Bedford Forrest and His Critter Company* (N. Y., 1931), and E. W. Sheppard, *Bedford Forrest, the Confederacy's Greatest Cavalryman* (N. Y., 1930). Similar materials may be found in B. W. Duke, *History of Morgan's Cavalry* (Cin., 1867); Sally R. Ford, *Raids and Romance of Morgan and His Men* (Mobile, 1864); U. R. Brooks, *Butler and His Cavalry, in the War of Secession* (Columbia, S. C., 1909); and Harry Gilmor, *Four Years in the Saddle* (N. Y., 1866). U. R. Brooks, ed.,

Stories of the Confederacy (Columbia, S. C., 1912), presents a composite picture of Confederate war reminiscences. The extent of human sacrifice to war is revealed in J. K. Barnes, ed., *The Medical and Surgical History of the War of the Rebellion* (6 vols., Wash., 1870-1888); B. A. Gould, *Investigations in the Military and Anthropological Statistics of American Soldiers* (N. Y., 1869); J. H. Baxter, *Statistics, Medical and Anthropological, of the Provost-Marshal-General's Bureau . . . during the Late War of the Rebellion* (2 vols., Wash., 1875); W. F. Fox, *Regimental Loss in the Civil War* (Albany, 1889); and T. L. Livermore, *Numbers and Losses of the Civil War in America* (Boston, 1901). Supplementary material will be found in such memoirs as Jonathan Letterman, *Medical Recollections of the Army of the Potomac* (N. Y., 1866); J. H. Brinton, *Personal Memoirs of John H. Brinton, Military Surgeon, U.S.V., 1861-1865* (N. Y., 1914); F. E. Daniel, *Recollections of a Rebel Surgeon* (Chicago, 1901); J. A. Wyeth, *With Sabre and Scalpel* (N. Y., 1914); and W. H. Reed, *Hospital Life in the Army of the Potomac* (Boston, 1866). An extensive body of information is found in the annual and special reports of the United States Sanitary Commission, much of which is summarized in C. J. Stillé, *History of the United States Sanitary Commission* (Phila., 1866); J. S. Newberry, *The United States Sanitary Commission in the Valley of the Mississippi* (Cleveland, 1871); and J. G. Forman, *The Western Sanitary Commission* (St. Louis, 1864). The enlistment of Northern women for relief work and their generous sacrifices are recounted in Frank Moore, *Women of the War: Their Heroism and Self-Sacrifice* (Hartford, 1866).

THE SOUTH IN WAR TIME

General studies of the Confederacy include J. C. Schwab, *The Confederate States of America* (N. Y., 1900); N. W. Stephenson, *The Day of the Confederacy* (*Chronicles of America Series*, XXX); and R. S. Henry's more recent *The Story of the Confederacy* (Indianapolis, 1931). They are effectively supplemented at various points by recent monographs of excellence, including F. L. Owsley, *State Rights in the Confederacy* (Chicago, 1925), and A. B. Moore, *Conscription and Conflict in the Confederacy* (N. Y., 1924). Important monographic articles by C. W. Ramsdell have appeared in the *Am. Hist. Rev.*, XXII, 794-810; XXXV, 758-777, and in the *Miss. Valley Hist. Rev.*, VIII, 231-249. D. L. Dumond, *The Secession Movement, 1860-1861* (N. Y., 1931), like the older work, Joseph Hodgson, *Cradle of the Confederacy* (Mobile, 1871), is largely political. Background for the blockade will be found in J. T. Scharf, *History of the Confederate Navy* (2d edn., Albany, 1894), and W. M. Robinson, jr., *The Confederate Privateers* (New Haven, 1929). The best collection of material on blockade running is F. B. C. Bradlee, *Blockade Running during the Civil War* (Salem, Mass., 1925). It can be supplemented by a number of personal narratives.

Among biographical materials that reflect the social forces at work in the Confederacy, especially useful are H. D. Capers, *Life and Times of C. G. Memminger* (Richmond, 1893), and Pierce Butler, *Judah P. Benjamin* (Phila., 1906), in telling of conditions at the Confederate capital. The aggressive qualities of two Civil War governors in their respective states are revealed in Herbert Fielder, *A Sketch of the Life and Times and Speeches of Joseph E. Brown* (Springfield, Mass., 1883), and Clement Dowd, *Life of Governor Zebulon B. Vance* (Charlotte, N. C., 1907). Three important recent biographies help to fill out this picture: Laura A. White, *Robert Barnwell Rhett, Father of Secession* (N. Y., 1931); P. S. Flippin, *Herschel V. Johnson of Georgia: State Rights Unionist* (Richmond, 1931); and Hamilton Basso, *Beauregard, the Great Creole* (N. Y., 1933). Life within the beleaguered Confederacy is further disclosed in a vast body of personal accounts. J. B. Jones, *A Rebel War Clerk's Diary* (2 vols., Phila., 1866), is valuable for the extent of its detail. An important diary may be found in Randolph Abbott Shotwell, *Papers* (J. G. deR. Hamilton, ed., 2 vols., Raleigh, 1929-1931). Other significant items are J. E. Cooke, *Wearing the Gray* (N. Y., 1867); F. G. De Fontaine (Personne, *pseud.*), *Marginalia,* or, *Gleanings from an Army Note-Book* (Columbia, S. C., 1864); T. C. De Leon, *Four Years in Rebel Capitals* (Mobile, Ala., 1890); Robert Stiles, *Four Years under Marse Robert* (N. Y., 1903); and J. S. Wise, *The End of an Era* (Boston, 1899).

The period is rich in accounts by aliens representing various viewpoints, largely sympathetic toward the South: W. C. Corsan (An English Merchant, *pseud.*), *Two Months in the Confederate States* (London, 1863); Bela Estvàn, *War Pictures from the South* (N. Y., 1863); A. J. Fremantle, *Three Months in the Southern States: April-June, 1863* (N. Y., 1864); [Catherine C. Hopley], *Life in the South: From the Commencement of the War* (2 vols., London, 1863); T. D. Ozanne, *The South as It Is* (London, 1863); Fitzgerald Ross, *A Visit to the Cities and Camps of the Confederate States* (Edinburgh, 1865); W. H. Russell, *My Diary North and South* (Boston, 1863); Heros von Borcke, *Memoirs of the Confederate War for Independence* (2 vols., Edinburgh, 1866); William Watson, *Life in the Confederate Army* (N. Y., 1888); and J. W. Massie, *America: The Origin of Her Present Conflict* (London, 1864).

A number of the best narratives come from the pens of women contemporaries, and constitute important sources in general, as well as for the war-time rôle played by their sex: Eliza F. Andrews, *The War Time Journal of a Georgia Girl, 1864-1865* (N. Y., 1908); Myrta L. Avary, *A Virginia Girl in the Civil War* (N. Y., 1917); Fannie A. Beers, *Memories: A Record of Personal Experience and Adventure during Four Years of War* (Phila., 1891); Belle Boyd, *Belle Boyd in Camp and Prison* (2 vols., London, 1865); Mary P. Branch, *Memoirs of a Southern Woman "Within the Lines"* (Chicago, 1912); Dolly S. L. Burge, *A Woman's Wartime Journal* (Macon, Ga., 1927); Mary B. Chesnut, *A Diary from Dixie* (N. Y., 1905); Sarah M. Dawson, *A Confederate Girl's Diary* (Boston, 1913); Mary A. H. Gay, *Life in Dixie during the War* (Atlanta, 1892); Susan R. Jervey and Charlotte St. J. Ravenel, *Two Diaries from Middle St. Johns, Berkeley, South Carolina, February-May,*

1865 (Pinopolis, S. C., 1921); Julia Le Grande, *Journal: New Orleans, 1862-1863* (Kate M. Rowland and Agnes E. Croxall, eds., Richmond, 1911); [Mary W. Loughborough], *My Cave Life in Vicksburg* (N. Y., 1864); Judith W. McGuire, *Diary of a Southern Refugee* (3d edn., N. Y., 1889); Sarah A. Pryor, *Reminiscences of Peace and War* (N. Y., 1905); Elizabeth McHatton-Riply, *From Flag to Flag: A Woman's Adventures and Experiences in the South during the War* (N. Y., 1889); C. J. Worthington, ed., *The Woman in Battle: A Narrative of the Exploits, Adventures and Travels of Madame Loreta Janeta Velasquez, otherwise Known as Lieut. Harry T. Buford, C. S. A.* (Hartford, 1876). The rôle of women is more generally presented in J. L. Underwood, *Women of the Confederacy* (N. Y., 1906), and M. P. Andrews, comp., *The Women of the South in War Times* (Balt., 1920).

No adequate study of Unionism in the South is as yet available. Union enlistments in Dixie are studied in C. C. Anderson, *Fighting by Southern Federals* (N. Y., 1912). The sufferings of the loyal element are recounted in memoirs like W. G. Brownlow, *Sketches of the Rise, Progress and Decline of Secession* (Phila., 1862); T. W. Humes, *The Loyal Mountaineers of Tennessee* (Knoxville, 1888); R. S. Tharin, *Arbitrary Arrests in the South, or Scenes from the Experience of an Alabama Unionist* (N. Y., 1863); and A. W. Bishop, *Loyalty on the Frontier* (St. Louis, 1863). E. C. Smith, *The Borderland in the Civil War* (N. Y., 1927), throws light on conditions in the Southern states that did not secede. On the guerrilla warfare that prevailed in many border regions material is available in W. E. Connelley, *Quantrill and the Border Wars* (Cedar Rapids, Iowa, 1910); Harrison Trow, *Charles W. Quantrell: A True History of His Guerrilla Warfare on the Missouri and Kansas Border* (Kansas City, 1923); John Scott, *Partisan Life with Col. John S. Mosby* (N. Y., 1867); and J. N. Edwards, *Noted Guerrillas, or the Warfare on the Border* (St. Louis, 1877). Other source material on the Confederacy may be located by the use of D. S. Freeman, *A Calendar of Confederate Papers, with a Bibliography of Some Confederate Pub-*

lications (Richmond, 1908), and C. N. Baxter and J. M. Dearborn, *Confederate Literature: A List of Books and Newspapers, Maps and Miscellaneous Matter Printed in the South during the Confederacy, now in the Boston Athenaeum* (Boston, 1917).

INDEX

451

MISTRESS COLUMBIA, WHO HAS BEEN TAKING A NAP, SUDDENLY WAKES UP AND CALLS HER NOISY SCHOLARS TO ORDER.

The Irrepressible Conflict

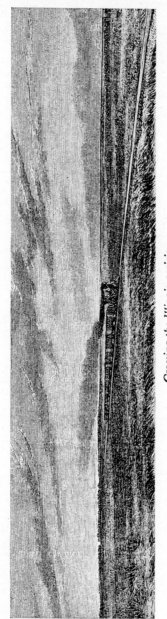

Crossing the Illinois prairie.

The St. Louis river front.

Transportation

An ideal plantation home

William Lowndes Yancey

James D. B. De Bow.

Southern Ideals

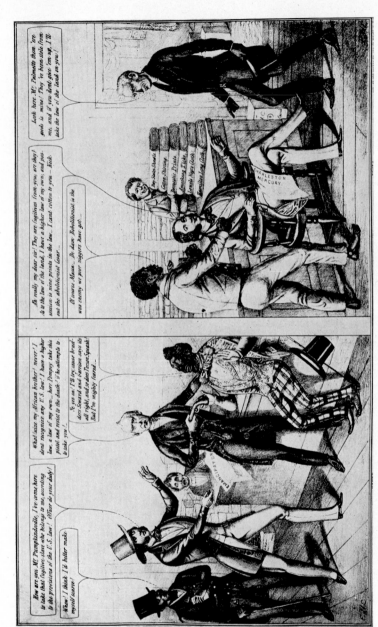

The South Threatens Reprisal

Vassar ~~Female~~ College,

Poughkeepsie. N. Y. "Spring Side" Aug 25th 1866

My dear Mrss Hale

Yours of the 22nd Current is just
received this morning, I send you by return post one
copy each of our College Circular & Catalogue" last issued,
I hope they will be in time for notice in the next number
of your "Lady's Book" viz any matter they may contain,
I thought our Clerk Mr Schard had sent you copies before
this, Students & Teachers all absent enjoying vacation
season, Mechanics & Domestic busy repairing & cleaning
ready for opening Soph term, I am spending the
hot months among the Evergreens & flowing water brooks at
Springside, our average temperature some 8 degrees
less that our City residence, my health is fair that
is only subject to occasional oscillations resulting

A Letter from Matthew Vassar

A Summer Resort

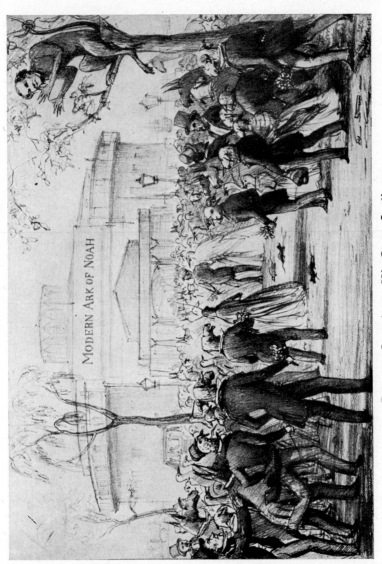

Barnum Laughs at His Own Audience

The Valley of the Yosemite — by Albert Bierstadt

A Camp Meeting

Reformers

Attorney-General Benjamin   Secretary Memminger   Secretary Walker   President Davis

Secretary Mallory   Vice-President Stephens   Postmaster Reagan   Secretary Toombs

The Confederate Cabinet—1861

Offering Substitutes

Political Brigadier-General and the masked battery.

Sherman's "Bummers" in South Carolina.

War in the Field

Washington in 1861.

A Southern cartoon on how to deal with extortioners.

Richmond in ruins.

The Collapse of the South